Documenting the Black

# Documenting the Black Experience

*Essays on African American History, Culture and Identity in Nonfiction Films*

Edited by NOVOTNY LAWRENCE

McFarland & Company, Inc., Publishers
*Jefferson, North Carolina*

Library of Congress Cataloguing-in-Publication Data

Documenting the black experience : essays on African
    American history, culture and identity in nonfiction
    films / edited by Novotny Lawrence.
        p.    cm.
    Includes bibliographical references and index.

    **ISBN 978-0-7864-7267-3 (softcover : acid free paper)** ∞
    **ISBN 978-1-4766-1963-7 (ebook)**

    1. African Americans—Civil rights—History—20th century.
    2. African Americans—Social conditions—20th century.
    3. United States—Race relations—History—20th century.
    4. Documentary films—United States—History and
    criticism.    I. Lawrence, Novotny, 1973– editor.

E185.61.D645  2015
323.1196'0730904—dc23                                        2014035788

British Library cataloguing data are available

On the cover: *top to bottom* Emmett Till, *The Untold Story of
Emmett Louis Till*, 2005; Venus Williams, 2000s; Dorothy
Dandridge, 1950s; *Rize*, 2005 (all images Photofest)

Printed in the United States of America

*McFarland & Company, Inc., Publishers
    Box 611, Jefferson, North Carolina 28640
    www.mcfarlandpub.com*

For Louteamer, Bobby, Verdie, and Leanna

# Table of Contents

*Acknowledgments*                                                    ix
*Introduction*
    Novotny Lawrence                                         1

## Part I. Civil Rights

The Scottsboro Boys' Experiences as Resource to Create a
More Perfect Union
    Joseph L. Smith                                          10

*The Clinton 12* and *Prom Night in Mississippi*: Conversations
in Integration
    Eric Pierson                                             29

A National Concern: Remembering and Teaching the Death
of Emmett Till
    Kevin E. Grimm                                           43

Fear Factor: When Black Equality Is Framed as Militant
    Winsome Chunnu-Brayda and Travis D. Boyce               57

## Part II. Sports

A "perpetual threat": *Unforgivable Blackness* and Jack Johnson
as a Transmedia Sports Icon
    Michael Graves                                           74

From Compton to Center Court: *Venus and Serena* and the Black
Female Experience in Professional Tennis
    Novotny Lawrence                                         92

## PART III. ELECTRONIC MEDIA

Immortalizing Dorothy Dandridge in Documentary, African
American Press and Mainstream Press
CHARLENE REGESTER 116

"Rated R because it's real": Discourses of Authenticity in *Wattstax*
MIKE PHILLIPS 132

A Glance at Herstory: Black Female Documentarians Navigating
Beyond the Normative Constraints in *A Question of Color* and
*My Mic Sounds Nice*
THERESA RENÉE WHITE, SARA TEKLE and
MELANIE SHAW 153

Documenting Grassroots History as a Means to Social Change:
*778 Bullets*, Community Engagement and the Legacy of
Rural Civil Rights
ANGELA J. AGUAYO 170

## PART IV. AND BEYOND: THE CONTEMPORARY BLACK STRUGGLE

Sundown Nation: Living in the Aftermath of an
American Holocaust
DAVID ROSSIAKY 188

*Portrait of Jason:* A Reappraisal
GERALD R. BUTTERS JR. 208

Dancing as Voice: Krumping and Clowning in *Rize* as Black
Vernacular Rhetoric
JOSHUA DANIEL PHILLIPS 221

Gender, the Streets and Violence: Ameena Matthews and
Violence Interruptions in *The Interrupters*
ASHLEY FARMER 238

*About the Contributors* 257
*Index* 261

# Acknowledgments

I would like to begin by thanking all of the contributors to this volume. Bringing this book to fruition has been a long journey, and through it all, the authors were patient and demonstrated a serious commitment to this work. In addition, I express my appreciation for Mary Lou Kowaleski for all of her work on this volume. Her insight and diligence made this collection even better than I could have envisioned.

I also thank my parents, William and Virginia Lawrence, for their love and support. And I thank my brothers, Cornell and Courtney, for their friendship, love, and guidance. Together we have grown from boys to men.

Additionally, I want to recognize my nieces and nephews, Rachael, Cheyenne, Jordan, Andrew, Alexis, and Alyson. Your love and respect mean a great deal to me, and I will continue to forge ahead in the struggle for equality with the hope of making the world a better place for you all.

I also express my deep gratitude to my wife, Sarah Lawrence, for her love and unwavering support. It means a great deal to me to know how much you believe in me and what we refer to as "the work." You remain my motivation and mean more to me that I could ever express. Thank you for all that you are.

Further, I want to acknowledge my godmother, Paula, whom we lost in 2013. Although you have left this earth, your caring and giving spirit endure. I will never forget your love and kindness.

I also thank Dr. Dafna Lemish for being a wonderful mentor and for counseling me as I was searching for a publisher for this volume. I greatly appreciate your guidance.

Thanks to all of my colleagues in the Department of Radio, Television, and Digital Media and in the College of Mass Communication and Media

Arts at Southern Illinois University. I feel very fortunate to be able to work with such a talented, dynamic, and creative group of people.

I also would like to acknowledge Father Joseph Brown, Professor Kevin Willmott, Dr. Peter Lemish, Dr. Derrick Williams, and Dr. Rachel Griffin for their support and sustained advocacy against oppression. Though the struggle is at times frustrating and difficult, I find great comfort in knowing that we are engaged in it together.

Additionally, thank you to the members of my extended family, who have always loved and cared for me unconditionally.

I want to express my appreciation for Lloyd Ballou, Germaine Brown, David Rooks, Dr. Larry Ehrlich, and Dr. Gregory Black. Your friendship and support mean a great deal to me.

Finally, I thank all of my students for making academe an exciting and fulfilling career.

# Introduction

## Novotny Lawrence

Because issues such as slavery and lynching are key to understanding the African American experience, I often reconsider my K–12 education and wonder why such atrocities did not occupy a more prominent space in my history classes. Rather than instruct me and my fellow classmates about such aspects of black life, among the most popular anecdotes that my teachers recounted to the class were that the first president of the United States, George Washington, had false teeth and that he chopped down cherry trees for some reason that I cannot even remember. Although I didn't consider it at the time, as I grew older and progressed further in my education, I found it incredibly disappointing that a teacher would privilege such pieces of information over the fact that Washington had been a slave owner. From my perspective, that kind of information is much more relevant for students as it provides even further evidence of how far-reaching the institution of chattel slavery actually was. While I fully understand that it is impossible for any instructor, class, or school for that matter to cover every detail in history, when I reflect upon my early school years, it is clear that much African American history was either glossed over or simply excluded from the curriculum; my students consistently inform me this is still the case today. That the black experience can be so easily dismissed when it has played and continues to play such a prominent role in the development of the United States always leads me to this question—How many ways can American society continue to tell African Americans that they are less valuable?

As a result of what I consider to be glaring omissions in my education, I have turned to many different sources to become more informed about the atrocities that have plagued black folk since they were initially transported to the United States against their will. Documentary films are among the most

1

valuable resources for filling in the gaps in history, a point that I set out to share with my students in the spring of 2008 when I taught a course on black-themed nonnarrative film. As I prepared my syllabus, I was thoroughly dismayed when I discovered that there was scant academic literature devoted to examining the black documentary experience. More often than not, scholars discussed African American documentarians either in passing or in stand-alone chapters in anthologies focusing more broadly on nonnarrative cinema. As an example, in his seminal text *Documentary: A History of the Non-fiction Film*, Erik Barnouw provides little attention to black filmmakers Marlon Riggs and Bill Miles, whose documentaries *Color Adjustment* (1992) and *Liberators: Fighting on Two Fronts in World War II* (1992) shed light on the black experience in television and the little-known story of an all-black tank battalion, respectively. Betsy A. McLane follows suit in *A New History of Documentary Film*.

Importantly, Phyllis R. Klotman and Janet K. Cutler's *Struggles for Representation: African American Documentary Film and Video* is the sole academic book to date devoted to the black documentary experience. In particular, the text examines "more than 300 nonfiction works by more than 150 African American film/videomakers that constitute the burgeoning African American documentary tradition."[1] Indeed, *Struggles for Representation* is significant as it brings attention to the production, content, and challenges associated with bringing a range of films, including *The Negro Soldier* (1944), *Eyes on the Prize* (1987), and *Midnight Ramble* (1994), as well as many others, to fruition.

Although *Struggles for Representation* marks an important contribution to documentary literature, much has occurred since its publication in January 2000. Significantly, in the early 2000s nonnarrative cinema experienced a renaissance, in large part due to the box-office success of Michael Moore's *Bowling for Columbine* (2002) and *Fahrenheit 9/11* (2004). In addition, technological advancements in the form of digital video cameras and fairly inexpensive home editing software have afforded more documentarians the opportunity to seize the means of production. As a result, there has been an influx of nonnarrative films over the last ten years, many of them, such as *Hip Hop: Beyond Beats and Rhymes* (2006), *American Blackout* (2006), *Thrilla in Manila* (2008), and *On the Shoulders of Giants* (2011), to name a few, centering on African American history, culture, and identity. That there is little to no literature discussing either these films or many produced before them means that there exists a significant void in documentary discourse that needs be filled.

Taking the aforementioned information into account, this collection is motivated by two primary concerns:

- Versions of history taught at the elementary, middle, high school, and at times college levels often exclude significant events from African American history, such as the murder of Emmett Till or the Ku Klux Klan's murder of four black girls when it bombed the Sixteenth Street Baptist Church in Birmingham, Alabama. Such events are integral aspects of history that continue to inform America's racial politics. Their exclusion from traditional accounts of history is a problem that this project addresses by bringing more visibility to documentaries focusing on such stories and thus the events themselves.
- Notable cinema books chronicling the history of documentary films and filmmaking follow a similar pattern, omitting the efforts of documentarians who have chronicled and continue to recount black-oriented stories. Therefore, this book also works to make documentary discourse more complete.

This volume is arranged in four parts that at times intersect given that the authors address issues of racism, oppression, and resistance. The first, "Civil Rights," brings attention to people and events that in mainstream civil-rights narratives either receive little attention or go unmentioned. The struggle for civil rights is often recounted in the national discourse using uplifting narratives centering on activists, such as Martin Luther King, Jr. and Rosa Parks, who do indeed warrant sustained attention for their advocacy during events such as the March on Washington and the Montgomery Bus Boycott, respectively. However, focusing on such stories should not come at the expense of more painful and potentially anger-provoking occurrences that are vital to understanding the depths of American racism and blacks' work to overcome it. The essays in the "Civil Rights" section focus on documentaries that bring attention to lesser-regarded events, working to provide a more full account of one of the most important periods in U.S. history.

In "The Scottsboro Boys' Experiences as Resource to Create a More Perfect Union," Joseph L. Smith focuses on Daniel Anker and Barak Goodman's *Scottsboro: An American Tragedy* (2001), which chronicles the inciting events, trial, and subsequent appeals of eight black male youth who were wrongfully accused of raping two white women. Importantly, Smith goes beyond discussing the event, drawing upon the writings of W. E. B. Du Bois to demonstrate how Anker and Goodman use black history and memory to question presuppositions that sustain legacies of racial injustice and also putting forth black visions of an American democracy committed to mutual flourishing and racial justice.

Eric Pierson addresses school desegregation in "*The Clinton 12* and *Prom*

*Night in Mississippi*: Conversations in Integration." Many narratives discussing the subject center on the events that took place in Little Rock, Arkansas, where after the ruling in the *Brown vs. the Topeka Board of Education* case, then–Arkansas governor Orval Faubus worked to prevent nine black students from entering Central High School. While this story occupies a prominent space in civil-rights lore, Pierson examines *The Clinton 12* (2006), which chronicles the story of Clinton, Tennessee, the first town to integrate its public schools after the *Brown* verdict, before shifting his focus to *Prom Night in Mississippi* to discuss school segregation in a contemporary context. Specifically, *Prom Night* centers on Charleston, Mississippi, a rural community where until 2008 the high school continued to hold separate proms—one for its white students and another for its black students, illustrating how in some communities segregationist practices sustain.

In "A National Concern: Remembering and Teaching the Death of Emmett Till," Kevin E. Grimm discusses the manner in which the PBS documentary *The Murder of Emmett Till* (2003) and *The Untold Story of Emmett Louis Till* (2005) bring a greater level of visibility to the story of the fourteen-year-old Chicago youth who during a vacation to Mississippi in 1955 was killed by two white men for allegedly whistling at one of their wives. Grimm provides insight into the production of the two films, the events surrounding Till's death, and the subsequent murder trial. He concludes his examination by offering educators strategies and valuable resources that they can use to teach Till's story to ensuing generations of students.

Winsome Chunnu-Brayda and Travis D. Boyce close out the "Civil Rights" section with "Fear Factor: When Black Equality Is Framed as Militant," which discusses how a segment of the white population has historically positioned the struggle for black equality as radical and dangerous. As a result, black activists and African Americans, more generally, have at times been met with violent resistance and covert acts of racism implemented out of a fear of black identity. Chunnu-Brayda and Boyce provide an overview detailing specific instances where black struggle has been framed as militant and then discuss *Scarred Justice: The Orangeburg Massacre 1968* (2009), which recounts incidents surrounding several South Carolina State University students who, while protesting a segregated bowling alley, were shot by police officers. Moreover, the authors connect their theme to contemporary politics using President Barack Obama's experiences on the campaign trail as well as his time in office to demonstrate that the fear of black identity continues to inform society.

The second part of this volume, "Sports," is dedicated to examining African American participation, achievement, and struggle in athletics. Indeed, sports have historically provided blacks with the opportunity to challenge dominant ideologies perpetuating fallacies about black inferiority, and at times African American athletes have transformed fields, rings, and courts into spaces of resistance. From Mohammad Ali's protest of the Vietnam War to the indelible image of Tommie Smith and John Carlos raising the Black-Power fist in silent protest at the 1968 Mexico City Olympics, sports have remained central to the struggle for black equality.

Michael Graves begins the exploration of African American sports documentaries in "A 'perpetual threat': *Unforgivable Blackness* and Jack Johnson as a Transmedia Sports Icon." As the title indicates, Graves focuses on Jack Johnson, the first African American world heavyweight boxing champion, who not only helped validate blacks when he defeated top white boxers but also during his illustrious career openly challenged society's racist conventions. Using Ken Burns' *Unforgiveable Blackness* in conjunction with the comic book *The Original Jack Johnson* and the Tom Russell Band's music lyrics, Graves investigates Johnson's career and his sustaining transmedia presence.

In "From Compton to Center Court: *Venus and Serena* and the Black Female Experience in Professional Tennis," I move away from the sports generally associated with blacks—football, basketball, and boxing—to an examination of tennis. In doing so, I discuss three African American female tennis players—Ora Washington, Althea Gibson, and Zina Garrison—to provide insight into the black female experience in tennis. The remainder of the essay focuses on Michelle Major and Maiken Baird's *Venus and Serena* (2012), bringing more attention to the Williams sisters' rise to tennis stardom, the racism that they have endured over the course of their careers, their impact on professional tennis, and the controversy surrounding the release of the documentary.

The third part of the book, "Electronic Media," comprises essays centering on blacks' historic struggle for representation in motion pictures as well as filmmakers' production of media that address key African American issues. Charlene Regester opens this exploration with "Immortalizing Dorothy Dandridge in Documentary, African American Press and Mainstream Press," which works to bring more recognition to one of the most important, yet oft overlooked female movie stars in the history of film. Using *Dorothy Dandridge: An American Beauty* (2003) along with commentary from the black press and mainstream press, Regester works to create a more complete narrative of Dandridge's life and Hollywood career that illustrates her immense popularity while subtly challenging readers to question why her memory resonates much more softly than her white counterparts, such as Marilyn Monroe and Elizabeth Taylor.

In "'Rated R because it's real': Discourses of Authenticity in *Wattstax*,"

Mike Phillips discusses Mel Stuart's *Wattstax*, a concert film conceived as a part of the 1973 Watts summer festival commemorating those who died in the 1965 Watts Rebellion. While the event was seemingly about black uplift, Phillips reveals ulterior motives illustrating that the concert organizers were attempting to capitalize off of the momentum of Hollywood's black exploitation film movement in order to solidify Stax Records as the dominant black label. Furthermore, he calls attention to the ways in which Stuart manipulated reality, creating a documentary that helped Stax Records shift from an integrationist record company to a separatist entity that epitomized the transition from the Civil Rights Movement to Black Power philosophies.

Theresa Renée White, Sara Tekle, and Melanie Shaw shift the focus from issues of authenticity, detailing the work of African American female documentarians Kathe Sandler and Ava DuVernay, in "A Glance at Herstory: Black Female Documentarians Navigating Beyond the Normative Constraints in *A Question of Color* and *My Mic Sounds Nice*." In particular, White, Tekle, and Shaw problematize the lack of attention that black female documentarians receive even though they have a history of producing significant work. As prominent examples, the authors discuss Sandler's *A Question of Color* (1993), which examines the color complex, and DuVernay's *My Mic Sounds Nice* (2010), which brings attention to black female rappers' experiences in an industry that is largely dominated by men.

Angela J. Aguayo continues along a similar trajectory, focusing on her own work in "Documenting Grassroots History as a Means to Social Change: *778 Bullets*, Community Engagement and the Legacy of Rural Civil Rights." Using her documentary short *778 Bullets*, which recounts the events surrounding a shoot-out that took place in the small college town of Carbondale, Illinois, between the police and members of the Black Panther Party for Self-Defense, Aguayo discusses the importance of documenting local histories. In doing so, she provides valuable insight into her mode of production, the challenges associated with addressing local histories, and how *778 Bullets* has served as a catalyst for members of the Carbondale community to come together to discuss the shoot-out and how race and class continue to impact the community.

The final part of this volume, "And Beyond: The Contemporary Black Struggle," features a mix of essays that explore documentaries examining issues from the past and present. Though each essay addresses different subject matter, the authors demonstrate that racism and the struggle for black equality endure. In "Sundown Nation: Living in the Aftermath of an American Holocaust," David Rossiaky uses *Banished: How Whites Drove Blacks Out of Town* (2006) to bring attention to sundown towns, or communities that became all white after their white residents forcefully drove out their African American populations. Discussing this disturbing phenomenon, Rossiaky explains the catalysts for the banishments, the process by which African Americans were forced to leave their homes, and how sundown communities functioned after becoming all white. Moreover, he makes clear that sundown towns are a hidden aspect of American racism that continue to have a profound impact upon blacks whose ancestors were forced to leave their homes decades ago.

Gerald R. Butters Jr. focuses on the black gay male experience in "*Portrait of Jason*: A Reappraisal." In particular, he explores Shirley Clarke's minimalist pseudo-documentary *A Portrait of Jason* (1967), which centers on the title character, a black gay man who identifies as a hustler and an actor. Heralded as a masterpiece at the time of its release, Butters deconstructs *Portrait of Jason*, demonstrating how the film perpetuates egregious gay stereotypes and promotes hostility toward members of gay communities. Given that in 2013 the film began being recirculated, Butters calls for a reevaluation of Clarke's filming methods, the film's authenticity, and its representation of black gay masculinity, an existence that remains highly taboo among a segment in the African American population whose negative attitudes and beliefs about gay black men function as a microcosm of U.S. society.

In "Dancing as Voice: Krumping and Clowning in *Rize* as Black Vernacular Rhetoric," Joshua Daniel Phillips highlights underprivileged South Central Los Angeles, California, youth who use dance as a mode of expression, resistance, and, more importantly, as an alternative to engaging in gang activity. Specifically, he discusses David LaChapelle's *Rize* (2005), which chronicles the evolution of krumping and clowning, two dance styles conceived of and popularized by South Central L.A. dance troupes. Phillips explains how the representation of black inner-city life presented in the documentary is a significant contradiction to Hollywood's narrative films that depict a reductive view of impoverished black communities. Additionally, he also highlights how *Rize* provides a voice to impoverished black youth, allowing them to speak out against the system that consistently relegates them to society's margins.

Finally, Ashley Farmer extends the discussion of inner-city black life in "Gender, the Streets and Violence: Ameena Matthews and Violence Interruptions in *The Interrupters*." She focuses on Steve James and Alex Kotlowitz's *The Interrupters*, a documentary that brings attention to the work of former gang members on the South Side of Chicago working to intervene in potentially violent situations as well as in the lives of youth engaging in gang activity. Though Farmer acknowledges the importance of all of the violence interrupters' work, she gives particular attention to Ameena Matthews, the lone female interventionist depicted in the film. In doing so, Farmer illustrates how

Matthews challenges widely accepted notions of black femininity and her attempts to help a young black female straddling the line between street life and the pursuit of her education.

This collection of essays is aimed primarily at college instructors teaching a range of courses that might include, but certainly are not limited to, documentary cinema studies and production, history, race, gender, and sports. However, it is important to note that the essays in this book are accessible; thus, middle and high school instructors can potentially use the volume in the education of their students as well. It is my hope that this book represents the first in a series that will help bring more attention to the black documentary tradition while filling in the gaps that exist in black history—which for the record is actually American history.

## Note

1. Klotman and Cutler, *Struggles for Representation*, xiv.

## Work Cited

Klotman, Phyllis R., and Janet K. Cutler. *Struggles for Representation: African American Documentary Film and Video*. Bloomington: Indiana University Press, 1999.

# PART I

# CIVIL RIGHTS

# The Scottsboro Boys' Experiences as Resource to Create a More Perfect Union

## Joseph L. Smith

The "Scottsboro Boys" incident remains virtually unknown in the larger history of struggle and resistance within the black experience in the United States. However, Daniel Anker and Barak Goodman's documentary *Scottsboro: An American Tragedy* (2001) is an important text that informs people unfamiliar with the event while also functioning as a call to remember this history. *Scottsboro* presents the story of Olen Montgomery, Clarence Norris, Haywood Patterson, Ozie Powell, Willie Roberson, Charlie Weems, Eugene Williams, Andy Wright, and Roy Wright. On March 25, 1931, the nine black teenagers were traveling by rail—in a boxcar as many thousands were reduced to—attempting to make lives for themselves during the Great Depression. However, their dreams of better lives turned into a nightmare after two white women accused all nine teenagers of raping them in one of the boxcars. The nine youths were tried and convicted of the crime in Scottsboro, Alabama, and they, thus, became known as the "Scottsboro Boys."

*Scottsboro: An American Tragedy* chronicles the tragic and complex story of the Scottsboro Boys' fight for freedom and provides audiences with an opportunity to enter into the historical context and into the personal lives of the nine youths and of their accusers. Directors Anker and Goodman extensively researched the history of the event and the subsequent trials. As Duke University history professor Nancy MacLean points out, "The production team has incorporated a wealth of primary source materials—rare moving film footage, good stills, dramatized readings of court testimony and newspaper editorials, even movement songs—and has involved several leading historians

10

of Scottsboro, including Dan Carter and Robin Kelly."[1] With this depth of resource material, the producers provide access to the nine accused young black men; their accusers, Victoria Price and Ruby Bates; the oppressive social-economic-political structures that the men faced; the interracial protests for equality; and the Communist Party USA, which brought the case to the attention of the international community and whose legal team, the International Labor Defense, spearheaded and funded the legal defense, led by Samuel L. Leibowitz. Without exhausting the depth of the documentary, this essay engages Anker and Goodman's work at the level of documenting the black experience, especially their use of black history and memory.

In the United States, documenting the black experience has historically played a role in creating the national consciousness and in influencing public policy in regard to racial-justice issues. There are two general approaches: one seeks to document the African American experience for the purpose of maintaining legacies of white supremacy and, thus, silencing black history and memory,[2] and the other to document the black experience for the purpose of using African American history and memory as resources in exploring more meaningful ways of democratic life.[3] This approach attempts to use black history and memory to question presuppositions that sustain legacies of racial injustice, while also putting forth black visions of an American democracy committed to mutual flourishing and racial justice. Anker and Goodman's documentary fits into and contributes to the latter approach of documenting the black experience.

*Scottsboro: An American Tragedy* acts as a resource to educate the political community for the purpose of provoking its viewers to reflect philosophically on the American democratic way of life.[4] The documentary accomplishes this, in part, by providing the Scottsboro Boys a platform to be heard. As this essay illustrates, the Scottsboro Boys' narrative challenges us to ask questions, such as what are the remaining tasks in achieving "our country and ending the racial nightmare" in our present historical context?[5] In order to more fully illustrate how *Scottsboro* is illustrative of the latter tradition of documenting the black experience, a Du Boisian reading of the documentary follows, and the film is placed within the oft proclaimed yet fallacious concept "postracial America."

A Du Boisian perspective provides a framework to treat *Scottsboro* as a text that acts as a "site of knowledge" for the purpose of guiding and influencing the development of democracy in relation to the legacies of white supremacy in the contemporary world. In order to understand why a Du Boisian read of the documentary is warranted, it is important to appreciate the contemporary political stakes in regard to documenting the black experience. For this reason, it is necessary to examine the use of black history and memory by scholars and laypersons in the contemporary public sphere. Specifically, this essay examines how President Barack Obama and political commentators Glenn Beck and Dinesh D'Souza use black history and memory. The question that this essay seeks to answer is, what does *Scottsboro: An American Tragedy* offer as a resource for influencing and guiding the future development of U.S. democracy? The essay addresses that question by (1) describing the one constant thread throughout the film, namely, the nine young black teenagers and their fight for racial justice,[6] (2) connecting themes found in this documentary to a larger context of the black experience, namely, W. E. B. Du Bois' challenge to intellectuals and public figures in regard to race and democracy, and (3) explaining how the documentary, as a site of remembering the history of struggle and resistance, is relevant today by explaining the current political stakes.

## The Scottsboro Boys and Racial Justice

The Scottsboro incident occurred in the Jim Crow south, a time and place where laws helped dictate the relationship between race and democracy as "separate but equal." Although the laws of each southern state and municipality varied, Jim Crow was maintained by racial conflict through random acts of terrorism white communities enacted upon black communities. Two of the mechanisms of terror were the brutal torture and lynching of black individuals, which were carried out by white males and witnessed as spectacle by white audiences of men, women, and children. A common justification of the torture and lynching by white communities was the criminalization of black bodies, especially males. The ultimate crime that black males were accused of was raping white women. In many instances, when African American men were accused of this crime, they were seized upon by an unruly white lynch mob that acted as judge, jury, and executioner by torturing and killing the accused. The preservation of Jim Crow through acts of terror and the criminalization of black males set the stage for the Scottsboro Boys.

*Scottsboro* opens with the image of a moving train that housed the unwanted and disadvantaged during the Depression. While the shot lingers, the film's narrator, actor Andre Braugher, provides insight about the people aboard the train, that they were "not the old or the young on it. Nor people with any difference in their color or shape. Not girls or men. Negroes or white, but people with this in common: people that no one had use for, had nothing to give to, no place to offer but the cars of a freight train, careening through ... town after town without halting."[7] The documentary quickly places these people within their historical context, highlighting the roles that race, class, and sexuality played in determining the Scottsboro Boys' fates.

On March 25, 1931, a Southern Railroad Corporation freight train left Chattanooga, Tennessee, and headed southwest into Alabama. Among the cargo were different groups of hobos seeking employment opportunities outside of their hometowns. All of the hobos were poor, but they self-segregated, using race and gender as means to establish distinct groups. As the freight train entered northeast Alabama, a racial confrontation broke out when a member of a group of white men walking along the top of the train stepped on the hand of black rider Haywood Patterson, almost knocking him off the train. Patterson said the white men began to assert their racial superiority: "We were just minding our business when one of [the white men] said, 'This is a white man's train. All you nigger bastards upload.' But we weren't going anywhere. So, there was a fight, and we got the best of it and threw them off."[8]

Word of the scuffle quickly spread to the next stop on the train's route, Paint Rock, Alabama, where a large posse of white men with guns and ropes waited for the group of black teenagers. When the train arrived in Paint Rock, the posse searched it, finding not only the nine black youth but also two white women who emerged from the freight cars. Twenty-one-year-old Victoria Price and seventeen-year-old Ruby Bates, traveling on the train out of economic necessity, claimed they had been raped by the African American teenagers.[9]

By the pervasive southern criteria of the time, neither woman met the standards commonly used to position white women as the epitome of womanhood, which was "concerned with preserving the purity of the superior race" and was based, in part, on the myth of a white Virgin Mary.[10] Among white men's most important responsibilities was to protect these symbols of the "superior" race's purity, these representations of the south itself, from becoming "stained." Thus, any attack on white womanhood was seen as an attack on the region, and the defense against this was one of the linchpins of legal segregation. As American history professor Robin Kelly states, "The protection of white womanhood might be the pivot around all of southern culture. Of the five thousand people who were lynched from 1880 to 1940, most of those were cases of black men accused of raping or sexually assaulting a white woman."[11] Although Price and Bates were at the lower realm of the hierarchy of white womanhood, the Alabama judicial system upheld southern culture.

Within whiteness itself was thought to be a hierarchy in which poor whites were deemed biologically feebleminded and prone to criminal tendencies and pauperism. Such characteristics, the American Eugenics Society argued, were "determined solely by heredity" and led the eugenicists to push for a public policy that would sterilize poor whites.[12] Price and Bates were at the bottom of the hierarchal structure of white womanhood, the very segment that the eugenicists advocated for sterilization.

Not only were both Price and Bates far from the prevailing construction of white womanhood but their daily lived experiences were also in direct contradiction with Jim Crow segregation laws, the embodiment of the widely held, yet farcical, separate but equal doctrine. For example, by age twenty-one, Price had already been married twice and "served time in the workhouse for adultery and vagrancy," behaviors that were associated with the "biologically degenerate" segment of the white population. Price and Bates, who both worked in one of the poorest-paying textile mills, located forty miles outside of Paint Rock in Huntsville, Alabama, received wages that were so low in 1931 they could only afford to live in the black section of town, where they occasionally had sex with black men and white men in exchange for food and clothing. Thus, Bates and Price were not representative of white womanhood. However, as soon as Price and Bates accused the black youth of rape, the women established themselves as symbols of pure white womanhood violated by savage black brutes, and white Alabama would respond with a vengeance.[13] The posse that awaited the Scottsboro Boys at the train depot was not permitted to respond with the violence that generally unfolded after white women made rape allegations against black men. One of the unique features of the Scottsboro Boys case was the attempt by the state of Alabama to prove that black people could receive a fair trial under its separate but equal policy. The Alabama legal system protected the black youth from the white posse that awaited them in Paint Rock. The young men were not lynched on the spot as a result of Price's and Bates' rape allegations but were taken to the county jail in Scottsboro, Alabama. A large, white lynch mob formed at the Scottsboro County jail as the word spread of the alleged crimes and location of the accused criminals. The mob's members threatened to break into the jail in order to retrieve the "niggers" if the county sheriff did not turn the alleged criminals over. In order to ensure that the black youths were tried in a legal courtroom, the Scottsboro County sheriff called Alabama governor Benjamin Meeks Miller to request protection from the National Guard, and troops were sent in to guard the prison for the safety of the nine teenagers.[14]

Although they were spared from the lynch mob, the Scottsboro Boys were tried in one trial after another from April 6 to 9, 1931, and figuratively lynched by the Alabama judicial system. James A. Miller, a professor of English and American studies at George Washington University, describes the first trial: "What distinguished the spectacle of Scottsboro from the 'classic' lynching scenario was the fact that the 'main event'—the public meting out of 'justice' and the 'period of mutilation'—occurred symbolically within the courtroom."[15] That is, a white judge presided over the Scottsboro Boys' trial, with an all-white jury, in front of an all-white audience that filled the courtroom to witness southern justice, all while a white mob stood outside the courtroom.

Lacking financial resources, the Scottsboro Boys hired a real estate lawyer, who only met with them for twenty minutes before the trial and advised them to plead guilty. During the proceedings, Price testified that six of the nine boys raped her, and Bates corroborated her story. All of the Scottsboro Boys were found guilty of rape, sentenced to death, and taken to Kilby Prison's death row, with the exception of thirteen-year-old Roy Wright, who was given a life sentence. This legal lynching by the Alabama judicial system sent a strong message to the state's black residents, ensuring them as well as others who followed the trial that blacks could not receive a fair trial in Alabama.

Over the next seventeen years, the Alabama judicial system demonstrated its lack of commitment to racial justice while upholding the tenets of Jim Crow segregation. In particular, the judicial system continued to find the Scottsboro Boys guilty of rape each time they appealed the original verdict. In 1937 after three additional trials, the charges were dropped against Montgomery, Roberson, Williams, and Roy Wright, but the remaining five were reconvicted. Between 1938 and 1946, Norris, Powell, Weems, and Andrew Wright were released on parole. In 1946, Patterson successfully escaped from jail. Now "free," the majority of the Scottsboro Boys led troubled lives in the north, which demonstrated the negative impact that prison had on them. Patterson killed a man in a bar fight, was found guilty of the crime, and died in a Michigan penitentiary at the age of thirty-nine. Andy Wright was arrested for allegedly raping a white woman in Albany, New York, only to be acquitted of the charges. In 1959, Roy Wright thought his wife was cheating on him and killed her and then himself.[16]

Despite the devastating impact of the sentences and imprisonment, one of the Scottsboro Boys, a lone voice among the vulnerable and disadvantaged, emerged, seeking justice by recounting the group's experiences. Only Norris had a successful life in which he rejoined society and started telling his story in the attempt to gain a pardon for all of the Scottsboro Boys. Norris responded to racial injustice by fighting for justice for himself and the other eight wrongfully convicted young black men. His efforts were not in vain, as in 1976, Norris received a pardon from Alabama governor George Wallace. *Scottsboro* ends with a clip of Norris, with tears in his eyes, speaking at a news conference about the pardon: "I have no hate or racism against any creed or color. I like all people, and I think all people accused of things of which they didn't commit should be free. I wish these other eight boys was [*sic*] around."[17]

## Du Bois and the Scholar's Role in Documenting the Black Experience

From a Du Boisian perspective, *Scottsboro* acts as a site of knowledge that documents the black experience by reaching down into the Scottsboro Boys' narrative and lifting them up to echo in our own context. By using the history and memory of the Scottsboro Boys, Anker and Goodman provoke the political community to think through how the young black men's narrative relates to racial injustice in contemporary society. In this sense, *Scottsboro* is a resource to guide and influence the development of U.S. democracy in relation to the legacies of white supremacy. To more fully articulate how a Du Boisian read provides for this interpretation, it is important to explain Du Bois' understanding of the role the scholar plays in creating sites of knowledge, especially in regard to documenting the black experience. Before explicating Du Bois' concept of the scholar is an explanation of the historical context in which he was writing.

Du Bois wrote in an era dominated by white supremacist ideologies. One of the aspects of white supremacist logics that Du Bois engaged was the way in which the black experience was documented by white supremacists or sympathizers of this logic. As Robert L. Harris rightly remarks about documenting the black experience prior to the 1960s, "White historians generally ignored black people in their treatment of American History. When they did consider them, the work was usually impaired by white supremacy."[18] This approach to documenting the black experience functioned in two ways: (1) it was used to justify the oppression of black people; and (2) it fueled the atrophy of the popular imagination regarding the possibilities and potentialities of U.S. democracy in regard to racial justice. One of the ways Du Bois responded to this approach of documenting the black experience was to employ black history and memory as a countermemory for the purposes of deepening democracy.[19]

Du Bois used history and memory in order to provoke white America to become self-reflexive in order to support the flourishing of black individuals within America and to deepen democracy. This is not to imply that Du Bois viewed the black community as devoid of agency, but, rather, he was well aware of the devastating impact of the systematic oppression of black people in America that was supported and sanctioned at the local, state, and federal levels. Throughout his entire career, Du Bois consistently attempted to unsettle white America's belief in black people's natural inferiority for the purpose of establishing a democratic pluralistic society in which different races could be co-creators in America's experiment with democracy. Du Bois' vision for American democracy was the flourishing of individuality within each race's community and extending the uniqueness of a specific race's gifts to another race. From his perspective, this would serve to deepen democracy because each race would be contributing to the public "good." As Du Bois states, "The vision of life that rises before these dark eyes has in it nothing mean or selfish," but, rather, has "the determination to realize for men, both black and white, the broadest possibilities of life, to seek the better and the best."[20] Thus, Du Bois' concern for individuality and democracy necessitated a dialogue with those who perpetuated white supremacist logics and with the popular imagination that it infected.

Du Bois' strategy to challenge white supremacist logics was to create countermemories that acted as indices of meaning that highlighted the possible actualities of more meaningful ways of life and emphasized the choices, in the past and in the present, that sustained and closed off potentialities within human history. This strategy focuses on the role of scholars within society as social and cultural critics who respond to the crises of their times. Although Du Bois does not make his conception of the scholar explicit, a working knowledge of it is essential to understanding countermemory as a strategy against white supremacist logics. Du Bois understood the function of scholars as the creators of the intellectual capital for an extremely important aspect of culture, namely Truth or sites of knowledge.[21] He claimed that in each era and within each nation, scholars must create their own Truths based upon history and memory (this includes all written records by previous generations), which serve as an index of meanings. As one example, African American Christians deliberately edited any biblical references to enslavement out of the theology they created upon their arrival in the United States. The truth of "received revelation" was judged through the gaze of blackness. Not even the Bible was exempt. As one of their songs says, "Everybody talking 'bout Heaven ain't going there."[22]

History and memory provide scholars with the necessary recorded facts required to build up Truths out of the doings and sufferings of past human experiences. Truth in this context refers to scholars properly using or gathering all the facts in order to have an adequate set of meanings for the purpose of gaining insight into specific contemporary social problems through understanding the historical development of these problems. By properly using the facts, Du Bois means that the use of history and memory ought to be scientific (gathering all the facts, including all the congruent and divergent sets of meanings) in order to have (as much as possible according to the available information of the past) "that accuracy and faithfulness of detail which will allow its use as a measuring rod and guidepost for the future of nations."[23] The purpose of the scholar, then, is to institute Truth in order for the possibility of human history moving towards and possibly establishing Right (justice) in the future.[24]

It is the scholars' Truths that influence and guide human behavior and institutions in responding to the crises of the times (this is not to claim that these Truths are the only Truths influencing and guiding societies). Thus, Du Bois' conception of the scholar is that she/he must be impartial in building up and in creating sites of knowledge in order for nations to have an adequate set of indices of meaning that are necessary to create the critical distance needed to gain perspective on their social ills and also in order to function as an incentive and provocation for nations to experiment with future possibilities of more meaningful ways of life.[25] The value of the sites of knowledge as representing or providing Truths is that these sites are major contributors to the creation of two aspects of the popular imagination within nations that guide and influence human behavior and institutions—namely, collective memory and moral imagination.[26]

The importance of the sites of knowledge on the popular imagination is that they constitute the collective memory and moral imagination of a nation. Collective memory provides populaces with a historical and broad understanding of who the "we" is within a nation. This means that collective memory provides specific populaces with a developmental account of the ideas and actions, and institutions built to attempt to satisfy the wants and needs of the "we" while also providing a critical consciousness of the meaning of the present that seeks to put forth a detailed, and specific, understanding and analysis of the unfulfilled (both past and present) wants, needs, hopes, and dreams that constitute the social conflicts that are in need of amelioration. In this way, collective memory influences the construction of the "we" by providing individuals within a nation a consciousness that highlights the choices that were made in the past to take one specific path rather than another in order to respond to a specific social ill (constituting who the "we" is, and what were and are "our" present problems) while also highlighting the divergent possibilities within a present social ill (the choices "we" have to choose from in order to create untried set/s of meanings that may resolve the problem). In turn, collective memory contributes to the moral imagination of a nation.

Moral imagination consists of a deliberation process that acts as a transformative guide for future behavior and the development of institutions. The moral imagination takes up all of the information that is provided by collective memory and requires individuals to think through and choose what is best to do in a particular situation. Individuals within a nation imagine a future that is different from the present and make choices out of the competing preferences from the actual possibilities within a present problematic situation and act on the choice.[27] *Choice* acts as a transformative guide that seeks to reorganize and reconstruct habits, behavior, and institutions in light of the broadest possibilities for individuals within a nation. Du Bois' conception of the role of the scholar to establish Truths for the purpose of guiding and transforming culture in order to potentially change sites of crises for the better is what allowed him to critique American scholars and laypersons.[28] Specifically, Du Bois would use this concept to criticize the documentation of the black experience by white supremacists or those who sympathized with their logic.

In the *Black Reconstruction* chapter "The Propaganda of History," Du Bois claims that a majority of white American scholars in the early part of the twentieth century falsified the facts of the Reconstruction period, 1860–80, in American history for the purpose of guiding and influencing the development of American democracy along the path of white supremacist logics.[29] The problematic social issue that the white American scholars were responding to was the continual "problem of black folk." These scholars gathered the facts and continued to produce white supremacist logics, which were a major contributor in creating the collective memory and moral imagination of the American populace. Additionally, Du Bois highlighted what the American population was being taught about the role black people played in and the general meaning of Reconstruction. In doing so, he explains that the majority of the textbooks (as sites of knowledge) had the following three theses: (1) all Negroes were ignorant; (2) all Negroes were lazy, dishonest, and extravagant; and (3) Negroes were responsible for bad government during Reconstruction.[30] Du Bois rightly believed that if the popular imagination of the American populace was solely based on white supremacist logics, the result was that the popular imagination would have an inadequate set of indices of meaning for the critical distance to understand the present and future development of American democracy, especially in relation to its darker citizens. Du Bois used countermemory in order to directly challenge white supremacist logics.

Du Bois put forth a countermemory based on slave biographies, black autobiographies, and black intellectual scholarship.[31] The countermemory was to act as a broader set of indices of meaning that sought to provoke the popular imagination to use different sets of meaning to judge and gain perspective of the present and future possibilities. Du Bois was also demanding that white American scholars fulfill their role in society by creating sites of knowledge that included the wants, hopes, and needs of the black community. In this way, Du Bois' countermemory seeks the broadest possibilities for the American populace by creating sites of knowledge that used history and memory for the purpose of guiding and influencing American democracy towards a possible better future for all:

> One reads the truer deeper facts of Reconstruction with a great despair. It is at once so simple and human, and yet so futile. There is no villain, no idiot, no saint. There are just men; men who crave ease and power, men who know want and hunger, men who have crawled. They all dream and strive with ecstasy of fear and strain of effort, balked of hope and hate. Yet the rich world is wide enough for all, wants all, needs all. So slight a gesture, a word, might set the strife in order, not with full content, but with growing dawn of fulfillment.[32]

*Scottsboro: An American Tragedy* contributes to Du Bois' conception of sites of knowledge, collective consciousness, and moral imagination in regard to documenting the black experience. Anker and Goodman's documentation of the Scottsboro incident acts as a site of knowledge that provides an account of the black struggle for racial justice. Specifically, the documentary allows us to see how the criminalization of black males was a justification for state violence against the Scottsboro Boys in order to preserve Jim Crow in the U.S. south. By reeducating us about the Scottsboro Boys, the documentary acts to enlarge our indices of meaning in regard to the legacies of white supremacy and, thus, is a site of knowledge. Further, the documentary builds up our collective memory of how the United States developed in regard to the relationship between race and democracy, while also providing black visions of democracy as expressed by Clarence Norris. The vision of democracy that Norris puts forth is one based on mutual flourishing and racial justice.

Lastly, the documentary builds up our moral imagination by giving Norris the final word. He challenges us to create a world in which all people wrongly accused of crimes are set free. In a contemporary context, audiences are asked to think through how the criminalization of and sanctioned state violence upon black bodies continue to plague African American communities throughout the United States. By building up this set of collective memory and moral imagination, we are given the task of thinking through how might we construct institutions and individual behaviors to remedy the violence upon and criminalization of black bodies that are linked to legacies of white supremacy in the future.

Some critical questions now are, How does *Scottsboro: An American Tragedy* act to broaden our set of indices of meaning? Why a Du Boisian read now? How does the film act as a resource for influencing and guiding the development of U.S. democracy? In order to suggest an answer to these questions, the documentary is placed within the current debate regarding the use of the documentation of the black experience.

## The Current Political States of Black History and Memory

When Barack Obama announced his candidacy for the democratic presidential nomination in 2007, a renewed public debate began regarding the purpose of documenting the black experience. This debate intensified with his 2008 election as the forty-fourth president of the United States. The conflict is over whether or not the United States has entered a "postracial America" as a result of the election of the country's first black president. Underlying the debate is a concern about the cultural resources that will guide and influence the future development of American democracy in regard to racial justice. One of the central questions underlying the discussions is, can black culture be a resource for guiding and influencing the future development of United States democracy? The remainder of this essay examines the answers put forth to this question by Obama, Beck, and D'Souza. However, before examining their responses, it is important to understand why a Du Boisian read is warranted and how *Scottsboro: An American Tragedy* acts as a vital resource for American democracy within this debate.

It is within the context of a postracial America that a Du Boisian read is warranted. As explained next, a Du Boisian read of *Scottsboro: An American Tragedy* is necessitated by proponents of a postracial America, such as Beck and D'Souza, who argue from a narrow set of indices of meaning that seeks to justify racial inequalities in contemporary America. Beck and D'Souza claim that the documentation of the black experience should only be used to highlight and signify that Dr. Martin Luther King, Jr.'s dream has been achieved.[33] This understanding of documenting the black experience is analogous with the white supremacist logics Du Bois was responding to, in regard to Beck and D'Souza arguing from a narrow set of indices of meaning that seeks to justify racial inequalities. For this reason, a Du Boisian read of *Scottsboro: An American Tragedy* creates the cultural capital to move society toward truth and potentially establish an American democracy committed to mutual flourishing and racial justice. Furthermore, *Scottsboro: An American Tragedy* acts as a vital resource in guiding and influencing the future development of American democracy because it provides a broader set of indices of meaning by giving the Scottsboro Boys a platform to be heard. In this way, the nine black men, especially Norris, act as a critique of and challenge proponents of a postracial America.

Significantly, President Obama addressed the postracial America question directly in his speech "A More Perfect Union." In this speech he rightly claims that we must remember how the United States developed in order to potentially resolve social ills in regard to legacies of white supremacy. For President

Obama, sites that document the black experience, such as *Scottsboro: An American Tragedy*, play a central role in educating U.S. citizens of the development of American democracy. By educating U.S. citizens of their past, *Scottsboro: An American Tragedy* acts to provide an index of meaning that aids in thinking through the tasks before the nation. It is in this sense that *Scottsboro: An American Tragedy* acts as a vital resource for future development of American democracy. The Scottsboro Boys are part of the black history and memory Obama makes reference to in highlighting the tasks before America in regard to racial justice and mutual flourishing.

President Obama argues that in order to address and ameliorate the complexities of race and move towards a more perfect union, the United States as a country must remember the development of its democracy in relation to race: "We do not need to recite here the history of injustice in this country. But we do need to remind ourselves that so many of the disparities that exist in the African-American community today can be directly traced to inequalities passed on from an earlier generation that suffered under the brutal legacy of slavery and Jim Crow." President Obama rightly believes that the current cycle of violence and neglect in urban black communities and the present disparities of the education and wealth gaps between blacks and whites directly relate to the history of segregated schools, legalized discrimination (especially as maintained by violence), and the lack of economic opportunities for black people during Jim Crow. He suggests that if America is going to resolve this "part of our union that we have yet to perfect," then we must begin by remembering our past in order to potentially secure a different future.[34] The use President Obama makes of black history and memory, as a cultural resource in moving towards a more perfect union, is what Beck and D'Souza mistakenly declare antidemocratic and anti–American and, thus, as a danger to "our" way of democratic life.

Public figures like Beck and D'Souza (the former president of Kings College in New York City) use the history of the struggle and resistance of black people in the United States to stir up white fears in regard to black culture influencing and guiding the direction of the United States. In other words, Beck and D'Souza are using their cultural influence for the purpose of defining the visions of democracy that are worth pursuing—visions that are reflected in media, education, and public policy. Specifically, they are concerned about the impending demographic shift and the election of a black president in regard to the possibility of nonwhite cultural resources serving as guides for the future development of the United States, especially visions and ideas of democracy found within black history and memory. Beck and D'Souza conclude that the use of black history and memory is dangerous and, thus, not valuable resources in guiding and influencing the development of U.S. democracy. In the dialogue that is culture, they seek to render the black voice mute and ineffective.

Beck and D'Souza put forth criteria that seek to set the limits and the proper use of black history and memory. The aspects of black history and memory they employ are the Civil Rights Movement, the Black Power Movement, and the decolonization movements in Africa. They put forth both a positive and negative conception of the use of black history and memory whereby positive perception is that America, as a country, has achieved King's dream with the passing of civil rights legislation; thus, for Beck and D'Souza and their followers, the proper use of black history and memory is to remind Americans of their achievement. They also advocate that we focus our memory on the moment when King states, "I have a dream my four little children will one day live in a nation where they will not be judged by the color of their skin but by content of their character."[35] For Beck and D'Souza, this statement represents the culmination of black history and memory, in the struggle for a deeper democracy, which was consummated when President Lyndon B. Johnson signed the Civil Rights Act of 1964. This trivialized understanding of the use of black history and memory serves as the basis on which to critique and to name those as a danger to "our" present way of life who seek to employ it for any other conclusion.

The negative conception paints important aspects of black history and memory as antidemocratic and anti–American and, thus, as a danger to U.S. democracy. Beck and D'Souza come to this conclusion by asserting that philosophies underlying antiracist and anticolonialist movements are a perversion of the founding traditional American values. One of the underlying philosophies they focus on is known as philosophy of liberation.[36] For them, philosophies of liberation pervert the traditional value of individualism. Specifically, Beck and D'Souza downplay black struggles against colonialism, racism, and racist public policies by reducing the meaning and memory of such struggles to an us-versus-them philosophy. According to Beck and D'Souza, philosophies of liberation put forth an oppressed/oppressor and victim/oppressor dichotomy in which the oppressed simply seek to invert the power structures.

Further, for Beck, philosophies of liberation lend themselves to terrorism because the victim can use any means for liberation against the oppressor.[37] What makes philosophies of liberation a danger to U.S. democracy, for Beck and D'Souza, is that any perceived connection to historic structures of domination to American post–civil rights era leads to historically oppressed peoples remaining loyal to the cause of overcoming the oppressor rather than focusing on personal character and individualism. Thus, Beck and D'Souza assert that philosophies of liberation are a danger to the United States and, as such, not a resource for the development of U.S. democracy. Beck and D'Souza use Obama's cultural heritage, which he outlines in *Dreams from My Father: A Story of Race and Inheritance*, to launch their negative conception of the use of black history and memory.

The central move of Beck's attack on President Obama is to reduce his cultural heritage of struggle and resistance to black liberation theology. Doing so allows Beck to offhandedly dismiss black history and memory in total (regardless if Beck's interpretation has validity or not). This became readily apparent when Beck used his now-defunct show to launch an attack on Obama's cultural heritage. Beck's efforts were so positively received that his attacks culminated in his Restoring Honor rally in Washington, D.C., on August 28, 2010. According to Beck, black liberation theology is the political perversion of Christianity, a perversion that lends itself to division and to the potential formation of terrorist groups in the United States. The reason Beck believes black liberation lends itself to terrorism is due to its insistence on inverting the power struggle from the "haves" to the "have-nots." More explicit, Beck asserts that black liberation theology creates a false dualism based on race, that is, the oppressor as white and the oppressed as black, that has been historically used by "terrorist" groups as a justification of violence against whites in order to bring about the inverted world, such groups as the Weathermen and the Black Panthers.[38] As Beck states,

> Liberation theology has completely perverted Christianity and teaching something radically different…. Another perversion is the concept of collective salvation. You've heard Barack Obama say that his "individual salvation depends on collective salvation." What does that mean? According to liberation theology, it means that salvation and redemption bought by Jesus comes in the form of political and social "liberation" for minorities from white oppression. Salvation is realized with minorities achieving economic and political parity, via redistribution of wealth with whites. Minorities are "saved" in the sense that white people constantly confess and repent of being racists and meet the economic demands of minorities, via redistribution as a consequence of some form of reparations…. [T]here are those in the country that need to divide us for power. They will make this about race. But this has almost nothing to do with race; it has everything to do with power.[39]

For Beck, this dangerous and antidemocratic cultural heritage must be remedied by taking back "our" country by a renewal of founding principles and ideas. This was the rallying cry for Beck's successful Restoring Honor rally.

D'Souza launched a similar attack on Obama's cultural legacy in a film titled *2016: Obama's America* (2012). In the film, D'Souza describes President Obama's apparently anticolonialist ideology as embedded in his cultural fabric, a cultural fabric woven together through his cultural genetics, particularly his Kenyan father. D'Souza attributes this to President Obama's education that he received from leftist teachers, such as Edward Said and Roberto Unger at Harvard University. Specifically, D'Souza argues that Obama's anticolonialist ideology informs his policy-making decisions that ultimately aim at weakening the U.S. economy. As Yeshiva University law professor Stanley Fish points out, D'Souza shows how Obama's ideology influences issues, such as

> debt, oil drilling, health care, the Middle East, Egypt, Libya, nuclear disarmament, global warming, financial regulation, Supreme Court appointments, you name it. In each instance Obama's view is explained by D'Souza as a logical extension of an anti-colonialist desire to take funds, goods and weapons away from the haves—the United States and its allies—and give them to the have-nots, to poor countries in general and Muslim countries in particular. Rather than laboring to maintain and increase American dominance, Obama, says D'Souza, is busy leveling the playing field so that no nation will have control of the world's resources and be in a position to call the tune.[40]

The positive and negative criteria Beck and D'Souza employ function to fuel the atrophy of the popular imagination in regard to racial justice in contemporary America. The popular imagination is atrophied due to Beck's and D'Souza's insistence that we have arrived at a postracial America, and, thus, we need to turn our attention away from the past and focus solely on individual character in order to reclaim and achieve "our" America. From this perspective, the documentation of the black experience, such as *Scottsboro: An American Tragedy*, seems to be obsolete, and, more important, "dangerous." We must pause here and reflect upon lessons learned from the Scottsboro Boys themselves, especially Clarence Norris.

*Scottsboro* evokes us to think through the tasks before us regarding legacies of white supremacy in creating an America democracy committed to mutual flourishing and racial justice. Anker and Goodman's documentary pulls us into the lives of the Scottsboro Boys. It is here that we are reminded of the development of U.S. democracy in relation to race and the tasks before us. Specifically, Norris challenges us to think through how the criminalization and state violence against the Scottsboro Boys continue to plague black individuals in contemporary America and calls us to muster the moral courage to think through and attempt to create a more perfect union. In this way, *Scottsboro: An American Tragedy* acts as a vital resource in guiding and influencing the future development of U.S. democracy.

## Notes

1. MacLean, review, 1199–200.
2. This is discussed later in the essay in two examples that are representative of this historical approach to documenting the black experience, namely, the historians Du Bois is criticizing and in the current context in regards to Glenn Beck and Dinesh D'Souza.
3. The section on Du Bois discusses this further.
4. My understanding of "our democratic way of life" is based on John Dewey and Jeffrey Stout. Please see Dewey, *Public and Its Problems*, and Stout's introduction in *Democracy & Tradition*, 1–15.
5. Baldwin, *Fire Next Time*, 105.
6. I want to make explicit that by bracketing the roles of the Communist Party, the legal trials, the "everyday people" that participated in national and international demonstrations (including the inter-racial demonstrations), the families of the boys, and so forth that I am not attempting to diminish their importance in the fight for racial justice. Rather, this essay is interested in the response of the young men themselves and the consequences of this event in their lives.
7. Anker and Goodman, *Scottsboro*, 1:47–2:29.
8. Ibid., 5:05–29.
9. Ibid., 11:51.
10. Berry and Blassingame, "Sex and Racism," 114–15.
11. Ibid., 15:41.
12. Taylor, "W. E. B. DuBois' Challenge," 92.
13. Anker and Goodman, *Scottsboro*, 1:47–2:29, 12:07–15, 13:06–20, 13:21–37.
14. Ibid., 9:35–48.
15. Miller, *Remembering Scottsboro*, 10.
16. Anker and Goodman, *Scottsboro*, 1:47–2:29, 1:20:04, 1:20:00–21:00.
17. Ibid., 1:23:27.
18. Harris, "Coming of Age," 107.
19. My understanding of "deepening democracy" is based on Judith M. Green, *Deep Democracy*.
20. Du Bois, *Autobiography*, 212.
21. Du Bois does not use the language "sites of knowledge." I use this phrase to make Du Bois' claim explicit that the Truths the scholars create function as major contributors of the consciousness of nations. I am also using the terms *Truth* and *sites of knowledge* as equivalences.
22. Brown, "Everybody Talking," 654.
23. Du Bois, Black Reconstruction, 714.
24. Ibid., 725.
25. Ibid., 722.
26. Du Bois does not use the language of *popular imagination, collective consciousness,* or *moral imagination* in *Black Reconstruction*. I use these terms to make explicit his claim that the sites of knowledge provide a populace with the relations between past facts and the present (a critical consciousness of present meanings). The critical consciousness of the relations between the past and the present influences and guides the continuous development of a nation, especially regarding the social, political, and economic aspects.
27. I have appropriated Dewey's conception of "dramatic rehearsal" that uses memory and constructive imagination to reconstruct habits. Dewey, *Human Nature and Conduct*, 140.
28. The term *layperson* refers to those that may not have had the tools and skills of professional scholars but published texts through their own economic means. See Du Bois' discussion of James Ford Rhodes in *Black Reconstruction*, 717–18.

29. Du Bois, *Black Reconstruction*, 711–29.
30. Ibid., 712.
31. Ibid., 715–21.
32. Ibid., 727.
33. See D'Souza, *Roots of Obama's Rage*, and Beck, "Glenn Beck: Black Liberation Theology."
34. "More Perfect Union."
35. King, *Testament of Hope*, 219.
36. Beck and D'Souza define philosophy of liberation based on the work of Dr. James Cone and Reverend Jeremiah A. Wright. See D'Souza, *Roots of Obama's Rage*, and Beck, "Glenn Beck: Black Liberation Theology."
37. See Beck, "Glenn Beck: Liberation Theology."
38. See ibid.
39. Ibid.
40. Fish, "Obama, D'Souza, and Anti-Colonialism."

## Works Cited

Anker, Daniel, and Barak Goodman, dirs. *Scottsboro: An American Tragedy*. Social Media Productions, 2001. DVD.

Baldwin, James. *The Fire Next Time*. New York: Vintage International, 1993.

Beck, Glenn. "Glenn Beck: Black Liberation Theology." July 12, 2010. *Glenn Beck*. http://www.glennbeck.com/content/articles/article/198/42831/.

_____. "Glenn Beck: Liberation Theology and Social Justice." July 13, 2010. *Glenn Beck*. http://www.glennbeck.com/content/articles/article/198/42891/. Also available at http://www.foxnews.com/story/2010/07/13/liberation-theology-and-social-justice/.

Berry, Mary F., and John W. Blassingame. "Sex and Racism." In *The African American Experience in a Pluralistic Society*, edited by Leonard Gadzekpo, 114–34. Dubuque: Kendall Hunt, 2010.

Brown, Joseph. "Everybody Talking 'Bout Heaven Ain't Going There." *Callaloo* 36 (Summer 1988): 651–55.

Dewey, John. *Human Nature and Conduct*. In *The Middle Works, 1899–1924*, vol. 14, edited by Jo Ann Boydston. Carbondale: Southern Illinois University Press, 1980.

_____. *The Public and Its Problems*. New York: Holt, 1927.

D'Souza, Dinesh. *The Roots of Obama's Rage*. New York: Regnery, 2011.

D'Souza, Dinesh, and John Sullivan, dirs. *2016: Obama's America*. Lionsgate, 2012. DVD.

Du Bois, W. E. B. *The Autobiography of W. E. B. Du Bois: A Soliloquy on Viewing My Life from the Last Decade of Its First Century*. New York: International, 2007.

_____. *Black Reconstruction; an Essay toward a History of the Part Which Black Folk Played in the Attempt to Reconstruct Democracy in America, 1860–1880*. New York: Harcourt, Brace, 1935.

_____. *The Souls of Black Folk*. New York: Norton, 1999.

Fish, Stanley. "Obama, D'Souza and Anti-Colonialism." August 27, 2012. *New York Times*. http://opinionator.blogs.nytimes.com/2012/08/27/obama-dsouza-and-anti-coloni alism/.

Green, Judith M. *Deep Democracy: Community, Diversity, and Transformation*. Lanham, MD: Rowman & Littlefield, 1999.

Harris, Robert L., Jr. "Coming of Age: The Transformation of Afro-American Historiography." *Journal of Negro History* 67, no. 2 (1982): 107–21.

King, Martin Luther, Jr. *A Testament of Hope: The Essential Writings and Speeches of Martin Luther King, Jr.* Edited by James M. Washington. New York: HarperCollins, 1986.

MacLean, Nancy. Review of *Scottsboro: An American Tragedy*. Directed by Barak Goodman and David Anker. *Journal of American History* 88, no. 3 (2001): 1199–200.

Miller, James A. *Remembering Scottsboro: The Legacy of an Infamous Trial*. Princeton: Princeton University Press, 2009.

Obama, Barack. "A More Perfect Union." Speech on race delivered during presidential campaign on national television, Philadelphia, Pennsylvania, March 18, 2008. Transcript. *NBC News*. http://www.nbcnews.com/id/23690567/ns/politics-decision_08/t/more-perfect-union/#.UYFPssqbV-0.

Stout, Jeffrey. *Democracy & Tradition*. Princeton: Princeton University Press, 2004.

Taylor, Carol M. "W. E. B. DuBois' Challenge to Scientific Racism." In *The African American Experience in a Pluralistic Society*, edited by Leonard Gadzekpo, 90–97. Dubuque: Kendall Hunt, 2010.

# The Clinton 12 and Prom Night in Mississippi

## Conversations in Integration

### Eric Pierson

Can segregation be eradicated from the fabric of a culture by simply making the practice illegal? *Berea College v. Kentucky*, *University of Maryland v. Murray*, *Westminster School District v. Mendez*, and *Sweatt v. Painter* are all significant legal cases centering on the question of desegregation. In *Berea College v. Kentucky*, Berea College, a private college admitting both black and white students, appealed a $1,000 fine for violating a state law prohibiting integrated education. In 1908, the U.S. Supreme Court ruled in favor of Kentucky, thus stopping Berea College from integrating until the 1950s. In *University of Maryland v. Murray* (1936), the Maryland Court of Appeals ruled that Donald Gaines Murray, who had been rejected from the university's law school solely on the basis of color, would be allowed to attend although he was to be segregated from the white students. The segregation of white and Mexican American students is the focus of *Westminster School District v. Mendez* (1947), a suit begun when five Mexican American fathers challenged the Orange County, California, school district's practice of placing children of "Mexican" ancestry into schools separate from white students. A federal court ruling in California struck down this segregation, and Governor Earl Warren signed into law the repeal of provisions that mandated segregation. *Sweatt v. Painter* (1950) was won in the U.S. Supreme Court by Herman Marion Sweatt, who, because the Texas State Constitution prohibited integrated education, had been denied admission to the School of Law at the University of Texas. Sweatt's suit successfully challenged the separate but equal doctrine.

29

These legal cases highlight the role that courts have played in moving the United States closer to becoming a more fully integrated society. Embedded in the legal arguments for ending segregation is the ideal that the United States would be a better nation once segregation was a thing of the past.

The struggle for equal treatment of black citizens under the law has been a long and tumultuous series of battles in what some would describe as a never-ending war. Beginning in 1619 when the first slaves arrived in Jamestown, Virginia, and continuing past the election of the first president of African descent, the history of race relations between blacks and whites has been shaped by moments of progress and periods of deep frustration at the slow evolution of change. The legal system has been an ever-present element in the dialogue regarding racial tensions, with many of the most important changes to race relations finally being settled or cemented by the Supreme Court of the United States.[1] These court cases are designed to resolve legal questions connected to equality, but should Americans look to the courts as sites of resolution for moral dilemmas?

At the heart of the discussions on equality is the interpretation of what the framers of the Constitution intended with the phrase "equal protection of the laws."[2] *New York Times* reporter Adam Liptak describes the dynamic within the Supreme Court as one of "different conceptions of equality. Some justices are committed to formal equality. Others say the Constitution requires a more dynamic kind of equality, one that takes account of the weight of history and of modern disparities."[3] The legal challenges make it more difficult to practice discrimination; however, the question remains, Do these rulings mean that discrimination disappears?

Two documentaries, *The Clinton 12* (2006) and *Prom Night in Mississippi* (2008), enable the examination of the way in which the Court's rulings in school desegregation has impacted understanding of equality over an extended period of time.[4] The Court's order to integrate public schools and other court rulings were not just about concerns regarding the inequalities in education; they were destined to impact the social fabric of communities throughout the United States.

The films offer opportunities to reflect upon the struggles of the past and assess the needs of the future. The documentaries exam moments in history separated by almost fifty years and highlight the continuum of the difficult conversations around educational segregation in America. The films help us to understand the complexities at the nexus of race and education in the United States. Both films aspire to "observe, describe or poetically evoke situations and interactions ... to enrich our understanding of aspects of the historical world by means of their representations ... grasp the implications and consequences of what we do."[5]

## The Clinton 12: *First Test for Desegregation*

Keith Henry McDaniel's *The Clinton 12* opens with archival footage of the bombing of Clinton High School, an event that left the facility unusable and the community shaken. Through a voice-over by James Earl Jones, viewers are introduced to the Clinton community as he frames the town's story and are informed that they are about the see "a story of courage and determination of reconciliation and resolve. The story of a community that stood shoulder to shoulder to uphold the law. This is the story of twelve black teenagers who faced the best and the worst in all of us. This is story of the Clinton 12," the moniker given to the twelve youth—Jo Ann Allen, Bobby Cain, Anna Theresser Caswell, Gail Ann Epps, Ronald Gordon Hayden, Minnie Ann Dickie Jones, William R. Latham, Alvah McSwain, Maurice Soles, Robert Thacker, Regina Turner, and Alfred Williams—who first integrated public schools in the U.S. south.

The bombing of the Clinton school and the immediate aftermath evoked a spirit of solidarity, reflecting a community committed to change; however, to really understand the dynamics of segregation in Clinton, it is necessary to revisit the town in the decade that preceded the *Brown v. the Board of Education of Topeka* verdict, when Clinton was unwilling to grant black citizens equal access to education. At the core of the documentary is the community's struggle to comply with the Supreme Court mandate, but there is also the awareness within the community that school integration is only a small portion of the changes that are about to impact the town. The people featured in the film do not seem driven by their own moral conviction that segregation must end but instead are motivated by the rule of law. The citizens depicted through the archival footage are either unwilling or unable to understand the moral impact of a social structure that supports and maintains a system of inequality. The Clinton residents see themselves as being on the right side of the integration conversation, yet a closer examination of the archival footage used throughout the film shows a much more complicated and arduous trek to an integrated Clinton.

Following the Supreme Court's ruling in the landmark 1954 case *Brown v. the Board of Education*, communities throughout the south began debating how, and in some cases if, they would comply with the order. *The Clinton 12* examines the struggles of a community as it responds to legal mandates designed to protect the rights of black citizens to equal levels of education. What makes the story of the Clinton 12 noteworthy is that Clinton, Tennessee, was actually the first town in the south to integrate a public high school in response to *Brown v. the Board of Education*. The film was produced by the

Green McAdoo Cultural Organization, whose mission is "to be an inclusive, community based, non-profit organization preserving the legacy of education in Anderson County with an emphasis on Clinton's (Tennessee) public high school desegregation."[6] The organization preserves the history of the events surrounding the Clinton 12 through a series of events and activities, including maintaining a museum and cultural center on the site of Green McAdoo Grammar School, holding annual tribute events, and producing *The Clinton 12* documentary. Although writer and producer McDaniel focuses on the ways in which the people of Clinton banded together to obey the law and integrate the high school, the film also offers the opportunity for a closer examination of the history of segregation in Clinton. This history is a complex and complicated story, as the people of Clinton tried to comply with the law while holding on to the remnants of the Jim Crow south.

While filmmaker McDaniel chooses to focus on Clinton post–*Brown v. Board of Education* and does not fully explore the pre-*Brown* attitudes, historian Janice McClelland believes that to understand the struggle over desegregation, one has to understand the social/cultural components of Clinton prior to the ruling: "The characteristics of the city's residents, the community's history of school segregation and of Jim Crow race relations, and the evident class divisions within the white population shaped the community's responses to the demand of integration and the controversy that followed."[7] The lawsuit *McSwain et al. v. County Board of Education of Anderson County, Tennessee*, filed in December 1950, was the opening salvo in the legal battle to integrate Clinton. The high school in Clinton would not accept black students, which forced those students of high school age to travel eighteen miles to a black high school in another county; the road to the black high school took the students daily past Clinton High School. For the black residents of Clinton, it was clear that black students were not being given the same access to education and educational resources as the town's white students. The lawsuit came shortly after the county school board had added upgrades to the Clinton Colored School, which included indoor restrooms, and had renamed it in honor of Green McAdoo, one of Clinton's black residents, who after serving fifteen years in the military had worked as a custodian at the Anderson County Courthouse for twenty-five years.[8] For many of Clinton's white citizens, the lawsuit was an unwarranted nuisance because the community had upheld the concept of "separate but equal"; thus, there was no need for a conversation regarding the integration of public schools.[9] As the lawsuit moved through the legal system, the school board made it clear to the white residents of Clinton that it would mount a vigorous challenge in an effort to avoid integrating the schools.

It would take two years before a judge would hear the suit the black citizens of Clinton filed. Judge Robert L. Taylor ruled in favor of the school board, supporting its assertion that the recent upgrades to the Clinton Colored School complied with the law of separate but equal and that the black high school students' travel to another county to attend school was "not aggrieved at present arrangements." Judge Taylor also used his ruling as an opportunity to scold the plaintiffs and remind them that segregation was the law of the land throughout the state of Tennessee and others.[10] The ruling made it appear as if the law had prevailed. Documents from the Anderson County School Board reported that it had spent over $7,000 in legal fees to avoid integration.[11]

The *McSwain* verdict and the school board's efforts to maintain segregated schools clearly demonstrate that the school board wanted to remain status quo and that the community's political leaders were neither interested in change nor willing to change. The school board's actions are critical to understanding Clinton's white citizens' attitudes. The board used the power of the courts to defend segregation and thus allowed the community to legally adhere to tradition, a strategy that permitted communities like Clinton to forgo the moral debates surrounding segregation. As a result, the residents could position themselves as law-abiding citizens as opposed to proponents of racism.

Important, that the *McSwain* lawsuit moved through the court system had ramifications far beyond Clinton, as other communities monitored the case in search of strategies for pursuing legal remedies to segregation. The National Association for the Advancement of Colored People (NAACP) was an active participant in the Clinton lawsuit, providing counsel and support to the town's black citizens. Thurgood Marshall, who would eventually argue the *Brown v. the Board of Education* case, was a member of the NAACP's legal team in the Clinton case. The NAACP's presence indicated that the organization considered the case in Clinton an important legal battle in the struggle against inequality. The organization spent a great deal of time and energy and money developing legal strategies to challenge segregation in education. The Clinton experience allowed the NAACP to see firsthand how communities might respond and the arguments and strategies that they might employ in defense of the racist status quo. Hence, *Brown v. the Board of Education*'s success can be attributed in part to the "trial runs" that occurred in towns like Clinton.

Although the Clinton school board prevailed in the lawsuit, its members seemed well aware that the fight over segregation was far from over and began taking steps to mitigate the potential impact.[12] While *Brown v. the Board of Education* was working its way through the court system, the school board took a prophylactic approach to avoiding change and approved another substantial upgrade of the Green McAdoo School, which included the addition of a new gymnasium that would house a regulation-size basketball court. This upgrade was nothing more than an attempt to make the Green McAdoo School more acceptable and thus placate Clinton's black residents. However, to an outsider looking in, it could be viewed as a sign that the white powers that be in Clinton were fully committed to providing the very best educational facilities to all of its students, regardless of color.

In *The Clinton 12*, McDaniel briefly mentions but fails to fully explore the *McSwain* lawsuit or its aftermath. These are glaring omissions from the narrative that prevent audiences unfamiliar with the historical events from fully understanding Clinton's racial politics. The absence of information regarding the struggles in Clinton prior to the court-ordered ending of segregation allows the filmmaker to create a narrative that is devoid of the complexities and difficulties surrounding desegregation. Clinton's white citizens are portrayed as law-abiding folks who are prepared to address the problems of segregation rather than as a community that has gone to great lengths to prevent the integration of its school system.

Instead of presenting a detailed, historical examination, the film presents a story where the good people of Clinton emerge as heroes fighting against villainous outside agitators who turned a peaceful transition to integration into a high-profile racial conflict. While the narrative structure simplifies the events that transpired in Clinton, the archival footage of the conflict communicates the depth of the struggle. The true power and understanding of the events come from this footage, where words and images help the audience see that what was happening in Clinton was a complicated social upheaval where old rules, traditions, customs, habits, and expectations were being forced to meet a changing cultural climate.

One of the reoccurring themes emphasized throughout *The Clinton 12* via some of the archival footage is that the town's white citizens supported integration. The high school principal, captain of the football team, and a prominent pastor are all featured in the footage expressing their support for the legal mandate of integration. For example, Principal D. J. Brittain frames the legal mandate as one of responsible citizenship: "We do not feel that if we allow our citizens to disobey this law that they are learning the right principles of citizenship."[13]

Significant, the aforementioned footage presents a skewed version of the truth. Missing from the archival footage presented in the film is the discussion of the moral obligation to treat black citizens as equals. This demand of a legal mandate versus moral obligation is never explored in the film and is only mentioned by the narrator as he attempts to present the black citizens' perspective.

The narrator, then, becomes the voice of Clinton's black population because the film does not include any archival footage of them speaking about the community's transition from a Jim Crow town to an integrated municipality. The only black voices prominently featured in the documentary frame the conflict in a manner that is influenced by the passage of time and reflection. The viewer does not get to hear them speak when they were in the midst of the struggle and the outcome was uncertain. The missing voices are a sign of the times as the blacks in Clinton were not asked to speak in the public forums at that time. Hence, viewers are left with only McDaniel's assessment of the mindset of the black community. The nonexistence of archival footage of the black voice is a subtle, yet powerful reflection of a period when blacks were silenced in the public debates that would profoundly influence their daily lives.

*The Clinton 12* spends a significant amount of time highlighting the rhetoric of John Kasper, who was well known as an opponent of integration and as an advocate of violence as a means to keep schools separate. While Kasper is clearly an outsider to the community, he quickly finds an audience for his racist rhetoric. News footage shows him winning over a segment of Clinton's white population by playing upon their fears of race mixing. Though miscegenation is only mentioned once in the film, history clearly demonstrates that it was often among the most powerful arguments used by anti-integrationists. Kasper makes a very powerful villain, and McDaniel uses him as the point of conflict. There is footage of him making the most incendiary racist statements. Furthermore, Kasper is framed as the racist outsider, which allows the citizens of Clinton, black and white alike, to be presented as heroes. If Clinton is, in fact, united in its support of the law and its desires to challenge outside agitators, where is the archival footage of this unity? There is no footage of blacks and whites together in formal settings like press conferences or interviews. When the community is given the opportunity to show its solidarity to the world, the opportunity is squandered.

A closer examination of Clinton's history reveals that Kasper did not have to look very far to find like-minded people. "It is not uncommon for people to blame 'outsiders' when serious controversies rack the peace and harmony of a community," McClelland states. "It is far too easy to point the finger at 'outsiders' rather than admitting that the problem might have internal origins."[14] Focusing on Kasper allows the filmmakers to use him as the dominant voice of dissent, which frees the community's racist white citizens who are instead presented as heroic. There is not a single frame of a local citizen offering opposition to integration. Viewers do not get any sense of how the white students felt about the process while it was happening. The black and white students that are interviewed work hard to present themselves on the right side of history. What about those persons who were harassing the students as they attended class? The principal speaks about organizing protection for the students while they are in school. Viewers hear from those providing protection but nothing from those students voicing opposition. What of the teachers who dissented to the process? Given the strong legal challenges of the past, it is unlikely that the local community was as unified as the filmmaker wants viewers to believe.

One of the most telling sequences in the film focuses on the attack on Reverend Paul Turner, a local white pastor who becomes the target of a physical assault after he shows his support for the black students by escorting them to school. As he returns from escorting the students, he is assaulted by several individuals, who severely beat him. Reverend Turner returns to his congregation shortly after the beating and preaches a powerful sermon to his all-white congregation. The beating, like the bombing, presents an opportunity for the community to come together and show solidarity. Instead, the old traditions of the segregated church remained firmly in place.[15] As the sequence includes multiple close-ups of the congregation, it is clear that the black community has not been invited to this sermon. Reverend Turner uses this moment to comment on the coming of integration: "Here in Clinton we are not especially against integration, we are not especially against segregation, but we are positively and defiantly against the disintegration of our community and our body politic that we cherish above all things, realizing that where anarchy prevails, none of us has anything of any value, and none of us has any freedom anymore."[16] Though Reverend Turner's sermon is heartfelt, the image of his segregated church service in the midst of racial turmoil reflects the struggles within Clinton. Simply put, the people of Clinton want to have a world where blacks and whites attend high school together, but they can't worship together. They are willing to compartmentalize the conflict of integrating the school as a legal issue while church is a social matter.

Clinton has the distinction of being the first public high school in the south to graduate black students, but the city still had work to do in the area of integration. It would be several years until the school system was fully integrated, and it was clear that the situation at the high school and the legal mandate were really the greatest motivators for the community to change. Clinton, then, is an excellent example of the rule of law forcing a community to address years of sanctioned or accepted discrimination. Segregation in Clinton would not have ended without legal intervention. The Green McAdoo School did not integrate until 1965. Once the spotlight and the national media leave a town like Clinton, the real tension once again takes center stage. Though Clinton was forced to allow integration within the schools, the town was not forced to become an integrated community. For many, the forced integration of schools was a crucial step toward a fully integrated society; however, a visit to schools in communities throughout the south would indicate that America is falling short in its quest for a fully integrated nation.

## Prom Night: *School Segregation in a Contemporary Context*

Paul Saltzman's *Prom Night in Mississippi* (2008) focuses on the small town of Charleston, Mississippi, a rural community that continues to struggle with race relations. For example, Charleston did not integrate the high school until sixteen years after the *Brown v. Board of Education* ruling. Though the schools in Charleston are fully integrated, the community clings to the racist traditions of the past by holding segregated senior proms, one for white students and another for black students. The practice is clearly a custom of a racist bygone era, but it is widely accepted in the town by blacks and whites alike.

*Prom Night* chronicles Academy Award winner and Charleston native Morgan Freeman, who challenges the high school's problematic tradition of holding segregated proms. More specific, he offers to pay for Charleston High School's dance on one condition—the prom must be integrated. While *Prom Night's* premise is relatively simple, during the shooting process, the filmmakers discovered that the school's separatist tradition functions as commentary on the community's racial politics. Thus, Freeman's intervention extends far beyond the prom, as it shakes Charleston's very foundation by challenging a host of other practices used to maintain segregation, albeit in a contemporary context.

As with Clinton, it is important to understand Charleston's history to place *Prom Night* within its proper context. When the film begins, audiences learn that this is not the first time that Freeman attempted to change the culture of his hometown. He initially offered to pay for Charleston High School's prom in 1997 only to have the school board refuse his proposition. Freeman makes the offer again a decade later, but this time he brings a camera crew with him, which seems to prompt the school board to allow him to speak with the students. The documentary crew records him as he addresses members of the senior class and makes the offer to pay for the prom. Freeman explains that there is no limit on the cost of the event, a point that excites the students. He continues by presenting his only condition—that the prom be integrated.

After Freeman outlines his parameters, the cameras capture the black students' enthusiasm and the discomfort that registers on the faces of some of the white students who are reluctant to go on camera to expound upon their uneasiness. Although the remainder of film almost entirely comprises interviews of those involved with organizing the prom, no student is willing to publicly speak against holding an integrated prom. There are several interviews with parents regarding the upcoming integrated prom. Their reactions seem to be ones of acceptance rather than full support. It is clear that not everyone in the community is onboard with the idea, but the people in the community are also aware that public displays of racism and bigotry are no longer acceptable.

Because public displays of racism and bigotry are politically incorrect, the filmmakers have difficulty finding anyone willing to speak on camera against an integrated prom. They do find one member of the community who speaks honestly regarding the situation, but his face is blurred and his voice is altered during his interview. Referred to simply as "Billy Joe," the young man offers a very powerful commentary on Charleston's racial politics and the integrated prom. He claims that traditions will be slow to change and that the racism and bigotry have been and always will be part of the community.

Billy Joe's insight regarding the community is evidenced by a group of white parents who decide to continue the tradition of a whites-only prom. They so strongly oppose an integrated prom that they even band together to initiate a lawsuit against the school board for changing the high school's racist practice. Despite their determination to continue segregation, the parents, who fear "being characterized as racist, bigots, or hypocrites," refuse to speak with the filmmakers about their opposition.[17] Instead, much like a Ku Klux Klan member hides behind a mask, these parents hide behind their attorney, who speaks on their behalf. In an interview with the filmmakers, the lawyer avoids mentioning race, instead claiming that the parents' concern about the integrated prom is really about losing of control over this important social event.

Much like Kasper in *The Clinton 12*, the white parents who oppose the integrated prom are framed as *Prom Night*'s villains. Throughout the film, pervasive racism is presented as a problem among this splinter group of parents, which suggests that the students in the film are somehow immune to their influence. That point is further emphasized in an interview where a student explains racism as a generational phenomenon rather than an issue that today's youth continues to grapple with. Moreover, by positioning what appears to be a small group of parents as villainous, the film functions in the vein of a traditional Hollywood narrative in which good prevails over evil, without fully acknowledging or exploring just how deeply social, economic, and political racism continues to impact the Charleston community and the United States more broadly.

Although *Prom Night* does not examine how deeply racism permeates the Charleston community, one of the film's strengths is that it makes clear that the segregated proms can in part be attributed to a polarizing issue that U.S. citizens across ethnic backgrounds remain divided about—miscegenation. Freeman mentions in the middle of the film that the old traditions and fear of race mixing are still a part of Charleston's culture: "Now we've avoided talking about the sexual aspects of this separation, but that separation is primarily black boys and white girls. It's like the bugaboo of sex has absolutely drowned out common sense in terms of how young people interact." Indeed, antimiscegenation laws and fear of race mixing have been a part of Mississippi's culture at least since it became a state in 1817. As recent as 2011, a survey by a Democrat pollster of Mississippi Republicans found that 46 percent want to ban interracial marriage.[18] Hence, what Freeman is trying to accomplish by integrating the high school prom runs counter to historic cultural practices and attitudes that remain intact in Charleston.

Although miscegenation remains a polarizing topic, it is not Charleston's order of the day. *Prom Night* demonstrates exceptions to the tradition by presenting interracial friendships where black and white students express great respect, concern, and admiration for their peers of other ethnic groups, with whom, in many cases, they have journeyed through all of their school years. Additionally, the film also includes interviews with an interracial couple, a white female and a black male, who attend the high school and contribute powerful stories and see themselves and the integrated prom as a catalyst for change. Though these stories provide an uplifting direction for the future, it is also apparent that racism is deeply woven into the fabric of the community.

Among the most powerful sequences in *Prom Night* is the filmmaker's documentation of the senior proms. Using a series of drawings, the film briefly recounts that the white prom was held out of town, with the parents taking effective measures to keep Saltzman's cameras away from the event. In contrast, Saltzman and Freeman are granted full access to the integrated prom, which they chronicle in much-greater detail. The event is presented as a complete success as concerns about choices of music, types of food, and security issues prove unfounded. Moreover, the film shows black and white students comfortably dancing and interacting with each other just as they do on school days when they take classes together. By the end of the evening, the teachers have moved onto the dance floor, creating an even-stronger image of a united community. The success of the prom should not be underestimated, as it shows that there is at least a segment of the community that is willing to defy its racist traditions. The integrated prom is bigger than a dance, as the prom is also symbolic of hope.

After viewing *Prom Night*, some viewers may be left with more questions than a single eighty-nine-minute documentary can answer. In particular, when integration came to Charleston, how difficult was the process? Other than the prom, what other remnants of the Jim Crow era are still being practiced? How do practices of racial discrimination become normalized social traditions? Because these questions remain, the presence of the camera highlights the overt racism attached to a segregated prom while forcing racism underground. No one in Charleston is ever forced to answer the charges of racism. Even with the cameras in place, the white parents still move forward with a prom specifically for their kids, which functions as the clearest indication of how strongly a segment of the community feels about mixed-race social events. That several of the white students attended both proms further demonstrates the complexity of the issue. Clearly, for those students, the dances represented an opportunity to celebrate with the black and white friends with whom they grew up and journeyed through school. However, in order to celebrate with all of their peers, they *had* to attend two proms, with one functioning as a bitter reminder that in the town, blacks remain unwelcome by some people.[19]

Clinton, Tennessee, and Charleston, Mississippi, are communities that reveal how the United States has worked and continues to work through the issue of school desegregation. *The Clinton 12* highlights legally mandated desegregation, while *Prom Night in Mississippi* provides a glimpse into a community struggling to overcome racism in a contemporary context, decades after the legal battles over school integration began. The conversations across the films indicate that legal remedies have a limited effect in changing people's hearts and minds. The citizens of Clinton integrated the schools because they were mandated to do so and not because of any real reflection upon the moral ills of discrimination. In Charleston, the community slowly integrated the school system while maintaining the social structures that enforce and entrench racial separation. Important, holding an integrated prom over fifty years after *Brown v. Board of Education* does not indicate that people are willing or able to do the right thing on their own. Year after year, the people of Charleston chose to keep old systems in place with very little community resistance. In many ways, the black and white communities both share some responsibility for maintaining the "tradition" of separate proms.

The conversation regarding black and white relations in America are part of a long and complicated historical continuum. When documentaries take these subjects on, it is impossible to tell the entire story within the time allocated. As both *Clinton 12* and *Prom Night* demonstrate, the documentaries at times end up telling their stories with individuals serving as surrogates for very complex and complicated social dynamics. Any documentary focused on a single moment of the racial conflict is only operating along the continuum of that conflict. The film can inform about the past, but it also can be part of a conversation about the present and the future.

It is critical that filmmakers understand that it is impossible to address racial dialogues without understanding the scope of the ground that must be covered. In the case of both of the documentaries in this essay, we have the seeds of a fuller historical context and examination of the depth of racial conflict in the United States. Documentaries that attempt to simply present the problem as a narrative of heroes and villains forfeit an opportunity for more detailed exposition on the subject.

These two films offer an interesting complement to each other, as they both center on the issue of race and education. Each demonstrates that the process of cleansing racism from the fabric of a community is always an ongoing process that requires a vigilant commitment. As recently as September 2013, the difficulty of this was underlined by events at the University of Alabama, Tuscaloosa. The university was integrated in 1963 but in the years since has maintained a system of segregated sororities.

The legal challenges make it more difficult to practice discrimination; however, the question remains, do these rulings mean that discrimination disappears? What these documentaries help us understand is that segregation has a long shelf life that can be effectively challenged when both legal and community pressures are applied. In Clinton, Charleston, and Tuscaloosa, change came when people stood up.

## Notes

1. *Dred Scott v. Sanford* (1857) declared that slaves were property and persons of African descent born in the United States were not citizens. *Loving v. Virginia* (1967) allowed blacks and whites to marry, a practice that had been outlawed in several states. *Plessy v. Ferguson* (1896) ushered in over fifty years of acceptable racial discrimination by institutionalizing the concept of "separate but equal"; *Brown v. Board of Education of Topeka* (1954) led to the end of racial segregation in public education and the end of the legal validation for the concept of "separate but equal."

2. Adam Liptak, "Supreme Court Weighs Cases Redefining Legal Equality," *New York Times*, June 23, 2013, A1, http://www.nytimes.com/2013/06/us/supreme-court-weighs-cases-redefining-legal-equality.html?_r=0.

3. Ibid.

4. McDaniel, *Clinton 12*; Saltzman, *Prom Night in Mississippi*.

5. Nichols, *Introduction*, 165.

6. Green McAdoo Cultural Center, "Preserving the Legacy: Mission Statement."

7. McClelland, "Structural Analysis," 296.

8. Spears, "Green McAdoo."

9. McClelland, "Structural Analysis," 299.

10. Green McAdoo Cultural Center, "Preserving the Legacy: The Story of Desegregation."

11. Anderson, *Children of the South*, 8.

12. McClelland, "Structural Analysis," 300.

13. McDaniel, *Clinton 12*.

14. McClelland, "Structural Analysis," 296.

15. Martin Luther King, Jr. in the Letter from the Birmingham Jail calls for churches to work together to fight segregation. His letter reflects his frustration at the churches' inability or in some cases unwillingness to join the fight for justice. He once referred to eleven o'clock on Sunday morning as the most segregated hour in Christian America.

16. McDaniel, *Clinton 12*.

17. Saltzman, *Prom Night*.

18. Public Policy Polling, "Barbour," para. 4.

19. Charleston should not be viewed as an anomaly. Other communities throughout the south also held segregated proms after the dawn of the new millennium. For example, Montgomery County High School in Mount Vernon, Georgia, hosted its first integrated prom in 2009. In Montgomery County, it was common for the black prom to be open to all students, a point that demonstrates that it was not blacks that had a problem with celebrating with whites.

## Works Cited

Anderson, Margaret. *The Children of the South*, 6th ed. New York: Farrar, Straus and Giroux, 1966.

Green McAdoo Cultural Center. "Preserving the Legacy: Mission Statement." Accessed August 6, 2013. http://www.greenmcadoo.org/contact.html.

_____. "Preserving the Legacy: The Story of Desegregation in Clinton, Tennessee." Accessed August 6, 2013. http://www.greenmcadoo.org/story.html.

Head, T. "Poll: Only 40% of Mississippi Republicans Think Interracial Marriage Should Be Legal." April 7, 2011. aboutwww. Accessed August 6, 2013. http://civilliberty.about. com/b/2011/04/07/poll-only-40-of-mississippi-republicans-think-interracial-marriage-should-be-legal.html.

McClelland, Janice M. "A Structural Analysis of Desegregation: Clinton High School 1954–1958." *Tennessee Historical Quarterly* 56 (Fall 1997): 296–309.

McDaniel, Keith Henry, dir. *The Clinton 12*. Written by McDaniel. Produced by Green McAdoo Cultural Organization. Oak Ridge: Secret City Films and HP Video, 2007. DVD. 86 min.

Nichols, Bill. *Introduction to Documentary*. Bloomington: Indiana University Press, 2001.

Public Policy Polling. "Barbour, Bryant Lead in Mississippi." *Public Policy Polling*, April 7, 2011. http://publicpolicypolling.blogspot.com/2011/04/barbour-bryant-lead-in-mississippi.html.

Saltzman, Paul, dir. *Prom Night in Mississippi*. Written by Saltzman. Produced by Patricia Aquino and Saltzman. New York: documramafilms, 2009. DVD. 90 min.

Spears, Alan. "Green McAdoo and the Clinton 12." Californiabuffalosoldiers.org, April 21, 2012. Accessed August 12, 2013. http://www.californiabuffalosoldiers.org/green-mcadoo-and-the-clinton-12/.

Totenberg, Nina. "Supreme Court Weighs the Future of Voting Rights Act." February 27, 2013. National Public Radio. Accessed August 12, 2013. http://www.npr.org/2013/02/ 27/173012038/supreme-court-weighs-future-of-voting-rights-act.

# A National Concern

## *Remembering and Teaching the Death of Emmett Till*

### Kevin E. Grimm

My parents, like many parents, used it as a warning: Don't let what happened to Emmett Till happen to you.—Keith Beauchamp, director, *The Untold Story of Emmett Louis Till*

On March 30, 2012, hip-hop artist Duran Butler appeared on CNN to discuss his song concerning the recent death of Trayvon Martin, a black teenager who was shot and killed while walking home one evening in Sanford, Florida. The title, "Skittles and Arizona," references the candy and the brand of iced tea Martin had been carrying when he died. In addition to addressing in the track the contemporary issues that the African American community faces, Butler also invokes a major event in the early Civil Rights Movement when he mentions Emmett Till. The CNN journalist interviewing Butler, Fredericka Whitfield, played the line before explaining that a number of people had noted the similarities between the deaths of Martin and Till, despite the intervening decades.[1] The two events are not exactly the same, to be sure, but the way that the 2012 death of a black male teenager immediately invokes images of Till's violent 1955 murder indicates Till's fate is widely known in early twenty-first century America.

Yet, Till's death had not always figured so prominently in the collective public memory of the United States. In fact, only a decade ago the events surrounding Emmett Till were largely unknown to the general public, and discussions of the beginning of the Civil Rights Movement rarely included his death. Two documentaries on the murder of Till helped change that trend. This essay analyzes the content of and reaction to Stanley Nelson's PBS documentary, *The Murder of Emmett Till* (2003), and Keith Beauchamp's documentary, *The Untold Story of Emmett Louis Till* (2005). Although the latter appeared in its finished form nearly two years after Nelson's film, Beauchamp had worked on his project for nine years and was thus widely known to be producing a film on the Till murder. Screenings of Beauchamp's film had also occurred as early as November 2002.[2]

## The Murder and the Documentaries

Despite several attempts to bring the story to the screen, almost a half-century passed before Till's 1955 murder became the topic of a film. Given the previous lack of interest in delving into the Till case, it is ironic then that by the time the disturbing events of his death were finally retold in motion-picture form, it was the subject of two documentary films released closely together. Prior to completing his film on Till, Nelson was a well-established documentary filmmaker. He had already made films on Pan-Africanist Marcus Garvey and the African American press, both of which received a number of nominations and awards.[3]

For director Beauchamp, making a documentary on Till's murder was very personal. In November 2002, *New York Times* journalist Brent Staples's editorial described how one of Beauchamp's childhood experiences had led him to make his film. When the director was young, he found the *Jet* magazine edition featuring the infamous picture of Till's distorted corpse, asked his parents about the event, and subsequently "grew up obsessed with this case." Staples further notes that "over the past several decades, Hollywood has turned away even famous producers who wanted to bring this story to film," but Beauchamp was now "casting new light on a crime that many thought would remain forever unpunished. The information in his film could conceivably change that, allowing law enforcement officials to achieve justice at last for Emmett Louis Till."[4] Staples's language highlights the importance of both films in bringing the murder of Till back into the national spotlight in late 2002 and early 2003, a period when Beauchamp's documentary began to be screened in theaters and Nelson's aired on PBS.

Both Beauchamp's and Nelson's films document the events surrounding the murder of Emmett Louis Till, which occurred in August 1955 during his visit to the South. Specifically, fourteen-year-old Till had traveled from Chicago to Mississippi to visit his great-uncle Moses (Mose) Wright and other members of his extended family. One day, along with his cousins and some friends, he entered a grocery store owned by Roy and Carolyn Bryant in the small town of Money. Carolyn was working the store alone, and although accounts differ on what exactly occurred, Till may have made a suggestive comment or wolf-whistled at her as he exited the establishment. Three days later Carolyn's husband and his half-brother J. W. Milam visited Wright's home in the middle of the night and demanded that he hand the child over. Wright pled with Bryant and Milam to let Till alone, but they persisted, even threatening Wright's life as they demanded to see his great-nephew. Wright conceded, and although the two white men were armed, he believed that they would just beat Till and bring him back to the house. Unfortunately, no one saw Till again until his body was discovered in the nearby Tallahatchie River three days later. His body was so mutilated that he could only be identified by his late father's ring, a keepsake that Till had worn with great pride.

Devastated, Till's mother, Mamie Till, shipped his body back to Chicago and held an open-casket funeral because, as she explained, she wanted to "[l]et the people see what I've seen."[5] She desired "the world to see this."[6] Indeed, the combination of the beating Till had endured and the onset of decomposition made his face look hideous. Over fifty thousand people, the vast majority of them African American, viewed Till's body. Shortly afterward, *Jet* magazine ran pictures of the corpse, helping spread the image of his mutilated body to an even larger audience.

Bryant and Milam were soon arrested and tried for kidnapping and murder. Wright was the prosecution's key witness, who, despite being surrounded by a room full of Bryant and Milam's peers, boldly identified them as the men that had kidnapped Till.[7] In addition, an African American teenager named Willie Reed testified that he had heard someone being beaten in a shed behind Milam's house on the night Till had been kidnapped and that he had seen Milam and Bryant there. Despite the overwhelming evidence against them, the all-white, all-male jury acquitted the two men after only an hour of deliberation. According to the foreman of the jury, they would have returned with the not-guilty verdict even sooner had they not been instructed "to make it look good."[8] African Americans, many whites, and people in the world at large were outraged at the miscarriage of justice. To make matters worse, a few months later Milam and Bryant, protected by double-jeopardy laws, sold their story to *Look* magazine, fully admitting their guilt.[9]

Both Nelson's and Beauchamp's films recount the events surrounding Till's murder, although the content and style of each differ slightly. Beauchamp's film chronicles a shorter account of Till's family life than Nelson's, and Beauchamp uses extended segments from his interviews with Till's mother. While Nelson utilizes a voice-over narration, Beauchamp doesn't, perhaps to create a deeper sense of connection between the audience and Till's friends and relatives, even including comments from Till's grandmother and cousins. Beauchamp spends less time on the actual trial than Nelson does and seeks to make Till's murder felt on a personal level. Alternatively, Nelson's relatively more intimate discussion of the events of the murder and the trial lead him to identify a number of new potential witnesses to the crime. In addition, Beauchamp mentions at the end of his film that in 2003, the U.S. Department of Justice and he began meetings to explore reopening the Till case; he follows with a CNN segment that describes how the Justice Department was reopening the case due in part to Beauchamp's film.[10]

Overall, however, the similarities between the films are more interesting and important than any differences. Both Beauchamp and Nelson place the Till murder firmly in the context of the beginning of the Civil Rights Movement, with Nelson explaining that the murder was equally as significant as the Montgomery Bus Boycott.[11] The two films also address the massive international anger over the case, a point that often goes unmentioned in conversations about Till's murder. When covering Bryant and Milam's trial, Nelson's film describes the numerous reporters in Money and notes, "The Associated Press fielded queries from Paris, Copenhagen, Tokyo. The Till case had become a major international news story." Likewise, when the jury returned with the not-guilty verdict, Nelson's film states over a picture of an article on the verdict from the French paper *Le Peuple*, "Reports of the acquittal made front-page headlines across the United States and set off an international firestorm. The life of a Negro in Mississippi, a European paper observed, is not worth a whistle."[12] Beauchamp also touches on the international impact of the murder by including comments by historian Raymond Lockett of the Southern University of Baton Rouge that the Jim Crow system in the American South looked much like apartheid in South Africa.[13] Both filmmakers thus expand the context of Till's murder to include the increasingly global opposition to white supremacy in the mid-twentieth century.

News of Till's death indeed reverberated around the world. During the 1950s, African Americans increasingly identified with African freedom movements, especially the widely publicized campaign led by the charismatic Kwame Nkrumah against British colonialism in Ghana. African leaders and populations alike paid attention to incidents of racial violence within the United States, and Till's murder undermined U.S. prestige abroad, especially in the decolonizing nonwhite world. Nonwhite populations distrusted a nation that allowed some of its nonwhite citizens to be murdered with impunity. Events such as Till's murder, therefore, severely complicated American efforts to orient Third World nonwhite nations toward the West in the Cold War. For instance, one report by the U.S. Information Agency, an organization President Dwight D. Eisenhower created in 1953 to spread positive images of the United States abroad, found in April 1956 that negative reactions to the Till murder and verdict existed in the Belgian Congo, British Ghana and Nigeria, Egypt, France, India, Israel, Italy, Lebanon, Norway, the Soviet Union, Thailand, and Turkey. Numerous other countries disapproved of American race relations in general.[14]

A bit of tension also marked the relationship between Nelson and Beauchamp, who were both committed to bringing Till's murder back into America's national consciousness. In particular, a point of contention between the two filmmakers was that PBS refused Beauchamp's film in favor of Nelson's, who was already an award-winning documentarian. In addition, in a 2003 interview with Robert Finn of the *New York Times*, Beauchamp suggested that it was he who had done "the investigative grunt work.... When Stanley did his film, he caught everyone after they'd already talked to me." Thus, according to Finn, "[i]n the rookie's view, the vet 'snaked' him."[15] When *New York Times* journalist Felicia Lee interviewed Beauchamp a year later, he explained that the making of the documentaries became "a competitive issue.... I don't want to talk bad about him [Nelson]—he knew I was working on this film. PBS turned me down many times; he's a known documentarian."[16]

Despite the tension between the filmmakers, Lee notes, "[N]either wanted to use the term 'rivalry' to describe their efforts." Instead, they "stressed that even though they were of different generations, they grew up as many African-Americans did, with Emmett Till's story etched into their minds and hearts as a symbol of black struggle."[17] In addition, both men were pleased that they had helped the nation refocus on the Till case. Beauchamp even said, "In the end, I'm kind of glad he [Nelson] did his film; it brought more attention to the case."[18] Indeed, they had played different roles in stimulating new interest in Till's murder. Nelson generated much publicity through his screenings and the airing of his documentary on PBS, and Beauchamp met directly with members of Congress and U.S. officials about reopening the case.[19]

## Reactions and Reopening

Both *Murder* and *Untold* stimulated a positive domestic response in early twenty-first-century America. Almost two months before Nelson's film aired on PBS on January 20, 2003, Rick Bragg of the *New York Times* traveled to Chicago to talk with Mamie Till Mobley about the murder. During the interview, she commented, "It looks like Emmett is surfacing once again." For Bragg,

Mamie was "the emotional anchor" of Beauchamp's documentary, which was being screened at the time. Bragg described Beauchamp as a man "haunted by an image of the murdered boy in an open coffin" and hinted that Mississippi officials were already, in late 2002, considering reopening the case to see if there had been other participants who could now be charged. Beauchamp believed up to "three other white and four black men" may have been involved, although he said the African Americans were probably "forced to partici-pate."[20]

The strong evidence presented in the two documentaries, that there may have been other possible participants in the murder, led to a new investigation into Till's death. According to *New York Times* journalists Eric Lichtblau and Andrew Jacobs, on May 10, 2004, R. Alexander Acosta, assistant attorney general for civil rights, Department of Justice, announced that the department would be reopening the case because "information uncovered in the filming of two documentaries on the 1955 killing suggested that people besides the two original suspects may have been involved." U.S. Representative Bobby Rush (D-IL), supported by the Congressional Black Caucus, had also proposed a resolution in Congress specifically requesting that the Department of Justice reopen the case. Simultaneously, U.S. Representative Charles Rangel (D-NY) and Senator Charles E. Schumer (D-NY) submitted a special request to U.S. Attorney General John Ashcroft to investigate Till's death. Along with the urging of activist Alvin Sykes, president of the Emmett Till Justice Campaign, the federal government was under immense pressure to reexamine the case after the two films seemed to indicate that Bryant and Milam were not solely responsible for Till's murder. Beauchamp held a screening of his documentary for a district attorney and a U.S. attorney in Mississippi in an effort to persuade them to reinvestigate the case. He also sought help from Schumer and Rangel and "met with the federal authorities to plead his case."[21] Although Nelson did not have such direct influence on U.S. officials, when he screened his film, he provided ten thousand postcards, by his own estimation, for his audience to send to the attorney general of Mississippi requesting a new investigation.[22] Thus, the films not only stimulated a new level of awareness about Till's death but they also created an opportunity to achieve at least a measure of justice. Both Nelson and Beauchamp "were jubilant" when they learned of the Department of Justice's decision to reopen the case.[23]

African Americans' reactions to the new investigation were "bittersweet," according to *Jet* magazine. In early 2004, Kweisi Mfume, head of the National Association for the Advancement of Colored People (NAACP), explained that the new focus on the case created "mixed emotions.... I am glad the case is being reopened, but it is sad that it has taken so long."[24] Other black American leaders reacted similarly. For example, the Reverend Jesse Jackson argued, "Justice this delayed is justice denied. Fifty years later is an injustice. But it is a good thing that it's reopened to remind us of the horror of state-fostered terrorism."[25] Coretta Scott King, widow of Martin Luther King, Jr., called the new investigation "long overdue but welcome" and labeled the case "a festering sore on our nation's soul."[26] Mississippi State Senator David Jordan, an African American representing the area of the state that includes Money and who had been at the trial of Milam and Bryant in 1955, also supported the reopening of the case.[27]

Despite the hope that a new investigation might at long last provide justice for Till and his family and despite the investigation itself, no criminal charges resulted. In late May 2005, officials exhumed Till's remains in order to identify his body because in 1955 lawyers for Milam and Bryant had based their defense primarily on the ridiculous notion that the corpse pulled from the Tallahatchie River was not Till's.[28] Milam and Bryant had died over a decade earlier, but Carolyn Bryant remained potentially culpable in the kidnapping and murder of Till. By March 2006, however, the Federal Bureau of Investigation (FBI) determined the statute of limitations regarding the murder had expired because the federal government could only prosecute civil rights violations up to five years after they occurred. The FBI subsequently gave the eight thousand pages of material that it had gathered to the district attorney in Greenville, Mississippi, for use in determining whether or not Carolyn Bryant, seventy-three years old by that time, should be charged with manslaughter in state court.[29] In late February 2007, a grand jury in Mississippi decided there was not enough evidence to bring her to trial. That decision, in the words of *New York Times* journalist Shaila Dewan, "effectively end[ed] any further prosecution of a crime that fueled the civil rights movement."[30] Although no one was ever convicted for Till's kidnapping and murder, Dewan's language makes it clear that Till's death is now an important aspect of the nation's collective memory of the Civil Rights Movement.

## *The Till Bill*

The two documentaries and the reopening of the Till case also revealed the need for stronger measures at the federal level to conduct new investigations into unsolved cases from the civil rights era. Thus, although no one was ever punished for Till's death, the discussions stimulated among the public and U.S. officials led to new inquiries into other past racial crimes. In addition to reopening the Till case, the FBI also canvassed its field offices for unsolved murder cases that appeared to be motivated by race; however, the authorization and the funding to pursue the numerous new investigations into old cases could only come from Congress. On February 8, 2007, U.S. Representative John Lewis (D-GA), a veteran of sit-ins during the civil rights era, introduced the Emmett Till Unsolved Civil Rights Crime Act. Lewis declared, "It is long overdue. The country is ready. The victims' families, friends, and loved ones have been suffering indefinitely, and Congress needs to act." In addition to seeking justice for those killed during the civil rights era, Lewis said that the measure would bring "healing." The bill enjoyed broad support, with over eighty representatives from both parties initially or eventually cosponsoring the measure.[31] Simultaneously in the U.S. Senate, Christopher J. Dodd (D-CT) and Patrick Leahy (D-VT) introduced a bill with similar language, receiving broad support from eighteen other senators.[32] The NAACP, American Civil Liberties Union (ACLU), and Southern Poverty Law Center were only a few of the numerous organizations to support the bill.[33]

The passage in both chambers of the Emmett Till Unsolved Civil Rights Crime Act of 2007, the House version, had significant implications. Within the division of the Department of Justice that deals with civil rights, the bill created a new Unsolved Civil Rights Era Crimes Unit, led by a new deputy chief. The unit would coordinate with state and local officials to investigate old civil rights cases occurring before 1970. The bill also granted the FBI a new Unsolved Civil Rights Crime Investigative Office, led by a deputy investigator, to conduct similar activities, and stipulated that until 2017 the unit would receive an $11.5 million annual budget to fund its investigations. An additional $2 million would annually go to grants to fund similar activities at the state and local levels. Creating two new offices both with a wide mandate for investigation of old cases and an appropriate budget indicated Congress was taking the reopening of unsolved civil rights cases quite seriously.[34]

In addition to the title, the language used during discussions of the bill clearly indicates that the measure had resulted from renewed interest stimulated by the two films. When Leahy introduced the bill in the Senate, he claimed, "Emmett Till's death served as a momentum for change. It inspired a generation of Americans to demand justice and freedom in a way America had never seen before."[35] A Senate report on the bill the following June from the Senate Committee on the Judiciary describes both the domestic and international impact of Till's death: "The racial violence commonplace in the American South became known to the world, and generated a widespread public outcry across America. Emmett Till's murder also inspired the modern civil rights movement." The House Committee on the Judiciary held a public hearing where a number of activists testified, including the widows of murdered civil rights leaders Medgar Evers and Michael Schwerner, Sykes of the Emmett Till Justice Campaign, an NAACP official, and the head of the Southern Poverty Law Center. Federal officials and politicians were listening closely to the people most involved in obtaining justice for Emmett Till and to those that unsolved civil rights crimes affected most directly.[36] With such massive support, the Till Bill easily passed the House of Representatives with a vote of 422–2.[37] While the Till Bill would not pass the Senate so easily, with Senator Tom Coburn (R-OK) blocking a unanimous vote for a year over financial concerns, the measure finally passed the following September, and President George W. Bush signed it into law on October 7, 2008.[38]

## Teaching Emmett Till

A number of websites dedicated to the story of Emmett Till emerged shortly after the releases of *Murder* and *Untold* and the passage of the Till Bill. The sites, which suggest diverse ways to teach the Till case, are products of the documentaries, demonstrating the American public's rediscovery of the case. Especially noteworthy is the website PBS created for Nelson's documentary *The Murder of Emmett Till*, which suggests different ways of presenting the case to students through the various lenses of history, civics, geography, and economics. The history section is especially effective, with one lesson recommending the teacher divide students into groups to analyze different topics involving race in the early twenty-first century. The students can thus connect the events surrounding Till's death to their own experiences. One case, for instance, asks students to think about candidate Bush's 2000 trip to Bob Jones University, which, according to the PBS website, at the time did not allow dating between blacks and whites. Other topics include Thomas Jefferson's relationship with Sally Hemings as well as the issue of reparations. In the civics section, the website suggests students read a series of Jim Crow laws and become familiar with the landmark U.S. Supreme Court cases *Plessy v. Ferguson* and *Brown v. Board of Education*. Lynching is also a topic listed for discussion. Regarding geography and economics, students can learn about African American migration among regions of the United States, the role of race in presidential elections, and the history of sharecropping. Students can even enter into discussions of class, working to answer the question of why poor blacks and poor whites have not organized together politically in American history. The PBS website thus helps teachers present Till's death to students from a variety of productive angles.[39]

Other websites also contain useful suggestions for teaching Till's death in a national context. Houghton-Mifflin Publishing constructed a site for Marilyn Nelson's book *A Wreath for Emmett Till*, which tells the story of the murder and the case in the form of poetry. The site's teaching guide recommends students perform research on lynching and Jim Crow laws in addition to the case itself. As with the PBS site, Houghton-Mifflin suggests teachers tie the Till case into current events, including a discussion of whether or not Till's killers were terrorists. Another potential topic listed is why the author and other poets were initially invited to the White House in 2004 but were later asked not to visit.[40]

Beyond publishers and those directly involved in producing the films, other institutions have shown interest in how to teach Till's death. Facing History and Ourselves, an organization explicitly devoted to challenging "racism, anti–Semitism, and prejudice," has constructed a site to teach themes found in Stanley Nelson's documentary. In a series of four excellent lessons, students can learn to analyze the reactions of both numerous groups and Americans as a whole to the crime, learn to place the murder in the larger contexts of lynching, anti-black violence, and the Civil Rights Movement and think about the impact and importance of Till's murder for future generations. The site twice mentions the larger global context of the case, noting the importance of Till's death as "part of the collective history of the United States and the world."[41]

Although the aforementioned websites provide many valuable suggestions on how to teach the death of Emmett Till, the international reaction to the case needs to be included more often. Till's death had an enormous impact on citizens around the globe, especially those in nonwhite nations, as the USIA report cited earlier indicates. America could not claim to be a country of freedom, justice, and equality as long as such blatant miscarriages of justice occurred. During the 1950s, ties of mutual understanding and support deepened between black Africans struggling for independence from their European colonizers and African Americans facing ongoing discrimination and violence. Thus, nonwhite populations in Africa viewed the failure to prosecute Till's killers as an indication of how white America might treat their own nations in international relations. Hence, not only did Till's death undermine American prestige abroad but it also threatened, along with numerous other contemporary episodes of American racial violence, the ability of the United States to attract nonwhite nations to the side of the West in the global Cold War. With that in mind, transnational racial connections and the Cold War environment are two useful international contexts within which teachers can place Till's death.

Even as the death of Emmett Till has become a central event in America's public memory of the Civil Rights Movement, the teaching of the case can still stir controversy. In February 2007 a seventh-grade class in Los Angeles created a presentation on the murder as a part of Black History Month. School administrators, however, were concerned that Till's murder, according to journalist Carla Rivera of the *Los Angeles Times*, "was too graphic for younger children and did not fit the mood of what was to be a celebratory event." The administrators blocked the event from taking place, and when students protested by writing letters, the school fired two teachers who signed one of the students' letters.[42] As the teachers perhaps recognized, presenting only positive events from the civil rights era obscures both the reality of the dangers African Americans confronted as well as their corresponding courage in the face of such threats.

Fortunately, the predominant public attitude toward Till's murder now seems to welcome the incorporation of his death into the canon of significant civil rights events. By retelling Till's largely forgotten story, *The Murder of Emmett Till* and *The Untold Story of Emmett Louis Till* stimulated a reopening of the Till case, increased awareness of Till's death among the American public, and helped prod Congress to eventually pass the Emmett Till Unsolved Civil Rights Crime Act, commonly known as the Till Bill. Until 2017, the measure provides authority and financing for the Department of Justice and the FBI to investigate unsolved cases from the civil rights era. Even more significant, due in large part to the way the two films retold Till's story, his death became more important in American public memory as an event that galvanized the early Civil Rights Movement. Analyzing both the way American public memory recovered the events of Till's death during the first decade of the twenty-first century and the way the Till case is now taught to secondary-school students reveals the widespread rediscovery of Till's murder as a central event in the Civil Rights Movement. In addition, emphasizing the way racial violence complicated America's efforts to attract nonwhite nations to the West in the globalizing Cold War of the 1950s and tracing the racial connections between victimized African Americans and colonized Africans will help students, and the entire nation, think more internationally about race and American history. Till's death must be seen as not just a national concern but a worldwide event in the twentieth-century struggle against white domination. Hence, America's public memory of the Civil Rights Movement will help its citizens better connect to those around the world still suffering oppression and racism in the early twenty-first century.

In June 2003, Brent Staples at the *New York Times* invoked journalist David Halberstam's quote that the Till murder constituted "the first 'media event of the civil rights era.'"[43] Keith Beauchamp was only twenty-three years old when he began working on his film on Till, which was his first, and he has continued to pursue the use of documentary filmmaking in the cause of civil rights. In 2011 he began work on a television series called *The Injustice Files*, which has begun airing on the Investigation Discovery Network, in which he works directly with the FBI unit that was created from the Till Bill to investigate old civil rights cases and present them to the American public.[44] Since the Till Bill was passed in large part due to the two documentaries on Till's death, Beauchamp has therefore been able to participate directly in the positive results his own filmmaking caused. Likewise, after his Till film, Stanley Nelson has continued his close relationship with PBS, producing pieces for them on the 1890 massacre at Wounded Knee and on the freedom rides that took place in the South during the 1960s. Overall, he has remained centered on African American topics and continues to receive awards for his works that often reveal very personal and untold stories about African Americans. In fact, his film on Till was clearly part of such a pattern of rediscovering some of the lost personal stories from the American Civil Rights Movement.[45] Both directors thus remain explorers of the powerful combination of documentary cinema and race as they continue to make films in the service of racial equality and justice.

## Notes

1. Whitfield, interview.
2. "A Premiere Screening of the Documentary Film 'The Untold Story of Emmett Louis Till,'" *New York Times*, November 10, 2002, H18.
3. "Stanley Nelson."
4. "Premiere Screening," H18; Brent Staples, "The Murder of Emmett Louis Till, Revisited," *New York Times*, November 11, 2002, A16.
5. *Murder of Emmett Till*, 29:00.
6. *Untold Story*, part 1, 29:45.
7. Fearing for his life, Wright left Mississippi immediately after testifying, never to return again.
8. *Murder of Emmett Till*, 45:15.
9. Ibid., 50:00. Willie Reed (who changed his name later to Willie Louis) passed away on July 18, 2013. See Carreras, "Emmett Till Case."
10. Untold Story; *Murder of Emmett Till*, part 2, 27:30.
11. *Murder of Emmett Till*, 2:50, 51:15; *Untold Story*, part 2, 29:00.
12. *Murder of Emmett Till*, 34:15, 48:00.
13. *Untold Story*, part 1, 3:45.
14. "World-Wide Press Comments," 4, 9, 17, 20, 22, 25–27, 30–31, 34–35, 43, 51, 56. The report also explores reactions to the bus boycott in Montgomery and the University of Alabama's expulsion of Autherine Lucy, the first African American who had enrolled at the school.
15. Robin Finn, "Bringing History to Life, and a Crime to Light," *New York Times*, May 21, 2003, B2.
16. Felicia Lee, "Directors Elated by Plan to Revisit 1955 Murder," *New York Times*, May 12, 2004, B4.

17. Ibid.

18. Finn, "Bringing History to Life," B2.

19. Lee, "Directors Elated"; Eric Lichtblau and Andrew Jacobs, "U.S. Reopens '55 Murder Case, Flashpoint of Civil Rights Era," *New York Times*, May 11, 2004, A1.

20. Rick Bragg, "Emmett Till's Long Shadow: A Hate Crime That Refuses to Give Up Its Ghosts," *New York Times*, December 1, 2002, C1.

21. Lichtblau and Jacobs, "U.S. Reopens '55 Murder Case," A1; "Emmett Till: Blacks React."

22. Lee, "Directors Elated," B4.

23. Ibid.

24. "Emmett Till: Blacks React."

25. Ibid.

26. Ibid.

27. Andrew Jacobs, "In Mississippi Delta Town, An Unwelcome Past Calls: Some Dread Reopening of the Till Case," *New York Times*, May 12, 2004, A17.

28. Stephen Holden, "Remembering a Boy, His Savage Murder, and Racial Injustice in Mississippi," *New York Times*, August 17, 2005, E5. See also Shaila Dewan and Ariel Hart, "F.B.I. Discovers Trial Transcript in Emmett Till Case," *New York Times*, May 18, 2005, A14.

29. Diana Schemo, "National Briefing: South," *New York Times*, March 17, 2006, A21.

30. Shaila Dewan, "After Inquiry, Grand Jury Refuses to Issue New Indictments in Till Case," *New York Times*, February 28, 2007, A16.

31. "2008 Bill Tracking H.R. 923"; 153 Cong. Rec., H312 (February 9, 2007) (Emmett Till Unsolved Civil Rights Crime Act of 2007 hereafter referred to as Till Act).

32. "2008 Bill Tracking S.R. 535."

33. 153 Cong. Rec. H6742–49 (June 20, 2007) (Till Act).

34. "2008 Bill Tracking S.R. 535"; "2008 Bill Tracking H.R. 923."

35. 153 Cong. Rec. S1789 (February 8, 2007) (Till Act).

36. House Committee on the Judiciary, H. Rep. No. 200, *Emmett Till Unsolved Civil Rights Crime Act of 2007*, 110th Cong., 1st sess. (2007); Senate Committee on the Judiciary, S. Rep. No. 88, 110th Cong., 1st sess. (2007) (all Till Act).

37. 153 Cong. Rec. H6749 (June 20, 2007) (Till Act).

38. 153 Cong. Rec. S12419 (October 2, 2007); 153 Cong. Rec. S15162–65 (December 12, 2007); 154 Cong. Rec. S9350–52 (September 24, 2008) (all Till Act).

39. "Teachers' Guide: Suggestions for Active Learning." *Plessy v. Ferguson* (1896) declared the principle of "separate but equal" valid in public schools; *Brown v. Board of Education* (1954) struck down that principle. The rumored romantic relationship between Thomas Jefferson and his slave Sally Hemings gained more popularity after DNA tests on descendants in 1998 seemed to prove that Jefferson likely fathered some of Hemings' children. "Sally Hemings," New York Times: Times Topics, *New York Times*, 2013, accessed March 28, 2013, http://topics.nytimes.com/topics/reference/timestopics/people/h/sally_hemings/index.html. Also, Houghton-Mifflin's site hints that the Bush administration feared the potential meeting would degenerate into an antiwar protest focused on Iraq.

40. "Teacher's Guide, A Wreath for Emmett Till."

41. "Emmett Till: A Series of Four Lessons."

42. Carla Rivera, "'Emmett Till' Poet Urges the Reinstatement of 2 Teachers," *Los Angeles Times,* March 22, 2007, http://articles.latimes.com/2007/mar/22/local/me-charter22. See also Erin Aubry Kaplan, "Tell Black History's Ugly Truth," *Los Angeles Times,* March 23, 2007, http://www.latimes.com/news/opinion/commentary/la-oe-kaplan23mar23,0,6186046.column.

43. Brent Staples, "Sins of the Fathers: Tracing the Gene of 'Intolerance' through Several Mississippi Generations," *New York Times*, June 8, 2003, B18.

44. "Keith Beauchamp."
45. "Stanley Nelson."

## Works Cited

Carreras, Iris. "Emmett Till Case: Willie Louis, Key Witness in the 1955 Murder of Teen in Miss., Dies at 76, Report Says." *CBSNEWS.* July 24, 2013. *CBS Interactive,* 2013. Accessed August 15, 2013. http://www.cbsnews.com/8301–504083_162–57595237–504083/emmett-till-case-willie-louis-key-witness-in-the-1955-murder-of-teen-in-miss-dies-at-76-report-says/.

"Emmett Till: A Series of Four Lessons." *Facing History and Ourselves,* 2012. Accessed June 25, 2012. http://www.facinghistory.org/resources/units/emmett-till-a-series-four-lessons.

"Emmett Till: Blacks React to Reopening of Tragic Case." *Jet,* May 31, 2004. Accessed May 14, 2012. http://findarticles.com/p/articles/mi_m1355/is_22_105/ai_n6152964/pg_2/?tag=content;col1.

"Keith Beauchamp 'The Injustice Files' Interview with Kam Williams." June 11, 2011. Lee Bailey's Eurweb.com Electronic Urban Report. *News Theme on Genesis Framework,* 2012. Accessed October 10, 2012. http://www.eurweb.com/2011/06/keith-beauchamp-the-injustice-files-interview-with-kam-williams/.

*The Murder of Emmett Till.* Directed by Stanley Nelson. Alexandria, VA: PBS Video, 2004. DVD.

"Stanley Nelson." *Firelight Media,* 2011. Accessed October 10, 2012. http://firelightmedia.tv/stanley-nelson/.

"Teacher's Guide, a Wreath for Emmett Till, A." *Houghton Mifflin Harcourt,* 2012. Accessed June 25, 2012. http://www.houghtonmifflinbooks.com/readers_guides/nelson_wreath.shtml.

"Teachers' Guide: Suggestions for Active Learning." American Experience: The Murder of Emmett Till. *WGBH Educational Foundation,* 1996–2009. Accessed June 25, 2012. http://www.pbs.org/wgbh/amex/till/tguide/index.html.

"2008 Bill Tracking H.R. 923." *LexisNexis Academic & Library Solutions,* 2008. Accessed June 21, 2012. http://web.lexis-nexis.com.proxy.library.ohiou.edu/congcomp/document?_m=75c90a4521451396976f4e9e9454b0c4&_docnum=2&wchp=dGLbVzV-zSkSA&_md5=f86fd7034d60f45c6640da07aabacaaf.

"2008 Bill Tracking S.R. 535." *LexisNexis Academic & Library Solutions,* 2008. Accessed May 16, 2012. http://web.lexis-nexis.com.proxy.library.ohiou.edu/congcomp/document?_m=75c90a4521451396976f4e9e9454b0c4&_docnum=3&wchp=dGLbVzV-zSkSA&_md5=b924b74c435b63df8b6e4617924a3c98.

*The Untold Story of Emmett Louis Till.* Directed by Keith A. Beauchamp. New York: Thinkfilm, 2005. DVD.

Whitfield, Fredericka. Interview with Duran Butler. *Blipsters: All Things Black, Hipster, and Blipster.* March 30, 2012. *CNN.* Accessed May 9, 2012. http://blipsters.tumblr.com/post/20185817445/duran-butler-on-cnn.

"World-Wide Press Comments on the Racial Problem in the U.S., 1956." Box 8, Memorandums, and Summaries, 1954–56, Intelligence Bulletins, Office of Research, Record Group 306, U.S. Information Agency, Records of the United States Information Agency. National Archives at College Park, College Park, Maryland.

# Fear Factor

## When Black Equality Is Framed as Militant

### Winsome Chunnu-Brayda
### and Travis D. Boyce

In 2009 California Newsreel released Judy Richardson and Bestor Cram's *Scarred Justice: The Orangeburg Massacre 1968*, a documentary about the killing of unarmed black student activists by white South Carolina Highway troopers.[1] Richardson and Cram shed light on the Orangeburg Massacre as one of many untold incidents that occurred during the Civil Rights Movement. Moreover, this film provides an insightful look at how whites have historically used fear to portray as peril those blacks who seek equality. As noted by Cram in an April 2008 interview in the *New York Times*, this film depicts how the prevailing viewpoint (that blacks seeking equality are dangerous) minimized the dead and wounded black youth of Orangeburg, leaving the tragedy in the margins of history—as compared to other, later events, such as the Kent State University shootings, which are considered historically pivotal.[2] This essay shows how the fear of blacks seeking equality is revealed in the documentary and how this method continues to be used today to suppress black political candidates. Finally, the essay concludes with a discussion on the change that must occur in the heart of the metastructure (the justice, economic, and government systems) of the United States.

*Scarred Justice* poignantly chronicles an event that took place in Orangeburg, South Carolina, in 1968. South Carolina State College (SCSC) students, along with students from neighboring Claflin University, were protesting a segregated bowling alley and had thrown objects at police and damaged businesses. The police began to beat the protestors and subsequently shot several

57

of them dead and wounded others. Eventually, the police went to trial. Even though the officers shot the students in their backs, the officers were acquitted of using unnecessary force. To make matters worse, Robert McNair, South Carolina's governor at the time of the incident, brought the activists to trial for inciting a riot. Specifically, he blamed the civil rights activists (particularly Cleveland L. Sellers Jr., formerly a member of the Student Nonviolent Coordinating Committee [SNCC]), for the conflict, claiming that the trouble was a result of their Black Power advocacy.[3]

The fact that equality sought by black people can be viewed by some whites as militancy, rather than as black enfranchisement, is highly problematic. This type of framing (which is used for suppression) paints the Orangeburg activists as responsible for what happened to them. The following section of this essay reviews the historical trend that some whites see blacks' pursuit of equality as militancy. This trend, illustrated in the documentary, has long been part of U.S. history and remains part of today's culture.

## The Historical Framing of Black Militancy Prior to 1968

During the antebellum era, many white southerners believed that blacks were content with the status quo, attributing any change in their happy attitudes as the work of outside agitators. After the Civil War (Reconstruction, 1865–77), blacks gained their freedom, citizenship, and voting rights, occurrences that heightened white anxiety because in several southern areas there was a black majority. As a result, numerous black politicians were elected into office, and blacks gained access to social and education venues.[4] Interesting, many whites saw this presence as an act of militancy (derived from the push of outsiders), which the whites believed could lead to a collapse of the United States. Certainly, black equality challenged the conventional African American stereotypes; many whites feared this change and fought to preserve inequality. For example, in 1895, South Carolina Senator Ben Tillman held a constitutional convention that stripped blacks of much of the progress they had gained, particularly their voting rights.[5] By the end of the nineteenth century, racial segregation was the law of the land.

Prior to the modern Civil Rights Movement (1954–68), civil rights activism in the United States was widespread. In the 1930s and 1940s, civil rights activists scored several important legal victories. In particular, they gained blacks access to graduate and professional education and voting rights (by the elimination of the white Democratic primary). Activists during World War II and the postwar United States also influenced federal legislation and presidential Executive Orders 8802 and 9981. Moreover, the activists organized grassroots movements to address the harsh realities of Jim Crow segregation, particularly drawing international attention to the 1931 Scottsboro Boys incident, where nine black youth were falsely accused and subsequently convicted of raping two white females. In 1954, the U.S. Supreme Court overturned the 1896 *Plessy v. Ferguson* decision, thereby ruling that racial segregation was unconstitutional.

Perhaps, one of the most glaring examples of this "outsider" mythology came in the aftermath of the 1955 lynching of Emmett Till, a fourteen-year-old Chicago native, who was murdered in Mississippi for reportedly flirting with a white woman. When speaking with the media regarding the incident, local Sheriff Clarence Strider explained, "We never have any trouble until some of our Southern niggers go up North and the NAACP talks to 'em, and they come back home. If they would keep their nose and mouths out of our business, we would be able to do more when enforcing the laws."[6] In this quote, Strider clearly implicates blacks seeking justice for the murder of a child as the crux of the problem rather than the white racism that was the catalyst for Till's murder.

In another example, in Clarendon County, South Carolina, the Reverend J. A. De Laine challenged school desegregation in the late 1940s in what would later be known as *Briggs et al. v. Elliot*, which became the legal narrative that ultimately in 1954 overturned racial segregation in *Brown v. Board of Education*. Interestingly, many white residents believed that De Laine and his associates (E. E. Richburg, J. W. Seals, and Edward Frazier) were part of a communist conspiracy. De Laine's daughter explained, "Some White farmers told their sharecroppers the four AME ministers were being paid by Russia to stir up strife."[7] This is yet another illustration of framing, in this case portraying the need for equality as the work of outside agitators. Ironically, the origins of the *Briggs et al. v. Elliot* case began simply with Reverend De Laine seeking equal facilities within the parameters of racial segregation. When the power structure did not comply, De Laine and his associates were forced to challenge and overturn segregation laws altogether. Incidents regarding school desegregation were not solely regulated to select areas but were occurring across the country. For example, in nearby Orangeburg County, the blacks who challenged segregation faced similar slander from the white power structure.

Because the Supreme Court ruled in 1954 that school segregation was illegal, in 1955 numerous black parents in Orangeburg petitioned for the town's schools to desegregate. To downplay the *Brown* ruling and the petition, the local newspaper, *Times and Democrat*, published several stories suggesting that Orangeburg's race relations were good. However, when the black parents persisted, whites formed a chapter of the White Citizens Council to put an end to their pursuit of equal access to education. Satirically known as the uptown Ku Klux Klan, the council was made up of prominent white citizens who used economic reprisals (as opposed to violence) as a weapon against anyone who challenged the racial status quo.[8] White businesses and suppliers terminated their contracts with black businesses in Orangeburg, sharecroppers were evicted, and black city employees were fired. In retaliation, students at SCSC boycotted food that whites supplied. Overwhelmed by constant student protests and negative media attention, Governor McNair pressured SCSC president Benner C. Turner into retirement. Turner, who was considered by students to be too conservative (and by McNair to be polarizing and the lesser of the two evils), was always fearful that students could ultimately get hurt as a result of their protests, a concern that foreshadowed the 1968 Orangeburg Massacre.[9]

Significantly, civil rights activists' philosophies shifted between 1954 and the late 1960s. By 1967, "Black Power," a phrase that began to gain traction when newly elected SNCC president Stokely Carmichael uttered it while participating in the 1966 March against Fear with Dr. Martin Luther King, Jr., was a popular slogan among youth. Keeping with the tradition of framing black resistance as dangerous, the media immediately positioned the slogan as militant, drawing a distinction between King's philosophy of nonviolence and Carmichael's aims. More specific, the media led U.S. citizens to believe that Carmichael was seeking to organize a violent black uprising. A week after the March against Fear, Carmichael appeared on the CBS Sunday morning political interview show *Face the Nation*, where he was grilled by three reporters who had taken his calls for Black Power out of context. Carmichael, who was very charismatic, successfully defended the philosophy, which was actually predicated upon self-sufficiency, prison reform, self-defense, and a sense of *possibility*.[10]

Although Carmichael effectively defended the tenets of Black Power, many whites still interpreted the slogan as a violent revolutionary movement that sought to overturn the government. *Scarred Justice* clearly articulates this fear by focusing on an April 1967 editorial in the *Times and Democrat*, in which a white Orangeburg businessman claims, "If Stokely Carmichael, or SNCC, or others of his kind, get a hold on the State College campus, Orangeburg could see disorders, property destruction, and even deaths and personal injuries that we have never seen before in our lifetimes."[11] Hence, as a result of the burgeoning Black Power Movement, the SCSC students engaged in the struggle for racial equality were stigmatized by some local whites as dangerous and violent.

Because the aforementioned sentiment reigned supreme, the students' true reasons for protesting in Orangeburg were either misunderstood or not given proper consideration. As John Stroman, a former SCSC student, explains, it was the town's "quiet approval of racism" that caused the students to protest. He fully recognized that students protested because of their frustration, not because of any "outside" ideals. In contrast, one witness, Carl Stokes, contended that Sellers was talking to the students and riling them up. (For his part, Sellers, presently president of Voorhees College, maintains his innocence.)[12]

Not only does the documentary paint a portrait of white fear but it also pinpoints an important reason why this fear continues—because America's big systems run on power. This was the case in the past, and it is true today, when the divide continues to steepen between rich and poor. The next section discusses the documentary's portrayal of the events, demonstrating how the fear of blacks (brought so stunningly to light in the film) was exploited by officials and the media.

## Scarred Justice: The Orangeburg Massacre 1968

*Scarred Justice: The Orangeburg Massacre 1968* is a valuable film that examines the concept of "framing fear." The filmmakers delve into very complex issues about fear in a way that is understandable. Using television clips, newspaper articles, and interviews, the filmmakers effectively communicate the intricacies of the violence as well as the social, economic, historical, and political factors that influenced the tragedy. As *Scarred Justice* relates, Orangeburg's population was predominantly black; yet, whites wielded most of the social, political, and economic power. Comparatively, blacks could only move freely in Afrocentric community spaces. However, because the city had two black colleges, South Carolina State College (SCSC) and Claflin University, the town did have a large, educated, black middle class.

In the year of the massacre, 1968, many Americans (white and some black) believed that civil rights had taken a radical turn; for them, Black Power meant violence. Historian William C. Hine has said that the white community in Orangeburg feared that they were in the hands of enraged militants and that rioting would eventually come to their town.[13] White shopkeepers armed themselves in preparation for possible rioting. Members of the black community had mixed feelings; middle-class blacks believed in gradualism, while young blacks wanted equality immediately.

Student activism and youth activism were not new to Orangeburg in

1968. In 1956, students at SCSC boycotted their classes (as well as select products served in the college's cafeteria) in wake of a local government and business backlash against blacks who had signed a petition requesting the immediate desegregation of Orangeburg's public schools. Moreover, at a campus protest, students also hung in effigy SCSC president Turner and then South Carolina Governor George Timmerman. By the mid–1960s, there were repeated marches in the town to desegregate social spaces, particularly a bowling alley whose owner refused to desegregate after many other businesses had already done so.[14] Governor McNair believed that students should use the court system (which was white) to address their grievances.[15] When the group of students attempted to desegregate the bowling alley, the owner told them that he did not need their business. The next night, the students returned with a larger group and gained entrance through a back door. The police told them to leave, but they refused. Meanwhile, a fire truck pulled up outside where approximately three hundred students had gathered. The students lit matches and taunted the police. Someone broke a window; then, pandemonium ensued when the police started beating some of the young black women. Unwilling to stand idly by while their friends were being tormented, the students retaliated by destroying several white-owned businesses.[16]

As a result of the small-scale riot, rumors spread that black militants were going to bomb Orangeburg's waterworks. In an attempt to prevent such an attack, the mayor and the city council met with the black students, but they were unable to reach a compromise.[17] The person framed as the chief militant was former SNCC program director and recent Howard University graduate Sellers, whose hometown is about twenty miles away from Orangeburg. Although he was no longer a member of SNCC, he had been with the organization when it advocated Black Power. Hence, because of his past affiliation with SNCC, it was easy for Orangeburg's white powers that be to frame him as *the* source of the black students' frustrations and actions at the bowling alley.

It is plausible that the Orangeburg County Massacre would not have occurred had the town's power structure taken measures to end all segregation in the town immediately after the small-scale riot. However, Jim Crow law remained the order of the day at the bowling alley, and tensions continued to run high. Two nights after the initial confrontation, students lit a bonfire just outside the gates of the SCSC campus and yelled at the police and the National Guard, who had been summoned to maintain law and order in the event that there was a black militant uprising. The National Guardsmen were armed with guns and a tank positioning its muzzle in the direction of the students. As the bonfire grew, Pete Strom, Orangeburg's police chief, sent in a fire truck to extinguish the blaze. Under the protection of sixty-six police officers, the fire-fighters worked to put out the fire. As the blaze died down, an unidentified protestor threw a banister, striking one of the white police officers, who responded by opening fire on the crowd of students. Hearing the gunfire, the students turned and fled for their lives, a few to no avail. In approximately ten to fifteen seconds, the officers shot and wounded twenty-five students (including Sellers, who was shot in the arm while taking pictures of the conflict) and killed three others. Further illustrating that the town was divided along racial lines, the wounded were taken to a segregated hospital.[18]

Speaking with the media after the incident, McNair and Strom held Black Power advocates responsible. Strom insisted that the town had never had problems until Black Power advocates arrived. Not only did McNair and Strom distort the facts surrounding the conflict between the protestors and the police but the media also failed Orangeburg's citizens by erroneously reporting that there had been an exchange of gunfire. As it was later discovered, Strom and the Federal Bureau of Investigation had covered up the actual events. Of course, the tragedy in Orangeburg was not isolated; it had erupted against a backdrop of nationwide social violence. There were race riots in Detroit, Vietnam protests, and the 1968 assassinations of King and Robert F. Kennedy. In 1970, Ohio's National Guard would open fire on antiwar (Vietnam) protestors on the Kent State campus. History long remembers the shootings at that college but not those at SCSC; *Scarred Justice* sheds light on a similar incident to Kent State that occurred years earlier, during which black students seeking social justice lost their lives.

Importantly, the documentary does not force an agenda; instead, it juxtaposes the massacre as reported by the various media outlets against the interviews with the people who were there. The contrast between the media and eyewitnesses allows the viewers the opportunity to assess the opposing narratives. Most important, historical documents support the facts in the film. *Scarred Justice* was made to provide a balanced perspective to a tragedy that had previously only been reported from a point of privilege. In chronicling the events surrounding the massacre, the film provides some vindication of Sellers, who is the only person arrested and convicted in connection with the Orangeburg Massacre. With that in mind, *Scarred Justice* briefly follows his son Bakari Sellers, who was, in 2006, one of South Carolina's youngest state legislators. Bakari Sellers represents a new generation of activists seeking justice for the 1968 incident. The film shows how young Sellers continues to work to correct the skewed historical narrative surrounding the event that occurred as a result of the fear of blacks' struggle for civil rights.

Although the Orangeburg County Massacre occurred over forty-five years ago, the fear that led to the conflict remains a part of contemporary American society. There are many examples; however, among the most notable is the vehemence toward the United States' first black president, Barack Obama. During the elections, his opponents portrayed him as a black militant, using rhetoric and fear tactics that are eerily reminiscent of those used against the college students who demanded justice in Orangeburg County. The next section discusses President Obama, articulating how during his campaigns, he was framed as militant determined to employ a black agenda that threatened to destroy the very fabric of American society.

## Framing of Obama as a Black Militant

During Obama's first presidential campaign, his opponents consistently and inaccurately framed him as a black militant. For example, author Mark Orbe notes that a young white male in Michigan told him that he learned on FOX News that Obama was pushing for Muslim-owned businesses to be tax exempt.[19] Additionally, several jokes surfaced about Obama (if elected) being the "redistributor in chief" (instead of the commander in chief), meaning that President Obama would be pursuing a Robin Hood approach to economic policy, where he would steal from the rich and give to the poor. Implicit in this socialist rhetoric is that many whites believe that the majority of Americans on welfare are black people who do not want to work.[20] In fact, about fifteen million black people are on welfare, and ninety-three million white people are on welfare. Each group represents about 38 percent of its respective population. Thus, despite the claims, one group is not disproportionally benefiting from government programs designed to help those in need.[21]

## Stoking of White Fear

A prevalent white fear at election time was that as president, Obama would take money from people who are working hard, to pander to those who are not making any meaningful contribution to the country.[22] Political science professor Horace Campbell offers a unique phrase to define the fear: he contends that the old, white working class was "awakened to the erosion of the investment in whiteness."[23] For example, Orbe maintains that a man in his thirties from a rural southern Ohio community told him, "The first thing I thought was the African Americans, the colored community, was going to take over.... I got the picture that the next time I walk in McDonald's, ... I would hear 'White boy, you get down and wash the dishes.'"[24] This young man expressed the same fear of black uprising (or takeover) as those who feared the Black Power Movement, making it clear that he has no real understanding of U.S. power and privilege. It is important to note that many viewed candidate Obama as someone who would serve blacks and not the entire country. So again, real problems—white racism, ignorance, and fear—were ignored, leaving Obama as the problem.

In addition, there was also a micro-fear that with Obama elected president, black people would exact revenge upon white people for years of past oppression. President Obama's opponents in the first campaign focused on his race in an attempt to increase white voters' fears. Certainly, the July 21, 2008, cover of the *New Yorker* magazine effectively illustrated the concept by parodying white fear (see Fig. 1). Specifically, artist Barry Blitt uses the cover to satirize Obama opponents' scare tactics. He shows the allegedly militant presidential candidate's and his wife's supposed true identities, depicting them in the Oval Office celebrating their arrival as if they've finally gained the power to turn the world upside down. For example, Michelle Obama sports a huge Afro hairstyle, carries an M-16 rifle, and wears army fatigues. This personal style is certainly reminiscent of how whites framed Black Power militancy during the 1960s and early 1970s, eras when African Americans wore Afrocentric clothes and sported natural hairstyles as symbols of pride and beauty. Moreover, the *New Yorker* artist positions candidate Obama as a foreigner by dressing him in sandals and traditional Muslim attire. This is further emphasized in a painting of terrorist Osama Bin Laden that hangs on the wall in the background and by an American flag that is burning in the fireplace.[25]

While the opposition's attempts to position Obama as a militant during the 2008 campaign ultimately failed, the opposition returned in 2012 to the strategy as President Obama ran for reelection. For example, conservative political commentator Dinesh D'Souza offered what he considers undeniable "proof" that President Obama is a militant Muslim, pointing out his support for a $100 million mosque scheduled to be built near the former World Trade Center site. Although President Obama clearly explained that his position is based on the Constitution's commitment to religious freedom, D'Souza contends that "Obama supports the Ground Zero mosque because to him 9/11 is the event that unleashed the American bogey and pushed us into Iraq and Afghanistan. He views some of the Muslims who are fighting against America abroad as resisters of U.S. imperialism."[26]

In his book *The Roots of Obama's Rage* and his film *2016: Obama's America* (2012), D'Souza boldly predicts that in Obama's second term, the president will make sure that white America is held accountable for years of prejudice

Fig. 1. Artist Barry Blitt parodies white fear. Cover, *New Yorker* magazine, July 21, 2008 (courtesy *The New Yorker*).

and domination. For D'Souza, President Obama's militant attempts to take over the banks and health insurance companies and to weaken the armed forces are meant to devastate the U.S. economic and military stability. It is interesting to compare D'Souza's film with *Scarred Justice*, which combines historical analysis with current interviews. While Richardson and Cram present the perspective of white officials and citizens, the media, and the black student protestors, D'Souza choses to focus solely on the right wing's point of view. *Washington Post* movie critic Michael O'Sullivan concludes that the film is a

> one-sided argument [that] ultimately stoops to fear-mongering of the worst kind, stating in no uncertain terms that, if the president is reelected, the world four years from now will be darkened by the clouds of economic collapse, World War III (thanks to the wholesale renunciation of our nuclear superiority), and a terrifyingly ascendant new "United States of Islam" in the Middle East. These assertions are accompanied by footage of actual dark clouds and horror-movie music.[27]

Sadly, despite D'Souza's one-sided approach, there are American citizens who remain all too willing to accept the distorted information as truth.

## Not One of Us

During the 2012 election, Republican presidential candidate Mitt Romney joined in the fear campaign against President Obama. In particular, while speaking at a campaign rally, Romney commented, "This is what an angry and desperate presidency looks like." Many media pundits and citizens alike interpreted Romney's description of Obama as racially coded rhetoric positioning him as the stereotypical "angry black man." Rebekah Metzler, a writer for *U.S. News & World Report*, discusses the commentary of Touré Neblett, an African American cohost on MSNBC's *The Cycle*, who said, "You notice he [Romney] said 'anger' twice.... This is part of the playbook against Obama, the 'otherization'—he's not like us.... You are like the scary Black man we've been trained to fear."[28] Though it is difficult to say with absolute certainty that Romney intended to categorize President Obama stereotypically, it is important to note the pundits and U.S. citizens' reaction to his speech were potentially a direct result of the right wing's consistent reliance upon fear to discredit him. In a time when racism has become much more covert, the segment of Republicans using fear tactics rather than arguing the issues actually create distrust from an important segment of the U.S. population.

As historian Charles Pete Banner-Haley points out, there are continuous issues of equality that black people grapple with, irrespective of time and place.[29] *Scarred Justice* provides a look at a specific time (1968) and place (South Carolina), recounting a violent tragedy that occurred because black students were seeking racial equality. Unfortunately, whites framed them as militant, attributing their dissatisfaction with segregation to outside agitators. By looking at history, it is possible to see that such framing has been a trend for decades prior to the Orangeburg County Massacre. Further, one can observe the same framing in contemporary culture, surrounding Barack Obama's 2008 presidential campaign, his first term, and his 2012 campaign.

What is to be learned from *Scarred Justice* and the framing that the film so distressingly illustrates? What can be done to stop such framing? Today, black people are apprehensive about many problems comparable to Orangeburg's desegregation dilemma, such as violence in their communities, substandard schools, and disenfranchisement at the local, state, and federal levels. Blacks are fighting to protect what they see as a loss of their identity due to continuous violence. They see their existence at stake, and some even see themselves as victims. Among all these issues, Banner-Haley maintains that race is still the most tenacious and pernicious crisis.[30] Such problems become amplified because of inequality and the lack of security among American citizens. Sociologist Jeffery Alexander contends that part of gaining and keeping power in the United States is about maneuvering constructed social binaries or the "extracivil realms." These extracivil realms are not necessarily central to governing, but they are crucial, such as "gender and family values ... whether one is god fearing and faithful ... whether one is of respectable ethnicity and racial stripe."[31] History professor Paul Zeleza describes leadership and human agency as being the most problematic factors in transforming intractable conflicts.[32] Hence, it was not Black Power that led to the Orangeburg Massacre but, rather, the exclusion of blacks. These social and political exclusions perpetuated the inequality that already existed. While there is a relationship between poverty and violence, there is also a relationship between inequality and violence. *Scarred Justice* clearly demonstrates that although inequality did not create the violence, inequality stimulated it.

After examining the historical and contemporary issues raised in *Scarred Justice*, it is apparent that the central narrative of the film is to create fear by framing blacks as militant. How can that linear narrative be decentered? Even the election of a black person as the President of the United States has not managed to change that metanarrative. The problem is more than just many fearful white people perpetuating the narrative. Rather, as *Scarred Justice* shows, there is a perpetuation of the narrative on a metastructural level (meaning at the level of society's largest and most powerful building blocks). As

Melissa Harris-Lacewell notes, the problem continues because of "structures of inequality codified in law and supported by government action."[33] These inequalities can trickle down to microstructural parts of society (businesses, churches, city councils, neighborhood-watch patrols, local school boards, and so forth).

Fearful framing may be eased if there is a change at the heart of the powerful U.S. metastructures (such as economics and government). The people in these dominant positions must come to realize that equality and humanity can strengthen the nation's potential. A rebuilding can take place, focused on human rights. Citizens want a decent life, with good schools and safe neighborhoods; these things help secure America's future. As the big institutions (the country's solid underpinnings) begin to embrace equality, the fear of change will diminish (whether it is the fear of college students demanding their civil rights or a black person running for president).

To be sure, planning to change the metastructures of the United States seems like a tall order, rather like writing a recipe for a whole new nation. But as former presidential candidate and U.S. Senator Adlai Stevenson, Jr. eloquently explained, "There is a new America every morning when we wake up. It is upon us whether we will it or not."[34] This suggests that things can be changed, depending on the strength and the will of the people. What must be addressed is why some whites fear blacks and how that fear can be proved baseless. In a democracy, fear of others has no place because it takes all of us working together to make a country with a good standard of living. From the large cornerstones of the nation, the idea can emerge that we are all stronger when we all have equal opportunity. This essential idea can then filter down to the microstructural parts of society, such as the streets of little towns like Orangeburg.

## Notes

1. *Scarred Justice.*
2. Tim Arango, "Films Revisit Overlooked Shootings on a Black Campus," *New York Times*, April 16, 2008, http://www.nytimes.com/2008/04/16/arts/16oran.html?page wanted=all.
3. *Scarred Justice.*
4. Dray, *Capitol Men*, 306; Tindall, *South Carolina Negroes*, 9.
5. Du Bois, *Black Reconstruction in America.*
6. "People & Events." See also *Eyes on the Prize: America's Civil Rights Movement*, vol. 1.
7. Gona, *Dawn of Desegregation*, 111–12.
8. Payne, *I've Got the Light*, 34–35.
9. Orangeburg business boycott: Hine, "Civil Rights and Campus Wrongs," 314; Boyce, "I Am Leaving," 218–19.
10. Blue and Murphee, "Stoke the Joke," 212–11.

11. See also *Eyes on the Prize*, vol. 4. For more information about national media coverage on the black separatist group the Nation of Islam, see *The Hate That Hate Produced*.

12. Hine, "Civil Rights and Campus Wrongs," 330, 13; Shuler, *Blood and Bone*, 93, 131; Sellers, "Orangeburg Massacre," 359–66.

13. Sellers, "Orangeburg Massacre," 359–66.

14. Ibid. See also Grose, *South Carolina at the Brink*; Hine, "Civil Rights and Campus Wrongs"; Shuler, *Blood and Bone*; Nelson and Bass, *Orangeburg Massacre*.

15. *Scarred Justice*.

16. Ibid.

17. Ibid.

18. Ibid.

19. Orbe, *Communication Realities*, 173.

20. Crary, "Obama 'Socialist' Claim Persists."

21. "Welfare Statistics."

22. "Who Racializes Welfare Reform."

23. Campbell, *Barack Obama*, 23.

24. Orbe, *Communication Realities*, 133.

25. "*New Yorker* Cover."

26. D'Souza, "How Obama Thinks."

27. Michael O'Sullivan, "In '2016,' Obama Is Fear Itself," *Washington Post*, August 24, 2012, http://www.washingtonpost.com/gog/movies/2016-obamas-america,1230760/critic-review.html.

28. Ibid.

29. Banner-Haley, *From Du Bois to Obama*.

30. Ibid., 2.

31. Alexander, *Performance of Politics*, xiii.

32. Zeleza, *Barack Obama*.

33. Harris-Lacewell, "Commentary."

34. Simpson, *Best Quotes*, 315.

## *Works Cited*

Alexander, Jeffery C. *The Performance of Politics: Obama's Victory and the Democratic Struggle for Power.* New York: Oxford University Press, 2010.

Banner-Haley, Charles Pete. *From Du Bois to Obama: African American Intellectuals in a Public Forum.* Carbondale: Southern Illinois University Press, 2010.

Blue, Mary, and Vanessa Murphee. "'Stoke the Joke' and His 'Self-Appointed Critics': A Clash of Values on Network Television News, 1966–70." *Media History* 15, no. 2 (2009): 205–20.

Boyce, Travis D. "I Am Leaving and Not Looking Back: The Life of Benner C. Turner." PhD diss., Ohio University, 2009.

Campbell, Horace G. *Barack Obama and the Twenty-First-Century Politics: A Revolutionary Moment in the USA.* New York: Pluto, 2010.

Crary, David. "Obama 'Socialist' Claim Persists on Right Despite Inaccuracies." June 4, 2012. *The Huffington Post.* http://www.huffingtonpost.com/2012/06/04/obama-socialist-claim-history_n_1568470.html.

Dray, Philip. *Capitol Men: The Epic Story of Reconstruction through the Lives of the First Black Congressmen.* Boston: Houghton Mifflin, 2008.

D'Souza, Dinesh. "How Obama Thinks." September 27, 2010. *Forbes Magazine.* http://www.forbes.com/forbes/2010/0927/politics-socialism-capitalism-private-enterprises-obama-business-problem_2.html.

———. *Obama's America: Unmaking the American Dream.* Washington, D.C.: Regnery,

2012. Film version of the book directed by Dinesh D'Souza and John Sullivan, *2016: Obama's America*, Salt Lake City: Rocky Mountain Pictures, 2012.

_____. *The Roots of Obama's Rage*. Washington, D.C.: Regnery, 2010.

Du Bois, W. E. B. *Black Reconstruction in America: An Essay toward a History of the Part Which Black Folk Played in the Attempt to Reconstruct Democracy in America, 1860–1880*. New York: Oxford University Press, 2007.

*Eyes on the Prize: America's Civil Rights Movement*. Vol. 1, "Awakenings, 1954–1956"; "Fighting Back, 1957–1962." Produced by Henry Hampton. 1986. Boston: Blackside, 2006. DVD.

*Eyes on the Prize: America's Civil Rights Movement*. Vol. 4, "The Time Has Come, 1964–1966"; "Two Societies, 1965–1968." Produced by Henry Hampton. 1990. Boston: Blackside, 2006. DVD.

Gona, Ophelia De Laine. *Dawn of Desegregation: J. A. De Laine and* Briggs v. Elliot. Columbia: University of South Carolina Press, 2011.

Grose, Phillip. *South Carolina at the Brink: Robert McNair and the Politics of Civil Rights*. Columbia: University of South Carolina Press, 2006.

Harris-Lacewell, Melissa. "Commentary: Why Holder's Speech Was a Failure." February 19, 2009. *CNN*. http://articles.cnn.com/2009-02-19/politics/lacewell.holder.remarks_1_eric-holder-unequal-schools-public-schools?_s=PM:POLITICS.

*The Hate That Hate Produced*. Broadcast July 13–17, 1959. WNTA-TV, *News-Beat*. Produced by Mike Wallace and Louis Lomax. *National Archive*. http://archive.org/details/PBSTheHateThatHateProduced.

Hine, William C. "Civil Rights and Campus Wrongs: South Carolina State College Students Protest, 1955–1968." *South Carolina Historical Magazine* 97, no. 4 (1996): 310–31.

Metzler, Rebekah. "Racism Shows Its Face in Presidential Campaign, Obama, Romney Matchup Takes On Wider Racial Implications, Some Say, with Both Sides to Blame." August 17, 2012. *U.S. News*. http://www.usnews.com/news/articles/2012/08/17/racism-shows-its-face-in-presidential-campaign.

Nelson, Jack, and Jack Bass. *The Orangeburg Massacre*, 2d ed. Macon: Mercer University Press, 1984.

*"New Yorker* Cover Satirizing Obama Raises Controversy." Narrated by Michael Eric Dyson and Eric Bates. July 14, 2008. *PBS News Hour*. http://www.pbs.org/newshour/bb/politics/july-dec08/obamacover_07–14.html.

Orbe, Mark P. *Communication Realities in a 'Post-racial' Society: What the U.S. Public Thinks about Barack Obama*. Lanham, MD: Lexington Books, 2011.

Payne, Charles M. *I've Got the Light of Freedom: The Organizing Tradition and the Mississippi Struggle*. Berkeley: University of California Press, 1995.

"People & Events: Clarence Strider (1904–1970)." American Experience. *Corporation for Public Broadcasting*. Accessed October 12, 2013. http://www.pbs.org/wgbh/amex/till/peopleevents/p_strider.html.

*Scarred Justice: The Orangeburg Massacre 1968*. Directed and produced by Bestor Cram and Judy Richardson. 2009. San Francisco: California Newsreel, 2009. DVD.

Sellers, Cleveland. "The Orangeburg Massacre." In *Toward the Meeting of the Waters: Currents in the Civil Rights Movement of South Carolina during the Twentieth Century*, edited by Winfred B. Moore Jr. and Orville Vernon Burton, 359–66. Columbia: University of South Carolina Press, 2008.

Shuler, Jack. *Blood and Bone: Truth and Reconciliation in a Southern Town*. Columbia: University of South Carolina Press, 2012.

Simpson, James B. *Best Quotes of '54, '55, '55*. New York: Thomas Y. Crowell, 1957.

Tindall, George B. *South Carolina Negroes, 1877–1900*. Columbia: University of South Carolina Press, 1952.

*2016: Obama's America*. Directed by Dinesh D'Souza and John Sullivan. Salt Lake City:

Rocky Mountain Pictures, 2012.

"Welfare Statistics." *Statistic Brain*, 2012. http://www.statisticbrain.com/welfare-statistics/.

"Who Racializes Welfare Reform." August 29, 2012. *National Review*. http://www.nationalreview.com/articles/315206/who-racializes-welfare-reform-editors#!.

Zeleza, Paul T. *Barack Obama and the African Diasporas, Dialogues, and Dissensions*. Athens: Ohio University Press, 2009.

# PART II

# SPORTS

# A "perpetual threat"

## Unforgivable Blackness *and*
## *Jack Johnson as a Transmedia Sports Icon*

### MICHAEL GRAVES

As the first African American heavyweight champion of the world, an affluent entrepreneur, and a black man who openly dated white women, Jack Johnson challenged white hegemony in the United States in the early 1900s. In *Unforgivable Blackness: The Rise and Fall of Jack Johnson* (2005), documentary filmmaker Ken Burns describes Johnson as a "perpetual threat" to white society as a result of these transgressions of racial and class boundaries at a time when African Americans were largely marginalized.[1] Given that fictionalized representations of the heavyweight champion also appear in an array of contemporary texts, including films, a Broadway play, a comic-book series, novels, a video game, and music, Johnson continues to challenge established hierarchies long after his death.[2] Yet, despite the continuation of Johnson's legacy in the popular-culture imagination, Burns presents Johnson's story as fixed, isolating the boxer's significance largely in the past. With that in mind, this essay examines Burns' construction of Johnson's iconoclastic persona in *Unforgivable Blackness* as well as his enduring transmedia presence, illustrating how his iconic status in popular culture persists because he functions as a symbol of racial pride, individualism and independence, and subversion of the established power structure.

Based on Geoffrey C. Ward's nonfiction book with the same title, *Unforgivable Blackness: The Rise and Fall of Jack Johnson* premiered on PBS over the course of two nights in January 2005. The name of both Ward's book and Burns' documentary is a reference to a W. E. B. Du Bois quote from the

National Association for the Advancement of Colored People's (NAACP) publication *The Crisis* (1914), in which the civil rights activist addresses the widespread animosity aimed at Johnson. As Du Bois eloquently observes, the vitriol stemmed not from Johnson's status as heavyweight champion or his controversial and often-adulterous relationships with white women but rather a racial stigma that was for dominant white culture both deplorable and untenable:

> Why ... this thrill of national disgust? Because Johnson is black. Of course some pretend to object to Johnson's character. But we have yet to hear, in the case of White America, that marital troubles have disqualified prize fighters or ball players or even statesmen. *It comes down, then, after all to this unforgivable blackness.*[3]

The two-part, 212-minute documentary chronicles the boxer's often-tumultuous life through archival motion-picture footage, photographs, and newspaper accounts as well as commentary by Johnson biographer Randy Roberts, boxing expert Bert Sugar, and writers Stanley Crouch and Gerald Early. Moreover, Burns vividly brings Johnson's story to life through the use of a talented cast of actors—most notably Samuel L. Jackson as Johnson—who passionately voice the film's central figures. Additionally, John Osborne and Brenda Ray's sound design and Wynton Marsalis's original music effectively augment the archival visual material, establishing a compelling sense of time and place. Burns thereby recounts Johnson's life in a gripping manner, with *Unforgivable Blackness* unfolding chronologically, charting the boxer's rise to prominence in part 1 and his subsequent fall from grace in the film's second half.

Johnson's unforgivable blackness, his offense to early 1900s white society, was so powerful that it continues to reverberate through contemporary popular culture. Yet, while Johnson was largely maligned within a racially oppressive Jim Crow America, contemporary artists and producers find in Johnson a folk hero of sorts. For example, Trevor Von Eeden's comic-book series, *The Original Johnson* (2009–11), traces the history of "the first psychologically free black man in American history," from Johnson's childhood in Galveston, Texas, to his death on June 10, 1946.[4] Furthermore, in the songs "Jack Johnson" (1994) and "Blue Black Jack" (2004) by The Tom Russell Band and Mos Def (Dante Terrell Smith), respectively, Johnson triumphs in the face of physical, racial, and class barriers, becoming a black "superhero."[5] Finally, the Broadway play *The Great White Hope* (1968) depicts African American boxer Jack Jefferson, a thinly veiled allusion to Johnson, struggling against deep-seated racist ideologies tied to his status as heavyweight champion and his interracial relationships with white women.[6]

Discourses of racial politics circulated around Johnson during his lifetime, and as the boxer's transmedia presence illustrates, Johnson continues to function as a cultural lens through which notions of race and class filter. Addressing the issues facing African Americans in 1900, Du Bois observes, "The problem of the twentieth century is the problem of the color line, the question as to how far differences of race ... are going to be made, hereafter, the basis of denying to over half the world the right of sharing ... the opportunities and privileges of modern civilization."[7] Issues of racial and class-based inequalities still dominate the popular imagination in the twenty-first century, and narratives centering on Johnson's defiance of white supremacy as well as his unapologetic individualism and rejection of authority enable contemporary scholars to interrogate these issues.

Richard Dyer's work on stardom, *Stars* in 1979 and *Heavenly Bodies: Film Stars and Society* in 1986, and on race, *White* in 1997, provides an approach for analyzing the construction of Johnson's transmedia persona. Utilizing a semiotic approach, Dyer in *Stars* observes that media stars function as complex signifiers. Constructed from an array of diverse media texts, ranging from films, promotional materials, and media commentary and criticism, a star's image or persona involves an intertextual process of signification shaped by the discourses surrounding the production and circulation of these texts.[8] A star study, therefore, examines representations of a star in the context of the ideological terrain of the time. Given that Ward's depiction of Johnson is constructed largely from newspaper accounts, a critical examination of Johnson's persona in *Unforgivable Blackness* reveals the inherent contradictions surrounding him, as both white and black societies projected conflicting notions of race and class onto the boxer.[9] Dyer demonstrates in *Heavenly Bodies* how star images provide a space for the negotiation of such ideological incongruities.[10] In other words, representations of Johnson's boxing matches, affluent lifestyle, and relationships with white women function as a way for audiences to resolve complex racial and class issues. Further, Dyer's examination of race in *White* highlights the ways in which whiteness is constructed and established as the societal norm. Dyer elucidates that only society's most privileged groups wield the freedom of nonconformity to this implicit norm.[11] Hence, Johnson represented a threat to the white establishment by violating the dominant ideology of white supremacy and transgressing the ideological boundary separating white and black societies in the early twentieth century.

While star studies of preeminent African American athletes emphasize their status as media celebrities as well as how this iconic position functions as a signifier of race, an examination of the interplay between fictive and nonfiction representations is also needed.[12] In Muhammad Ali's fights and public appearances, for instance, David W. Zang argues that the boxer "embraced ... his blackness" and in doing so became a symbol of the rejection of firmly established racial beliefs.[13] Further, Douglas Kellner highlights the ways in which Nike and major media conglomerates exploited Michael Jordan's star image for the promotion of products, such as shoes, clothing, and films, in ways that both transcended and called attention to race.[14] Yet, more work is needed to interrogate the complex interplay between the transmedia construction of athletes' star images, focusing both on the individual as an athlete and the individual as a character in popular culture. Such an examination illuminates signification occurring across time periods, authors, and media platforms. Hence, using a semiotics-informed star-studies approach, the current study explores the ways in which transmedia representations of Johnson in *Unforgivable Blackness*, *The Original Johnson* comic books, the songs "Jack Johnson" and "Blue Black Jack," and *The Great White Hope* represent shifting ideologies centering on racial pride, individualism and independence, and subversion of the established order. As social and cultural discourses shift, producers employ Johnson's persona to rearticulate these issues, and, therefore, Johnson becomes a powerful and fluid signifier—a perpetual threat—through which conceptions of race and class are challenged, reconfigured, and even reinforced.

## Racial Pride

As one of the most visible African Americans of his time, Jack Johnson became a fluid signifier onto which both whites and blacks projected conflicting notions of racial superiority in the early 1900s. Reviled by the majority of white America and championed by large segments of black society, Johnson represented both animosity and pride in a racially torn America. Born in Galveston, Texas, in 1878, Johnson began boxing as a teenager, ultimately becoming the first African American heavyweight champion of the world in 1908 and retaining the title until 1915. Despite his talent, dedication to the sport, and boxing victories, Johnson struggled mightily to gain the opportunity to even contend for boxing's most prestigious title. Although African American boxers could compete for other, lesser titles, the "twisted logic of white supremacy" dictated that the heavyweight championship of the world was the sole property of the white race, a point Burns establishes early on by quoting Jack London.[15] "This contest of men with padded gloves," London proclaims, "is a sport that belongs unequivocally to the English-speaking race. It is no superficial thing, a fad of a moment or a generation. It is as deep as our consciousness and is woven into the fibers of our being."[16] Such a stance paradoxically positioned black boxers simultaneously as marginalized, nonentities as a result of their nonwhite status, as well as potentially dangerous threats to white hegemony at the beginning of the twentieth century. Edwin Bancroft Henderson, a noted advocate for African American athletes at that time, articulates this point when he asserts that if an African American boxer defeated a white champion, for instance, the victory for disposed black people would be literal and symbolic, illustrating that they could also achieve equality in other spheres of American life.[17] Burns reinforces this view, establishing the heavyweight championship as one of the most coveted titles of the time.[18] Given the potentially paradigm-changing repercussions of an African American heavyweight champion, the boxing establishment restricted the title to whites, with black pugilists competing instead for the unofficial Negro heavyweight championship.

Boxing's color line was originally drawn when reigning heavyweight champion John L. Sullivan refused to fight black boxers, and it continued with the succeeding heavyweight champion, Jim Jeffries, who made his support of the racist tradition known when he announced, "The title will never go to a black man, if I can help it." True to his word, he retired without either losing a match or facing a black boxer in the ring.[19] Burns highlights the rationale for Jeffries's standpoint, displaying the ways in which the white media subverted black boxers' positive attributes. The stamina of the most successful of black pugilists, commentators argued, was the result of an animalist inferiority enabling them to withstand great acts of physical punishment. In the face of such racist theories, it was with the following heavyweight champion, Tommy Burns, that a black boxer would ultimately obtain the opportunity to compete for the heavyweight title.

After winning the Negro heavyweight championship, Johnson tenaciously pursued Burns for a chance to fight for the official title, and although he initially denied the legitimacy of a black contender—just as Sullivan and Jeffries had before him—the combination of Johnson's dogged determination and Johnson's victories over other white boxers compelled him to acquiesce.

Described in *Unforgivable Blackness* as the "first great battle of an inevitable race war," the 1908 Burns-Johnson fight proved to be remarkably one-sided, as Johnson knocked Burns to the ground within seconds.[20] Further illustrating his superior physical prowess, Johnson conversed with people in the crowd as he fought Burns and even smiled in response to the torrent of bigoted remarks hurled from the champion's corner. In fact, the true fight occurred outside the ring, an ideological battle expressed in the language of the press and white boxing fans. Pejoratively described as a "butt nigger" and "a giant Ethiopian" by the media, Johnson exposed the hypocrisy of a white

America eager to keep African Americans subjugated.[21] In the face of the white crowd's racist epithets and the insults, Johnson's prideful smile came to signify not only the boxer's inflated ego but also a willful defiance of the period's white supremacist doctrine.

Johnson so resoundingly trounced Burns that the police were compelled to stop the fight, with Johnson declared the winner. For the first time in the history of boxing, an African American man held the heavyweight-championship title. The significance of Johnson's achievement, however, extended beyond the realm of boxing. Johnson biographer Roberts contends that his victory over Burns marked "the moment it all starts to fall apart for white society," with Johnson delivering the first blow to long-standing white-supremacist ideologies.[22] In fact, Johnson's achievement so threatened white America's hegemonic dominance that police also ordered the motion-picture cameramen to stop filming the final moments of the bout, thereby sparing the world "the spectacle of a black man knocking out a white man."[23] By both denying Johnson the opportunity to knock Burns out and preventing the recording of this historic event, the authorities attempted to preserve white racial dominance.

Yet despite such efforts, Johnson's attainment of the heavyweight championship title was indeed viewed as a powerfully threatening symbol of African American mobility. A *Boxing Magazine* writer of the time, for instance, bemoaned a sense of lost power: "[W]e shall never quite regain it, because the recollection of our temporary deposition will always remain to inspire the colored peoples with hope."[24] Although such discourses of race surrounded the title fight, Johnson did not view his accomplishment in those terms: "To me, it was not a racial triumph, but almost immediately, a hue and cry went up because a colored man was holding the championship."[25] Although Johnson downplayed his symbolic power, Ken Burns establishes the prevailing image of the pugilist as a signifier of racial pride by citing the popular press of the time, and this tradition continues. As depicted in the pages of *The Original Johnson*, the Burns-Johnson fight represents a point of irreversible social change in American society. Further, the chorus of the Tom Russell Band's "Jack Johnson" highlights the racial animosity targeted at the boxer, with much of white society seeking not only Johnson's pugilistic defeat but his death as well. Hence, as the first African American heavyweight champion, Johnson's transmedia persona is inextricably and paradoxically linked with racial pride on both sides of the color line. In this way, representations of the boxer challenge the logic of white supremacy.

Echoing the racial significance of Johnson's possession of the heavyweight-championship title, the outcome of the Burns-Johnson fight marks the beginning of the so-called era of White Hopes, in which a string of white boxers attempted to literally and figuratively put Johnson back in his place by knocking him from atop the boxing hierarchy. While many white fighters assumed the White Hope mantle, no boxer embodied the notion more than retired former heavyweight champion Jeffries. Just as Johnson represented racial pride for marginalized blacks, Jeffries's powerful physique, which was the subject of a series of myths, came to signify the white race's perceived dominance.[26] In addition, because he was undefeated when he left boxing, many whites believed that Jeffries was still the true heavyweight-boxing champion of the world. As such, white America urged Jeffries, who was living out his retirement on his farm, to return to the ring and defend the white race's honor. Novelist London even anointed Jeffries the savior of the white race: "Jim Jeffries must now emerge from his alfalfa farm and remove that golden smile from Jack Johnson's face. Jeff, it's up to you. The White Man must be rescued."[27] For white America then, Jeffries was the Great White Hope, the fighter who stood the best chance of returning the title to its "rightful" side of the color line.

Coaxed out of retirement by a sense of duty and a lucrative contract, Jeffries agreed to fight Johnson.[28] Whereas for whites, the Johnson-Jeffries fight for the title of heavyweight champion of the world represented the opportunity to reassert their racial dominance, the bout became the manifestation of many economically and socially marginalized blacks' struggle for racial equality. It was fitting, then, that the fight was held on the Fourth of July, as the event functioned as a symbolic act of independence or continued subjugation, respectively, for both whites and blacks, with Jeffries described as the "Hope of the White Race" and Johnson labeled as the "Negroes' Deliverer."[29] Although Johnson was reluctant to view his successes in the ring through a racial lens, Jeffries understood that the outcome of the fight would come to represent the physical dominance of either race: "I realize full well just what depends on me and I am not going to disappoint the public. That portion of the white race that has been looking to me to defend its athletic supremacy may feel assured that I am fit to do my very best."[30] Yet, as an article appearing in the *New York Times* suggests, in the eyes of the media and the public, the significance of the Johnson-Jeffries bout extended beyond physical superiority to broader notions of racial equality: "If the black man wins, thousands and thousands of his ignorant brothers will misrepresent his victory as justifying claims to much more than physical equality with their white neighbors."[31] Fearing the Great White Hope's potential defeat at the hand of a black man, the validity of the logic linking Jeffries's physical superiority in the ring with the white race's hegemonic dominance was paradoxically denied to African Americans.

Further illustrating the apprehension surrounding a shift toward an uneasy racial equality, numerous groups lobbied civic leaders in San Francisco, California, to stop the Johnson-Jeffries bout.[32] Ultimately moved from San Francisco to Reno, Nevada, the Johnson-Jeffries title fight took place on July 4, 1910, and the event captivated the public imagination in a way that remained unsurpassed until Charles Lindberg's historic transatlantic flight seventeen years later.[33] Much to the dismay of the largely white audience, Johnson utterly dominated Jeffries, breaking his nose, bruising his eyes until they were almost completely shut, and in the fifteenth round ultimately knocking him down, for the first time in Jeffries's career. Jeffries's corner eventually stopped the fight after Johnson knocked him to the canvas several more times during the same round. Johnson had defeated the Great White Hope and, in doing so, had given Jeffries the only loss in his storied career. As such, African Americans found in Johnson a symbol of great racial pride in which images of him standing triumphant over the bloodied representative of the white race signified a refusal to submit to dominant white culture.

Anticipating black reaction to the fight, an article appearing in the *Los Angeles Times* the day following Johnson's win was quick to dissuade African Americans: "A word to the black man: Do not point your nose too high. Do not swell your chest too much.... Remember, you have done nothing at all. You are just the same member of society you were last week.... No man will think a bit higher of you because your complexion is the same as the victor at Reno."[34] For white America, then, Johnson's attainment and successful defense of the heavyweight-championship title constituted much more than a victory in the athletic sphere.

Indicative of Johnson's power as a conflicting symbol for both white and black America, the response to the Johnson-Jeffries fight was explosive. Whereas blacks celebrated the fight's outcome, whites responded to Jeffries's loss with violence, leading to a slew of deadly race riots across the United States.[35] Throughout his life, Johnson transgressed racial boundaries in ways that continued to evoke similar reactions. Yet, while Johnson's athletic victories were a source of great pride and dignity for black America, Johnson's affluent lifestyle and association with white women would eventually alienate both white and black societies, alike.

## Individualism and Independence

In addition to threatening white America's racial superiority, Johnson challenged social mores and class boundaries by openly dating white women and attaining a level of wealth and prestige uncharacteristic of African Americans at that time. His individualism, independence, and his refusal to let the strictures of Jim Crow America dictate his behavior are central aspects of *Unforgivable Blackness*. Burns constructs a persona of a man who lived freely during one of the most "racially oppressive periods in American history."[36] However, while the African American community championed Johnson's physical prowess as a signifier of racial pride, his relationships with white women as well as his refusal to adhere to the dominant social etiquette of his time evoked harsh reactions from both whites and blacks. Hence, competing notions of freedom and class surrounded Johnson—both during his lifetime and in more contemporary texts—in ways that challenged, reconfigured, and even reinforced race and class ideologies.

In contrast to the economically and socially marginalized lifestyle of most contemporaneous African Americans, Johnson lived a highly affluent and visible lifestyle. Leveraging his athletic successes for financial gains, he became a successful businessman by securing lucrative contracts for the motion-picture rights to his fights, working as a vaudeville performer, and opening a nightclub. Johnson's expensive automobiles, gold teeth, and flamboyant clothing were signifiers of his privilege, and his penchant for extravagance was matched by his inflated, boastful personality. Although his wealth and behavior further granted Johnson celebrity status, his lifestyle threatened white and black societies, alike. Black leaders, for instance, wanted Johnson to be more humble in public.[37] Roberts contends that leaders, such as Booker T. Washington, "feared that Johnson challenged an order they wished to placate and that his emancipated lifestyle eventually would cause a violent white reaction."[38] Burns highlights the tension between Washington and Johnson through archival footage and testimony, emphasizing Washington's acceptance of the separation of the races and Johnson's willful commingling with whites.[39]

While Johnson's unapologetic individualism often enflamed tensions from both sides of the color line, his most threatening violation of such boundaries was his romantic and sexual relationships with white women, a transgression that ultimately led to his downfall. At a time when even the appearance of a sexual liaison with a white woman could result in the lynching of a black man, Johnson married three white women over the course of his life and engaged in sexual relationships with numerous others.[40] When Burns first introduces Johnson in *Unforgivable Blackness*, the boxer is described as "the Black Peril," one of several racial epithets applied to the boxer during his career.[41] Referring to the fear of black men raping white women, the notion of "black peril" was part of a larger, racist view of blacks, within early American society, as dangerous, hypersexualized beings.[42] Viewed through the distorted lens of black peril, black men's alleged uncontrollable desire to engage in miscegenation posed a threat to white America. The undercurrent of the black peril is evident in a photograph appearing in the *Chicago Sunday Tribune* in which a young white girl implores Jim Jeffries to fight Johnson and thereby protect her from the sexual threat that African American men represented. Von Eeden reinterprets the photograph in *The Original Johnson*, with the young girl signifying a perceived danger that was often met with deadly force. Johnson was, in fact, the target of death threats and attacks, and these relationships were hazardous for the white women involved, as well. Nine prostitutes lost their jobs at Chicago's prestigious Everleigh Club brothel after clandestinely associating with the boxer, and his white wives often became outcasts, ostracized by both whites and blacks.[43] Moreover, many African Americans "were very uncomfortable" with Johnson exclusively courting white women.[44] Following his marriage to Etta Duryea, for instance, the African American *Nashville Globe* expressed its opposition to the union, deeming it an act of betrayal to the black race:

> It is reported that Jack Johnson has married a woman who is not a member of his people. If that report is true, then Jack Johnson is wrong, entirely wrong. And that point of order is raised and sustained by every sensible and self-respecting Negro in this country.... *If he could not find a woman of his race suitable for his wife, then he ought to have died a celibate.*[45]

In stark opposition to the prevailing ideologies on both sides of the color line in the early 1900s, Johnson defiantly declared, "I shall claim the right to select the woman of my choice. Nobody else can do that for me. I am not a slave, and I have the right to choose who my mate shall be without the dictation of any man."[46] Johnson's slave rhetoric is fitting, given that he became a signifier of independence and individualism by breaking early 1900s taboos. His willful transgression is rendered more powerful when one considers, as Burns soberly highlights, the prevalence of lynchings—sometimes resulting from the mere speculation of an interracial romance—in early twentieth-century America.[47] Yet, Johnson refused to subordinate to such oppressive conditions, a position of independence afforded by his celebrity status. As a racially underprivileged, yet economically elite member of society, Johnson refused to conform to the prejudiced views projected onto African Americans.

The white establishment refused to grant a black man such independence, ultimately undertaking a judicial campaign that resulted in Johnson's incarceration. In other words, when the threat of violence and legitimate boxing efforts yielded little results, the focus shifted to legislation. "The 'White Hope' had failed," Johnson details in his autobiography, "and when [future efforts by 'White Hopes'] proceeded with so little success, other methods were taken to dispose of me."[48] One such method was the June 25, 1910, passage of the Mann Act, a new federal law aimed at combating prostitution and white slavery. Named for its sponsor, Illinois Congressman James Robert Mann, the act prohibited the transportation of women across state lines "for the purpose of prostitution or debauchery or for any other immoral purpose."[49] Although not conceived as a means to prohibit consensual, romantic relationships, the Justice Department used the Mann Act to persecute Johnson for his transgressions. In 1912, as a consequence of traveling with a white woman named Belle Schreiber, Johnson was arrested and ultimately convicted for violating the Mann Act.[50] As this treatment suggests, Johnson threatened white hegemony in the early twentieth century by violating social conventions and attaining a degree of economic independence that was uncharacteristic for the majority of black men of that era.

In the popular-culture imagination, Johnson continues this lifestyle, challenging entrenched racist beliefs and in the process reconfiguring race-based and class-based notions of individualism and independence. Despite his sizable wealth, for instance, Johnson is denied passage on the *Titanic* due to the color of his skin in the lyrics of the Tom Russell Band's "Jack Johnson."[51] Moreover, Johnson's attire and automobiles, signifiers of the boxer's affluence, figure significantly in Mos Def's "Blue Black Jack." Whereas Johnson's unapologetic individualism and independence enflamed both sides of the color line during his own lifetime, these qualities now afford him a superhero persona of sorts. Mos Def's use of "super man" to describe Johnson in the lyrics of "Blue Black Jack" is indicative of the pugilist's mythic status in contemporary culture, emphasizing both an enviable materialistic lifestyle and a preternatural ability to freely traverse both sides of an oppressive color line in early twentieth-century America. Johnson's almost superhuman socioeconomic mobility is also evident in *The Original Johnson*, with the boxer depicted as a flying, caped figure. In this way, Johnson's superhero or folk-hero status stems not from an athletic prowess but from an ability to circumvent barriers of race and class erected on both sides of a racially divided America.

Johnson's unapologetic defiance of the social mores centering on the dating of white women, a violation that ultimately brought about his downfall, is also a central aspect of the boxer's transmedia persona. Tellingly, Von Eeden depicts Johnson having sex with a white woman, "his enemy's most prized possession," after Johnson, as the caped figure, battles his many opponents in a dream.[52] Moreover, as portrayed by James Earl Jones in *The Great White Hope*, the Johnson-esque Jack Jefferson is prosecuted for a Mann Act violation after traveling with his white companion. In a manner akin to the response from both white and black societies during Johnson's lifetime, Jefferson's romantic relationship in *The Great White Hope* reinforces Jim Crow–era conceptions of race. A character labeled simply as "Negro," for example, contends that "the deportment of this man does harm to his race. It confirms certain views of it you may already hold: that does us harm. But it also confirms in many Negroes the belief that his life is the desirable life, and that does us even greater harm."[53] By publicly cavorting with white women, Johnson alienated both blacks and whites, and the weight of this defiance of social etiquette continues to resonate through the popular-culture imagination. Yet, despite being prosecuted for such transgressions, Johnson continued to rebel against the established order following his Mann Act conviction.

## Subversion of the Established Power Structure

Throughout his life, Johnson steadfastly rejected authority. Emblematic of this resistance, Johnson fled the United States in 1913, living in Europe and Mexico for the following eight years rather than endure imprisonment for violating the Mann Act. While living in Europe as a fugitive from U.S. law and in desperate need of money, Johnson agreed to fight Jess Willard, a white contender, in Havana, Cuba, on April 5, 1915. Displaying support for their potential racial savior, many in attendance waved white flags, and while Johnson clearly challenged white dominance, he also came to signify a wider subversion of the established order. As a New Negro, Johnson rejected Jim Crow laws and attitudes dictating the separation of the races and the institutionalized subjugation of African Americans. Moreover, as a famous pugilist, Johnson also represented a new morality that challenged the puritanical values expressed by powerful religious and reform groups opposing boxing, the consumption of alcohol, and the influx of immigrants. By circumventing "rules meant to tie him down," Burns argues Johnson constituted "a danger to the natural order of things."[54] For the dispossessed, then, Johnson functioned as a signifier of resistance to unequal social structures.

As a sociopolitical force advocating for the equal treatment of African Americans, the New Negro Movement challenged fixed racial hierarchies and stereotypical notions of black culture.[55] Largely advanced in the arts, the New Negro Movement rejected stereotypical depictions of African Americans in favor of positive images of black culture in ways that instilled a sense of racial pride and assertiveness. The New Negro Movement transpired largely in the North as African Americans fled the oppressive conditions of the Jim Crow South, and for many New Negroes, Johnson became a symbol of this new social order. In contrast to prior strategies of capitulation, Davarian L. Baldwin maintains that "the many masks and strategies of deference and accommodation were collectively discarded as a new aggressive race consciousness emerged through the events surrounding" Johnson's triumphs in the boxing ring.[56]

Furthermore, for religious and reform groups during the Progressive Era, boxing's glorification of violence represented a threat to society, particularly children, and the sport was met with vocal protests. The opposition to boxing by organizations, such as the International Law and Order League, was part of a larger "Purity Crusade" aimed at eradicating a wide range of illicit behaviors including prostitution and the consumption of alcohol.[57] Championing what they saw as traditional American values—namely, white, Christian morality—reform groups regarded boxing as an "immigrant sport" that appealed to those with radically different views and encouraged a multitude of objectionable behaviors.[58] As the sport's reigning heavyweight champion, Johnson therefore epitomized a new morality that rejected Christian moral authority and threatened the hegemonic position of whites by providing marginalized individuals, such as African Americans and immigrants, an opportunity for social mobility.

Given the discourses of sociopolitical change surrounding Johnson, significant incentive existed to find a White Hope who could defeat him and thereby reduce his symbolic power. Writer Stanley Crouch contends that "returning the [heavyweight championship] title back to its rightful ethnic group connects to the lost cause of the South ... and all of those desires to get things back to 'normal' [with whites] on top and [blacks] below."[59] For those seeking such a reestablishment of power, Willard provided perhaps the best opportunity. Nicknamed the "Pottawatomie Giant," the six-foot-six, 230-pound Willard, who was ten years Johnson's junior, was the largest of the White Hopes.[60]

Although Johnson fiercely attacked Willard in the early rounds, he began to lose stamina in the ninth as Willard seemingly absorbed his punishing blows. Sensing his imminent defeat after the twenty-fifth round, Johnson instructed a member of his staff to escort his wife from the event, and in the twenty-sixth round, Willard knocked Johnson to the canvas, where he remained, thereby losing the heavyweight-championship title. Through archival newspaper articles, Burns highlights the prevailing notion that "Jess Willard had restored pugilistic supremacy to the white race."[61] Indicative of the immeasurable threat Johnson represented to extant racial hierarchies, seven years passed before the white establishment permitted an African American boxer to compete for any boxing title, and it was not until twenty-two years after Johnson's defeat that an African American boxer contended for the heavyweight championship.[62]

Yet, because the potential existed that Johnson could have risen and continued fighting during the Johnson-Willard bout, rumors circulated that Johnson intentionally threw the fight—a suggestion that the defeated champion also perpetuated. Although Burns raises the possibility that the fight's outcome was predetermined, this speculation is not seriously considered in *Unforgivable Blackness*. In the pages of *The Original Johnson*, however, Von Eeden finds "clear evidence of the biggest hoax ever perpetrated against a blindly unsuspecting public, in the history of all sports" in the fight's most circulated image, a still image of Johnson shielding his eyes from the sun as he lay on the canvas.[63]

Upon returning to the United States, Johnson served a year in the federal prison in Leavenworth, Kansas. Even while incarcerated, Johnson opposed the established order. As one prison guard detailed, "This prisoner does not get up for the a.m. count. This is a daily occurrence, and *he seems to think the guard's orders do not apply to him*.... He comes in [the] hall when [he is] ready, asks no permission ... goes where he pleases ... asks no permission."[64] Johnson did, in fact, believe the rules did not apply to him. Before his death in 1946, the aging Johnson viewed his life as a continual struggle against authority, remarking, "You've now seen something that a lot of people didn't want to see.... I was a brunette in a blonde town, but, gentlemen, I did not stop stepping."[65] By refusing to acquiesce to social conventions restricting relationships between whites and blacks and by rejecting sociocultural boundaries imposed onto him, Johnson rejected established power structures.

Quite simply, Jack Johnson was a threat. At a time when white America deemed African Americans physically inferior, Johnson became the first African American heavyweight champion of the world. In an age characterized by the economic and social marginalization of African Americans, Johnson attained an exceptional level of wealth and prestige. During a period when the mere appearance of relationship between a black man and a white woman could result in a lynching, Johnson openly courted and married white women. Hence, Johnson challenged and reconfigured notions of race and class in early 1900s America, becoming a potent symbol of a new racial pride, independence, and resistance. Yet, while Johnson transgressed race and class boundaries in a manner that challenged white supremacy, his relationships with white women ultimately reinforced racial boundaries, as both white and black societies largely condemned his behavior. The reaction by both white and black America to Johnson's willful disregard of the prevailing social etiquette of the day rearticulated a strict separation of the races.

Finally, although Burns presents Johnson's significance in *Unforgivable Blackness* as fixed, isolating the boxer's relevance largely in the past, Johnson continues to challenge established hierarchies in the work of contemporary producers. In the music of Mos Def and the Tom Russell Band, the pages of *The Original Johnson*, and on the Broadway stage, Johnson functions as a fluid signifier, rendering him a perpetual threat. Once characterized by an unforgivable blackness, Johnson's provocation of early 1900s white society now functions as an unforgettable blackness.

## Notes

1. *Unforgivable Blackness*, part 1.

2. As a character, Jack Johnson appears in the novels *The Big Blow* (2000) and *The Killings of Stanley Ketchel* (2005), and an adaptation of *The Big Blow* is currently in development at Ridley Scott's Scott Free Productions. Johnson is also playable character in EA Sports' *Fight Night Champion* (2010). Johnson is a central character in Lead Belly's "The Titanic" (1912), and Miles Davis's album *A Tribute to Jack Johnson* (1971) honors the pugilist.

3. W. E. B. Du Bois qtd. in Ward, *Unforgivable Blackness*, viii, emphasis added.

4. Von Eeden, Freeman, and Hillsman, *Original Johnson*, book 1, 1.

5. Mos Def, "Blue Black Jack."

6. Although Sackler's play centers on a heavyweight champion named Jack Jefferson, the protagonist shares many similarities with Johnson, including a penchant for smiling and taunting opponents. Like Johnson, Jefferson successfully defeats an aging White Hope in Reno, violates the Mann Act, and ultimately loses the heavyweight title to an imposing white boxer in Havana. Further, Jefferson dates a white woman who eventually commits suicide.

7. W. E. B. Du Bois qtd. in Runstedtler, *Jack Johnson*, 6.

8. Dyer, *Stars*, 60–66.

9. With the exception of Johnson's autobiographical material, Ward notes that "there are no Jack Johnson 'papers' upon which to draw." However, Johnson appeared in a myriad of newspaper articles and cartoons throughout his lifetime. *Unforgivable Blackness*, xi.

10. Dyer, *Heavenly Bodies*.

11. Dyer, *White*, 12.

12. Andrews, "Fact(s) of Michael Jordan's Blackness"; Kellner, "Sports Spectacle, Michael Jordan, and Nike"; Zang, "The Greatest"; Lewis, "Don't Believe the Hype."

13. Zang, "Greatest," 292.

14. Kellner, "Sports Spectacle."

15. Zang, "Greatest," 292.

16. Jack London qtd. in *Unforgivable Blackness*, part 1.

17. Wiggins, "Edwin Bancroft Henderson," 272.

18. Specifically, Bert Sugar maintains the mantle of heavyweight champion "was the singular, most important title in the world, outside of being a general or a president." Moreover, Gerald Early argues the holder of the heavyweight-championship title became the "emperor of masculinity … a hero figure." *Unforgivable Blackness*, part 1.

19. Jim Jeffries qtd. in *Unforgivable Blackness*, part 1.

20. *Australian Star* qtd. in *Unforgivable Blackness*, part 1.

21. *Unforgivable Blackness*, part 1.

22. Randy Roberts qtd. in *Unforgivable Blackness*, part 1.

23. Jack Newfield qtd. in *Unforgivable Blackness*, part 1.

24. *Boxing Magazine* qtd. in *Unforgivable Blackness*, part 1.

25. Jack Johnson qtd. in *Unforgivable Blackness*, part 1.

26. It was believed that Jeffries once drank a case of whiskey in two days, thereby curing himself of pneumonia. In addition, myths circulated that Jeffries was so strong he could shatter a person's hand just by shaking it and that he never punched challengers as hard as he could, for fear of killing them.

27. Jack London qtd. in Roberts, *Papa Jack*, 68.

28. For his participation in the fight, Jeffries would receive at least one-third of the total purse—and two-thirds if he won—which exceeded one hundred thousand dollars. In addition, Jeffries was paid a ten-thousand-dollar signing bonus. For the time, this was an unprecedented sum of money for a boxing match.

29. Roberts, "Year of the Comet," 49.

30. Jim Jeffries qtd. in *Unforgivable Blackness*, part 1.

31. *New York Times* qtd. in *Unforgivable Blackness*, part 1.

32. In addition to a growing reform movement opposing the sport of boxing, race figured heavily into the resistance to the Johnson-Jeffries fight.

33. Roberts, "Year of the Comet," 57.

34. *Unforgivable Blackness*, part 1.

35. Zang, "Greatest," 292.

36. Wiggins and Miller, *Unlevel Playing Field*, 74.

37. Ibid., 78.

38. Roberts, "Year of the Comet," 53.

39. Burns attributes Johnson's stance to his position as a "New Negro," which is discussed in the next section.

40. Dray, *At the Hands of Persons Unknown*, 71–76.

41. *Unforgivable Blackness*, part 1.

42. Genovese, *Roll, Jordan, Roll*; Cornwell, "George Webb Hardy's"; Thomas, *Sexual Demon*.

43. Etta Duryea, Johnson's first wife, committed suicide because, in part, of the extreme loneliness resulting from this treatment.

44. *Unforgivable Blackness*, part 2.

45. *Nashville Globe* qtd. in *Unforgivable Blackness*, part 1, emphasis added.

46. Jack Johnson qtd. in *Unforgivable Blackness*, part 2.

47. Between 1901 and 1910, Burns observes, 846 people died as a result of lynching in the United States; 754 of these individuals were African Americans. *Unforgivable Blackness*, part two.

48. Johnson, *Jack Johnson*, 186.

49. *Unforgivable Blackness*, part 2.

50. This was the second time the government filed Mann Act charges against Johnson. On October 18, 1912, Johnson was arrested for traveling with a nineteen-year-old white woman named Lucille Cameron. When Cameron refused to testify against Johnson, prosecutors dropped the charges. Johnson and Cameron later married.

51. Tom Russell Band, "Jack Johnson." Russell's "Jack Johnson" is a homage of sorts to Lead Belly's "Titanic" (1912), a song that references Jack Johnson and addresses racial issues. Russell mentions Lead Belly by name and incorporates elements of "The Titanic" in the song.

52. Von Eeden, Freeman, and Hillsman, *Original Johnson*, 56.

53. Sackler, *Great White Hope*, 73–74.

54. *Unforgivable Blackness*, part 1.

55. Nadell, *Enter the New Negroes*; Gates and Jarrett, *New Negro*; Pochmara, *Making of the New Negro*.

56. Baldwin, *Chicago's New Negroes*, 4.

57. Streible, "History," 237.

58. Roberts, "Year of the Comet," 50.

59. Stanley Crouch qtd. in *Unforgivable Blackness*, part 2.
60. Willard hailed from Pottawatomie County in Kansas.
61. *New York Times* qtd. in *Unforgivable Blackness*, part 2.
62. *Unforgivable Blackness*, part 2.
63. Von Eeden argues that Johnson's movement, specifically shading his eyes from the sun as he lay on the canvas, indicates that Johnson was still knocked out and therefore willingly lost the boxing match on purpose.
64. Officer Fowler qtd. in *Unforgivable Blackness*, part 2, emphasis added.
65. *Unforgivable Blackness*, part 2. Jackson's remarks are recounted by Stanley Crouch near the conclusion of the documentary.

## Works Cited

Andrews, David L. "The Fact(s) of Michael Jordan's Blackness: Excavating a Floating Racial Signifier." *Michael Jordan, Inc.: Corporate Sport, Media Culture, and Late Modern America*, edited by Andrews, 107–52. Albany: State University of New York Press, 2001.

Baldwin, Davarian L. *Chicago's New Negroes: Modernity, the Great Migration, and Black Urban Life*. Chapel Hill: University of North Carolina Press, 2007.

Cornwell, Gareth. "George Webb Hardy's *The Black Peril* and the Social Meaning of 'Black Peril' in Early Twentieth-Century South Africa." *Journal of Southern African Studies* 22, no. 3 (1996): 441–53.

Dray, Philip. *At the Hands of Persons Unknown: The Lynching of Black America*. New York: Modern Library, 2003.

Dyer, Richard. *Heavenly Bodies: Film Stars and Society*. London: Macmillan, 1986.

_____. *Stars*. London: BFI, 1979.

_____. *White*. London: Routledge, 1997.

Gates, Henry Louis, Jr., and Gene Andrew Jarrett, eds. *The New Negro: Readings on Race, Representation, and African American Culture, 1892–1938*. Princeton: Princeton University Press, 2007.

Genovese, Eugene D. *Roll, Jordan, Roll: The World the Slaves Made*. New York: Vintage, 1976.

Johnson, Jack. *Jack Johnson: In the Ring and Out*. Chicago: National Sports, 1927.

Kell8ner, Douglas. "The Sports Spectacle, Michael Jordan, and Nike Unholy Alliance?" In *Michael Jordan, Inc.: Corporate Sport, Media Culture, and Late Modern America*, edited by David L. Andrews, 37–63. Albany: State University of New York Press, 2001.

Lewis, Thabiti. "Don't Believe the Hype: The Racial Representation of Mike Tyson in Three Acts." In *Fame to Infamy: Race, Sport, and the Fall from Grace*, edited by David C. Ogden and Joel Nathan Rosen, 45–60. Jackson: University of Mississippi Press, 2010.

Mos Def. "Blue Black Jack." *The New Danger*. Geffen Records. October 12, 2004. CD.

Nadell, Martha Jane. *Enter the New Negroes: Images of Race in American Culture*. Cambridge: Harvard University Press, 2004.

Pochmara, Anna. *The Making of the New Negro: Black Authorship, Masculinity, and Sexuality in the Harlem Renaissance*. Amsterdam: Amsterdam University Press, 2011.

Roberts, Randy. *Papa Jack: Jack Johnson and the Era of White Hopes*. New York: Free Press, 1983.

_____. "Year of the Comet: Jack Johnson versus Jim Jeffries, July 4, 1910." In *Sport and the Color Line: Black Athletes and Race Relations in Twentieth-Century America*, edited by David K. Wiggins and Patrick B. Miller, 45–62. New York: Routledge, 2004.

Runstedtler, Theresa. *Jack Johnson, Rebel Sojourner: Boxing in the Shadow of the Global Color Line*. Berkeley: University of California Press, 2012.

Sackler, Howard. *The Great White Hope*. New York: Dial Press, 1968.

Streible, Dan. "A History of the Boxing Film, 1894–1915." *Film History* 3, no. 3 (1989): 235–57.

Thomas, Greg. *The Sexual Demon of Colonial Power: Pan-African Embodiment and Erotic Schemes of Empire*. Bloomington: Indiana University Press, 2007.

The Tom Russell Band. "Jack Johnson." *Hurricane Season*. Philo Records. February 22, 1994.CD.

*Unforgivable Blackness: The Rise and Fall of Jack Johnson*. "Part 1: Rise." Aired January 17, 2005. Directed by Ken Burns. Arlington, VA: PBS Home Video, 2005. DVD. 110 minutes.

*Unforgivable Blackness: The Rise and Fall of Jack Johnson*. "Part 2: Fall." Aired January 18, 2005. Directed by Ken Burns. Arlington, VA: PBS Home Video, 2005. DVD. 102 minutes.

Von Eeden, Trevor, George Freeman, and Dan Hillsman II. *The Original Johnson*. Book 1. San Diego: IDW, 2009.

_____, _____, and _____. *The Original Johnson*. Book 2. San Diego: IDW, 2011.

Ward, Geoffrey. *Unforgivable Blackness: The Rise and Fall of Jack Johnson*. New York: Alfred A. Knopf, 2004.

Wiggins, David K. "Edwin Bancroft Henderson, African-American Athletes, and the Writing of Sport History." In *Sport and the Color Line: Black Athletes and Race Relations in Twentieth-Century America*, edited by David K. Wiggins and Patrick B. Miller, 271–88. New York: Routledge, 2004.

Wiggins, David K., and Patrick B. Miller, eds. *Sport and the Color Line: Black Athletes and Race Relations in Twentieth-Century America*. New York: Routledge, 2004.

_____, and _____. *The Unlevel Playing Field: A Documentary History of the American Experience in Sport*. New York: Routledge, 2004.

Zang, David W. "The Greatest: Muhammad Ali's Confounding Character." In *Sport and the Color Line: Black Athletes and Race Relations in Twentieth-Century America*, edited by David K. Wiggins and Patrick B. Miller, 289–303. New York: Routledge, 2004.

# From Compton to Center Court

## Venus and Serena *and the Black Female Experience in Professional Tennis*

### Novotny Lawrence

When aficionados and commentators discuss significant moments in the history of women's professional tennis, many cite the iconic Battle of the Sexes match that was contested on September 20, 1973, in the Houston Astrodome. In an era when male players, such as Ilie Nastase and John Newcombe, garnered more attention and prize money than their female counterparts, five-time Wimbledon Ladies Champion Billie Jean King, who was twenty-nine, squared off against fifty-five-year-old former tennis professional Bobby Riggs in a contest where the winner would earn $100,000. While the paycheck was hefty, the implications of the match superseded money and the sport of tennis. As Susan Ware explains in *Game, Set, Match: Billie Jean King and the Revolution in Women's Sports*, the King-Riggs match was significant in part because of the outlandish media hoopla leading up to the event and because the match itself provided the perfect distraction for Americans who were sick of focusing on economic and political issues, such as Watergate, inflation, and the energy crisis. More important, the Battle of the Sexes became a significant moment in the Women's Liberation Movement.[1]

Although the King-Riggs contest became a part of the struggle for gender equality, its conception was not initially politically motivated. The Battle of the Sexes came to fruition when Riggs, who had an affinity for gambling, decided to challenge a top female professional tennis player as a means to "get a piece of the action—and the money—gravitating toward tennis in the open era." He set his sights on King, who initially declined his challenge, a move that led Riggs to approach Margaret Court, the top-ranked female player in the world. As Ware recounts, "Thinking it would be just a Sunday afternoon exhibition match with a tidy pay off, she accepted. Like so many opponents before and after her, Court underestimated Bobby Riggs, whose 6–2, 6–1 demolition of her on May 13, 1973, became known as the Mother's Day Massacre."[2] Upon hearing the results, King knew that she had to uphold the honor of women's tennis by facing Riggs.

In the weeks leading up to the Battle of the Sexes, the match received a great deal of media attention, gaining political significance along the way. Riggs, who realized that making sexist comments would garner him the attention that he loved, berated King and the struggle for women's rights. Among his more colorful quotes are, "I plan to bomb Billie Jean King in the match and set back the Women's Lib movement about another twenty years," and "The best way to handle women is to keep them barefoot and pregnant." Rather than fire back at Riggs, King comfortably assumed the underdog role: "Up until now, I've always been the heavy. You know, I'm the leader. I'm responsible for women's tennis. For once, I'm the underdog. I love it."[3] By the time Riggs and King played, the match had gained such grandiose media hype that the event paled in comparison. King controlled the tempo, won the best of five sets contest routinely, 6–4, 6–3, 6–3, and proved that female athletes deserve an equal amount of respect as their male counterparts.

While King's effort warrants sustained celebration, many commentators often frame, more often than not, it as *the* moment that women gained equality in professional tennis. Unfortunately, this "great white woman" narrative is often retold at the expense of African American female tennis players who had been working to gain respectability in the sport long before King and Riggs ever set foot on the court in the Houston Astrodome. That this occurs is even more disappointing when considering that black women's involvement in tennis has always been political. Moreover, as a result of race, class, and gender, "poor black women's players faced triple oppression because they rarely received equal support in the world of tennis."[4] Thus, African American females' journeys to equality have been arduous, and their story deserves a more prominent place in the annals of tennis lore.

This essay works to help fill the gap that exists in women's tennis history. In particular, the piece begins with an overview of the careers of three prominent African American female tennis players who overcame adversity and paved the way for ensuing generations of black players. The second half of the essay centers on Michelle Major and Maiken Baird's *Venus and Serena* (2012), which chronicles the Williams sisters' 2011 campaign on the Women's Tennis Association (WTA) tour. In doing so, the film provides an intimate look at Venus and Serena Williams' rise to tennis prominence, their relationship, and the racism that they have endured over the course of their careers.

## Historical Overview

Although tennis is generally associated with affluent whites, African Americans actually have a long-standing tradition in the sport. However, "[b]ecause the written history of the sport has focused on specific individuals and organizations involved in early play, it is unclear why blacks were attracted to the game in the first place." What history does reveal is that three developments in tennis occurred quickly for African Americans: "First, a number of blacks were playing the game by the 1890s. Second, upon its founding in 1881 the United States National Lawn Tennis Association (USNLTA), which later became the USLTA and then the USTA, barred blacks from participating in professional tennis so racial segregation in tennis was also set by that time. Finally, among blacks, tennis was very much a pursuit of the upper classes."[5] Thus, in the 1890s the game gained a great deal of traction with African Americans who had access to education at historically black colleges, such as Tuskegee and Howard, that offered tennis to its students and to numerous black tennis clubs like Baltimore's Monumental Tennis Club and Washington, D.C.'s Association Tennis Club.

Although historically black colleges and clubs afforded blacks opportunities to compete in tennis, the game progressed to new heights among African Americans on November 30, 1916, when a group of African American businessmen, college professors, and physicians founded the American Tennis Association (ATA). The organization's "primary objectives were

- to bring black tennis enthusiasts and players into close and friendly relations,
- to improve the standards of existing clubs,
- to hold an annual national championship tournament,
- to regulate the dates of local and regional tournaments to avoid conflicts,
- to appoint referees and officials for each event, and
- to promote the standard of the game among black players.[6]

Importantly, while the USNLTA banned blacks from playing in its events, the ATA had no such rules for white players, a point that further demonstrates how white resistance and racism fostered notions of separation and black inferiority. After its formation, the ATA would become the preeminent black tennis organization, hosting tournaments featuring popular African American players, such as Margaret Peters, Roumania Peters, James Trouman, and Emanuel McDuffle.

Of all the players to participate in ATA events, Ora Washington (1898–1971) was perhaps the most fascinating, though her accomplishments are virtually unknown in tennis lore and popular sports discourse, more broadly. As Nathan Aaseng recounts in *African American Athletes*, a young instructor at the Young Woman's Christian Association (YWCA) introduced Washington to tennis as a means to help her overcome the grief that consumed her as a teen after her sister died.[7] She put all of her energy into the game, winning her first African American National Tennis Tournament in 1924 over Dorothy Radliffe. Washington was such a dominant player that she would go undefeated over the next twelve years,[8] compiling a winning streak explained in part in a *Chicago Defender* article that asserts: "Her superiority is so evident that her competitors are frequently beaten before the ball crosses the net."[9] Indeed, Washington was so superior that she continued to excel on the tennis court in 1929 when she began competing in the ATA against the top African American tennis players. Though strong, the opponents were no match for Washington, who won the ATA's singles tennis title seven straight years before taking a yearlong break from the sport. After her hiatus, Washington returned to competition and once again won the ATA singles title.[10]

Importantly, Aaseng notes, "Washington's career closely overlapped with that of white U.S. tennis star Helen Wills Moody, who won seven Wimbledon singles titles from 1923 to 1931 and eight U.S. Open singles titles from 1927 to 1938, including four consecutive seasons in which she won both prestigious championships." Given Washington's and Moody's dominance against their respective opponents, a match between the two would have garnered a great deal of excitement from tennis aficionados and U.S. residents, more broadly. However, Moody would not even consider the idea, and neither the U.S. Open nor the Wimbledon organizers would open their tournaments to African Americans until several years later. Thus, skewed racial politics robbed tennis fans the honor of seeing the sport's two most dominant female players face off and ultimately played a major role in Washington's retirement from the sport. Aaseng summarizes that she was so accomplished that she rarely received any real competition from the ATA's other black players and eventually left tennis to focus on basketball, a sport at which she also excelled.[11]

Although Ora Washington was never permitted to compete against whites, Althea Gibson broke professional tennis's color line on her way to becoming one of the most notable players in tennis history. Gibson was born on August 25, 1927, in Silver, South Carolina, to Daniel and Annie Gibson, who were poor cotton sharecroppers.[12] After having several bad harvests, in 1930 the Gibson family relocated to Harlem, New York, which at the time presented more opportunities for blacks.[13] Her road to tennis glory began one summer morning when she began playing paddle tennis on her neighborhood street with a friend. Gibson became so adept at the game that she caught the eye of Harlem bandleader Buddy Walker, "who worked as a supervisor on the play street to earn money between gigs."[14] Impressed by her ability, Walker gave Gibson her first tennis racquet and later introduced her to Fred Johnson, the one-armed head tennis professional at the prestigious Cosmopolitan Club, who helped further hone her skills.[15]

Gibson was a natural at tennis, and by the age of fifteen, she won the ATA's New York State Junior Championship. In the ensuing years, she was a force on the tennis court, becoming the most dominant player in ATA history from 1947 to 1956 when she won ten consecutive singles titles. Unfortunately, as Cecil Harris and Larryete Kyle-Debose explain in *Charging the Net: A History of Blacks in Tennis from Althea Gibson and Arthur Ashe to the Williams Sisters*, few outside of black tennis even noticed Gibson's accomplishments.[16] As she recalls in her 1958 autobiography, "Winning the [ATA] championship got me three or four lines of type at the bottom of the page in the *New York Times*. The *New York Daily News*, which has less space, didn't mention it all."[17]

The scant attention that Gibson received from the white press for her accomplishments highlighted two important points. First, it was a glaring reminder that African Americans were second-class citizens whose triumphs against other African Americans, no matter how significant, were unworthy of national attention. Second, it illustrated that in order for Gibson to truly earn respect for her tennis prowess, she would have to defeat top white professionals in the sport's most prestigious events. To do so, the USLTA would have to permit Gibson to play in its tournaments, which the organization went to great lengths to keep all white. For example, when Gibson would apply to their events, the organization would conveniently lose her entry applications, claim that the applications arrived too late, or deny her entry based on the fact that she had not played enough USLTA tournaments.[18]

Although the USLTA's actions were frustrating, Gibson and the ATA continued pressing the organization to allow her to participate in its events. In June 1950, she received unsolicited support from four-time U.S. Nationals Champion and 1939 Wimbledon Champion Alice Marble, who, in an open letter that appeared in the July 1950 issue of *American Lawn Tennis Magazine*, challenged the USLTA's racist practices.

> If tennis is a sport for ladies and gentlemen, it's also time we acted a little more
> like gentle people and less like sanctimonious hypocrites. If there is anything left

in the name of sportsmanship, it's more than time to display what it means to us. If Althea Gibson represents a challenge to the present crop of women players, it's only fair that they should meet the challenge.... She is not being judged by the yardstick of her ability but by ... her pigmentation.... The entrance of Negroes into national tennis is inevitable as it has proven to be in baseball, in football, or in boxing.[19]

Marble's letter, in conjunction with the ATA's persistent advocacy and a burgeoning shift in public perception, coerced the USLTA to adopt the gradual approach to eradicating its racist policies. Beginning in 1950, the organization allowed Gibson to enter into its smaller events before allowing her to transition to its more prestigious tournaments later that same year. In her first USLTA matches, Gibson announced herself to the world and proved that black females belonged on the tennis tour. She performed consistently well, either defeating or playing soundly against top white female players, such as Barbara Knapp and three-time defending Wimbledon Champion Louise Brough.[20]

After establishing herself on tour, Gibson soared to new heights in the ensuing years, capturing several prestigious tournaments, becoming the top-ranked female player in the world, and earning some of sport's top honors. In 1956, a year when Gibson triumphed at more tournaments than any other player, she won the French Open title and was the Wimbledon runner-up.[21] She was so determined to take the title at the All-England Club the following year that she chose not to defend her French Open title so that she could focus on her grass-court game.[22] Gibson's preparation paid off when on July 6, 1957, she became the first African American player to capture the Wimbledon title when she defeated Darlene Hard 6–3, 6–2 in front of a capacity crowd that included Queen Elizabeth II.[23] With her victory, Gibson also integrated the prestigious All-England Club, which granted Wimbledon champions automatic membership. While little was written about that aspect of Gibson's win, it is of great importance as it signals how far-reaching Gibson's accomplishment was.

Ironically, while Gibson made great strides that challenged white-supremacist ideologies, she was uncomfortable with assuming the role of the great black savior. In her autobiography, *I Always Wanted to Be Somebody*, Gibson explains:

> I am not a racially conscious person. I don't want to be. I see myself as just an individual. I can't help or change my color in any way, so why should I make a big deal of it? I don't like to exploit it or make it the big thing. I'm a tennis player, not a Negro tennis player. I have never set myself up as a champion of the Negro race.... I shy away from it because it would be dishonest of me to pretend to a feeling I don't possess.... I try not to flaunt my success as a Negro success. It's all

right for others to make a fuss over my role as a trailblazer, and, of course, I realize its importance to others as well as to myself, but I can't do it.[24]

Despite Gibson's sentiments, it is impossible to discount the impact on tennis
and the world at large of her myriad accomplishments, which include but are
not limited to winning multiple Grand Slam tournaments and numerous other
titles, being named the Associated Press's first black Female Athlete of the Year
in 1958, becoming the sport's highest-paid female player regardless of ethnicity
in her era, and being inducted into the Tennis Hall of Fame.

Although Gibson's story is often pushed to the margins of popular
accounts of tennis history, in 1990 when Zina Garrison became just the second
African American female to make it to a Wimbledon final, she demonstrated
that her legacy sustains. Garrison's road to the concluding match in tennis's
most prestigious event began on November 16, 1963, in Houston, Texas, where
she was born to Ulysses and Mary Garrison. Unfortunately, Garrison's father
passed away when she was just five months old, leaving her mother to raise her
on her own.

By the time that Garrison was in grade school, it was obvious that she
was a talented athlete. In "Garrison's Biggest Rally Came off the Court," Alex
Fineman explains, "At eight, she was playing fast-pitch softball with 14- and
15-year-olds. While growing up, she would routinely win at track meets. The
hand-eye coordination and speed that came from those two sports made her
a natural for tennis."[25] Indeed, Garrison's athletic ability allowed her to quickly
pick up the game of tennis, which she began at ten years old, a late age for a
future professional tennis player. Former ATA Champion John Wilkerson was
her tutor.[26] Just four years after taking up the sport, Garrison earned national
attention when she was the runner-up in the USTA National Girls' 14s and
became the first African American girl to be ranked number 1 in the state of
Texas. In 1980 at age sixteen, she won the USTA National Girls' 16 title, and
the following year she captured junior titles at Wimbledon and the U.S. Open
on her way to becoming the top-ranked junior player in the world.[27]

Having achieved such great success as a junior player, Garrison decided
to forgo her senior year of high school to turn professional, joining iconic
players such as Chris Evert, Martina Navratilova, and Pam Shriver on the WTA
tour.[28] Although she did not achieve the same level of success as Gibson, Garrison had a solid career in which she claimed multiple singles and doubles
titles and became the first African American female to be ranked in the WTA
top 10.[29] For example, in 1985 she earned what was at the time the biggest win
of her young career when she defeated Evert in the final of the Sunkist WTA
Championships.[30] Later the same year she won the first grass-court title of her

career, taking home the trophy from the Family Circle New South Wales Open.[31] Garrison also won the bronze medal at the 1988 Olympics in Seoul, Korea, and found success in doubles at the event as well, teaming with Shriver to win the gold medal.[32]

While the aforementioned accomplishments should not be understated, the defining moment of Garrison's career was playing in the 1990 Wimbledon final. In order make it to tennis's biggest stage, she had to overcome Monica Seles and Steffi Graf, who at the time were two of most dominant players in professional tennis. After defeating both players in three-set thrillers, Garrison advanced to the finals, where she faced Navratilova, who had already established herself as one of the greatest players in tennis history. Garrison was unable to overcome her opponent's skill and experience, and in seventy-five minutes she lost the match routinely 6–4, 6–1. Although she would have loved to have had her name etched on the Wimbledon trophy, Garrison made another significant advancement for African Americans as she became just the second black female player to compete for the title. She played the final match in front of her predecessor, Althea Gibson, who traveled to England specifically to watch the match.[33]

It is important to note that the aforementioned section is not intended to be the comprehensive account of the black female tennis experience. That story is recounted more thoroughly in such texts as Sundiata Djata's, *Blacks at the Net: Black Achievement in the History of Tennis*, and Harris and Kyle-Debose's, *Charging the Net*. Rather, this brief narrative sheds light on three African American females who made important strides for subsequent players but rarely receive the recognition that they deserve in mainstream accounts of tennis history. Though victims of America's skewed racial politics, Washington helped demonstrate that black females could play tennis at a high level, Gibson broke the color line on her way to illustrating that African Americans were indeed equal to their white counterparts, and Garrison brought a renewed visibility to African American female tennis players, once again proving their viability in the sport. Therefore, in their own unique ways, Washington, Gibson, and Garrison paved the way for *Venus and Serena*, which is the focus of the remainder of this essay.

## Venus and Serena

*Venus and Serena* was written, produced, and directed by Maiken Baird and Michelle Major, both of whom had established themselves in the media industry long before embarking on this ambitious project. Baird gained prominence producing documentaries, such as *Smallpox Curse* (2001) and *Client 9: The Rise and Fall of Eliot Spitzer* (2010); from 2002 to 2010, Major worked for *Good Morning America*, producing 496 episodes of the show.[34] The duo initially conceived of *Venus and Serena* in the summer of 2007 during a brainstorming session. In an interview with *Life and Times'* Quinton Peterson, Baird explains, "[W]e were just throwing ideas around and this idea came up, we both were very [passionate] about making a film about these two sisters and finding out more about them.... So, it took us about three years to get a meeting with Venus in the summer of 2010. Then we managed to convince her and the people she was with at the time, her agent and [one of] her sisters." Major adds, "Basically, Venus liked the idea. We had a great conversation with her and after that meeting she green-lit the project and everybody else automatically came on board. Serena, the young sister—as you see in the film— she follows her big sister. So big sister made the decision, little sister agreed and everybody else came after that, there was not really a big persuasion with the rest of the family."[35] After gaining permission to document Venus and Serena Williams, Baird and Major spent the entire 2011 tennis season with the sisters, recording over 450 hours of footage that they would use in conjunction with archival materials to bring the one-hundred-minute documentary to fruition.

*Venus and Serena* opens on an interview with the Williams sisters as adolescents before they came into national prominence. A reporter positioned off camera asks the girls what they'd like to be when they grow up, a question to which they both respond " a tennis player." The screen goes black before the opening credits begin rolling throughout a montage that starts when an image of Serena as an adult fills the screen as an omniscient voice comments, "One of the greatest mysteries of modern American history, I think, is how two girls from Compton could go down as among two of the greatest tennis players ever." The montage proceeds, via archival materials from 1992 to 2010, to show the sisters' ascension to greatness. It features images of them practicing in their impoverished inner-city neighborhood in Compton, California, as young girls, footage from their early professional matches, and their victories at Grand Slam tournaments. Talking-heads interviews with a range of people, including comedian Chris Rock, former president Bill Clinton, and tennis-legend-turned-commentator John McEnroe discussing Venus's and Serena's importance, are interspersed between the footage, demonstrating how far-reaching their appeal and impact have been on professional tennis. The entire montage is set to Wyclef Jean's "I'm Ready," a hip upbeat track that, in conjunction with the archival materials and interviews, helps relate the excitement surrounding the Williams sisters.

Although the opening credits end with a title card explaining that Baird and Major spent the entire 2011 season with Venus and Serena Williams, the film encompasses more than that time frame. In doing so, the filmmakers deviate from the chronological narrative style often employed to document historical figures. Instead, *Venus and Serena* weaves back and forth between the present and the past, providing a rarely seen glimpse into the Williams sisters' professional and private lives. For example, after the opening credits, the film begins with Serena, who at the onset of the 2011 season was unable to play tennis due to injury. More specifically, she discovered that she had a blood clot in her lung that could have led to her death had it not been diagnosed and operated on in time. Hence, Serena's arc follows her as she works to recover from the injury and her return to the courts at the Wimbledon and the U.S. Open Championships.

In contrast, when audiences are introduced to Venus, she is in Melbourne, Australia, to compete in the first Grand Slam tournament of the 2011 season, the Australian Open. Unfortunately, her season takes an unexpected turn for the worse when in her second-round victory against Germany's Andrea Petkovic, she sustains a hip injury. Although she attempts to play her third-round match, the injury is too painful, making it impossible for her to compete at the highest level. Venus is forced to forfeit the match and finds herself working to return to action as well.

Because the aforementioned arcs comprise a majority of the documentary, and Venus's and Serena's struggles over the 2011 season were well publicized, this essay focuses more heavily on the story that unfolds between those narratives via interviews and archival footage. It is in those moments that tennis fans and those unfamiliar with the sport can gain more insight into the Williams sisters' rise from Compton to center courts around the globe, their relationship, and the personal and professional hardships that they have endured.

Maiken and Baird briefly recount the Williams sisters' early years, using archival video footage. In particular, they tell of how their father, Richard Williams, began grooming them to be professional tennis players on the public tennis courts in their Compton neighborhood when they were very young. Because the family did not have a great deal of money, he would visit country clubs and beg for their old tennis balls, which he would use to train his daughters. Richard Williams's methods were unconventional, as he had Venus and Serena work on their ground strokes by throwing footballs and had them practice martial arts and ballet and run while pulling tires behind them to work on their speed, agility, and footwork. Throughout their training, Richard boasted about his daughters' tennis prowess to reporters and sportswriters, garnering a great deal of attention. As a result, Venus (to a larger extent) and Serena had captured the imaginations of tennis enthusiasts before they ever turned pro.

Interestingly, Baird and Major subtly challenge the traditional accounts of Venus's and Serena's training, which credit Richard (and their mother, Oracene Williams) for making his daughters successful professional players. Coach Rick Macci, who at the time of the sisters' development was working with some of the best young players in the country at his Macci International Tennis Academy in Haines City, Florida, is oft overlooked, leaving a significant gap in the Williams sisters' narrative. Baird and Major work to fill that void by interviewing Macci in *Venus and Serena* and including his account of his involvement with the Williams sisters. Macci explains that when the girls were young, Richard contacted him and asked him to assess his daughters' tennis abilities. Although he lived in Florida and had never taken a trip to connect with any potential tennis prodigies, Macci flew out to California to watch Venus and Serena showcase their talent. He was initially unimpressed by their games but decided that they were worth the investment when during a bathroom break, Venus made the first ten feet of the trek to the restroom while walking on her hands and did backward cartwheels the remainder of the way. Upon seeing Venus's athletic prowess, Macci decided to coach the Williams sisters: "I funded the project. I moved the whole family from California. I put Richard on the payroll 'cause he left his security business in California." Macci relates that his relationship with the family came to an end after Venus won her first professional tournament in Oakland, California, at the age of fourteen. At that point she became a media sensation and signed a $12 million endorsement contract with Reebok, giving the Williams family the financial security that they needed to move into a residence with tennis courts in Palm Springs, Florida. He concludes his interview, "The foundation was laid by Richard. The rest of it was taken to the mountain top by Rick Macci."

Despite Macci's assertion, which the documentary substantiates to a degree in archival video footage in which Richard can be heard referring to him as coach, he is rarely mentioned as a part of the Williams sisters' success. In fact, when in an interview the filmmakers ask Venus if there are any other coaches in her life that she would like to talk about, she disregards Macci when she responds, "I would consider all of my sisters my coaches.... I worked with Billie Jean King and Zina Garrison so I would consider them both influences on my life and my game." When asked directly about Macci, Venus states, "We did work with Rick for a few years, but I think my dad was the one with the most revolutionary ideas as far as changing the game. We worked with my dad from conception until now." Although there is reluctance to fully acknowledge

Macci, Harris and Kyle-Debose, in *Charging the Net*, lend credibility to his assertions.

> Although Mr. and Mrs. Williams laid the foundation on which two future champions were built, they list themselves as the coaches of record for Venus and Serena for the same reason that people by vanity license plates: because they can. The truth is, a pair of amateur coaches, no matter how much they adored their daughters, could not have turned them into world-class players, indeed world champions, without helping hands. Truly experienced coaches were sought to provide schooling in the more technical aspects of the game. First, Rick Macci ... worked with the girls for a year and a half during their adolescence. But the relationship soured.[36]

Although we may never know the full story behind the Williams-Macci relationship, what becomes increasingly clear in *Venus and Serena* is that the sisters have shared a very special bond since childhood. Baird and Major rely upon footage from the sisters' adolescent years to begin exploration of their relationship, and it remains a constant theme as the documentary weaves between the past and the present. In the early footage, a reporter asks the girls how they feel when they are on the tennis court. Venus responds, "I feel good," and Serena immediately copies her older sibling, repeating the same answer. The film immediately cuts to Serena in an interview with the filmmakers in which she comments, "What didn't I do to try to copy Venus when I was younger? I mean her favorite color was my favorite color. Her favorite animal was my favorite animal. She wanted to win Wimbledon, I wanted to win Wimbledon." In the film, author Gay Talese further discusses the bond the sisters share: "I know they're not twins, but in a way they are and their whole life experience has been in the shadow of another person. There's very little that's happened to either one of them that the other has not been privy to, maybe even an eyewitness to."

As the documentary progresses, viewers learn that when Venus and Serena are not traveling to compete in tennis tournaments, they occupy a home together in Bradenton, Florida. The filmmakers provide a rare glimpse into their private lives with footage from 2011 that shows Venus and Serena spending time together during their respective recovery periods hanging out with friends, performing karaoke, and discussing the future. Perhaps the scene that relates the sisters' closeness most effectively is one in which Serena informs Venus that she is planning to get married. Venus congratulates her upon hearing the news and immediately asks Serena where she plans to live after she ties the knot. Realizing that she will have to move out of the home that they share, Serena immediately backs off her marriage talk.

Although the coverage of Venus's and Serena's personal lives is not overly extensive, it effectively captures the bond that they share, which has always made it extremely challenging for the two to compete against one another. As their older sister Isha Price explains in the documentary, "Venus is an extreme protector so Serena always had to win or she always had to be the princess." Their different personalities have informed their matches against one another since they were children. For example, when Serena was eight years old, she entered a tournament in which Venus was playing without her father's permission. The two advanced to the finals, which Venus won 6–2, 6–2. However, afterward she traded her gold trophy for Serena's second-place trophy, telling her little sister that she actually preferred silver to gold.[37]

Their personalities, in conjunction with them being sisters and the most dominant players on the WTA tour, made their match in the 2001 U.S. Open final compelling. Serena Williams had proven that she could win at the venue four years earlier, when at seventeen years old, she became the first African American woman to win a major title since Althea Gibson when in the final Serena defeated the world's top player, Martina Hingis. Serena continued to amass titles in the ensuing years, firmly cementing herself as the second-best player on the WTA tour. On the other hand, Venus had ascended to the top of the women's game in 2000, when she captured her first Grand Slam titles at Wimbledon (which she successfully defended in 2001) and the U.S. Open, feats that earned her a reported $40 million endorsement deal with Reebok. At the time, it was the most lucrative deal in sports history that a female had ever signed.[38] By September 2001, the Williams sisters were two of the most recognizable athletes in the world, regardless of the sport.

Given Venus and Serena Williams' status and the underlying theme of a sibling rivalry, there was great interest in the 2001 U.S. Open Final from tennis fans and the general public alike. CBS was acutely aware of the buzz surrounding the match and took what was at the time a huge risk when it reworked its Saturday night lineup so that it could air the match in primetime. The network's gamble paid off, as the final garnered huge ratings from home audiences, who, while tracking the competition on the scoreboard that appeared in the corner of the television screen during the broadcast, may not have thought twice about the fact that to differentiate the players from one another it simply read Venus and Serena, rather than V. Williams and S. Williams. Importantly, that detail aided in putting the sisters in a class with other popular culture icons, such as Prince, Madonna, and Cher, all of whom are simply known by one name.

In addition to the primetime broadcast, the atmosphere and the celebrities who attended the match also demonstrated just how popular Venus and Serena had become. As Djata recounts, the match was "the scene of black royal procession much like the scenes at the All-Star Games of the Negro Leagues. The Harlem Gospel Choir and Diana Ross performed. Highly visible personalities, such as Vanessa Williams, Spike Lee, Rick Fox, Sean Combs, Robert Redford, Joe Namath, Sarah Jessica Parker, Jay Z, and Brandy, attended."[39]

In the end, the buildup to the 2001 U.S. Open Final proved to be more of a draw than the competition itself. The spectators were subdued throughout the match as if unsure of how to react when either Venus or Serena won a point. In *Venus and Serena*, Isha, who was among the fans, discusses the difficulty of the moment: "It was a very tense and hard thing to watch. It's stressful to watch them play because you want them both to win. You feel there's a little guilt, like okay I can't clap for Serena. I can't clap for Venus." Perhaps as a result of nerves, their strong relationship, or a combination of both, neither of the Williams sisters played her best tennis that evening. In a match that lasted just sixty-nine minutes, Venus routinely defeated Serena 6–2, 6–4 to capture her second straight U.S. Open title. Still, the match marked a seminal moment for women's tennis that should forever be remembered because it was the first time that a tennis match had been played in primetime since the famous Battle of the Sexes match. Moreover, it was a significant moment for African Americans as it was the first time that two black players had ever contested a Grand Slam Final. That they did so in the stadium named after African American tennis legend and civil rights activist Arthur Ashe only adds to its relevance, making it another victory in the struggle for black equality.

Venus and Serena have made several advancements for African American tennis players and female athletes, more broadly, and at times they have done so in the face of resistance. There was a tremendous backlash against the sisters almost immediately after they joined the WTA tour. In the documentary Venus relates, "When we first came out, I think Serena and I were criticized more than some of our counterparts who weren't African American." Indeed, commentators and other players frequently questioned the sisters' training techniques, their attitudes, and whether their matches against one another were fixed, and engaged in more subtle acts that could also be construed as racist. For example, in her quarterfinal match against Venus at the 1997 U.S. Open, Romania's Irina Spirlea intentionally bumped into her during the changeover and then laughed about it as the two were waiting to resume play. Clearly, Spirlea's actions were unsportsmanlike, but they are even more deplorable considering that at the time of the incident, Venus was only fourteen years old while Spirlea was a twenty-three-year-old woman. After going on to lose to Williams, Spirlea was unapologetic in her postmatch interview: "She thinks she's the f*cking Venus Williams and she's not gonna turn. I'm sorry she feels that way." Not only did Venus defeat Spirlea on the court but she also upstaged her off the court in answer to a question in her postmatch interview about the bumping incident when she calmly responded, "It's not really a big thing to me."

In addition to the Spirlea incident, Baird and Major also revisit what is perhaps the most notable incident of racism that the Williams family has experienced on tour to date—the 2001 Indian Wells (California) Final, which occurred six months prior to Venus and Serena Williams' historic U.S. Open Final. Although the episode took place during the finals, it actually began to take shape the night before when Venus was forced to withdraw from her semifinals match against Serena approximately five minutes before it was scheduled to be played, an occurrence that meant that her sister would automatically advance to the final match the following day. The timing of her withdrawal was unfortunate as it happened fairly soon after WTA players Elena Dementieva and Hingis began suggesting that Richard Williams predetermined whether Venus or Serena would win their matches against the other. Hence, Venus's withdrawal, which was well within WTA regulations, only added more fuel to the proverbial match-fixing fire.

Despite the ridiculous speculation surrounding the outcome of the Williams sisters' matches against one another and the general disappointment that fans tend to experience when a match is cancelled, what transpired during the Indian Wells Final between Serena and Belgium's Kim Clijsters remains disturbing. Major and Baird use video footage obtained from a British sports outlet to revisit the moment. It all began when the predominantly white crowd in attendance booed Richard and Venus as they entered the stadium to take their seats. As they continued making their way down to Serena's player's box, the video footage shows Richard pause and look in the direction of a fan before continuing to his seat, where he tells Venus, "A guy just called me a nigger. Told me he would skin my ass alive or something." To make matters worse, as Serena and her opponent walked onto the court, the crowd booed vehemently. Isha recounts, "Serena's looking up in the stands trying to find it, like what am I missing. And then it dawned on her, that it was her." As the events transpire, the commentator in the video footage observes, "An American crowd booing an American family.... You have to say that it does smack of a little bit of racism."

The fans continued their raucous behavior throughout the entire match, cheering Serena's mistakes and wildly applauding Clijsters' efforts. Early on, the audience's behavior affected Serena, who fought back tears for much of the first set. Impressively, she eventually gained her composure and was able to overcome the hostile crowd and her opponent, winning the match 4–6, 6–4, 6–2. Much like Venus had done nearly four years earlier after the Spirlea incident, Serena took the high road in her speech during the trophy ceremony: "I would like to thank everyone who supported me, and if you didn't, I love you guys anyway."

Because of the way that they were treated on that day, the Williams sisters have boycotted the Indian Wells tournament ever since. Discussing her decision not to play in the event, Serena makes it clear to Major and Baird that her stance is very much about the ongoing struggle for black equality: "You look at people like Martin Luther King and Malcolm X, and Rosa Parks. If they didn't believe and stand for what they believed in, we wouldn't have the freedoms that we experience today. What I had to go through is so small compared to what they had to go through and if I can't stand up for something like this then ... who am I and what have they taught me in history?"

Though *Venus and Serena* recounts the Indian Wells incident in detail, the film does not address the fact that the Williams sisters' ongoing boycott of the event continues to receive media attention. Instead, Major and Baird present it as yet another testament to the Williams sisters' strength, determination, and perseverance and then move on to the documentary's next segment. What is important to note is that as time has passed, a segment of sports analysts have begun questioning Venus and Serena Williams' continued boycott of the tournament, with others remaining in staunch support of their decision not to play at Indian Wells.

A pair of articles by *Sports Illustrated*'s Bruce Jenkins and Elizabeth Newman perfectly articulates the ongoing Indian Wells debate. In "It's Time for Williams Sisters to Return to Indian Wells," Jenkins opens, "Arthur Ashe spent a lifetime confronting racism with calm and measured logic." This is telling because whether intentional or not, it reveals how from his perspective as a privileged white man, the appropriate manner in which racism should be handled by those who encounter it—calmly and measured. Jenkins continues by acknowledging that the crowd at the 2001 Indian Wells tournament behaved poorly.

> Let's be clear on one thing: What happened that day in 2001, before and during the final between Serena and Kim Clijsters, was one of the ugliest scenes in the sport's history. You didn't have to be in the stands (and I was not) to be appalled and disgusted by the crowd's hostile response to Venus, who showed up to watch after pulling out of her scheduled semifinal against Serena two days earlier, or to the Williams family in general. I believe I would be haunted, as well, by the sights and sounds lingering in memory.

After making such a powerful and empathic statement, Jenkins asserts that it is time for the Williams sisters to "let bygones be bygones" and, ultimately, concludes, "After 12 years, I no longer see dignity or integrity in the Williams' stance, only stubbornness and a grudge. I find that disappointing, and a little bit sad."[40]

Jenkins's article reveals that he lacks a critical understanding of racism, its functioning, and the impact that it has on those who are subjected to it, a point that Newman directly addresses in "Calls for Williams Sisters to Return to Indian Wells Are Wrong."

> I have read several editorials (including one by Bruce Jenkins at SI.com) suggesting that Venus and Serena should suck it up and move on, that they should set aside all of the pain and embarrassment from that fateful day and be the bigger people for the good of the sport. Sure, each plea for the sisters to come back to Indian Wells is written with a convenient eloquence and soft undertone so as not to overtly offend. They are often written by white male critics who have never experienced the complexities of race and discrimination and who use patronizing language like, "I know I can't begin to understand what it felt like for the sisters in that moment, but I am disappointed that after all this time they can't just get past it." If the sisters were to read such commentary, they would likely roll their eyes and respond, "It's been 12 years, people, why can't *you* get past it?"

Newman continues by reminding readers of just how nasty the crowd acted on that day: "For two hours, the packed stadium of 15,000 mostly white fans viciously booed as she began her final against Kim Clijsters. The crowd booed and heckled Serena after every point she won and cheered her double faults and unforced errors. When she finally won the match, the boos drowned out any applause. When she held up the trophy, the boos became even more intense as the shouts of condemnation grew louder."[41] Importantly, Newman puts the onus on those who committed the atrocities rather than those who endured them, demonstrating that whether or not people agree with the boycott, it is important that they respect the Williams sisters' decision to stand against racism.[42]

As *Venus and Serena* moves beyond the discussion of Indian Wells, it focuses more heavily on the sisters' 2011 season, while also mixing in brief discussions about the tragic murder of their older sister Yetunde Price, who in September 2003 was shot to death in an apparent case of mistaken identity, and about their relationship with their father and their parents' divorce. Through it all, the family remains close as they journey through a season that was full of disappointment and challenges. For example, after performing inexplicably poorly at Wimbledon, Venus is diagnosed with Sjogren's syndrome, an autoimmune disorder, that not only affects her 2011 campaign but that she will have to manage throughout the remainder of her life. In the meantime, Serena returns to the court only to lose early at Wimbledon and in the final of the U.S. Open.

Despite a disappointing 2011 season, *Venus* and *Serena* ends on an uplifting note as video footage and title cards reveal the Williams sisters' major accomplishments during the 2012 campaign. Serena wins the Wimbledon Championships and takes the gold medal in women's singles at the Olympics. She continues her domination, teaming with Venus to earn the Olympic gold medal in women's doubles as well. Although the Williams sisters are approaching the end of their careers, the film reestablishes the fact that they remain forces to be reckoned with.

## Venus and Serena: *The Aftermath*

Since *Venus and Serena* premiered at the prestigious Toronto Film Festival in September 2012, Major and Baird have been embroiled in rumor, speculation, and litigation. Controversy initially began when reports emerged claiming that Venus and Serena Williams had withdrawn their support for the documentary because they were unhappy with the way that the filmmakers portrayed their father. The allegations gathered momentum when neither of the sisters attended the film's premier at the Toronto Film Festival, even though the event organizers had shifted the date of the initial screening to accommodate their schedules. Venus refuted reports about her dissatisfaction with the final cut, expressing support for the documentary and citing scheduling conflicts for her lack of attendance. Serena also publicly supported the film, going so far as sending Major and Baird recorded apologies for her absence to play for audiences at the Los Angeles and New York premiers.[43]

In addition to premiering amid controversy, *Venus and Serena* opened to middling reviews that speak to the challenges associated with bringing new insights to audiences familiar with two of tennis's biggest icons. David Rooney of the *Hollywood Reporter* expresses appreciation for the array of talking-heads interviews that Major and Baird include in the documentary and the access that they were able to gain to Venus and Serena Williams. However, he explains, "beyond generic impressions concerning the hunger for victory and continued success, the documentary reveals surprisingly little, indicating that it's perhaps too sanctioned to be entirely effective. We get enough glimpses to know that the Williams sisters are vibrant, funny, determined women, but seeing them goof off with a karaoke machine during rare downtime is not the same as getting to know them."[44] In his review titled, "Champions Face Challenges, Too," the *New Times'* A. O. Scott continues along a similar trajectory:

> [T]ennis fans will find much to enjoy but very little that they haven't already seen or heard. The story of how Venus and Serena changed tennis—pushed,

coached and nurtured by their father, Richard, and their less talkative but no less determined mother, Oracene—is a remarkable chapter in the history of race and sports in America. The version told here is detailed but also superficial, since Ms. Baird's and Ms. Major's intentions and methods are more promotional than journalistic.[45]

As if the speculation surrounding Venus and Serena Williams' support for the documentary and the mediocre reviews were not disappointing enough for Major and Baird, the filmmakers have also encountered legal resistance from the USTA. In particular, on June 14, 2013, the organization filed a lawsuit against the filmmakers claiming that in *Venus and Serena*, they used unauthorized footage. The segment in question is of Serena's infamous outburst at a line judge during her semifinal match against Clijsters at the 2009 U.S. Open, which the USTA feels reflects poorly on professional tennis.[46]

Major and Baird have been vocal about their disappointment over the lawsuit, asking that tennis fans express their dissatisfaction with the USTA. For them their struggle against the organization is a free-speech issue. In "An Open Letter to the Tennis Community," the filmmakers note:

> We ask for your support in our fight against the efforts of the United States Tennis Association (USTA) to deny our first amendment rights of freedom of speech and freedom of the press and to censor our documentary, *Venus and Serena*, about the remarkable lives of the Williams sisters.
>
> When we began our work, we expected to have the cooperation of the USTA as we prepared to tell the world, for the first time in a full-length documentary, the story of two of the greatest American stars in tennis history. And we were fully prepared to fairly compensate USTA for any USTA-controlled film footage that we used in the film.
>
> Remarkably, though, USTA refused to sell us the rights to the footage of their greatest icons unless we agreed to censor our film. In particular, USTA demanded that we not include footage that we believed was important to the complete telling of this incredible story.[47]

Alex Gibney, *Venus and Serena*'s Oscar-winning executive producer, has also voiced his concern over the USTA's lawsuit.

> The USTA's efforts to censor this film about America's most inspiring female athletes don't change the fact that my colleagues were entirely within their legal rights to use a small amount of widely seen footage. The concept of fair use is vital to filmmakers trying to tell truthful stories and embodies the essence of the first amendment of the U.S. Constitution. Indeed, without the fair use doctrine, copyright itself would be unconstitutional. By its actions, the USTA is assaulting the very principle of free speech.[48]

As of the writing of this essay, the USTA's case against Major and Baird remains in litigation. As the filmmakers and their executive producer explain, its resolution will have far-reaching implications on *Venus and Serena* and documentarians, more broadly.[49]

As this essay illustrates, African Americans have a long-standing, yet relatively unknown, tennis tradition. From the creation of the ATA to the accomplishments of great female players, such as Ora Washington, Althea Gibson, and Zina Garrison, blacks have endured in a sport that continues to elevate white accomplishment over that of their black counterparts, who had to overcome great resistance just to step onto the same courts with them. Were it not for the efforts of the aforementioned female tennis legends, change may have occurred even more slowly, leaving black tennis players outside of the fence looking in rather than competing on the highest level. Baird and Maiken's *Venus and Serena* extends the African American tennis legacy; however, not only is it significant because it provides insight into the careers of two of tennis's most iconic stars, regardless of ethnicity, by demonstrating their rise to tennis prominence, relationship, and struggles with racism, but the film is also notable in that it fills a significant gap in tennis's lily-white dominant discourse, illustrating how imperative it is that filmmakers continue to document the black experience.

## Notes

1. Ware, *Game, Set, Match*, 1.
2. Ibid., 3, 4.
3. Ibid., 4.
4. Djata, *Blacks at the Net*, 24.
5. Ibid., 2, 3.
6. "American Tennis Association," para. 1.
7. Aaseng, *African-American Athletes*, 229.
8. Ibid.
9. "Doug Turner, "Ora Washington Lead Men and Women Tennis Players in Ratings of 1930s," *Chicago Defender*, March 14, 1931, 9.
10. Aaseng, *African-American Athletes*, 229.
11. Ibid.
12. Harris and Kyle-Debose, *Charging the Net*, 49.
13. Djata, *Blacks at the Net*, 28.
14. Harris and Kyle-Debose, *Charging the Net*, 50.
15. Wiggins and Miller, *Unlevel Playing Field*, 260.
16. Harris and Kyle-Debose, *Charging the Net*, 53–54.
17. Gibson, *I Always Wanted to Be Somebody*, 50.
18. Ibid., 54.
19. Qtd. in Knapp, *Book of Sports Virtues*, 152.
20. Harris and Kyle-Debose, *Charging the Net*, 55–56.
21. Djata, *Blacks at the Net*, 32, 34.
22. Ibid., 35.

23. "Althea Gibson."
24. Gibson, *I Always Wanted*, 158.
25. Fineman, "Garrison's Biggest Rally."
26. Djata, *Blacks at the Net*, 91.
27. Ibid.
28. Fineman, "Garrison's Biggest Rally."
29. The WTA was founded in 1973, years after Althea Gibson had retired from tennis.
30. Djata, *Blacks at the Net*, 93.
31. Ibid.
32. Fineman, "Garrisons Biggest Rally."
33. Djata, *Blacks at the Net*, 96.
34. "Maiken Baird"; "Michelle Major."
35. Peterson, "'Venus and Serena.'"
36. Harris and Kyle-Debose, *Charging the Net*, 21.
37. Djata, *Blacks at the Net*, 129.
38. Wiggins and Miller, *Unlevel Playing Field*, 421.
39. Djata, *Blacks at the Net*, 127.
40. Jenkins, "It's Time."
41. Newman, "Viewpoint."
42. Although to a lesser extent than in years past, the ridiculous match-fixing allegations began to swirl around the Williams sisters again in February 2014. In particular, both sisters advanced to the semifinals of the United Arab Emirates' Dubai Duty Free Championships, where Venus defeated Caroline Wozniaki, and Serena lost to Alize Cornet. After Serena's loss, a fan inquired to ESPN about whether Serena lost her match on purpose so Venus could go on to win the title. For more information about these allegations, see Archuleta, "Serena Williams Accused."
43. Thompson and Savage, "Navigating Documentary."
44. Rooney, "Venus and Serena."
45. Scott, "Champions Face Challenges, Too."
46. Gardner, "Venus and Serena Documentary Suit."
47. Major and Baird, "Open Letter."
48. Ibid.
49. Gardner, "Venus and Serena Documentary Suit."

## Works Cited

Aaseng, Nathan. *African-American Athletes*. New York: Infobase, 2003.
"Althea Gibson Wins Wimbledon." This Day in History: Sports. *A&E Television Networks*. http://www.history.com/this-day-in-history/althea-gibson-wins-wimbledon.
"The American Tennis Association (ATA)." *Black Tennis History*. http://www.blacktennis history.com/the-american-tennis-association-ata/.
Archuleta, Greg. "Serena Williams Accused of Throwing Match to Avoid Playing Venus? Dubai Scenario Rekindles Past Accusations of Match-Fixing." March 6, 2014. *Sports World News*. http://www.sportsworldnews.com/articles/10194/20140306/serena-williams-accused-of-throwing-match-to-avoid-playing-venus-dubai-scenario-rekindles-past-accusations-of-match-fixing-video.htm.
Djata, Sundiata. *Blacks at the Net: Black Achievement in the History of Tennis*. Vol. 1. New York: Syracuse University Press, 2006.
Fineman, Alex. "Garrison's Biggest Rally Came off the Court." Sportscenter Biography. *ESPN Classic*. http://espn.go.com/classic/biography/s/Garrison_Zina.html.
Gardner, Eriq. "Venus and Serena Documentary Suit Could Shape News Access to Sport

Events." June 18, 2013. *Hollywood Reporter*. http://www.hollywoodreporter.com/thr-esq/venus-serena-lawsuit-showtime-doc-570519.

Gibson, Althea. *I Always Wanted to Be Somebody*. New York: HarperCollins, 1958.

Harris, Cecil, and Larryete Kyle-Debose. *Charging the Net: A History of Blacks in Tennis from Althea Gibson and Arthur Ashe to the Williams Sisters*. Chicago: Ivan R. Dee, 2007.

Jenkins, Bruce. "It's Time for Williams Sisters to Return to Indian Wells." March 12, 2013. *SI*. http://sportsillustrated.cnn.com/tennis/news/20130312/williams-sisters-indian-wells-venus-serena/.

Knapp, Fritz. *The Book of Sports Virtues: Portraits from the Field of Play*. Skokie, IL: ACTA, 2008.

"Maiken Baird." *IMDB*. http://www.imdb.com/name/nm1930582/?ref_=ttfc_fc_dr1.

Major, Michelle, and Maiken Baird. "An Open Letter to the Tennis Community." The Blog. June 19, 2013. TheHuffingtonPostwww. http://www.huffingtonpost.com/michel le-major-and-maiken-baird/usta-venus-and-serena-documentary_b_3466253.html.

"Michelle Major." *IMDB*. http://www.imdb.com/name/nm3238760/?ref_=tt_ov_dr.

Newman, Elizabeth. "Viewpoint: Calls for Williams Sisters to Return to India Wells Are Wrong." March 15, 2013. *SI*. http://sportsillustrated.cnn.com/tennis/news/20130315/williams-sisters-indian-wells-serena-venus/.

Peterson, Quinton. "'Venus and Serena' Documentary Explores the Training and Bond of the Williams Sisters." May 3, 2013. *Life + Times*. http://lifeandtimes.com/behind-williams-sister-documentary-venus-and-serena.

Rooney, David. "Venus and Serena: Toronto Review." September 17, 2012. *Hollywood Reporter*. http://www.hollywoodreporter.com/review/venus-serena-williams-tennis-toronto-review-371071.

Scott, A. O. "Champions Face Challenges, Too: 'Venus and Serena,' a Documentary about the Williams Sisters." May 9, 2013. *New York Times*. http://www.nytimes.com/2013/05/10/movies/venus-and-serena-a-documentary-about-the-williams-sisters.html?_r=0.

Thompson, Anne, and Sophia Savage. "Navigating Documentary 'Venus and Serena' with the Williams Sisters Was Not Easy." May 10, 2013. *Indiewire*. http://blogs.indiewire.com/thompsononhollywood/venus-and-serena.

Ware, Susan. *Game, Set, Match: Billie Jean King and the Revolution in Women's Sports*. Chapel Hill: University of North Carolina Press, 2011.

Wiggins, David K., and Patrick Miller. *The Unlevel Playing Field: A Documentary History of the African American Experience in Sport*. Urbana: University of Illinois Press, 2003.

# PART III

# ELECTRONIC MEDIA

# Immortalizing Dorothy Dandridge in Documentary, African American Press and Mainstream Press

## CHARLENE REGESTER

Despite the star status that Dorothy Dandridge achieved as a black actress in 1950s Hollywood, today she is virtually ignored and forgotten compared to her white contemporaries, such as Elizabeth Taylor and Marilyn Monroe, who have been continually revered in the public discourse. The disproportionate attention that white actresses such as Taylor and Monroe receive does not compare to the sparse attention given to Dandridge. Although Dandridge receives minimal attention for her accomplishments relative to these white actresses, scholars, historians, and filmmakers continue to resurrect and reconstruct this black icon. This essay explores how Dandridge is presented in Ruth Adkins Robinson's documentary *Dorothy Dandridge: An American Beauty* (2003), the 1950s black press, and the mainstream press. More specifically, this essay exams *Jet* magazine because of the extensive coverage that it provided to Dandridge throughout her career; also considered are the *New York Times* and the *Los Angeles Times* because they are the national papers that extensively covered Dandridge's career, unlike other mainstream periodicals (primarily magazines) that ceased thoroughly following her after her 1954 Academy Award nomination.[1] While comparing newspaper to magazine coverage is fraught with its own complexities, this examination will provide an understanding of how Dandridge was constructed in the 1950s print media relative to contemporary visual media, as both are central to providing a complete profile of this oft-dismissed actress.

*Beauty* provides a visual reconstruction of Dandridge and attempts to achieve authenticity and realism in that it avoids presenting Dandridge as exclusively hypersexualized, as opposed to the black and mainstream press, which were more preoccupied with exploiting her hypersexuality to promote their own self-interests and appropriate her as a star. In order to more fully comprehend how *Beauty* reconstructs Dandridge, it is important to consider the documentary process. Discussing nonnarrative cinema, Albert Maysles surmises:

> We can see two kinds of truth.... One is the raw material, which is the footage.... Then there's the other kind of truth that comes in extracting and juxtaposing the raw material into a more meaningful and coherent storytelling form.... In a way, the interests of the people in shooting and the people in editing ... are in conflict with one another, because the raw material doesn't want to be shaped. It wants to maintain its truthfulness. One discipline says that if you begin to put it into another form, you're going to lose some of the veracity. The other discipline says if you don't let me put this into a form, no one is going to see it and the elements of truth in the raw material will never reach the audience.[2]

The struggle between form and content emerges as *Beauty* utilizes on-camera interviews with coworkers, film footage, photographs from her life, and newspaper reports to capture who Dandridge was. These sources are woven together by the narrator, actor Obba Babatundé, who guides the story and infuses it with meaning.[3]

*Beauty* begins as the camera pans out revealing an empty theater prior to focusing on one of the most outstanding black actresses of the 1950s era to grace the silver screen. Next, multiple images of Dandridge traverse the screen, including a picture of her in her signature role as Carmen Jones (*Carmen Jones*, 1954); an image of her as a presenter at the 1954 Academy Awards ceremony, where she was competing for best actress; and an image of her as a sultry nightclub singer dressed in a long form-fitting gown. During this brief introduction, the theater remains empty, perhaps in an attempt to visually symbolize the silence in history regarding her contributions, the scant attention or scholarship devoted to this actress, or the void that existed in her private life due to the insurmountable obstacles she faced. The theater's absence of attendees suggests that viewers of the documentary are the spectators occupying the seats, reflecting what theorist Gilles Deleuze characterizes as "including the viewer in the film," in another attempt to forge an intimate connection between contemporary audiences and this star, who has paled in the public's memory.[4]

As *Beauty* unfolds, Babatundé explains that he intends to introduce viewers to someone with whom they may be unfamiliar, suggesting that although Dandridge is missing from the Hollywood canon, younger generations should know exactly who she was. The film then shows Dandridge as a nightclub singer, a moment that subtly alludes to the fact that many black actresses, like Lena Horne and Hazel Scott, were established singers before transitioning to motion pictures. Shifting her position from standing on stage to lying on a couch suggests how Dandridge made the transition from singer to actress and invites reference to E. Ann Kaplan's "The Couch Affair." While the title of the essay is a play on Hollywood's practice of exploiting women's sexuality to elevate their acting careers, the couch also refers to the psychiatrist who psychoanalyzes the patient. This, however, is not to suggest that the metaphor of the couch implies that Dandridge used sex to obtain roles, nor to connote that she as a patient became the object of the voyeuristic gaze of a psychoanalyst. Instead, the couch affair metaphor is a fitting tribute to Dandridge because she achieved a level of stardom and became synonymous with white screen stars similarly photographed on the couch. Moreover, the metaphor of the couch is significant because it represents the possibility for engaging in a psychoanalytic study of Dandridge in view of her professional and private struggles. Kaplan contends, "It is precisely the hair-thin line between emotional problems resulting from racism, family context, economic deprivation, and social role models, and those resulting from unconscious reasons specific to the individual and the immediate relationships that is so difficult to draw here: for the psyche is inseparable from the political."[5] For Dandridge, her psyche also remains inseparable from her political and personal struggles.

Consistent with Kaplan's metaphor, *Beauty* depicts Dandridge lying on the couch while surrounded by three elegantly dressed black men, who stand behind her in white shirts and wear black ties and jackets, as she sings "My Baby Knows Where My Heart Belongs." Her demeanor, coupled with the song's lyrics, hints at her hypersexualized image. But more than that, *Beauty* uses this iconic image to establish Dandridge similar to her white contemporaries who appeared in pinup photos that connote their A-list status. Film scholar Richard Dyer argues that the pinup is central to the way a star's image is constructed. Drawing on the work of Thomas Hess, Dyer claims, "The body is evident beneath the costume, but not its details.... There is a dialectical pressure at work, between the voyeuristic public which wants to see more and more, and that same public which, in its social function, supports codes and laws that ban any such revelations."[6] In this instance, Dandridge's sexuality is appropriated on-screen in much the same manner as a pinup connotes stardom, and she uses her singing to reinforce this hypersexualized image.

In reconstructing Dandridge, *Beauty* provides a shot of her wearing a mink wrap to cover her long gown. She sings the lyrics, "You do something to me that nobody else can do," and when she removes the wrap to reveal her Tstrap gown, her sexuality is emphasized. The narrator suggests that while Dandridge is a "goddess" and "magical," she is also talented and charismatic, two qualities that allowed her to become a "trailblazer" and "pioneer." Dandridge's characterization as magical and talented is consistent with Dyer's critique that "stars are stars because of 'talent,' ... 'striking photogenic looks, acting ability, presence on camera, charm and personality, sex-appeal, attractive voice and bearing.'" However, Dyer admits that this alone does not constitute stardom because struggle is also a signifier of stardom, as in the case of actress Marilyn Monroe, who symbolized the exploitation "of woman as spectacle in film."[7] The documentary shifts from Dandridge's hypersexualization to the struggles she faced as a trailblazer and a pioneer. Babatundé professes in the documentary that her road to stardom was "paved with *more* potholes [than red] carpet[s]," yet her "beauty and talent could not be denied."

*Beauty* features historian Alan Gansberg, who expounds on Dandridge's struggles and reveals that she was reared by a lesbian divorcée whose lover violated Dandridge physically and emotionally, perhaps to provide an explanation for some of her complexity. (This, of course, is not to imply that someone reared in these circumstances could not emerge unscathed or achieve a state of "normalcy.") Dandridge seemingly was scarred and anguished by these circumstances, according to actress Jasmine Guy, who claims that the actress internalized her abuse and assumed the role of the victim as a result. In critiquing Dandridge, Guy reflects on an earlier interview conducted with actress Diahann Carroll, who warned her to be cautious in making such accusations and judgments without considering the mores and restrictions imposed on 1950s women.

Shifting from Dandridge's personal struggles to the early years of her career, *Beauty* reflects on the World War I era, which led into the flapper age, a period that signaled a renewed consciousness among women in their quests to achieve liberation and an era that may have strongly influenced her mother, Ruby Dandridge, also an actress, who worked in radio, film, and television. Most notable is the rarely seen film footage of Ruby and Dorothy when Dorothy and her sister, Vivian, performed as the Wonder Children and the Dandridge Sisters. Attributing Dandridge's early training to Ruby, who had a considerable influence on her daughter, *Beauty* later implies that Dandridge's "troubled" formative years were overcome with successes that could not have been achieved without her mother. But Dandridge was determined to cultivate her own career, and she refused to assume the stereotypical roles her mother popularized; Dandridge defied beliefs articulated by actor Clarence Muse, who claimed that she was "too pretty" and "not dark enough" for available Hollywood roles. Dandridge challenged these views and navigated her own direction, leading her to land parts in movie shorts ("soundies"), roles that provided the early training needed to become an accomplished actress.

Transitioning from her public to private life when she married Harold Nicholas, *Beauty* addresses Dandridge's first marriage and features a wedding photo that includes several well-known black actors. Fayard Nicholas, Harold's brother, gives his assessment of the marriage and reports that while Dandridge desired security and domesticity, Harold traveled extensively and sought the nightlife, two opposing positions that contributed to the dissolution of their short-lived marriage. According to Fayard, the breaking point occurred following the birth of their daughter, who was born "severely brain damaged," an event that represented Dorothy's "biggest personal tragedy." Even though the marriage dissolved, *Beauty* attempts to balance the deteriorating marriage with rarely seen photos of the young couple and their daughter to display a family that was intact at one point. But what emerges is the representation of a woman who could not escape life's fate, thus speaking to Dyer's assessment that "ordinariness is the hallmark of the star."[8]

Dandridge, despite her difficulties, was a woman who utilized her talent to resurrect herself. She responded to her failures, according to *Beauty*, by returning to the nightclub circuit. As a divorced mother with a daughter in need of care, she renewed her desire to perform. Publicly, she gained popularity on stage, but, privately, she became introverted and withdrawn. Dandridge as a nightclub singer to some extent parallels Horne, in that while Horne allegedly created distance and aloofness with her audiences and whose "performance worked to unperform the sexual subjectivity that [they] expected," Dandridge reversed Horne's strategy in that rather than being introverted publicly, she seemingly became introverted privately, to "[withhold], rather than make accessible, a sexualized and racialized subjectivity."[9]

Establishing Dandridge's cross-over appeal as a performer and competitor to white stars, *Beauty* indicates that Dandridge began to appear in films such as *Tarzan's Peril* (1951), in which she exuded such presence and sexuality that one reviewer declared, Tarzan virtually "forgot" about Jane when Dandridge was paraded on-screen. This film, among others, prepared her for one of the most significant and successful roles of her career, the coveted lead in *Carmen Jones*, a film where the relationship between star and character is perceived to be the "perfect fit" and where "all the aspects of a star's image fit with all the traits of a character."[10] *Beauty* claims that some cast members characterized Dandridge as distant. In response to this allegation, dancer Carmen de Lavallade explains that Dandridge was misunderstood by cast members, but, without a doubt, she claimed the role as her own. On the other hand, actor Joe Adams asserts that although she was aggressive on-screen, offscreen Dandridge revealed a much softer and more vulnerable side. Thus, *Beauty* explores how Dandridge was perceived by her peers, but the black and mainstream press focused more intently on the film's production and reception.

Dandridge's story then unfolds through a series of interviews conducted with performers (some with whom she worked) including actor Joe Adams, dancer Fayard Nicholas, actor Brock Peters, actress Jasmine Guy, actor Laurence Fishburne, and actress Rolonda Watts, among others. The interviews are accompanied by visual records of Dandridge's stage and screen performances, both of which hint again at her hypersexualization as well as her struggles to become a renowned actress. Adams refers to Dandridge as "magnificent" and as "a lady with a golden soul," seemingly to suggest that aside from her on-screen talent, offscreen she was genuine and kind-hearted. While Adams speaks to Dandridge's personality, Fishburne describes her significance to black film history: "She is of singular importance because she was the first black woman who was able to lead with her sexuality." This was a feat in and of itself, yet doing so perpetuated myths regarding the hypersexualization of black women. It was not just that Dandridge appropriated hypersexuality; it is that Dandridge was not allowed to be defined as something other than the quintessential stereotype. Acknowledging the dilemma that Dandridge faced, Peters affirms her strengths and is complimentary of her beauty both on- and off-screen. He reveals that she possessed such natural beauty that she did not need to have her photographs professionally altered. Collectively, these actors formulate an image of Dandridge that intertwines her private and public profiles while providing insight into her personality.

Complementing the interviews with visual representations, *Beauty* presents a photograph of Dandridge posing in a strapless gown, and the narrator explains that she was as visually striking as she was internally conflicted. At this point, the documentary shifts to explore the numerous obstacles she faced that led to her vulnerability and fragility. This is the first time that the documentary specifically hints at Dandridge's personal troubles, yet it shies away from delving deeply into this part of her life so that her significance as an actress will not be overshadowed by the difficulties she confronted. This is in stark contrast to the black press and mainstream press that at times took every opportunity that they could to expose and exploit her struggles.

## Dandridge's Struggles in the Black and Mainstream Press

Dandridge encountered personal struggles that became well known when she was embroiled in a libel suit against *Confidential* magazine, which she believed misrepresented and threatened her public image. The magazine insinuated that Dandridge had an illicit affair with a white male at Lake Tahoe, Nevada.[11] Responding to *Confidential*'s character assassination and demonstrating how she sought to resurrect her image, *Jet* reported that when she attended court, she wore "a trim beige shantung suit [revealing] the solemn look of a woman wronged in print," yet the "curvesome actress-singer ... Dandridge took the witness stand to defend her virtue at the Los Angeles criminal libel trial of scandal-happy *Confidential* magazine."[12] Dandridge, reportedly, found the experience "humiliating,"[13] and her more conservative dress demonstrates how she sought to rebel against the immoral image that the gossip magazine had fabricated. Also, Dandridge was involved in a legal suit against similarly demoralizing incriminations suggested by *Hep* magazine, whose scandalous article titled "Dorothy Dandridge—Her 1,000 Lovers" may have raised the ire of *Jet*, which attempted to extricate her from such allegations by garnering sympathies from its readers.[14]

Equally vigorous in investigating the smear campaigns the gossip magazines leveled against Dandridge, the *Los Angeles Times* also covered her legal battles and reported that *Confidential*'s libel suit was based on an article titled "What Dorothy Dandridge Did in the Woods," a report that provided a false and damaging representation of the actress. Dandridge, in dispute of these allegations, claimed the article was "published 'through evil motive and malice'" and was designed to "injure, disgrace and defame her by imputing to her 'a laxity of moral character.'"[15] Dandridge eventually received an out-of-court settlement, which was meager compensation for the damage inflicted to her image and certainly inadequate to reverse the harm caused to her public profile.[16]

## *Carmen Jones* in the Black and Mainstream Press

Intent on appropriating its black star, *Jet* magazine frequently reported on Otto Preminger's *Carmen Jones*, which was based on Bizet's opera. In preparation for the lead role, Dandridge worked on her vocalizations and reportedly "added six notes to her voice range after being coached for one and a half years in Hollywood by Lawrence Russell."[17] Despite the preparations, she was denied the opportunity to perform her own songs, which were instead recorded by white opera singer Marilyn Horne.[18] According to the *New York Times*, white "operatic voices" dubbed the singing of both Dandridge and costar Harry Belafonte (whose voice was dubbed by Laverne Hutcherson).[19] The *Los Angeles Times* suggested, "[R]ather than put some of the members of [his] cast for

*Carmen Jones* into a precarious position as vocalists, [Preminger] has arranged for some extraordinarily interesting voice-doubling—a normal procedure."[20] Imprecise in its reporting, the *New York Times* remarked, "Neither [Dandridge nor Belafonte], it seems, was dismayed at having stronger, opera trained voices 'dubbed' off-screen."[21] But *Jet* implied that Dandridge was dissatisfied with this decision.[22] More important, that Horne's and Hutcherson's voices substituted for these black actors speaks to a "dubbing [designed] to create a kind of phantasmic body that register[s] visually as black but sound[s] 'white' in terms of the material qualities of its 'voice.'"[23] Because Dandridge's voice, in particular, was dubbed by a white opera singer, it seems that filmmakers were counting on her body to carry the weight of blackness, while the white sound emanating from her voice connected her to whiteness, making her accessible to Eurocentric audiences.

Even though Dandridge and Belafonte did not actually sing in *Carmen Jones*, the film was extremely popular. When Dandridge was cast in *Carmen Jones*, she landed a plum role that called for an irresistible, enticing, and untamable characterization; she possessed the qualities to bring this character to life in a role where she nearly emasculates her on-screen lover.[24] Promoting the film, *Jet* featured Dandridge and Belafonte on its September 30, 1954, cover and characterized them as "Hollywood's first Negro screen lovers."[25] Referring to Dandridge as "luscious" and Belafonte as "handsome," *Jet* compared them to white Hollywood screen couples, such as Clark Gable and Lana Turner and Katharine Hepburn and Spencer Tracy. Making such comparisons to white romantic relationships was an attempt to humanize African Americans, since blacks all too often were dehumanized, and *Jet* believed that Hollywood had previously miscast blacks as romantic leads.[26]

While *Jet* celebrated the film's romantic relationship, *New York Times'* Bosley Crowther characterized the film as "emotionally superficial, inconsistent with the depth of its theme, and ... musically false and incongruous, as far as the natural rhythms of its characters are concerned."[27] Moreover, he referred to Dandridge as "a tight-dressed Beale Street tramp who is brassy, aloof and artificial, with little sense of genuine longing warmth."[28] Crowther's critique certainly seems rather harsh given that Dandridge received an Academy Award nomination. Philip Scheuer of the *Los Angeles Times* was much more complimentary: "Dandridge is the sizzling, sexy Carmen.... [S]he seduces [Joe] with such finality.... Some of Carmen's purpler passages with Joe are guaranteed to startle you out of your composure. Remember, this gal's a heat wave with a lotta livin' to do."[29]

Less concerned with critiquing the film and more concerned with lobbying for Dandridge to win the Academy Award, as she stood to become the first African American actress nominated in the Best-Actress category, *Jet* worked to garner support for Dandridge to receive the Oscar, featuring her on its March 10, 1955, cover with a caption announcing that she was being considered for the award.[30] According to *Jet*, given that Dandridge had already received numerous awards for her Carmen portrayal, she deserved this one.[31] While complimenting Dandridge for her nomination, *Jet* was critical of Hollywood's historic exclusion of African Americans from consideration for the Best-Actress Oscar and questioned, "How good are Dorothy Dandridge's chances for an Oscar?"[32] While Dandridge was the "first" African American to be nominated in the Best-Actress category, *Jet* admitted that she faced stiff competition from white actresses Grace Kelly (*Rear Window* and *Country Girl*), Judy Garland (*A Star Is Born*), Audrey Hepburn (*Sabrina*), and Jane Wyman (*Magnificent Obsession*). Yet, in spite of her competition, *Jet* reassured its readers that "many observers think her chances are excellent,"[33] as did several gossip columnists, such as Hedda Hopper, Sheilah Graham, Louella Parsons, and Army Archerd. Alerting its readers that winning would be difficult, *Jet* reported that Preminger, not so optimistic, cautioned, "'I can only hope Dorothy gets the Oscar.'"[34] In the end, neither the press's nor Preminger's hopes for Dandridge were enough as Kelly won. Still, because Dandridge was included in the running is a major milestone for black film performers that warrants recognition.

## *Dandridge's Interracial Screen Roles*

Although Dandridge did not win the Oscar, she received additional movie offers after her nomination. Interestingly, most of the roles she was offered featured her in interracial films rather than films like the all-black spectacle that firmly positioned her on Hollywood's A-list. *Beauty* relates that Dandridge was invited to appear in Twentieth Century–Fox's *The King and I* (1956) but was discouraged from accepting the role by Preminger, who attempted to control every aspect of her life. Because of his influence and dominance, Dandridge was reportedly alienated from friends and family. *Beauty* contends that Dandridge, now facing a paucity of screen roles, appeared in two low-budget European productions, a development that coincided with her second marriage to Jack Denison, a white restaurant owner. Unfortunately for Dandridge, Denison was abusive, and the relationship was strained, which may have contributed to her dependency on prescription drugs and alcohol.

Returning to the screen to divert attention away from her personal disappointments, Dandridge appeared in *Tamango* (1958), which also features her in an interracial romance as the concubine to a white slave trader, whom she betrays by allying herself with black rebellious slaves. To promote the picture, *Jet* proclaimed in a November 15, 1956, article headline, "Dorothy Dandridge to Incite Film Riot" and featured her on its October 31, 1957, cover. Expounding on her role and reviewing her screen career, *Jet* noted that several of her recent films had characterized her as a screen vixen who managed to lure and captivate her (black and white) male costars. *Jet* opined:

> Winsome Dorothy Dandridge kicked off one shoe in the movie *Carmen Jones*, poised a manicured tootsie under the hot breath of Harry Belafonte and commanded "Blow, Boy," she launched herself on a career as the most torrid Negro siren in screen history. In her recent film, *Island in the Sun*, she virtually charms the British accent right off handsome white actor John Justin. But it is in her latest movie [*Tamango*] that the honey-colored beauty assumes her hottest role ... [where she] cabins-up with white actor Curd [*sic*] Jurgens in order to make life on board [a slave ship] more bearable.[35]

*Jet*'s commentary regarding *Tamango* is significant on multiple levels. First, the black magazine refused to let the public forget her most notable role in *Carmen Jones*; second, it characterized her as a charmer to her white costar in *Island in the Sun*; and third, it depicted her as hypersexualized when she "cabins-up" with her white costar in *Tamango*, clearly demonstrating how the black press exploited these representations to appropriate Dandridge as a star.

In stark contrast, the *New York Times* characterized *Tamango* as "too inflammatory" due to its interracial theme but acknowledged that the film was a "hit" in Detroit and that it had been exhibited in southern cities (San Antonio, Texas, Charlotte, North Carolina, and Columbia, South Carolina) previously averse to liberal-themed pictures.[36] At the same time, the *New York Times* warned, "Polemicists for racial equality on the screen and the simply curious may find something enticing about the prospect of a Teuton-like Curt Jurgens making intense love to Dorothy Dandridge, a Negro, in *Tamango*."[37] The *Los Angeles Times* reported, "Aside from its violence and its hints of miscegenation, *Tamango* ... is thought to have little to offer.... That ... Dandridge is torn between her passionate master and her own people seems remote from all reality."[38]

Much like *Tamango, Island in the Sun* (1957) also centered on miscegenation, a taboo subject that filmmakers seemed compelled to normalize in the mainstream, using Dandridge as its primary vehicle to do so. In this feature, the actress is cast in a romantic relationship with white costar John Justin. Celebrating Dandridge's film, *Jet* featured a photo of the interracial couple on its December 13, 1956, cover with the caption, "They make love, but can't kiss in new movie."[39] Strategically, *Jet* was attempting to expose the cinema industry's cautious approach to depicting interracial relationships on-screen. Characterizing the film as scandalous, *Jet* suggested that even though the picture hinted at intimacy between blacks and whites, such intimacy could not be visibly shown on-screen. In a similar vein, the *New York Times* referred to the film as controversial when the producer, Darryl F. Zanuck, claimed that it was provocative not only because it depicted "race relationships," but also because it hinted at a more dangerous proposition: "miscegenation, which the Production Code stipulates, must be handled at the discretion of the producer."[40]

Developing a reputation for popularizing interracial roles, Dandridge was cast in *Malaga* (1960; originally, *A Moment of Danger*), another film that resulted in her photo being featured on *Jet* magazine's July 23, 1959 cover. This time, *Jet* claimed that at least she is kissed by her white male costar—a first for the screen. While the publication acknowledged that the film was progressive in its display of interracial intimacy, at the same time, the magazine characterized the film as regressive because of its treatment of Dandridge, who suffered "deep purple bruises on her body" when physically assaulted by her white male costar, a point that was made either to garner sympathy from its readers or suggest how the black body was under assault.[41]

## Porgy and Bess *in the Mainstream Press*

Gaining notoriety as an actress through the fabrication of these interracial roles, Dandridge returned to the all-black cast *Porgy and Bess* (1959), a film where she attracts the attention of three black male suitors: Crowne, Brock Peters; Porgy, Sidney Poitier; and Sportin' Life, Sammy Davis, Jr. This was Dandridge's final major film, which, according to *Beauty*, may have signaled her demise and was perceived by many blacks as antithetical to the Civil Rights Movement. Notable, *Jet* remained rather silent on the film for fear of dividing the black community, while the mainstream press provided extensive coverage. For example, *Los Angeles Times'* Hopper reported that the Screen Directors Guild board of directors "called a virtual strike against Samuel Goldwyn as a result of Goldwyn firing [director Rouben] Mamoulian from *Porgy and Bess* and then refus[ed] the board's invitation to appear before it to explain why he took such action."[42] Hopper explained that black actors Sidney Poitier, Pearl Bailey, and Dandridge had released a statement indicating that until the dispute was resolved, "[W]e would rather not discuss *Porgy and Bess....* When this is done, we hope there will be no further need to discuss the artistic interpretation of the script, as this was originally worked out by Mamoulian, which is our major concern."[43] Adding to the controversy, the *Los Angeles Times* reported that black actor Leigh Whipper, in response to the firing of Mamoulian, unequivocally declared, "As president of the Negro Actors Guild of America, I will not participate in any project that may prove derogatory to my race."[44]

When Preminger was hired to replace Mamoulian as director of *Porgy and Bess, Beauty*, there were claims that he "bullied" Dandridge and "left her crying on and off the set." Following the film's completion, *New York Times'* Crowther admiringly stated, "The great values in this lyric drama of the Negro residents of Catfish Row ... are colorfulness, vitality and the eloquence in the music that expresses its characters' joys and sorrows."[45] Crowther was more critical later in the same article: "Dandridge is too sinuous and sleek and got up to look too much like Kiki to give a fully satisfying portray of Bess." Yet, he concluded, "for the most part, this is a stunning, exciting and moving film, packed with human emotions and cheerful and mournful melodies." When the film premiered on the west coast, *Los Angeles Times'* Philip Scheuer suggested that Dandridge has "moments of real trouping, such as when she is tempted against her will by Sportin' Life's promises," yet he ended his critique, "She is, of course, a beauty."[46] The divide between the black and mainstream press in its reception of *Porgy and Bess* is glaringly apparent; many blacks opposed the film, and *Jet* provided scant coverage (with *Ebony* magazine condemning its stereotypical representations), while the mainstream press was much more laudatory of the film, yet oblivious to the damage inflicted on the black screen image.[47]

## Beauty's *Final Analysis of Dandridge*

According to *Beauty*, Dandridge suffered abuse during the production of *Porgy and Bess*, which was compounded by the fact that she was forced into bankruptcy after being swindled of her finances, targeted by the Internal Revenue Service, physically assaulted by Denison, and faced with the institutionalization of her daughter when she could no longer financially provide for her private care. On September 8, 1965, Dandridge was found dead of an apparent drug overdose in her apartment after she had negotiated a return to the screen in Mexico, a death that "may be as significant as the films [she] made," as premature death at times becomes another marker of stardom.[48] *Beauty* reveals that Dandridge had preplanned her funeral and stipulated that she desired to be cremated. At the star's funeral, Harold Nicholas and white actor, Peter Lawford, were among those in attendance, but many did not attend, including Vivian Dandridge (her sister), Cyril Dandridge (her father, who had been given the wrong date by her mother), and Preminger. The documentary ends with interviews from actress Watts and dedications by actress Halle Berry, who in 2001 was the first black woman to win the Academy Award for Best Actress. While Watts affirms Dandridge's significance yet vulnerability, Berry dedicates her Academy Award to the memory of Dandridge. When Berry receives her award, she holds her Oscar tightly and raises it high to suggest that it really belongs to Dandridge, who was denied this honor nearly fifty years earlier.

Hence, *Beauty* becomes a useful tool for reconstructing Dandridge's contributions to black cinema history, exposing the dilemma of being a black actress in a white, male-dominated industry and demonstrating how she ushered in the civil rights era, paving the way for other black actresses. *Beauty* is unique, as it contains rarely seen film footage and provides opinions of Dandridge by her contemporaries. Although these are its strengths, the documentary is beset with a few weaknesses. Dandridge is reconstructed primarily through the voices of men, and as a result, the documentary potentially participates in her further marginalization rather than liberation. Despite this shortcoming, *Beauty* is a valuable document that attempts to reveal Dandridge in all of her complexity and contradictions. In comparison, the black press celebrated her accomplishments and lobbied for her to win the Academy Award, and the mainstream press reviewed her films, explored her struggles, and exposed the difficulties associated with her films. Collectively, these sources expand the discourse surrounding Dandridge and stardom for an African American actress who emerged in the 1950s era.

As *Beauty* ends, the camera zooms in on a photo of Dandridge (the same photo that graces the cover of her biography by Donald Bogle) lying on a couch, solidifying her stardom and place in Hollywood film history and further invoking Kaplan's metaphor of the couch affair. Kaplan contends, "Black women's repressions and displacements, and the underlying reasons for black women's triple marginalization (behind not only white men, but white women and black men) requires yet more analysis." This metaphor is an appropriate way to end this discussion and to provide resonance for reading Dandridge, as it suggests that we, as spectators, are similarly positioned on the couch as we attempt to become conscious of our unconscious rendering of this black star.[49]

## Notes

1. Dandridge appeared in *Life* magazine articles "Shy No More: Singing Beauty Sheds Inhibitions and Squirms Her Way to Success," November 5, 1951, 65–70, and "Life Story in Song," March 23, 1953, 129. She was featured on the cover of *Life* magazine on November 1, 1954. She appeared in *Time* magazine articles "Two for the Show," May 2, 1955, 42, and

"Eye and Ear Specialist," February 4, 1952, 50. Dandridge was covered in *Cosmopolitan* magazine by Louella Parsons in an article, "Dorothy Dandridge Stars in a Great New Movie," December 1954, 4–5. Black publications in which she was featured include *Ebony*, *Our World*, and *Jet*, among others. Dandridge was featured on the cover of *Ebony* March 1966, June 1962, April 1953, and April 1951.

2. Giannetti, *Understanding Movies*, 151.

3. Babatundé played Dandridge's real-life husband Harold Nicholas in a fictionalized dramatization of her life, *Introducing Dorothy Dandridge* (1999).

4. Deleuze, *Cinema 2*, 3.

5. Kaplan, "Couch Affair," 487.

6. Dyer, *Stars*, 58.

7. Ibid., 18, 59.

8. Ibid., 48.

9. Vogel, "Lena Horne's Impersona," 24.

10. Dyer, *Stars*, 145.

11. Gladwin Hill, "2 Film Actresses Testify on Coast," *New York Times*, September 4, 1957, 40; "Confidential Aide," 62.

12. "Dandridge Defends," 60.

13. Ibid., 61.

14. "Dandridge Files New Suit," 65.

15. "Dorothy Dandridge Files $2,000,000 Suit against *Confidential* Magazine," *Los Angeles Times*, March 27, 1957, B1.

16. "*Confidential* Pays $10,000," *New York Times*, May 23, 1957, 39.

17. "Dorothy Dandridge Wants Own Voice," 57.

18. Ibid. See also Smith, "Black Faces, White Voices."

19. Thomas M. Pryor, "Allied Artists Signs Producer," *New York Times*, May 26, 1954, 35; Edwin Schallert, "Vanessa Brown's 'Moll' to Costar Guinness; Vocalists Aid *Carmen*," *Los Angeles Times*, July 3, 1954, 11.

20. Schallert, "Vanessa Brown's 'Moll,'" 11.

21. "On the 'Bright Road' of 'Carmen' and 'Joe,'" *New York Times*, October 24, 1954, X5.

22. "Dorothy Dandridge Wants Own Voice," 57.

23. Smith, "Black Faces, White Voices," 37.

24. "*Carmen* in CinemaScope," *New York Times*, July 25, 1954, X5.

25. "Dorothy Dandridge & Harry Belafonte," cover, 60–61.

26. Ibid., 60.

27. Bosley Crowther, "Negroes in a Film: *Carmen Jones* Finds American Types Singing a Foreign Opera Score," *New York Times*, October 31, 1954, X1.

28. Ibid.

29. Philip K. Scheuer, "*Carmen Jones* Vital, High-Voltage Musical," *Los Angeles Times*, November 2, 1954, B6.

30. "How Good," cover.

31. "Dandridge Cops New Honors," 61; "Dorothy Dandridge: Hollywood Experts," cover.

32. "How Good," 58–59.

33. Ibid., 59.

34. Ibid., 60.

35. "Dorothy Dandridge's Hottest Movie," [60–61].

36. A. H. Weiler, "By Way of Report," *New York Times*, September 13, 1959, X9.

37. "*Tamango*, From France," *New York Times*, September 17, 1959, 48. The film was banned in some regions. "Dandridge Film [*Tamango*] Banned by French in Algiers," *Jet*, May 1, 1958, 59.

38. Richard Griffith, "Unshocked New York Praises 'Look Back,'" *Los Angeles Times*, September 26, 1959, 14.

39. "Why Dandridge Can't," cover.

40. Stephen Watts, "Hove to On *Island in the Sun*," *New York Times*, January 20, 1957, 101. The film endured opposition. See "Picket *Island in the Sun* in Georgia; Klan Blamed," *Jet*, July 24, 1958, 61; "Ala. WCC Demonstrates against *Island in the Sun*," *Jet*, July 31, 1958, 61; "*Island in the Sun* Picketed, Banned in Atlanta," *Jet*, November 7, 1957, 54; "South Africans Rap Cutting of *Island in the Sun*," *Jet*, August 21, 1958, 60.

41. "Dandridge Makes Toughest Movie," 60.

42. Hedda Hopper, "Stars Comment on *Porgy* Row," *Los Angeles Times*, August 5, 1958, B1.

43. Ibid.

44. "Leigh Whipper Resigns *Porgy* Role in Protest," *Los Angeles Times*, August 7, 1958, B30.

45. Bosley Crowther, "Screen: Samuel Goldwyn's *Porgy and Bess* Has Premiere at Warner," *New York Times*, June 25, 1959, 20.

46. Philip K. Scheuer, "Decorum the Password at Premiere of *Porgy*," *Los Angeles Times*, July 16, 1959, 2.

47. Thompson, "Why Negroes Don't Like *Porgy and Bess*," 50.

48. Dyer, *Stars*, 70.

49. Kaplan, "Couch Affair," 509.

## Works Cited

Bogle, Donald. *Dorothy Dandridge: A Biography*. New York: Amistad, 1997.

"Confidential Aide Says Dandridge Story True." *Jet*, September 12, 1957, 62.

"Dandridge Cops New Honors for Movie Acting." *Jet*, February 3, 1955, 61.

"Dandridge Defends ... Says Magazine Story Untrue." *Jet*, September 12, 1957, 60–61.

"Dandridge Files New Suit Against *Hep* Magazine." *Jet*, September 12, 1957, 65.

"Dandridge Makes Toughest Movie of Her Career." *Jet*, July 23, 1959, 60.

Deleuze, Gilles. *Cinema 2: The Time-Image*. Trans. Hugh Tomlinson and Robert Galeta. Minneapolis: University of Minnesota Press, 1997.

"Dorothy Dandridge: Film Star Suffered Bruises in Moment of Danger." *Jet*, July 23, 1959, cover, 60.

"Dorothy Dandridge: Hollywood Experts Rate Screen Beauty High as a Possible Academy Award Winner." *Jet*, March 10, 1955, cover.

"Dorothy Dandridge: Romance Seems to Have By-Passed Beautiful Film Star: Is Dorothy Dandridge Afraid of Love?" *Jet*, February 16, 1956, cover, 60–62.

"Dorothy Dandridge & Harry Belafonte: They Are Being Boomed as Hollywood's First Negro Screen Lovers." *Jet*, September 30, 1954, cover, 60–61.

"Dorothy Dandridge to Incite Film Riot." *Jet*, November 15, 1956, 61.

"Dorothy Dandridge Wants Own Voice in New Movie." *Jet*, April 22, 1954, 57.

"Dorothy Dandridge's Hottest Movie." *Jet*, October 31, 1957, cover, [page number illegible, probably 60–61].

"Dot Dandridge Says 6 Male Adorers in Her Life." *Jet*, May 17, 1956, 61.

Dyer, Richard. *Stars*. London: British Film Institute, 1979.

Giannetti, Louis. *Understanding Movies*, 6th ed. Englewood Cliffs, NJ: Prentice Hall, 1993.

"How Good Are Dorothy Dandridge's Chances for an Oscar?" *Jet*, March 10, 1955, cover, 58–60.

"Is Dorothy Dandridge Afraid of Love?" *Jet*, February 16, 1956, 60–62.

Kaplan, E. Ann. "The Couch Affair: Gender and Race in Hollywood Transference." *American Imago* 50, no. 4 (1993): 481–514.

"People Are Talking About." *Jet*, March 8, 1956, 46.

Robinson, Ruth Adkins, dir. *Dorothy Dandridge: An American Beauty*. Written by Robinson. North Hollywood, CA: Passport Video, 2003. DVD. 60 mins.

Smith, Jeff. "Black Faces, White Voices: The Politics of Dubbing in *Carmen Jones*." *Velvet Light Trap* 51 (Spring 2003): 29–42.

Thompson, Era Bell. "Why Negroes Don't Like *Porgy and Bess*." *Ebony*, October 1959, 50.

Vogel, Shane. "Lena Horne's Impersona." *Camera Obscura* 23, no. 1 (2008): 11–45. doi: 10.1215/02705346-2007-022.

"Why Dandridge Can't Kiss Her White Film Lover." *Jet*, December 13, 1956, cover.

# "Rated R because it's real"

## *Discourses of Authenticity in* Wattstax

### MIKE PHILLIPS

On August 20, 1972, approximately one hundred thousand spectators gathered at the Los Angeles Coliseum for an all-day benefit concert produced by the Memphis-based Stax record label. The event, called Wattstax, was a part of that year's Watts Summer Festival, an annual commemoration of those who died in the 1965 Watts Rebellion. For an entrance fee of only one dollar, attendees were treated to performances from nearly the entire Stax roster, including the Staple Singers, the Bar-Kays, and Carla Thomas. Isaac Hayes, who at the time was riding high on the unprecedented success of his *Shaft* (1971) soundtrack, was the headliner. As a motorcade of security officials on motorcycles escorted Hayes into the stadium, emcee Jesse Jackson instructed the crowd, who had earlier stormed the field during Rufus Thomas's set, that if they did not remain in their seats, the concert would come to an abrupt end. Though by all accounts there were no violent incidents at the event, the specter of civil unrest still loomed over the proceedings. The emphasis on order within the Coliseum was not simply a practical matter for the concert's organizers; it also grew out of public-relations considerations. Seated upstage was a white cameraman capturing the performance for the festival's eponymous documentary, which was produced by Stax and Columbia Pictures and helmed by white Hollywood director Mel Stuart. It was imperative for Stax that this monumental undertaking run smoothly in order to produce a marketable film.

When Hayes took the stage, Jackson slowly removed the performer's hat to display his iconic shaved head that filled the cover of his 1969 album, *Hot Buttered Soul*. As the familiar, muted wah-wah guitar line and sixteenth-note high-hat beat of "Theme from *Shaft*" began to swell, Hayes lifted his arms, fists clenched. His robe fell away to reveal his signature vest made of golden chains, symbolizing both the legacy of slavery and the material prosperity of the new black superstar. *Shaft* had given Stax the marquee artist it had been missing since the death of Otis Redding nearly five years earlier, and the label had carefully tailored Hayes's image to present a larger-than-life figure who, like John Shaft, could vicariously enact the frustrated aspirations of young black consumers. The Wattstax concert and documentary were in large part an attempt by Stax to capitalize on Hayes's association with *Shaft* and his resultant incarnation as "Black Moses," the title bestowed upon him in his subsequent LP. Perhaps the clearest illustration of this strategy was Stax's use of the same boldly distinctive typeface in the promotional materials for both films. If one prong of this marketing campaign was the creation of a black superhero, the other prong was a public-relations push within urban black communities of which the Wattstax concert was the most spectacular example. While proceeds from ticket sales were donated to community organizations, it is sometimes unclear whether the concert was staged for the residents of Watts or for the movie cameras. According to a *Los Angeles Times* review of the event, Isaac Hayes "did two takes of 'Shaft,' ostensibly because of recording difficulties."[1]

Even before the concert took place, members of the black community criticized the 1972 Watts Summer Festival for having become too commercialized, and it is easy to understand how Wattstax could have exacerbated such misgivings.[2] These kinds of concerns about authentic black artistic expression and community solidarity had become increasingly important as African Americans gained wider representation in movies, television, and popular music since the time of the Watts Rebellion. The emergence of Hollywood's black exploitation (blaxploitation) cycle—films produced between 1970 and 1975 by black and white filmmakers to capitalize upon the black film audience[3]—provided especially rich discursive ground for debates over the meaning of black urban realities and their representations in the mainstream culture industries. As film historian Paula Massood contends, a "specific and highly identifiable urbanscape" was a key characteristic of this cycle.[4] In the controversy in the black press over blaxploitation, proponents argued that the settings and situations expressed some basic truths about ghetto life, while critics complained that the outlandish exploits of the films' heroes bore no relation to actual conditions.

*Wattstax* attempted to please blaxploitation fans and critics alike by providing a gritty urban milieu and soulful soundtrack along with a sense of realism and social conscience. Beyond being simply a concert film, *Wattstax* purports to be a realistic portrait of "the black experience" through its man-on-the-street–style interviews with South Central residents. Radio spots even promoted the film as "rated R because it's real."[5] This phrase is a literal invocation of documentary objectivity that also alludes to the fact that the film's "R" rating was handed down solely due to the colorful language employed by interviewees. It further draws a link between *Wattstax* and blaxploitation by clearly hearkening back to promotional materials for *Sweet Sweetback's Baadasssss Song* (1971) that proudly proclaimed, "Rated X by an all-white jury." More generally, it conjures up a tenuous alliance between verisimilitude and authenticity. Produced during the peak of the blaxploitation cycle, *Wattstax* displays all of the conflicts and contradictions inherent in the entertainment industry's attempt to package and market the black community's "authenticity" to both black and white consumers.

This strategy, of which Stax was an early and ardent advocate, sought to capitalize on the unprecedented expansion of black consciousness in the late 1960s and early 1970s. This market trend ironically reached its peak just as the Black Power Movement was rapidly dissipating and as Stax was about to collapse. The consumer base that Stax had helped to build, especially through its great successes in selling blaxploitation soundtrack albums, was rapidly assimilated into the mainstream as the major record companies began to buy up independent R&B labels. The emphasis on realism and authenticity in the marketing materials for *Wattstax* is striking evidence of the tensions and anxieties produced by the mainstreaming of black culture through motion pictures and popular music. To understand the stakes of the *Wattstax* project and the manifold discursive negotiations that occur both within the film and between the film and its sociopolitical milieu, it is important to first examine the historical context in which it was produced.

## Black Nationalism and Black Capitalism

Founded in 1957 by white banker Jim Stewart and his sister, Estelle Axton, Stax was initially conceived as a country-music label. However, when R&B singer Rufus Thomas and his daughter Carla provided the fledgling company with its first hit records, it became clear that Stax's path to success was through what would later be called "soul music." The label's particular brand of soul grew out of free interaction between black and white musicians, exemplified by the house band, Booker T. & the M.G.'s, which featured two black members, Booker T. Jones (organ) and Al Jackson, Jr. (drums), alongside two white members, Steve Cropper (guitar) and Donald "Duck" Dunn (bass). By

1965, the company was flourishing: A mutually beneficial distribution deal with New York R&B label Atlantic Records had Stax's marquee artist, Otis Redding, poised to become a major star. However, when Warner Brothers bought Atlantic in 1967, Jim Stewart discovered that he had unwittingly signed away all of Stax's master recordings. In December of that year, the twenty-six-year-old Redding died tragically in a plane crash. Soon after, Stewart sold his company to the Gulf+Western conglomerate and began to turn over the label's day-to-day operations to its African American marketing executive, Al Bell.

At the same time that Martin Luther King, Jr.'s assassination at the Lorraine Motel less than three miles from the Stax studio led to a growing mistrust of any white involvement in the Civil Rights Movement, whose center had already begun to shift from the rural South to the urban North and West, Bell began to move Stax away from the earlier model of interracial cooperation to an increasingly Afrocentric orientation. While he had briefly worked and marched with King's Southern Christian Leadership Conference (SCLC) in Georgia during 1959 and 1960, he parted ways with that organization because he preferred a strategy of economic empowerment to one of civil disobedience.[6] Bell took over the reins at Stax just as black nationalism was beginning to gain acceptance in unexpected corners of American politics.

Soon after the death of Dr. King, who had become increasingly critical of American capitalism and had begun to argue for systemic economic change, presidential candidate Richard Nixon recognized an opportunity to bring African American activists back into the capitalist fold. In a nationally broadcast speech on April 25, 1968, only three weeks after King's death, Nixon outlined his "black capitalism" program:

> What most of the militants are asking for is not for separation, but to be included in—not as supplicants, but as owners, as entrepreneurs—to have a share of the wealth and a piece of the action. And this is precisely what the Federal central target of the new approach ought to be. It ought to be oriented toward more black ownership, for from this can flow the rest—black pride, black jobs, black opportunity, and yes, black power, in the best, the constructive sense of that often misapplied term.[7]

Nixon's rhetoric clearly indicates that one of the major goals of the initiative was to co-opt the Black Power Movement, which had made significant inroads in gaining the favor of African Americans in the time since the Watts Rebellion. In May 1968, Nixon met secretly with Roy Innis and Floyd McKissick of the Congress of Racial Equality (CORE), which had recently shifted from an integrationist to a black nationalist stance and subsequently supported his candidacy. By 1972, even the Black Panther Party had at least partially embraced black capitalism by promoting the growth of small businesses, though the Panthers demanded that entrepreneurs donate a percentage of profits to the community. While Nixon's black-capitalism initiative ultimately produced more rhetoric than concrete results, it was undeniably effective. As political scientist Robert Weems explains, although Nixon's Office of Minority Business Enterprise "provided only limited assistance to black businesspeople and none of the various independent proposals for black economic development came to fruition, the period's discourse regarding Black Capitalism helped Nixon accomplish his larger ideological objective of 'containing' domestic black radicalism."[8]

Jesse Jackson, a King aide who was present at the Lorraine Motel when the civil rights leader was assassinated and who would serve as one of the emcees at the Wattstax concert, initially expressed opposition to Nixon's plan, calling it a "gimmick." However, it soon became obvious that his reformist agenda was perfectly in line with the spirit of Nixon's discourse. A 1972 *New York Times Magazine* profile noted, "Jesse decries capitalism and the devastation it has brought to blacks and many whites. But he is, at bottom, a capitalist, preaching that the system, with reform, can be made to work for the blacks and the poor."[9] While serving as the head of the Chicago chapter of the SCLC's Operation Breadbasket from 1966 to 1972, Jackson had successfully pressured several South Side businesses through boycotts or the threat of boycotts to hire more African Americans. In essence, his strategy was to demonstrate the collective political power of the black community by displaying its viability as a lucrative consumer market. In a 1970 interview, Jackson estimated African Americans' buying power at $36 billion per year and forcefully asserted his vision of black consumers' strong bargaining position vis-à-vis the white CEO: "We are the margin of profit of every major item produced in America from General Motors cars down to Kellogg's Corn Flakes. If we've got his margin of profit, we've got his genitals."[10]

Only weeks before the Wattstax concert, Jackson founded a new organization called Operation PUSH (People United to Save Humanity) that would attempt to implement his strategy nationally. PUSH's first major initiative was a headline-grabbing attack on the Hollywood film industry that denounced the industry's discrimination against African Americans in its hiring practices and also joined the debate over the content of blaxploitation films. "We'll raid studios," Jackson proclaimed. "We will take on these films of vulgarity, violence and vanity, those films that project into the minds of our children the images of killers rather than healers, of dope pushers in the vein rather than hope in the brain."[11] Yet Jackson maintained a close relationship with Stax, the same label that, as discussed below, was instrumental in developing the market for blaxploitation soundtracks. In the spring of 1971, Jackson invited Isaac Hayes to address a PUSH meeting and then tour Chicago jails and hospitals, carrying with him the Oscar he had won for the *Shaft* score.[12] Jackson even released a spoken-word album, *I Am Somebody*, on Stax in 1970. The poem that gave the album its title became a staple of his public-speaking repertoire, and he famously recited it to open the Wattstax festivities.

Jackson's imprimatur, through his reputation for promoting black business, helped to foster the impression that the event at the Coliseum was a strictly black-produced affair. Yet the truth is closer to Brian Ward's assessment that "Wattstax was a conspicuous example of continued black economic dependency."[13] While it is true that all of the event's producers and security officials as well as the vast majority of performers and spectators were black, Stax was still technically owned by Jim Stewart at the time, and the company was being financed by loans from white-owned banks. Furthermore, *Wattstax* producer David Wolper maintains that Columbia Pictures allotted $500,000 to the film project, while *Billboard* reported that the Schlitz Brewing Company, already a sponsor of the Watts Summer Festival for several years, underwrote the rental of the Coliseum.[14] These accounts contradict Al Bell's assertion that Stax "was able to go to LA, where you had all the giant corporations, and get the musicians out there, hire Mel Stuart, take a stadium and finance the production, then get Columbia to distribute it, and not ask any of them for any money."[15] Bell's claims about complete economic independence are reminiscent of the fantasies of black empowerment that characterize the blaxploitation cycle, which Stax played a major and underappreciated role in promoting through its involvement in the production and marketing of soundtrack albums.

## The Memphis Sound Goes to Hollywood

Soon after Bell took the reins at Stax, he attempted to steer the label into the lucrative motion-picture soundtrack market via its new parent company, which also owned Paramount Pictures. Although ultimately not as fruitful as Bell envisioned, the G+W deal did result in one memorable soundtrack album: *Up Tight* by Booker T. & the M.G.'s. Released in December 1968, *Up Tight* was director Jules Dassin's black-cast version of John Ford's *The Informer* (1935). Cowritten by Dassin, Ruby Dee, and Julian Mayfield, the remake's milieu is shifted from the Irish Republican Army in 1920s Dublin to the Black Power Movement in 1960s Cleveland. Shot in Hough, a neighborhood still strewn with the rubble of its own July 1966 uprising, the story takes place on the night of King's funeral and opens with documentary footage of the public memorial service. *Up Tight* thus participates in the partially realist aesthetic of the blaxploitation cycle through the juxtaposition of actual urban space with a narrative derived from Hollywood models. Yet in the same way that the film focuses on the King assassination as the end of an era, the soundtrack by the integrated M.G.'s, with its dominant gospel elements and countrified guitar licks, seems to be looking backward. By this time, Bell had already recognized that the rapidly shifting black political consciousness would also require new modes of cultural expression and new methods of marketing to urban consumers.[16]

The key figure in this shift in Stax's marketing strategy was Larry Shaw, whom Bell hired as vice president of advertising and publicity in January 1970. It was Jesse Jackson who introduced Bell to Shaw, who had acted as a consultant for Operation Breadbasket while an executive at the Chicago firm Vince Cullers Advertising. Jackson's organization, which successfully encouraged the distribution of products manufactured by black-owned companies, also had a hand in making Cullers the first black advertising firm with a nationwide reach. When he joined Stax, Shaw was on the cutting edge of "segmented marketing," a strategy predicated upon what are commonly known in the advertising industry as "psychographics," or variables based on a target market's cultural attitudes and lifestyles. Stated simply, the idea was to sell the black community on its image of itself. For example, one Cullers campaign titled, "Wantu Wazuri Beautiful People," helped to elevate Afro-Sheen to the top of the hair-care market simply by using Swahili words to connect the product to the prevailing black-nationalist sentiment. Likewise, Shaw had cornered the black cigarette market for Newport with a radio ad invoking "The Bold Soul in the Blue Dashiki." In Shaw, Bell saw a savvy and sophisticated manipulator of public opinion who could help move Stax away from what Bell referred to as their "'Bama" image. His choice of words is precise: *'Bama*, short for Alabama, is a pejorative epithet that arose during the Great Migration as a way for Northern, city-dwelling African Americans to differentiate themselves from their newly arrived, Southern, rural counterparts.

Ironically, Shaw's first major ad campaign attempted to penetrate Northern urban markets by touting Stax's Southern credentials. The "Memphis Sound" campaign evoked an idyllic, agrarian past: "Stax, deep in the fertile soil of the southern United States has cultivated and nurtured an energy that has its roots firmly planted in America and its branches spreading the continents of the world [*sic*]. The Memphis Sound: Soul Music, an energy with a message that has no regard for political preference, ethnic background or ideologies. Check it out.... It's the real thing from Memphis U.S.A."[17] This emphasis on authenticity is in line with a trend in American advertising dating back to the first decade of the twentieth century. Cultural historian Miles Orvell associates the emergence of a discourse of authenticity with urbanization and the rise of consumerism: "One might imagine that the concept of authenticity begins in any society whenever the possibility of fraud arises, and that fraud is at least possible whenever transactions—whether social, political, commercial, or aesthetic—routinely occur, especially when the society becomes so large that one usually deals with strangers, not neighbors."[18] In this sense, Stax's problematic evocation of its Southern "roots" nostalgically hearkens back to a time before the commoditization of black cultural products. The ad fetishizes Stax recordings as authentic, organic products that arise independently of capital and mass production. This assertion must be understood in the context of the growing popularity of black music and blaxploitation films and the increasing possibility of cooptation by the mainstream culture industries.

As popular music scholar Kembrew McLeod has demonstrated, "When faced with the very real threat of erasure via misrepresentation by outsiders ... community members attempt to protect their culture by distinguishing authentic and inauthentic expression."[19] The implied counterfeit that Stax posed itself against in the Memphis Sound campaign was Berry Gordy's Detroit-based Motown Records. Motown's polished, poppy style had successfully crossed over into the Top 40, while Stax singles were still generally confined to the R&B charts. The dichotomy between the two companies' musical styles and marketing strategies is encapsulated in the placards that adorned their respective studios: Motown was "Hitsville, U.S.A.," and Stax was "Soulsville, U.S.A." Though the Memphis Sound campaign paid lip service to racial unity, some statements by Shaw make it clear that the ads were primarily addressed to an African American audience. Stax regularly bought space in the pop-culture–focused *Jet*, but only for this campaign did the label buy a full-page spread in the more prestigious, middle-class–oriented *Ebony*. "We did that ad to render that [idea as] an institution," Shaw explained, implying that the thrust of the campaign was to instill the image of Stax's authenticity among African Americans, even if, like many *Ebony* subscribers, they were not necessarily in the label's target market. He explicitly frames the campaign's tagline, "Everything is everything," meant to invoke the indefinable essence of "soul," as a direct challenge to the readily identifiable, heavily produced Motown sound.[20]

The Wattstax concert was in part an outgrowth of this rivalry. Just months before the event at the Coliseum, Gordy had relocated Motown's headquarters to Los Angeles in a bid to break into major-label territory and gain access to the Hollywood film industry. At that time, Motown already had a picture in production with Paramount: *Lady Sings the Blues*, a bowdlerized

Billie Holiday biopic starring Diana Ross. Stax had followed a different path into the movie business, at first eschewing feature production and instead concentrating on the burgeoning motion-picture soundtrack market. When Stax's relationship with Gulf+Western came to an end in 1970, Bell, now the head of an independent label, was still itching to break into the movie business. He made a deal to release Earth, Wind & Fire's soundtrack to Melvin Van Peebles's *Sweet Sweetback's Baadasssss Song* in April 1971. This surreal, picaresque tale about a sexually potent, heroically violent rebel introduced one of the cornerstones of the blaxploitation cycle: a black protagonist besting white adversaries. *Sweetback* also helped to institute the practice of synergistic marketing between black films and their soundtracks. As Bell noted, "soundtrack albums have a ready-made market if you know how to reach the people," and in this case, Stax implemented the novel approach of selling the album in theater lobbies after screenings.[21]

In a sense, though, this practice had a precedent in the Satellite Record Shop that Estelle Axton had run in the old lobby of the movie theater that housed the Stax recording studio. Ironically, the much-vaunted "Stax sound," which would find its greatest success in a motion-picture soundtrack album, owed its unique character to the acoustic irregularities produced by the sloping floor of an empty movie theater. In 1960, Stax's founders considered purchasing at least three recently shuttered South Memphis cinemas before settling on the former Capitol Theater. Throughout the previous decade, many small houses like the Capitol had been driven out of business by upheavals in the motion-picture industry arising from the success of television, concomitant with the exodus of white city-dwellers to the suburbs and away from urban theaters. The resultant precipitous decline in ticket sales, which reached their lowest postwar level in 1971, would eventually lead Hollywood to search for alternative revenue streams. One such untapped market was a burgeoning black audience, which by the mid–1960s accounted for 30 percent of the urban moviegoing public, though African Americans made up only 15 percent of the total U.S. population. Despite mounting pressure from the National Association for the Advancement of Colored People (NAACP) and other groups throughout the 1960s, Hollywood had continued to resist producing black-themed films and hiring black actors, directors, and crew members: In 1969, only 6 percent of industry trade union members were African Americans. It was only when the demands of political-pressure groups began to merge with the major studios' economic interests that Hollywood relented. As cinema scholar Ed Guerrero has so aptly stated, Hollywood "changes only when forced to do so by the combined pressures of multiple influences, no matter how just or important any single condition may be."[22]

Stax found itself uniquely positioned to take advantage of Hollywood's new interest in black-themed films due to its signature sound's perceived authenticity, which owed much to Shaw's marketing prowess. *Sweetback* became the first project for Shaw's consortium of black-owned marketing firms, Communiplex, which had been retained by MGM "to handle creative concepts in marketing and promotion" for *Shaft*.[23] Communiplex's *Shaft* campaign refined *Sweetback*'s model and exponentially expanded the market for blaxploitation films and soundtracks. Though each film grossed roughly $10 million in its first year of distribution, the *Sweetback* record sold only 100,000 copies during that period, while Isaac Hayes's double-LP score to *Shaft* sold twenty times that number within six months of its release.[24] As wildly successful as the *Shaft* album was, the marketing push by Communiplex went far beyond ticket and record sales. A feature story in *Ebony* complained that "black pockets are now being emptied on such sideline items as *Shaft* suits, watches, belts, and sunglasses, leather coats, decals, sweatshirts and night shirts, beach towels, posters, after shave lotion and cologne. At the rate things are going, black audiences will at least be the best-dressed, nicest-smelling film-goers anywhere."[25] It is clear that consumers were buying not only art and entertainment but a lifestyle as well. The fantasy of masculine power and geographic mobility represented by John Shaft, a character who moves seamlessly between the backstreets of Harlem and the bohemian Greenwich Village scene, became symbolically attainable through the conspicuous consumption of *Shaft* merchandise.

Stax's marketing strategy in the wake of the *Shaft* windfall was analogous to blaxploitation's situating its heroes in an urban milieu. The label was determined to penetrate urban markets and to once and for all rid itself of the 'Bama stigma. The label's next big campaign after the Memphis Sound was its highly coordinated August 1971 invasion of Chicago media and retail outlets, called "Stax Sound in Chi-Town." As the campaign's title suggests, Stax had moved from a rhetorical approach meant to induce nostalgia for an agrarian past to an on-the-ground approach that emphasized the physical presence of its stars in an urban setting. Stax historian Rob Bowman reports that "a bevy of Stax stars descended on the city," appearing in record shops and department stores as well as on local television and radio. Bell made a deal to place records in every Sears outlet in the city for the duration of the promotion, in an attempt to show that Stax products could sell just as well in mainstream retail outlets that catered to a largely white clientele as in the independent shops that traditionally served the African American community.[26]

We can easily identify a paradox at the heart of this campaign: It was an attempt to identify Stax with a black, urban milieu, a field that would come to be identified with "real" black experience, but partially in the interest of attracting a white audience. White spectators' newfound interest in representations of the black ghetto was partially a result of the intense media coverage of the Watts Rebellion and the series of urban uprisings that followed over the next three years. Massood cites this phenomenon as "one of the most important circumstances influencing the creation of specific urban cinematic codes" that would later be employed in blaxploitation films.[27] The complicated history of media representations of the Watts Rebellion and their entrance into wider discourses of racial politics had a profound effect on both the form and content of *Wattstax*.

## Consumption and Containment

On the evening of August 11, 1965, an all-too-routine traffic stop led to a cataclysmic release of the tensions that had long festered among the African American communities of Los Angeles. Around 7:00 p.m., a California Highway Patrol officer pulled over twenty-one-year-old Marquette Frye on the outskirts of Watts. Accounts differ as to what exactly transpired, but it is clear that there was an altercation between the police and Frye's mother. Within twenty minutes, an estimated fifteen hundred people had gathered at the scene. A rumor quickly spread that the police had assaulted a pregnant woman, and in response, some of the onlookers began to throw rocks and bottles. The violence rapidly engulfed Watts, and when the dust settled four days later, thirty-four people were dead, and a thousand more injured. There had been roughly four thousand arrests and approximately $200 million worth of property damage.[28]

As noted above, the events in Watts were thoroughly documented on national television. Some of this footage is included in the opening montage of *Wattstax*, which gives way to a discussion among several young men about the events of 1965 and their impact on the neighborhood. One of them states of the uprising, "That's the only way we communicate with whitey, man." Yet what exactly was being communicated depended on the divergent readings of different audiences. Massood argues that the news coverage acted as "a momentary 'warp' in the surface of the nation's racial repressed," with white and black spectators reading the broadcast images in almost opposite ways.[29] To many whites watching the fires spread on television, the violence in Watts was perplexing, especially since President Lyndon B. Johnson had signed the Voting Rights Act of 1965 into law less than a week earlier. The events in Los Angeles seemed to fly in the face of the apparent successes of the Civil Rights Movement, and a flood of discourse in news media, academic publications, and government reports attempted to account for this apparent paradox.[30] Such explanations were unnecessary for many African American spectators, who recognized the root causes underlying the televisual images of urban violence, including persistent discrimination in housing and hiring practices, pervasive unemployment, and lack of access to public transportation. The de facto segregation that accompanied the development of suburbs and "white flight" away from urban centers severely limited both geographic mobility and economic opportunity for the citizens of Watts, formerly a rail hub until manufacturing industries began to leave the city center just as the largest wave of Southern black migrants was arriving in Los Angeles in the late 1940s.[31]

There are intimations of this lack of mobility in a *Wattstax* sequence in which blues singer Little Milton lip-synchs to "Walking the Back Streets and Crying" in the disused rail yard near the Watts Towers. The atmosphere of decay in this sequence recalls a statement in the preceding interview segment in which another of the aforementioned group of young men asserts that "the blues is past tense," while other, older interviewees wax philosophical in accents more apparently tinged with southern inflections. Any suggestion of the history of that generation's trials quickly falls away in the transition to the next sequence, Johnnie Taylor's performance of "Jody's Got Your Girl and Gone" in the one-chord funk style recently innovated by James Brown. Taylor had been scheduled to appear at Wattstax but was bumped due to time constraints, so he instead performed a set for the movie cameras at the Summit Club in Los Angeles. The beginning of the sequence shows a series of expensive cars rolling up to the door of the club, their passengers emerging outfitted in the type of flamboyant attire that characterizes the heroes of blaxploitation films like *Super Fly* (1972) and *Willie Dynamite* (1974). These men, too, are among the predominantly young demographic that actively participated in the Watts Rebellion and that was now being marketed as a lifestyle of conspicuous consumption by companies like Stax and Communiplex.

This nightclub sequence also highlights the close relationship between performer and audience that a setting like the Coliseum largely precluded. The master of ceremonies at the Summit Club that evening was Rufus Thomas, then fifty-five years old, who was often billed as "the World's Oldest Teenager." Thomas had gotten his start in show business with the Rabbit Foot Minstrels' traveling tent show and had subsequently served as an emcee at every black venue in Memphis. He was undoubtedly the most experienced showman on the Stax roster, and he seems to have been able to work a crowd of any size. Oddly enough, Thomas had performed in Watts just days before the uprising. On the nights of August 8 and 9, a capacity crowd of seven hundred had packed the 5/4 Ballroom to hear Thomas, his daughter Carla, Wilson Pickett, and William Bell, all accompanied by the M.G.'s. The popular local radio DJ Magnificent Montague served as the emcee. Between acts, Montague worked the crowd with a catchphrase that had become a common expression in Watts: "Burn, baby, burn."[32] In this context, it at once signified satisfaction with a down-and-dirty performance and acted as an exhortation to the following act to surpass the previous performer's level of intensity. By the following Wednesday, it would become the motto of the uprising, shouted on the streets and emblazoned on walls. The youth of Watts had transformed this catchphrase from a metaphorical cry of joy into a literal expression of defiance.

The apparent link between these two usages was a sentiment of participatory fervor that is clearly expressed in Montague's introduction of Thomas: "He'll light the fires of happiness! He makes you wanna burn! ... He needs no introduction! He needs no publicity! He needs no promotion! He only needs you to give a big round of applause. I wanna hear you say, one time, loud and clear, on the count of three: one, two, three, *burn* !"[33] Montague's stage banter emphasizes the close relationship between performer and audience: His assertion that Thomas "needs no publicity" suggests that he was well known within that particular space and also implies the possibility that others outside of that space would, somewhat distastefully, need to be told who he was and were thus excluded from the unmediated experience shared between Thomas and the crowd. The participatory aspect in Montague's address also indicates the sense of intimacy that would have been characteristic of small clubs like the 5/4 Ballroom.

When Thomas performed at the Wattstax concert in the Coliseum seven years later, his commanding onstage presence would be put to very different uses. After initially inviting the audience onto the fenced-off field in front of the stage, Thomas was instructed by the producers to coax the spectators back into their seats, which he did with great skill and humor, as can be seen in *Wattstax*. This scene is reminiscent of the onrush of gate-crashers in *Woodstock* (1970), with the important difference that Thomas is able to control the crowd. Implicit in the attention devoted to this event in the film are the specter of civil unrest and the potential for the concert to devolve into a repeat of the events it was meant to memorialize. Tommy Jacquette, a founder of the Watts Summer Festival, recalled that the Los Angeles Police Department had suggested that the event be moved from the festival's usual venue, Will Rogers Park, to the Coliseum because "they didn't want to see that many black people in Watts 'uncorralled!'"[34]

In aesthetic terms, the relationship between performer and audience becomes distant and in a sense alienated in the contained space of a stadium, with the spectator taking on the role of a consumer of entertainment rather than a participant. In an early critical assessment, Thomas Cripps likens *Wattstax* to the "race films" of the 1920s and 1930s:

> [I]n race movies the blacks knew they were segregated and so did their occasional white directors, who had a distinct feeling of straying into another world. Thus, clichéd one- and two-shots against a gray wall, or parallel cutting to a jivey dance routine in some seedy Negro saloon, were signals of black society in a motion picture frame. To blacks they meant "this movie is about 'us'" and was shot in private. *Wattstax*, through the use of the Los Angeles Coliseum ... evoke[s] the same image.[35]

Yet the major difference that escapes Cripps is that race films were intended specifically for black audiences, while the black-themed films of the early 1970s attempted to attract black and white spectators alike. Seen in this light, the confines of the Coliseum foreclose the urban space that is integral to blaxploitation films' perceived sense of authenticity. Cripps is closer to the mark when he calls the interview segments "a visual plea for credibility" that attempt to recoup that lack.[36]

## *Authority and Authenticity*

Given the truth claims made by the publicity materials for *Wattstax*, it may come as a surprise to learn that Stuart hired actors to be interviewed for the film: "I decided to protect ourselves, because I didn't know how good it was going to be, to have some actors at the time, because maybe they'd be a little more articulate."[37] Stuart's reservations about Watts residents' level of erudition were ill-founded, as the finished product shows. The practice of hiring actors as interviewees also reflects Bell's concerns about professionalism, his desire to find the "best in the business" to produce this film. Stuart's and Wolper's status as Hollywood professionals meant that they had the equipment and experience to produce a film that would be taken as a legitimate document in the eyes of the mainstream viewing public. As Mark Baker and Houston Baker observe, "The post and privilege of documentation is financed by power," in this case by Columbia Pictures. Furthermore, "[o]nly the original, official, legal seal of professionalism—whether inscribed or merely implied by the overall process of production—creates a document."[38] This "seal" is present here in both senses, explicitly in the corporate logo of the torch-bearing goddess Columbia that precedes the film proper and implicitly through the participation of industry veterans Stuart and Wolper. In this sense, their involvement bolsters *Wattstax*'s claims to documentary accuracy, their previous collaboration on the fantastic excess of *Willy Wonka and the Chocolate Factory* (1971) notwithstanding.

Stuart recounts a story from the production of the film that starkly illustrates the Bakers' point. When *Wattstax* associate producer Forrest Hamilton, then head of Stax's Los Angeles office, took Stuart to a Watts venue to see Richard Pryor perform, the two were stopped at the door by a burly, ill-tempered man who grabbed Stuart and exclaimed, "What is this honky doing in my club?" The three-hundred-pound Hamilton threw their assailant against the wall and answered, "He's got expertise, motherfucker!" The man responded, "Shit, man, I didn't know you had expertise! Come on in, man. Come on in."[39] This anecdote indicates Stuart's desire to be accepted as a chronicler of everyday ghetto life and for his "expertise" or professional status to afford him a connection with his subjects. Yet it is patently clear that it is Hamilton's intervention that actually grants him entry into the nightclub and metaphorically into the community of Watts.

In actuality, much of the interview footage in *Wattstax* was shot by black film crews from outside the industry. One African American crew member, Larry Clark, reports that the producers had initially assigned these interviews to "pretty much a White Hollywood crew," who were quickly "run out of South Central." After dispatching a similarly unsuccessful professional black crew, they finally discovered a group of filmmakers, including Clark, who lived in and around Watts and who were better able to develop a rapport with interviewees.[40] Their creative presence within the film results in a multiplicity of discourses, as the interview footage was shot in two different styles: in contrast to Stuart's controlled, composed interviews, Clark used a direct-cinema approach. He recounts how he would begin interviews without the camera rolling and only shoot film once the subject had become sufficiently relaxed not to notice the camera.[41] At the time, he was a student at the University of California, Los Angeles, where he was one of a cohort that has become known as the L.A. School of Black Filmmakers or the L.A. Rebellion. The experience of interviewing Watts residents for this film certainly falls in line with what novelist and filmmaker Toni Cade Bambara cites as one of the major tenets of the L.A. School: "The community, not the classroom, is the appropriate training grounds for producing relevant work." Yet the corporate funding and industrial production of the picture seem to contradict another maxim: "Accountability to the community takes precedence over training for an industry that maligns and exploits, trivializes and invisibilizes Black people."[42]

Clark dramatizes the tension between politically engaged cultural expression and commercial considerations in his 1977 UCLA thesis film, a feature titled *Passing Through*. He was not the only *Wattstax* alumnus involved:

actor/interviewee Ted Lange cowrote the screenplay, and Roderick Young is credited as a cinematographer on both films. *Passing Through* chronicles the political awakening of Eddie Warmack, a jazz saxophonist recently released from prison, who decides to form his own record label in order to circumvent the exploitative, white–mob-controlled music industry and give black musicians financial and creative control over their own performances. The ensuing conflict between the musicians and the record-company gangsters builds to a violent showdown, with Warmack emerging victorious. The film clearly adopts some narrative elements of blaxploitation films, but it does so in favor of allegorically linking revolutionary impulses with cultural nationalism. Clark often weaves documentary footage into the diegesis of *Passing Through*, as when images of the Attica prison uprising are intercut with a flashback to the murder of a white gangster that led to Warmack's jail sentence.[43] Manthia Diawara cites Clark as employing "a mixed form of fiction and documentary in which the documentary element serves to deconstruct the illusion created by the fiction and makes the spectator question the representation of 'reality' through the different modes."[44] In contrast, *Wattstax* resolutely presents itself as a document of a "happening" and of "the black experience," despite the many fictional devices it employs.

According to Ntongela Masilela, the members of the L.A. School were attempting "to find a film form unique to their historical situation and cultural experience, a form that could not be appropriated by Hollywood."[45] *Wattstax*, on the other hand, attempted to employ Hollywood "expertise" in the interest of reaching a wider (read: whiter) market. Similarly to "Stax Sound in Chi-Town," *Wattstax* attempted to conjure up an association between Stax and black urban space not only to expand its black consumer base but also to exploit the rising popularity of representations of urban blackness among young, white consumers. *Variety* noted Columbia Pictures' policy of distributing the film in each major city to both a black-oriented theater and a "non-inner-city site appealing to young audiences." Advertisements in Los Angeles newspapers touted *Newsweek* critic Arthur Cooper's characterization of the film as a "welcome gift to white America," while a print ad for smaller markets advised the consumer, "You can't judge a movie by its color." When Vincent Canby's *New York Times* review criticized *Wattstax* for being merely a concert film, Mel Stuart wrote a letter to the editor in which he lambasted Canby for "mislead[ing] a potential white audience."[46] It is telling, and rather unexpected, that Stuart should focus on the perceived appeal of the interview segments over the concert footage. His consternation implies that the unprecedented crossover success of the *Shaft* soundtrack was less a function of Isaac Hayes's musical talent than an indication of the touristic desire on the part of white audiences for an experience of the black ghetto.

In terms of the film's attempt to communicate with a white audience, the segments featuring Richard Pryor are the most revealing. These brief cutaways are actually all part of the same long riffing session that Stuart filmed in an empty Watts club in one afternoon. As the film repeatedly cuts back to this scene, we are often shown a medium two-shot of Pryor seated at the end of the bar as we look over the shoulder of a white man, presumably Stuart. This spatial arrangement places Stuart in the position of mediating a white spectator's confrontation with the acerbic observations of Pryor, who was not yet the superstar that he would soon become.

It is telling that Stuart referred to Pryor's role in the film as analogous to that of the Chorus figure who opens Shakespeare's *Henry V* with a direct address to the audience.[47] In his plea for the spectators' forgiveness for the stage's inadequacy in presenting momentous historical events, the Chorus simultaneously emphasizes the fact of the play as a performance and acts as a conduit for the audience's entry into a fictional world. Pryor likewise opens *Wattstax* with a speech to the camera, but he complicates his relationship to this role in a brief monologue featured later in the film: "When [white people] found out that niggers could talk, other than *no-wah-ho*, they got scared to death. Like, one day some whitey said, 'Nigger, talk!' 'Well, motherfucker, I've been wanting to tell you something.' 'I beg your pardon?!'" By responding to a demand for a performance with a disarming direct address, the black interlocutor turns "whitey's" fascination to repulsion and transplants him from a position of detached observation into an unexpected dialogue. This rupture in the scene's power dynamic imbricates both parties in relationship that involves both historical continuity and the potential for change. Yet Pryor sets forth this fictional situation in an actual situation where he is addressing not the audience but Stuart, who maintains his spectatorial position within the scene and his discursive dominance as the director of the film. In this sense, Pryor is indeed like Shakespeare's Chorus in that he remains caught between performance and communication.

Literary scholar Herman Beavers argues that Pryor's "cool" persona enacts "quiescence" in the sense that it "create[s] both agreeability and satisfaction out of potentially volatile icons through the conscious manipulation of information as it resonates at the level of signs, symbols, myths, and social rituals" and thus "work[s] out a drama whereby numerous constituencies reach a state of satisfaction within the arena of race relations." This mode of discourse overtly addresses social inequities but also diffuses the potential for violent confrontation by emphasizing the nature of the utterance as a performance.

Beavers suggests, "Cool ... is important to the mainstream because its postulation of a style of resistance is easily transformed, in advertising for example, into the consumption of goods and services that signify nonconformist behavior, a refusal to be co-opted by the mainstream."[48] Pryor's central position in *Wattstax* indicates that the film as a whole partakes in this tension between resistance and quiescence, between authenticity and assimilation.

These concerns animate all of the various discourses that reverberate throughout the film, providing the viewer with a window into the contentious cultural climate that accompanied the widespread success of blaxploitation films and their soundtracks. By the time of the Wattstax concert, the major record labels already had their sights on the lucrative African American market that Stax had helped to cultivate. Within a few years, they had successfully taken over most of the independent R&B labels, and the production of *Wattstax* only slightly preceded the precipitous decline and eventual demise of Stax Records. Nonetheless, the film is unique as an industry-produced documentary about African Americans made during a time of profound questioning around the meaning of being black. During the period between the emergence of blaxploitation and the industry takeover of black music, the assimilation of black cultural products into mainstream markets created a complex discourse of authenticity that remains relevant to the contemporary production and consumption of African American art forms.

## Notes

1. Lance A. Williams, "Wattstax Concert at Coliseum," *Los Angeles Times*, August 22, 1972, G8.

2. See Celeste Durant, "7th Watts Summer Festival Ends with Parade, Discontent," *Los Angeles Times*, August 21, 1972; Tyler, "Rise and Decline."

3. Lawrence, *Blaxploitation Films*, 18.

4. Massood, *Black City Cinema*, 84–85. I thank Massood for her insightful comments on an earlier draft of this essay.

5. "Street Talk Earns 'R,'" 5.

6. Bowman, *Soulsville*, 81.

7. Weems, *Business in Black and White*, 115.

8. Ibid., 111–26, 154–55, 7.

9. Ibid., 155; Serrin, "Jesse Jackson," 15–16.

10. "Jesse Jackson," 17.

11. Paul Delaney, "A Job Drive Is Set by Jesse Jackson," *New York Times*, July 30, 1972, 39.

12. Larry Shaw has acknowledged that as with many of Stax's promotions during this period, this was both a gesture of solidarity and a public-relations maneuver. Bowman, *Soulsville*, 233.

13. Ward, *Just My Soul Responding*, 402.

14. Wolper, *Producer*, 182; Freedland, "50,000 Wattstax Ducats Sold," 3. Stax artist Rufus Thomas appeared in a Schlitz commercial in the same pink outfit that he wore at Wattstax. See *Respect Yourself*; Attrep, "Sonic Inscription of Identity," 121–25.

15. James Maycock, "Loud and Proud," *Guardian* (London and Manchester), July 20, 2002, 30.

16. In 1970, the Staple Singers contributed two performances to the soundtrack (not a Stax release) for *The Landlord*, Hal Ashby's directorial debut. The film follows the fortunes of a bored young WASP who buys an apartment building in a Brooklyn ghetto. For a thorough production history and analysis of both *Up Tight* (variously styled *Uptight!* or *Up Tight!*) and *The Landlord*, see Sieving, *Soul Searching*.

17. Bowman, *Soulsville*, 201. Ellipses in original.

18. Orvell, *Real Thing*, xvii.

19. McLeod, "Authenticity within Hip-Hop," 148.

20. Bowman, *Soulsville*, 201.

21. Ibid., 221–22. According to Al Bell, Stax used a similar strategy to promote *Wattstax* star Richard Pryor's 1974 LP *That Nigger's Crazy*: "We worked the record in poolhalls, barbershops, beauty parlors, and in the streets across America by getting instant play at small record shops. We went after that record strictly on the grass-roots level using word of mouth." George, *Death of Rhythm and Blues*, 139.

22. Bowman, *Soulsville*, 8; Leab, *From Sambo to Superspade*, 234; Guerrero, *Framing Blackness*, 82–86.

23. Bowman, *Soulsville*, 222.

24. *Sweetback* cost $500,000 to produce, while *Shaft* had a budget of $1.2 million. See Guerrero, *Framing Blackness*, 86, 92. For soundtrack sales numbers, see Freedland, "Melvin Van Peebles," 44; "Hayes' 'Shaft' Hits," 58.

25. Mason, "New Films," 62. Part of this quotation also appears in Guerrero, *Framing Blackness*, 97.

26. Bowman, *Soulsville*, 235.

27. Massood, *Black City Cinema*, 83.

28. Horne, *Fire This Time*, 54–56, 3.

29. Massood, *Black City Cinema*, 83.

30. For a concise overview of the sociological corpus on the events in Watts, see Thompson, "Urban Uprisings: Riots or Rebellions?," 109–17.

31. See Horne, *Fire This Time*, 35–36; Wild, *Street Meeting*, 205; Banham, *Los Angeles*, 173; Scott, "Cities and Suburbs," 267.

32. Bowman, *Soulsville*, 75–76.

33. Magnificent Montague, "Stage Announcements," recorded August 8 or 9, 1965, on *Funky Broadway*.

34. Maycock, "Loud and Proud."

35. Cripps, *Black Film as Genre*, 153.

36. Ibid., 107.

37. Quoted in Kubernik, *Hollywood Shack Job*, 58. One of these interviewees, future *Love Boat* star Ted Lange, also played pimps in the blaxploitation films *Trick Baby* (1972) and *Friday Foster* (1975).

38. Baker and Baker, "Uptown Where We Belong," 211–12.

39. Quoted in Kelly, "Living Word," 121.

40. Ibid., 119. Clark also recalls going out to shoot street arrests and following a squad of police officers into a bar, where they shook down the owner and took money from the cash register. This footage was lost after having been sent to a lab for processing; Clark suspects LAPD involvement in the disappearance. See Tony Cooper, "'Black Woodstock' Back on TV, DVD," *San Francisco Chronicle*, September 3, 2004, F2.

41. Clark, "Cast & Crew Commentary."

42. Bambara, "Reading the Signs," 119.

43. James, *Most Typical Avant-Garde*, 323–25; Horak, "L.A. Rebellion."

44. Diawara, "Black Spectatorship," 219.

45. Masilela, "Los Angeles School," 108–10. In this respect, the L.A. School was heavily influenced by and theoretically in solidarity with cinematic movements like Brazil's Cinema Novo, which emphasized aesthetic experimentation and revolutionary consciousness. Incidentally, informal screenings of *Wattstax* played a key role in the emergence of black consciousness in Brazil in the early 1970s. See Hanchard, *Orpheus and Power*, 113.

46. "Wolperized Black-Angled Ballyhoo," 5. *Wattstax* ads appear in the *Los Angeles Times*, February 27, 1973, G13, March 3, 1973, A6, and March 4 1973, P21; *Wisconsin State Journal*, May 4, 1973, 71; and "Movie Mailbag," *New York Times*, May 6, 1973.

47. Quoted in Kubernik, *Hollywood Shack Job*, 60.

48. Beavers, "Cool Pose," 280n3, 258.

## Works Cited

Attrep, Kara Ann. "The Sonic Inscription of Identity: Music, Race, and Nostalgia in Advertising." PhD diss., University of California, Santa Barbara, 2008.

Baker, Mark Frederick, and Houston A. Baker Jr. "Uptown Where We Belong: Space, Captivity, and the Documentary of Black Community." In *Struggles for Representation: African American Documentary Film and Video*, edited by Phyllis R. Klotman and Janet K. Cutler, 211–49. Bloomington: Indiana University Press, 1999.

Bambara, Toni Cade. "Reading the Signs, Empowering the Eye: *Daughters of the Dust* and the Black Independent Cinema Movement." In *Black American Cinema*, edited by Manthia Diawara, 118–44. New York: Routledge, 1993.

Banham, Reyner. *Los Angeles: The Architecture of Four Ecologies*. New York: Harper and Row, 1971.

Beavers, Herman. "'The Cool Pose': Intersectionality, Masculinity, and Quiescence in the Comedy and Films of Richard Pryor and Eddie Murphy." In *Race and the Subject of Masculinities*, edited by Harry Stecopoulos and Michael Uebel, 253–85. Durham: Duke University Press, 1997.

Bowman, Rob. *Soulsville, U.S.A.: The Story of Stax Records*. New York: Schirmer Books, 1997.

Clark, Larry. "Cast & Crew Commentary." *Wattstax*. Directed by Mel Stuart. Burbank, CA: Warner Home Video, 2004. DVD.

Cripps, Thomas. *Black Film as Genre*. Bloomington: Indiana University Press, 1978.

Diawara, Manthia. "Black Spectatorship: Problems of Identification and Resistance." In *Black American Cinema*, edited by Diawara, 211–20. New York: Routledge, 1993.

Freedland, Nat. "50,000 Wattstax Ducats Sold." *Billboard*, August 19, 1972, 3.

———. "Melvin Van Peebles: Multi-Media Maverick." *Billboard*, January 9, 1972, 44.

*Funky Broadway: Stax Revue Live at the 5/4 Ballroom*. Stax SCD-8567-2, 1991. Recorded August 8 and 9, 1965. CD.

George, Nelson. *The Death of Rhythm and Blues*. New York: Penguin, 1988.

Guerrero, Ed. *Framing Blackness: The African American Image in Film*. Philadelphia: Temple University Press, 1993.

Hanchard, Michael George. *Orpheus and Power: The* Movimento Negro *of Rio de Janeiro and São Paulo, Brazil, 1945–1988*. Princeton: Princeton University Press, 1994.

"Hayes' 'Shaft' Hits Wax Listing Jackpot." *Jet*, December 2, 1971, 58.

Horak, Jan-Christopher. "L.A. Rebellion: *Passing Through*." *UCLA Film & Television Archive*, 2011. Accessed August 8, 2013. http://www.cinema.ucla.edu/la-rebellion/films/passing-through.

Horne, Gerald. *Fire This Time: The Watts Uprising and the 1960s*. Charlottesville: University Press of Virginia, 1995.

James, David E. *The Most Typical Avant-Garde: History and Geography of Minor Cinemas in Los Angeles*. Berkeley: University of California Press, 2005.

"Jesse Jackson: One Leader among Many." *Time*, April 6, 1970, 14–16, 27.

Kelly, Michael. "The Living Word." *Wax Poetics*, Winter 2005, 111–24.

Kubernik, Harvey. *Hollywood Shack Job: Rock Music in Film and on Your Screen*. Albuquerque: University of New Mexico Press, 2006.

Lawrence, Novotny. *Blaxploitation Films of the 1970s: Blackness and Genre*. New York: Routledge Press, 2007.

Leab, Daniel. *From Sambo to Superspade*. Boston: Houghton Mifflin, 1975.

Masilela, Ntongela. "The Los Angeles School of Black Filmmakers." In *Black American Cinema*, edited by Manthia Diawara, 107–17. New York: Routledge, 1993.

Mason, B. J. "The New Films: Culture or Con Game?" *Ebony*, December 1972, 60–62, 64, 66, 68.

Massood, Paula. *Black City Cinema: African American Urban Experiences in Film*. Philadelphia: Temple University Press, 2003.

McLeod, Kembrew. "Authenticity within Hip-Hop and Other Cultures Threatened with Assimilation." *Journal of Communication* 49, no. 4 (1999): 134–50.

Orvell, Miles. *The Real Thing: Imitation and Authenticity in American Culture, 1880–1940*. Chapel Hill: University of North Carolina Press, 1989.

*Respect Yourself: The Stax Records Story*. Directed by Robert Gordon and Morgan Neville. Beverly Hills, CA: Concord Music Group, 2007. DVD.

Scott, Amy. "Cities and Suburbs." In *The Columbia Guide to America in the 1960s*, edited by David Farber and Beth Bailey, 263–72. New York: Columbia University Press, 2001.

Serrin, William. "Jesse Jackson: 'I Am ...' Audience: 'I Am ...' Jesse: 'Somebody' Audience: 'Somebody.'" *New York Times Magazine*, July 9, 1972, 15–21.

Sieving, Christopher. *Soul Searching: Black-Themed Cinema from the March on Washington to the Rise of Blaxploitation*. Middletown, CT: Wesleyan University Press, 2011.

"Street Talk Earns 'R.'" *Variety*, February 7, 1973, 5.

Thompson, Heather Ann. "Urban Uprisings: Riots or Rebellions?" In *The Columbia Guide to America in the 1960s*, edited by David Farber and Beth Bailey, 109–17. New York: Columbia University Press, 2001.

Tyler, Bruce M. "The Rise and Decline of the Watts Summer Festival, 1965 to 1986." *American Studies* 31, no. 2 (1990): 61–81.

Ward, Brian. *Just My Soul Responding: Rhythm and Blues, Black Consciousness, and Race Relations*. Berkeley: University of California Press, 1998.

Weems, Robert. *Business in Black and White: American Presidents and Black Entrepreneurs in the Twentieth Century*. New York: New York University Press, 2009.

Wild, Mark. *Street Meeting: Multiethnic Neighborhoods in Early Twentieth-Century Los Angeles*. Berkeley: University of California Press, 2008.

Wolper, David, with David Fisher. *Producer: A Memoir*. New York: Scribner, 2003.

"Wolperized Black-Angled Ballyhoo for 'Wattstax'; Columbia's Angles." *Variety*, February 7, 1973, 5.

# A Glance at Herstory

*Black Female Documentarians Navigating*
*Beyond the Normative Constraints*
*in* A Question of Color *and*
My Mic Sounds Nice

THERESA RENÉE WHITE,
SARA TEKLE and MELANIE SHAW

Black history can be both lost and sustained, as well as serve as the connection between historical consciousness and political social change. Manning Marable reminds us, "Too often the study of history is an exercise in nostalgia or political myth-making rather than an honest interaction with the raw materials of the past." As a result, "artifacts, memorabilia, and archives of the great black forerunners in the fight for freedom and democracy are seriously endangered, and precious little is being done about it. Priceless records, films, photographs, and crucial documents that reveal the inner stories of remarkable African-American men and women are rapidly being destroyed."[1]

Preservation issues are particularly problematic in the educational system in the United States, as, in theory, this is where the populace should be introduced to the rich and textured history of African Americans. However, the limited exposure to authentic narratives of African American contributions has been detrimental in terms of stifling the knowledge base of those interested in learning about the black experience, particularly in kindergarten through twelfth grade. Classroom curriculums have had an unsettling reputation for muting or omitting African American narratives and histories from lessons and learning materials. In fact, until the mid–1960s, historical representations highlighted in many traditional K–12 textbooks largely focus on the white, Anglo-Saxon experience.[2] Early classroom textbooks dating back to the first decades of the twentieth century rarely mention African Americans; however, when the books do, the accounts are imbued with racist implications and commentary. African Americans were firmly excluded from the collective American identity; instead, they were portrayed only in their capacity as slaves. Histories of blacks as Americans were left out of the curriculums and replaced by the discussion of slavery as an institution rather than the group itself.[3]

With the explosion of the Black Power and black consciousness movements of the 1960s came a call to update, rewrite, and reform the one-dimensional, exclusionary K–12 historical narrative. Until that point, the National Education Association (NEA) remained exclusionary, and textbooks remained static in their omission of African American histories. However, textbooks published later in the decade tell an entirely different story,[4] and the amount of attention devoted to African Americans and multiculturalism grew tremendously. Not only do black exemplars appear more frequently in classroom texts but these exemplars are also now portrayed more positively and accurately. Discussions of African American doctors, politicians, and soldiers allow African Americans to be associated with traits such as intelligence, selflessness, and patriotism rather than laziness, unintelligence, and selfishness.[5]

Despite the changes made to K–12 curriculums and textbooks, many scholars continue to argue that there is a "lack of complexity found in African American historical narratives."[6] Critiques of black history in K–12 curriculums insist that narratives in textbooks only focus on noncontroversial, one-dimensional histories and heroic figures that limit students' knowledge and context of understanding racial inequalities, power, and black history.

Though school curriculums have undoubtedly changed from extreme exclusion in the twentieth century to standards more acceptable today, it is necessary that textbooks and curriculums be revisited and revised to provide a more nuanced look into African American history that extends beyond slavery, Reconstruction, and heroic black figures. Moreover, it is important that we acknowledge the curriculums' dearth of information on black women and make efforts to address their contributions and include them as part of the conversation.[7] This essay addresses the gap in the African American historical narrative in standardized curriculums by breaking through this intellectual gridlock and highlighting the cultural contributions of two African American female documentary filmmakers. In particular, Kathe Sandler and Ava DuVernay, who have gained access to, and control of, the means of production and circulation of their cultural projects, are discussed. Sandler's and DuVernay's efforts to illuminate communal values and subjectivities of African Americans in their groundbreaking documentary films, *A Question of Color* (1993) and *My Mic Sounds Nice: The Truth about Women in Hip Hop* (2010), respectively, are the subjects of this essay.

## The Documentary Film Genre

Nonfiction films serve as a means to document life stories and preserve and disseminate spoken and visual memories, offering eyewitness accounts to help verify historical facts and also to personalize the underlying truths of the written record. Documentary films can be used as research tools and methodologies that explore the visual means of communication about social and cultural worlds and can thus augment missing narratives in the trajectory of the black experience.

From the beginning, African American documentaries have addressed a broad spectrum of concerns, using a diverse array of narrative and counternarrative strategies. Documentaries made by, and for, African Americans often make connections to real people and events, as well as political and social issues. Phyllis R. Klotman and Janet K. Cutler point to this trend: "African American documentaries like other Afro-diasporic works have much to say about links to Africa, the impact of slavery and colonization, patterns of displacement, migration and settlement, and the issue of race throughout the Americas, the Caribbean and Europe."[8]

The documentary tradition, though it is the film method considered to be one of the greatest forms of self-expression and one that uses personal narratives and takes subjects and scrutinizes them for the purpose of investigation and observation, has, in many respects, marginalized films created by African American females, particularly prior to 1970. Most early documentaries were made by African American males and focused on black soldiers in battle. These include Peter P. Jones's *For the Honor of the Fighting 8th Illinois Regiment* (1914), and Carlton Moss's *The Negro Soldier* (1944). Documentary films made by, and about, African American women have been largely absent from the black cultural landscape.

Until the early 1970s, black female filmmakers were not generally considered viable artists by the cinematic community; however, the award-winning documentaries and docudramas produced by a pioneering generation of black women have positioned these women as a force to be reckoned with. Lewis Jacobs posits, "In the United States, the single most conspicuous development in the seventies was the arrival of scores of women filmmakers, many of them young and fresh out of college film courses, but demonstrating by their assertiveness and keenness, [they reflected] an important new source of film talent."[9]

With the emergence of the Women's Movement in the 1970s, African American women began to assert their creativity by chronicling their history and cultural contributions. Klotman and Cutler note that among those who have created early film portraits of African Americans are independent filmmakers Carroll Parrott Blue, who directed *Conversations with Roy DeCarava* (1983), an intimate expose that examines the life and work of one of the foremost photographic artists of the twentieth century, and Barbara McCullough, director of *Fragments* (1980), a film that features the ritualized performance of McCullough and her fellow artists.[10] This generation of documentarians has reacted against perceived preachiness, looking instead for a style that is visually stimulating, imaginative, and challenging and one that decolonizes the gaze.[11]

There has been a significant body of writing focused on fiction films produced by African Americans, including critical assessments focusing on the narrative films of African American artists, such as Kasi Lemmons and Julie Dash. Some of the more notable examples include Frederick Luis Aldama's *Postethnic Narrative Criticism: Magicorealism in Oscar "Zeta" Acosta, Ana Castillo, Julie Dash, Hanif Kureishi, and Salman Rushdie*, and Mark Reid's *New Wave Black Cinema in the 1990s*. Much of this writing examines and critically analyzes the narrative structure of the filmmakers' productions while seeking to understand how the aspirations, challenges, and oppression that African Americans have historically experienced have been articulated on the silver screen. Less examined by scholars and critics, however, is the work of a cadre of African American females working in the documentary tradition. This genre has enabled independent filmmakers to use their cameras to explore the intersections of race, class, and gender, producing work that reflects and explores alternative images of the black female.

In an area of cinematic representation that has traditionally excluded, marginalized, and displaced black women, Sandler and DuVernay have positioned themselves as the articulators of the black woman's cultural and sexual images, increasing the opportunity to advance our understanding of black women's cultural history and the social determinants molding their lives. Sandler and DuVernay have used imaginative ways to construct worlds that mimic, and comment on, and at the same time interrogate, subvert, and posit alternatives to the status quo.

Although the work of female black documentarians oftentimes shares perspectives found in some of their male counterparts' productions, the women's films tend to exhibit a compelling gendered worldview that tends to express women's sexuality and subjectivity in provocatively unique ways. Their films focus on productive images of black women working from their own experiences, interests, and realities. These films are often characterized by shifts in the dominant language and formula of films most recognized in the Hollywood genre. The films exemplify alternative systems of thought, which, in many cases, reject traditional Hollywood aesthetics in their push toward re-presentations of the marginalized black female.

A major objective of this essay, then, is to explore the multiple definitions of black female identity, race, sexuality, and subjectivity and the nonfiction approach to cinematic representations in Sandler's commentary on race in *A Question of Color* and DuVernay's expose on black female MCs in *My Mic Sounds Nice*. This essay uses Douglas D. Kellner's Cultural Studies multidisciplinary paradigm, which takes into account the political, social, and cultural issues prevalent during the making of the film and explicates relevant issues related to race, class, culture, and gender. Moreover, the paradigm provides a theoretical space that emphasizes how cultural texts are read and how meaning is constructed from these readings.[12] The perspectives advanced by the aforementioned black female documentary filmmakers address an array of matters crucial to understanding various facets of black life.

## *Kathe Sandler:* A Question of Color

A protégé of famous documentarian St. Clair Bourne, Kathe Sandler is a Guggenheim award–winning independent filmmaker whose works include *Beah: A Black Woman Speaks* (2003), *The Friends* (1995), which garnered her the first-prize award in the cross-cultural category at the Black Filmmaker's Hall of Fame, and *Remembering Thelma* (1981), which received the best biography of a dance artist award from the New York Dance Film and Video Festival. *A Question of Color* remains her most recognized work, though she is currently working to complete her forthcoming documentary *When and Where We Enter: Stories of Black Feminism*.[13]

*A Question of Color*, produced by Independent Television Service (ITVS) and distributed by California Newsreel and Jane Balfour Films, was written by Sandler and Luke Charles Harris and directed by Sandler. As the title indicates, *Color* confronts the issue of skin color and color consciousness in the black community. Sandler journeys through time, beginning with the era of slavery and ending in the early 1990s, to discuss skin color, the black community's historical, emotional, and psychological burden.

*Color* confronts the turmoil associated with "colorism" in black America. Sandler's exploration begins with slavery, apartheid, and the institution of racism to discuss how the caste system that operates based on how closely one fares to the European ideal has defined the black self-image. Her interviewees discuss how looking "more white" potentially helped blacks during chattel slavery. Whites created beauty conventions crafted in their own self-image to ensure a racial hierarchy that would mark them as superior. Based on these ideals, "slave owners used skin color as a basis to divide enslaved Africans for work chores and to create trust and animosity among them, minimizing chances for revolt."[14] The Eurocentric standard of beauty was impressed upon Africans, and "negroid" features were regarded as alien and unattractive.[15] Lighter skin and softer-textured hair were used at times to determine duties and social status, even among slaves. Therefore, the obsession with conforming to European ideals began very early on with the Africans' arrival to the "New World" when color, in lieu of race, became the most salient, defining American characteristic.[16]

The interviews and commentary in *Color* provide a comprehensive context in which to understand the far leap the world has taken with regard to black and African physical characteristics. Interesting, the authors found no documentation prior to the slave trade that suggests discriminatory attitudes toward black skin. In actuality, some early Western cultures "extolled the beauty of dark skin and did not hesitate to do so publicly."[17] Early poems document Westerners praising African hair and dark skin tones. Frank Snowden recapitulates a poem from Asclepiades, one of the first Westerners, "Gazing at her beauty, I melt like wax before fire. And if she is black, what difference to me? So are coals when we light them, they shine like rose-buds."[18]

*Color* was released at a pivotal time in American history. New music, political outcries, and community uprisings during the 1990s presented another turning point in black consciousness and responsiveness to social injustices. During the 1960s and 1970s, African Americans experienced a new revolution of empowerment through the Black Power, Black Nationalist, and Civil Rights Movements. However, during the 1990s, the African American community shouldered the responsibility of deciding if they would create new transformation movements or remain static in the ways in which they regarded color consciousness and forward mobility. For instance, during that time, the world witnessed the 1992 Los Angeles riots, one of the largest, most violent racial upheavals in the history of the nation. The unrest erupted after the acquittal of four Los Angeles Police Department officers who were videotaped brutally beating Los Angeles civilian Rodney King. "The violence and anarchy lasted three days leaving 55 people dead and more than 2,000 injured" and sparked tensions among ethnic groups, law enforcement agents, and the black community.[19] As an act of responsiveness, new forms of hip-hop and gangsta rap were created with the intent of illuminating the social ills prevalent in black communities across America. This gangsta rap subgenre of hip-hop encapsulates the struggles of the period and differs greatly from the party-oriented rap music created in the 1970s.

Hip-hop was first introduced to America in the 1970s as a musical and artistic form of expression that fused poetry and live or recorded instrumentals. Although the earliest forms of hip-hop were "lyrically apolitical," by the late 1980s, rap and hip-hop had taken a different direction. Songs recorded by rap groups, such as Public Enemy, began to embody strong political resistance and espoused a new "radical social consciousness."[20] That struggle continued into the 1990s, with lyrics that raised consciousness about police brutality; however, new party music surfaced as well. Many of these records featured "scantily clad, sexually overcharged video vixens."[21] This particular configuration of female sexuality almost always fits a certain profile—a fair-skinned model with long, curly hair.[22]

The 1990s afforded black music the opportunity to create new standards of beauty in a more color-conscious and socially conscious atmosphere; however, mainstream hip-hop and rap music reverted to age-old standards that considered Eurocentric features and light complexions ideal for black women. With the prevalent media reinforcing this standard of beauty, the issue of color consciousness, once again, became a salient issue in the black community. *Color*, being one of the first to address color consciousness in the black community, contributed to the dialogue in new and provocative ways.

Although *Color* is a product of the 1990s, a time when the black community was less subjected to overt and blatant colorism, such as the "brown-paper-bag test," a ritual once practiced by certain African American sororities and fraternities who discriminated against people who were "too black" (i.e., darker than a paper bag), intraracism within the black community was still a monumental issue. Even today, empirical studies suggest little change in the preference for lighter skin among African Americans. Though researchers have noted that the pressure for lighter skin and Eurocentric features is more prevalent among African American women than it is for African American men, both groups are affected by colorism.[23] Furthermore, the notion of femininity and womanhood in America has been closely linked to whiteness and purity.[24] Culturally, virtues such as piety and purity have become synonymous with whiteness; everything "white" has become "ladylike," and everything associated with "blackness" is quite the contrary.[25]

Sandler interviews scores of African Americans of all ages, skin tones, and backgrounds to examine the skin-color hierarchy that exists, but that is rarely discussed in the black community. The film opens with an elderly brown-skin African American woman explaining, "If you're white, you're all right. If you're yellow, you're mellow. If you're brown, stick around. If you're black, get back!" A darker-skinned woman then explains how the mother of a man she was dating rejected her because she was "too dark."

After this powerful opening, *Color* explores the consequences of being too dark in black America, with then Tuskegee mayor Johnny Ford and the fifth president of Tuskegee University, Dr. Benjamin Payton, who explain the effects of colorism in the black community. Both were the first dark-skinned, black men to hold their positions, which, they explain, is not coincidental. According to testimony in the documentary, leadership positions in the black community were traditionally held by lighter-skinned African Americans, and those who looked white were elite. The effects of colorism hold true even today, as dark-skinned blacks in the United States are more likely to have lower socioeconomic status, more punitive relationships with the criminal justice system, and diminished prestige and are less likely to hold elective office compared to lighter-skinned blacks.[26]

The issue of color extends far beyond success and opportunity in the black community. It is an ideology that weighs heavily on the self-esteem and self-worth of both male and female African Americans. This is apparent when Sandler interviews two black teenage boys who are best friends and a rap duo. One of the young men has a fair complexion, and the other has dark skin. They discuss the fact that girls usually gravitate towards the light-skinned boy, and though the lighter male insists that he and his friend "are above the issue of color," the darker friend painfully struggles with his appearance, doing such things as wearing colored contacts to appear "less black." He explains, "We don't even discuss it, and we're best friends." He later reveals that he feels a sort of resentment toward his friend for having a lighter complexion.

Although Sandler discusses the effects of colorism among black men, she pays particular attention to the effects of the color bias among black women. For women, light skin is not only closely associated with European standards of beauty but it also, in conjunction with European features, is almost required to fit the mainstream standard of beauty in the United States.[27] For darker-skinned women, terms like "skillet blonde," "liver lips," and "tar baby" are painful reminders of the white supremacy established during slavery and colonialism. Moreover, such terms also reinforce the need to succumb to a standard that is not traditionally or naturally black or African. Sandler uses her documentary to expose the burdens placed upon black women in America. The interviewees discuss how their darker skin has at times left them feeling desexualized or devalued, while lighter-skinned women discuss the exclusion they experienced by some darker-skinned women who held a great deal of resentment towards them.

In the next stage of the documentary, Sandler transitions into the 1960s Black Power Movement, a unique period of social and political consciousness that transformed the ways African Americans regarded their personal appearances. During this period, Afrocentric features and nappy hair took on new meanings, becoming acceptable and cool and important ways of symbolizing one's commitment to the struggle for Black Power. These new exercises in black liberation were social and political, sending strong messages about black pride and black dissatisfaction. For example, James Brown perfectly articulates the period in his song "Say It Loud, I'm Black and I'm Proud." Additionally, *Color* features a clip from a speech by the Reverend Jesse Jackson, where he endorses black peoples' natural image: "The natural hair that you wear means that you're going to quit being fictitious, not only in your hair but in your life." Thus, embracing one's blackness in America was not only a social awakening but also a form of resistance against the dominant culture.

As *Color* progresses to the 1990s, it becomes clear that the influx of social and political consciousness prevalent in the 1960s has begun to fade. Once again, white standards of beauty have overshadowed the strong urge for Afrocentricity and black pride within the African American community. Although social consciousness resurfaced in new forms in the 1990s, the majority of black Americans reverted to old stereotypes, as rap singers praised the light-skinned girl with curly hair, and more and more black women opted for cosmetic surgery to acquire more Eurocentric features.[28] The film ends with narration by Sandler, who urges the black community to confront color consciousness and celebrate the varying shapes, characteristics, and shades of blackness.

Although *Color* was released in the 1990s, in 2014, colorism, its influences, and effects are still key issues. The conversation surrounding color biases in the black community has become more open as individuals in the community have addressed it. Films like Jeff Stilson's *Good Hair* (2009), featuring comedian Chris Rock, and Bill Duke and D. Channsin Berry's documentary *Dark Girls* (2011) effectively confront the black community's deep-seated biases regarding hair, color, and facial features. Like Sandler, these filmmakers have used the documentary genre as a platform for voicing serious concerns within the black community. These films provide evidence that the conversations aroused by Sandler's documentary are still worthy of discussion. As African Americans reach for bleaching creams and flat irons to look "less ethnic," it is important that the black community continue to address color consciousness in order to improve self-perception and self-worth.

## *Ava DuVernay:* My Mic Sounds Nice

Although men are the main focus in a significant number of documentary films examining hip-hop, it is critical to give recognition to the women that have equally aided in molding the musical genre into the global art form that it has become. *Style Wars* (1983), *Rhyme & Reason* (1997), *Free Style, the Art of Rhyme* (2000), and rapper Ice T's documentary *Something from Nothing: The Art of Rap* (2012) examine the contributions that have shaped contemporary hip-hop.

The disparate view of African American female rappers in hip-hop continues to be challenging, and the lack of equal visual representation in documentaries looking at this genre of music is scarce. Though many African American females are considered hip-hop pioneers, their skills as B-girls (a person devoted to the culture of hip-hop who participates in the dance style of breakdancing or breaking), MCs (a mic controller, someone with enough flow and skill to be considered a master of the art of rap), and graffiti artists have been overlooked, and, thus, these females are not considered among the great rap artists. Scholars Guillermo Rebollo-Gil and Amanda Moras closely examine hip-hop music lyrically, as well as culturally, to ascertain whether the musical genre encourages misogynistic behavior or if the vulgar content consistently featured in the music influences the amount of violence re-created by the genre's followers. The authors explain, "Rap or Hip Hop music has always been feminine. Since its creation, black male rappers have expressed their love and devotion for the art form they practice in ways very much akin to the traditional manner in which heterosexual men attempt to woo heterosexual women."[29]

Significant, men continue to dominate hip-hop, often diminishing the art form to a patriarchal and misogynistic genre. In addition, male dominance consistently defines and reproduces what many consider to be rap culture's true characteristics. Rebollo-Gil and Moras explore this notion in critiquing author Danyell Smith's work. They quote Smith: "Women's lyrics are often still viewed by men and women themselves as not valid.... [W]omen's versions of reality are somehow suspect."[30] From this assertion, one might assume that a woman's work in hip-hop will never be fully accepted, because in the rap game, men will always hold the upper hand because their lyrics are perceived as more credible.

Notably, Run DMC, A Tribe Called Quest, Public Enemy, Kanye West, Jay-Z, and Waka Flocka Flame are all examples of African American men or male groups who have, at some point, been at the forefront of the rap industry. With the exception of Missy Elliot, recognition of African American women in hip-hop has been relatively nonexistent, compared to their successful, black, male counterparts. Ironically, during the 1980s and 1990s, female performers, such as Roxanne Shanté, MC Lyte, Queen Latifah, Lauryn Hill, and the phenomenal duo Salt-N-Pepa, were at the forefront of the burgeoning musical genre. Though the rap landscape has changed dramatically since that time, DuVernay's *My Mic Sounds Nice* is an important film that will sustain, ensuring that the aforementioned rappers will remain a part of hip-hop's legacy.

In 2012 DuVernay became the first African American woman to win Best Director at the Sundance Film Festival for *Middle of Nowhere* (2012). Prior to receiving this prestigious distinction, DuVernay's filmography comprised *This Is the Life* (2008), *Compton C Minor* (2009), and *I Will Follow* (2011), which when considered in conjunction with *Middle of Nowhere*, demonstrates her commitment to telling stories about the African American experience. *My Mic Sounds Nice* is no exception as the filmmaker uses the documentary form to explore the untold stories surrounding black women's experience in hip-hop. Although the film did not win any notable awards, *My Mic* did receive one nomination from the Black Reel Awards in 2011 for Best Documentary.

In *My Mic*, DuVernay cultivates the idea that hip-hop has evolved into another commodity used to mischaracterize women as sexual deviants. She closely examines what it means to be a female MC in the industry and scrutinizes the idealized sexual image of women in this musical genre. DuVernay begs the questions, "Where are all the female MCs hiding? What happened to black female rappers such as Lady of Rage, MC Lyte, Rah Digga, and Roxanne Shanté?"

As *My Mic* unfolds, the answers to these questions become excruciatingly clear. In particular, the emergence of hypersexualized MCs like Lil' Kim, Foxy Brown, and Nicki Minaj made female rappers relying upon their lyrical skills expendable, pushing them to the margins of the hip-hop industry. That artists like Lil' Kim and Foxy Brown lack the musical ability of less sexual artists is a moot point. In essence, they produce music that is good enough to satisfy mainstream audiences while providing fans with the erotic fare that has become a staple of male rappers' music and videos. These artists' very presence on the hip-hop landscape had a tremendous impact on the industry as record executives worked to standardize the overtly sexual female performer. In *My Mic*, Eve, a prominent rapper who began her career in the 1990s, addresses this issue: "Being a female in the industry you were encouraged to show a little more leg, a little more ass, a little more whatever." Interestingly, rappers Queen Latifah, Lauryn Hill, and others have gained name recognition without exploiting their sexuality, demonstrating that the industry's reliance upon hypersexual female rappers is misguided. Unfortunately, the more Minaj's popularity grows, the more lyrically gifted female rappers are becoming vestiges of the bygone hip-hop era.

Although there have been many African American women that have risen to fame throughout the twentieth century and into the twenty-first, whether their short-lived stardom occurred in cinema or mainstream hip-hop culture, these black females' rise in popularity has been extremely transient. Throughout the years, it has been made unquestionably clear that an African American woman's contribution to the mainstream media is just as expendable as her image. In *My Mic*, a handful of female MCs sit down in front of the camera to reveal their stories of struggle and false hope in a world that has been continuously dominated by men. Rah Digga speaks eloquently about the differences between African American females and men as they compete in the rap industry: "We really had to rhyme like one of the guys in order to be taken seriously." Moreover, African American female rappers Eve, Trina, and Missy Elliott further explain that male dominance at the most notable record labels also makes it extremely difficult for females to ascend to prominence within hip-hop. Thus, the industry is patriarchal, functioning as a microcosm of American society.

Just as males holding positions of authority have historically made it tougher for women to gain traction in the corporate workforce, in hip-hop the same holds true. For example, thugged-out, outlandish male performers espousing lyrics that degrade women are consistently upheld over their female rap counterparts. *My Mic*, deconstructs the differences between black women and men in hip-hop by showing the viewer that in patriarchal America there is an imbalance between female MCs and hardcore male rappers. Author Tricia Rose discusses what she believes to be the root of feminine and masculine differential treatment in the rap industry, highlighting misogyny and sexism as the leading factors contributing to the lack of black women who are considered successful rappers. Rose states, "The fact is that although sexism is a systemic American problem, when it comes to the regular, sustained, celebrated misogynistic images of black women, hip hop stands center stage. It is the biggest black popular arena with the greatest number of highly sexually exploitative and dehumanizing images of black women."[31] Coincidently, in *My Mic*, Salt-N-Pepa reaffirm the author's contention when they explain that sexism is the root of any woman's struggle in the rap industry: "Hip-hop is so misogynistic. It's so male oriented. It's so hard. It's so masculine, that if a woman does not have something really, really unique and special that stands out amongst all the testosterone, then it's just a difficult genre to survive in."

Although the 1980s gave birth to only a small handful of female MCs, that era featured a range of musical and stylistic approaches as well as acceptance of a rapper's gender. In *My Mic,* hip-hop journalist and author Joan Morgan reflects on the time when she believed females in hip-hop reigned supreme: "In the 80s hip-hop belonged to the streets and in the streets we were a presence, and in the streets we were B-Girls. We had a very empowered position that allowed for diversity." Several female MCs throughout the documentary support Morgan's claim, noting that one can look at MC Lyte, who first emerged in the late 1980s, as a prime example. As one of the most influential female hip-hop veterans, MC Lyte illustrates the grit and grime of her struggle as a female rapper. In the documentary, she engages the audience, recounting the life-changing experiences she underwent as she evolved into a leading female MC: "When I started rapping, I came up in a time when it was all about change, provoking thought and inspiring a nation of people." Today, however, the primary recognition of an aspiring African American female MC is through sexually exploitative images and the hypersexualized, materialistic persona depicted of women and girls in the media.

Further confirming MC Lyte's assertion is female MC Roxanne Shanté, who in *My Mic* also speaks about the disparities that rap continues to reproduce: "Long before there was glam squads and your lipsticks and you knew your budget for your clothing, you went straight [on stage in] what you wore outside; if you had a show and the show time didn't give me enough time to change, then I wore what I had on, because at the end of the day it was about talent."

The talent that Shanté speaks of can be traced back to the formative years of female development. For instance, Kyra Danielle Gaunt examines childhood playground games, such as double Dutch, Miss Mary Mack, and patty-cake, and relates these adolescent diversions to hip-hop and rap. It is within these youthful pastime activities that many African American little girls familiarized themselves with musical rhymes and playful rhythmic dances. These innocent and familiar playground activities, which have been socially connected to femininity, are also the foundation of popular hip-hop lyrics in Nelly's "Country Grammar (Hot Shit)." In particular, Nelly borrows from the adolescent clapping game Down Down Baby, originally popularized by little girls, and transforms the song into a hypermasculine anthem characterized by gunplay and drug use. Examining the rapper's masculine twist on a rhyme that is heavily associated with little girls, Gaunt asks the age-old question, "What comes first, the chicken or the egg?" The author closely considers the connection between the lyrical content of male-dominated rap songs and the sweet melodies of innocent, female childhood games, exploring how misogynistic lyrics have taken content from playground chants that women played as girls. Gaunt speaks to that paradox, contending:

> Hip-hop is a contradictory space for women. On one hand, it offers young women the possibility of a "popular" or social identification with an African American group-consciousness through musical participation. On the other hand, hip-hop uses these same musical and cultural practices—making beats with technology, rhyming or rapping, and encoding ethnicity and gender (black and male)—in ways that deny the former agency and authority of women and girls, which deny things feminine.[32]

Because hip-hop is male dominated, it is seemingly easier for men to masculinize something as innocent as double Dutch and patty-cake. Gaunt contends that women's lyrics that are directly related to femininity run the risk of being rejected by their male counterparts, as is evidenced by many comments of the interviewees in *My Mic*. Thus, not only do we see inequalities related to women in hip-hop, but now we also see these disparities in early childhood through the denunciation of the games that young African American girls play.

Coincidentally, the same year that the BET Network debuted DuVernay's documentary to the public, female MC Nicki Minaj released her first mainstream album, *Pink Friday* (2010). Her physical image alone evokes the overarching question asked throughout the documentary concerning the whereabouts of female rappers and the misrepresentation of their images. As one examines Minaj's sexual image and sexually demeaning lyrical content, is it safe to say that her hypersexuality is what gives her the edge and propels her to reign supreme as a female rapper?

Unfortunately, according to author Cheryl Keyes, "women of rap still face overt sexism regarding their creative capabilities."[33] DuVernay's documentary, as well as other films that share similar observations, recapitulates the importance of recognizing the absence of strong female MCs in the hip-hop industry. Although rap superstar Minaj has become widely famous for her outrageous style (the MTV News Hip-Hop Brain Trust voted her the number 6 Hottest MC in the rap game), her explicit sexuality represents only a minuscule component of black female identity and subjectivity. The interviewees in DuVernay's documentary illuminate the fact that hip-hop continues to be male dominated, misogynistic, and sexist and that a woman's body becomes her most valuable asset once she sells her soul to hip-hop.

Rebollo-Gil and Moras concur with this assertion: "Rap music is situated in a predominately white and patriarchal culture industry, constraining the expression of black women."[34] *My Mic* creatively explores the inequality that female MCs have had to overcome in order to make a positive name for themselves. For many women in hip-hop, the likelihood of a sustained career is slim. In fact, surviving in any industry as a woman of color still proves to be the hardest struggle for females worldwide. *My Mic* provides an outlet for women to critically analyze the enduring lack of female hip-hop MCs and invites the viewer to take measures to bring about change in hip-hop's male-dominated industry, which can ultimately help reshape the future of the black female experience in this genre.

Notably, both Sandler's and DuVernay's documentaries extend the conversations about crucial issues relevant to the black community. While doing so, they establish themselves as cultural producers and disseminators of knowledge related to the black experience, thus contributing to the limited exposure to authentic narratives of African Americans, in general, and African American female documentarians, more specifically. These documentarians have created unique cultural artifacts that help to preserve the untold perspectives of *herstory*, which ultimately contributes to the collective American identity and to students' knowledge of race, subjectively, and the black historical narrative.

## Notes

1. Marable, *Living Black History*, xiv, xviii.
2. Kook, "Shifting Status," 154.
3. Brown and Brown, "Silenced Memories," 141.
4. Ibid., 143.
5. Hughes, "Hint of Whiteness," 204.
6. Brown, and Brown, "Silenced Memories," 141.
7. Ibid., 144.
8. Klotman and Cutler, *Struggles for Representation*, xv.
9. Jacobs, "From Political Activism," 516.
10. Klotman and Cutler, *Struggles for Representation*, xxiv.
11. "Conversations with Roy DeCarava."
12. Kellner, *Media Culture*, 101.
13. "Kathe Sandler."
14. Hunter, "If You're Light," 177.
15. Ibid., 175.
16. Hall, "Euro-Americanization of Race," 117, 116.
17. Ibid., 118.
18. Snowden, *Before Color Prejudice*.
19. "Name Synonymous."
20. Nielson, "Here Come the Cops," 349.
21. Ralph, "Hip-Hop," 143.
22. Hill, "Skin Color," 77.
23. Ibid., 79.
24. Hochschild and Weaver, "Skin Color Paradox," 643; Hunter, "If You're Light," 181.
25. Hunter, "If You're Light," 175.

26. Ibid., 178.
27. Ibid., 180.
28. "Plastic Surgery Is Growing."
29. Rebollo-Gil and Moras, "Black Women and Black Men," 118.
30. Ibid., 127.
31. Rose, *Hip Hop Wars*, 133.
32. Gaunt, *Games Black Girls Play*, 102.
33. Keyes, Empowering Self, 258.
34. Rebollo-Gil and Moras, "Black Women and Black Men," 129.

## *Works Cited*

Brown, Keffrelyn, and Anthony Brown. "Silenced Memories: An Examination of the Socio-ocultural Knowledge on Race and Racial Violence in Official School Curriculum." *Equity & Excellence in Education* 43, no. 2 (2010): 141–44.
"Conversations with Roy DeCarava." *Icarus Films*, July 31, 2010. Accessed January 15, 2012. http://www.icarusfilms.com/cat97/a-e/conversa.html.
"Country Grammar Lyrics: Nelly." LyricsManiawww. Accessed October 31, 2012. http://www.lyricsmania.com/country_grammar_lyrics_nelly.html.
Gaunt, Kyra Danielle. *The Games Black Girls Play: Learning the Ropes from Double-Dutch to Hip-Hop.* New York: New York University Press, 2006.
Hall, Ronald. "The Euro-Americanization of Race: Alien Perspective of African Americans vis-á-vis Trivialization of Skin Color." *Journal of Black Studies* 36, no. 1 (2005): 116–18.
Hill, Mark. "Skin Color and the Perception of Attractiveness among African Americans: Does Gender Make a Difference?" *Social Psychology Quarterly* 65, no. 1 (2002): 77–91.
Hochschild, Jennifer, and Vesla Weaver. "The Skin Color Paradox and the American Racial Order." *Social Forces* 86, no. 2 (2007): 643–70.
Hughes, Richard. "A Hint of Whiteness: History Textbooks and Social Construction of Race in the Wake of the Sixties." *Social Studies* 98, no. 5 (2007): 201–8.
Hunter, Margaret. "'If You're Light You're Alright': Light Skin Color as Social Capital for Women of Color." *Gender and Society* 16, no. 2 (2002): 175–93.
Jacobs, Lewis. "From Political Activism to Women's Consciousness." In *The Documentary Tradition*, 2d. ed. edited by Jacobs, 514–16. New York: Norton, 1979.
"Kathe Sandler." *Women Make Movies*, October 2009. Accessed January 15, 2012. http://www.wmm.com/filmcatalog/makers/fm7.shtml.
Kellner, Douglas D. *Media Culture: Cultural Studies, Identity and Politics Between the Modern and the Postmodern.* New York: Routledge, 1995.
Keyes, Cheryl. "Empowering Self, Making Choices, Creating Spaces: Black Female Identity via Rap Music Performance." *Journal of American Folklore* 113, no. 449 (2000): 255–69.
Klotman, Phyllis R., and Janet K. Cutler. *Struggles for Representation: African American Documentary Film and Video.* Bloomington: Indiana University Press, 1999.
Kook, Rebecca. "The Shifting Status of African Americans in the American Collective Identity." *Journal of Black Studies* 29, no. 2 (1998): 154–78.
Marable, Manning. *Living Black History: How Reimagining the African-American Past Can Remake America's Future.* New York: Basic Books, 2006.
"A Name Synonymous with Racial Divides" *Europe Intelligence Wire*, June 19, 2012, 1.
Nielson, Erik. "'Here Come the Cops': Policing the Resistance in Rap Music." *International Journal of Cultural Studies* 15, no. 4 (2012): 349–63.
"Plastic Surgery Is Growing in the Black Community." *American Society for Aesthetic Plastic Surgery*, June 18, 2012. Accessed January 16, 2012. http://www.surgery.org/consumers/plastic-surgery-news-briefs/plastic-surgery-growing-black-community-1036892.

Rebollo-Gil, Guillermo, and Amanda Moras. "Black Women and Black Men in Hip Hop Music: Misogyny, Violence, and the Negotiation of (White-Owned) Space." *Journal of Popular Culture* 45, no. 1 (2012): 118–32.

Reed, Mark. "New Wave Black Cinema in the 1990s." In *Film Genre 2000: New Critical Essays*, edited by Wheeler Winston Dixon, 13–28. New York: State University of New York Press, 2000.

Rose, Tricia. *The Hip Hop Wars: What We Talk About When We Talk About Hip Hop.* New York: Basic Books, 2008.

Snowden, Frank. *Before Color Prejudice.* Cambridge: Harvard University Press, 1983.

# Documenting Grassroots History as a Means to Social Change

## 778 Bullets, *Community Engagement and the Legacy of Rural Civil Rights*

### Angela J. Aguayo

Growing up as first-generation Chicanos in Los Angeles, my brother and I would sit around the breakfast table with my father after his night shift, and sometimes we would talk about history. At the same time we began learning about California history in grade school, my father started taking classes at East Los Angeles College. As a Mexican immigrant, my father was particularly inspired when we started learning about California history. Thanks to his life experience and Movimiento Estudiantil Chican@ de Aztlán (MEChA), a student group that he encountered on campus, the breakfast table became a place to deconstruct social studies lessons.

"Did you know that California was stolen from Mexico?" my father asked one morning.

It was the first moment that I remember questioning the authority of textbooks, teachers, myths, school lessons, politicians, and the government. What I could not quite articulate at the time is the sticky and complicated way the duality of history functions and that the hegemonic precision of certain stories take more precedence and legitimacy over others.

At a tender age, I learned there was a capital *H* history that is official, institutionalized, sanctioned, documented, and often disconnected from my life. There was also the people's history, undocumented, often oral, renegade in its impulse to speak truth to power, handed down, and unsanctioned. These stories felt more connected to my life and the people who came before me. These are the stories that are often left on the cutting-room floor of official, capital *H* history. I find myself grappling with the duality of history in my class-room, on production shoots, and with my research. Upon every reading of cap-ital *H* history, I am reminded of what is absent, privileged, and sanctioned.

Documentary production has always involved modes and variations of history.[1] Early films—called actualities—documented simple events like a train arriving at a station or news events that were not easily accessible because of geography and the infancy of travel. The power of documentary as a mode of influence emerged in the early twentieth century and punctuated the capacity of the genre to trouble the dominant historical narratives, suggesting a mul-tiplicity of perspectives and subject positions. During this time, documentary was initially conceived by John Grierson as the way to fix a troubled democracy by legitimizing with documentary representation those who lacked a political voice.[2] The documentary camera has often resided comfortably in places where cultural representation has stepped in for the lack of political voice. Although there have been moments to the contrary, documentary continues comfortably as a channel of the people's history.

What investigators of all types often assume is that grassroots people's history is sitting there waiting to be documented. History that is excluded from official, public, and institutionalized documents comes with a unique set of circumstances that provide opportunities and challenges for rethinking historical memory. For most of cinema history, the media makers fortunate enough to learn the craft and acquire the equipment to produce visual media have historically come from a privileged class.[3] There is a question of whether filmmakers can really gain access and/or exposure to these grassroots stories easily unless they are from the community or adopted into it. Counter-history is often silent and tied to long-ago-buried trauma. These histories are the kinds of narratives that require trust and shared motives. These kinds of connec-tions—between filmmaker and the community—are not easily forged, espe-cially when the creative team does not have an organic connection to the community. The media production industry is far from reflecting a diverse world, which is why documenting the black experience continues to be a crit-ical project.

This essay addresses these issues of documenting grassroots history, the African American experience, and social change as it is represented, initiated, and facilitated through the documentary camera. These concepts are explored through analysis of the preproduction, production, and distribution of *778 Bullets*, a documentary short that I completed in 2011. This film chronicles a remarkable and largely unknown incident in November 1970 between police and the Black Panther Party in the small college town of Carbondale, Illinois. Specifically, the local and state police, in the presence of the members of the Federal Bureau of Investigation (FBI), fired 778 rounds of ammunition into an off-campus rental house occupied by students and local residents, some of whom were assumed to be members of the southern Illinois chapter of the Black Panther Party. Using archival material, newspaper accounts, witness testimony, and experts in the field, *778 Bullets* recovers a little-known history of resistance and resilience of the human struggle for self-determination.

The Carbondale shoot-out was unlike other police raids of known Black Panther residences across the country, such as the police ambush of Bobby Hutton in Oakland, California, in 1968 and the December 1969 murders of Fred Hampton and Mark Clark. In November 1970, the Carbondale Black Panthers were nervous as a result of Hampton's and Clark's recent assassinations in Chicago. To protect themselves, members took defensive measures that included placing sandbags around the house to stop bullets and learning how to properly use gas masks and firearms. When attacked in November 1970, they shot back. The Carbondale shoot-out remains one of a few instances of many attacks across the country in which police violence toward Black Panthers did not end in fatalities.

The dominant memory of the Black Panther Party would have people believe that the organization was mostly constructed around violence and existed only in major urban cities; *778 Bullets* documents a more rural presence of radical politics and the struggle for civil rights. The documentation of this history extends our understanding of the presence of the Black Panther Party in places as unlikely as small-town Illinois and provides a countermemory of the organization, which was committed to public service and willing to engage in peaceful resolution to violent police engagement. While this history has value in terms of a historical contribution and academic significance, the production team was also invested in exploring how this story might also have local community interest and political influence. What is intriguing and notable is that *778 Bullets* has connected with the community in which this story happened, spurring a local social movement and several important community events that continue to facilitate public deliberation about undocumented local history. The community screenings of *778 Bullets* included grassroots partnerships with churches, organizations, and activists. At the Church of the Good Shepherd in July 2013—days after the not-guilty verdict in the George Zimmerman shooting of Trayvon Martin—the documentary was screened, which brought forth a spontaneous call to action. Since that moment, a growing social movement continues to evolve from the screenings of the film.[4]

The scholarly discussion of social-change documentary is largely silent about the production process as a site of agitation and is mostly focused on the screen as the primary site of meaning construction. What is largely missing from the research is an account of media events that mobilize publics for political engagement throughout the creative process of production. Even though social change can be difficult to map, the work toward typologies, identifiable strategies, contextual circumstances, and common themes of this documentary work are necessary, and a more rigorous mapping of rural civil-rights struggle is urgent and potentially emancipatory. Using notes taken while in the field documenting civil-rights history, video documentation of audience members responding to the documentary, primary-research documents, and other production notes, the remainder of this essay explores the possibilities for social change as it is represented, initiated, and facilitated throughout the documentary process. It is a cogenerative inquiry in which local and professional knowledge interacts, producing valid and contextually centered knowledge production.[5] First explored are challenges in the process of representation and the documentation of grassroots history. Next, this essay examines how a documentary may initiate social change by creating a space for activist engagement. Finally, grounding the ability of a documentary to help facilitate social change in the case of *778 Bullets*, criteria are offered to better direct the study and engagement of the activist media publics that emerge from the documentary audience.

## Representation and Resistance

The history of the Black Panthers in rural southern Illinois is remarkable and largely undocumented. The Black Panther Party emerged on the West Coast in 1966 in an effort to protect black neighborhoods from police brutality and serve other community needs. The Black Panthers were a revolutionary, socialist organization whose politics spread to major urban cities throughout the country.[6] Most Carbondale residents at the time and a generation removed are not aware of what happened in November 1970. The police shoot-out with the Carbondale Black Panthers is the kind of thing that people don't talk about in polite or mixed-race company; it is one of those stories that time covered up and no one worked hard to preserve.

Public memory of the Civil Rights Movement is by nature partial and frequently punctuates the early nonviolent aspects of the Civil Rights Movement.[7] In local communities and national discourses, Rosa Parks and Martin Luther King, Jr. are memorialized a great deal, and so do films that depict nonviolent civil rights protests. While the pursuit of civil rights was a radical concept, the nonviolent methods of the early movement and leaders like Parks and King were not threatening in comparison to organizations like the Black Panthers. In terms of public memory, diminutive media attention is paid toward the waning concern for nonviolent commitments and the emerging influence of socialism and black nationalist philosophies starting around 1964 and 1965. More than just a shift in emerging philosophies, civil rights activists—including King shortly before his death—began critiquing the endemic roots of capitalism and the histories of imperialism, which has systematic roots in the exploitation and marginalization of the African American community in the United States historically. Groups like the Black Panther Party began asking what they could do to serve the needs of their local community without the help of the government, suggesting resistance is oppositional but also productive.

Depictions of the Black Power Movement are typically sanitized of any radical critique.[8] When the emergence of the Black Power Movement does occupy the media screen or historical record, images of Black Panthers dressed in black and carrying weapons is usually the primary visual discourse that emerges. The slogan "black power" had a polarizing effect, empowering the black community but also stirring fear among others. The fear of black power and the Black Panther Party, in particular, was articulated as a real threat by the government and across public culture.[9] At the height of this tension, J. Edgar Hoover, director of the FBI, secretly waged a war on the Panthers, declaring the organization the nation's biggest threat.[10]

Southern Illinois is a bit of a crossroads for race relations stretching back to the migration of slaves from the south to the north. The railway lines easily carried people from one region to another. Southern Illinois also was a main corridor for freed slaves migrating north from the dark-belt region, bordering the Mississippi River, a strip of counties that held more than 70 percent of their residents in slavery.[11] Carbondale is located not too far from the line that divided a slave state from a free state, setting the stage for a unique culture of integration and segregation that warrants more intense study and documentation. *778 Bullets* is an attempt to understand the rural imprint on civil rights in addition to how these narratives unfolded outside the typical backdrops of the larger civil rights narratives in the south and in major urban cities.

The early stages of *778 Bullets* were built around a curiosity about how the Panthers' radical politics emerged in the rural Midwest, a rarely documented activist landscape. The production crew comprised a random, yet diverse collection of undergraduate and graduate students, two multiracial (one was me, Chicana and white), three African American, and one white. I would meet with the group almost every Friday for a year. We had heard rumors about the Carbondale Black Panther Party, but we could neither find record of the organization nor its rumored shoot-out with the police. In the process of collecting research, we began to realize that by skill or identification, the white student was afforded much more access to the spaces around collecting materials in formal institutions, such as public archives, libraries, and at the courthouse. This engagement with the racial makeup of the production crew and collection of information for the documentary made for interesting observations about the local cultural politics. Generally, it matters who shows up to ask questions and inquire about public documents in the production process, both for our benefit and to our detriment.

For the people who experienced the shoot-out of November 1970, it was deeply traumatic. Hundreds, possibly thousands, of bullets were fired throughout a multi-hour gunfight in the middle of the early morning. Stray bullets were fired into the black community while many children were sleeping in striking distance. I wanted the audiences viewing the film to experience what it might have been like for the northeast Carbondale residents who experienced the shoot-out. Therefore, the sounds of 778 bullets extend throughout the documentary, so that the audience is not allowed to escape the gunfight. Intentionally, the sound of the gunfire is omitted when the voices of the community emerge to speak of what they witnessed. My goal was for the audience to be held in the consciousness of being under constant physical attack throughout the story. Before significant issues of how to represent this history could be considered, access to the community members who experienced the shoot-out and their willingness to share their experiences were sensitive endeavors.

## Grassroots History: Access, Response, and Organizing

Gathering the initial interviews to qualify and elaborate upon the primary historical research was difficult. The process of understanding the conflicting emotions that arise from sharing such a traumatic history took a long while to fully understand. In my experience, it is not the fear of social or political retaliation that keeps most people from talking, especially in an environment that favors free-speech rights. The concern is about contributing to the public record, a process requiring a vulnerability to recount the events and yet no guarantee of anything positive or transformative materializing from reliving that pain. For many, these traumas have been tucked away because living with them front and center is neither productive nor empowering, as one of my interviewees reminded me. I continue to ask community members if they would be willing to contribute their story, with almost everyone stopping to think before responding. From what I gather, that thinking is often about what they are willing to share outside a close circle of trusted friends and family, considering what traumas they are willing to air in public.

The documentation of countermemory experienced by marginalized people whose histories are largely ignored is a delicate terrain that must be carefully navigated. The question of "in whose interest" the story is being constructed must take precedence. This is a heavy obligation; one that I don't take lightly and I don't always get right. There is a rich history of media practitioners acting in ways that are often uncritical, willing to sacrifice social justice and systematic analysis in exchange for recording trauma for quick, professional gain. Researchers of all varieties frequently descend upon marginalized communities for study, collect data, and disappear. This has led to what Gubrium and Harper identify as "research fatigue," or fueling a general distrust by the subjects of academic researchers.[12] For good reason, there is often a concern about motives for recording historical memory and trauma from those who are being documented. This kind of distrust runs deep in the Carbondale community. From the perspective of many longtime residents, Southern Illinois University (SIU) has been apathetic about its mission to serve the community. For many, our production team represented the university, and thus, our engagement with the community opened many long-buried grievances about the institution's gradual move away from its commitment to the community.

Margaret Nesbit, one of the participants that we sought early on for guidance and information, significantly influenced our intentions. She was clear about helping us remember that history is important if we connect it to the present. Nesbit is a community activist and the director of the local children's reading program. The home in which she lived with small children and her husband was a few doors down from the November 1970 shooting at 401 North Washington. Her brother, Elbert Simons, negotiated the cease-fire between police and the Black Panthers in the early morning hours. Nesbit has a rich legacy of being committed to civil rights issues in Carbondale. Because of her experiences, we needed her insight and guidance to tell this story. She insisted that members of the production team attend city council meetings and other community events before she agreed, one year later, to grant us an interview about her perspective on the shooting. She permitted us to interview her on one condition. Nesbit was not interested in talking about history as a way of looking back, but as an opportunity to move forward. This is not an uncommon request I have found in the practice of doing production work on the people's history. Reliving trauma and documenting stories of people who have been systematically marginalized from capital *H* history might benefit from or require that the story has some impact on current social conditions.

Because she is a respected community leader, Nesbit's participation in *778 Bullets* was a critical step in engaging other community stakeholders as a means to gain access to others' stories. As documentary filmmaker Jean Rouch is often attributed with saying, video making is a means to a shared anthropology.[13] The opportunity to contribute to the dominant narrative of historical memory is perhaps the most influential aspect of documentary discourse. Combined with a critical capacity, the people's history is empowering. For these reasons and many others, gathering the people's history is challenging and for some people a threatening proposition. I anticipated a strong reaction to *778 Bullets*, but not so early on in the production process.

In the early stages, the production team was simply sharing rare archival materials and a few difficult-to-obtain interviews, and thus, we were mostly unsure if we had a story. Preproduction included coordination with public events about significant acts of local protest and attempting to generate interest in civil rights and oral history. We hoped for an interactive community discussion where a perspective of history was placed upon the screen and podium for debate and where experts provided historical context and local community members spoke about their experiences. Our hope was to prompt historical connections for the audience and invite discussion and contribution to what is already known about the topic at hand.

Importantly, our big break came when we located the primary court documents surrounding the Carbondale Panther shoot-out at the same time several university departments and student groups were hosting a two-day event on historical radical activism at SIU. The symposium at SIU was organized by me, Robbie Lieberman, then chair of the History Department, and Jeffrey Haas, a civil rights lawyer who is noted for proving that the FBI murdered Hampton, was our guest speaker. Haas had just released his new book, *The Assassination of Fred Hampton: How the FBI and the Chicago Police Murdered a Black Panther*, with two chapters on the Carbondale shoot-out. In one of his first cases as a lawyer, Haas had represented the Carbondale 6, a name given to the Black Panthers by the local and national news after they were arrested on forty-two counts of attempted murder and aggravated assault.

The two-day event on radical activism in the local area spanned historical moments surrounding the antiwar movement in May 1969 and the active Civil Rights Movement, punctuated by the Black Panther shoot-out in November 1970. The event was widely attended, and a thought-provoking discussion emerged with significant contributions from the off-campus community. The newspaper coverage was positive, but the online responses to the news articles were not so generous. Although the local paper eventually removed the comments, they included attacks on my character and indictments of only doing "partial" history. After news coverage of the events circulated, our coproducer, who grew up in the area, returned to the courthouse to finish copying court documents. She was met with critical comments about how *778 Bullets* was an attempt to rewrite history. Finally, we met with one of the first police officers on the scene that evening in November 1970 who is now a local family lawyer. He was cold and challenged our approach to history. I explained that the objective of the project was to recount history from the perspective of the Black Panthers inside the house and from the vantage point of the members of the community who experienced the police violence because of their proximity to the event. Again, I was confronted with idea that official police records should stand in for legitimate truth and the final word. Often, there is a propensity to deny alternative narratives in contrast to official records, rendering counternarratives illegitimate while documented history remains unquestioned.

It is important to note that most of the initiating of activist engagement with the documentary camera begins well before the documentary short is available for view. From the very beginning, the concept of *778 Bullets* and participatory culture of production grew together. It began with gathering a community, gaining access and consent, including stakeholders, and creating the conditions for public dialogue as a part of the development process of the film itself. The early preproduction process of *778 Bullets* was so rich with opportunities for community engagement and documenting the black experience that the documentary quickly expanded into the Rural Civil Rights Project. The project is a long-term, multidisciplinary program encouraging new kinds of knowledge production using participatory visual and digital methods and archiving of rural civil rights history as a means of community engagement.

Next, how does documentary practice help create *sustained* engagement on the micro level, defining and redefining the concept of community as an inclusionary practice?

## Initiating the Public Space for Engagement

Since its inception at the beginning of the twentieth century, the documentary genre has been theorized as having the potential to invigorate a troubled democracy.[14] Little theoretical and conceptual clarity is available about what it means for documentary to engage the process of social change. As suggested by the editors of a recent special issue on documentary forms, functions, and impacts, "scholars need to consider more deeply the important dimensions that distinguish a film that engages and empowers publics."[15]

In my own study and practice, activist documentary has come to distinguish an impulse to conceptualize the camera as a tool for social justice in terms of the production, representation, and distribution of the documentary. In moments of political and social crises, historically, the genre has intervened in the political process in a variety of ways. In the 1930s, the Workers Film and Photo League documented massive labor strikes and protests with workers' newsreels. Recently, the genre has experienced a rebirth. Now, activists are on the Internet, documenting massive protests against the forces of economic globalization and (re)telling history. My experience with street-tape culture and social change led me to question how we documentary filmmakers and scholars could rethink our approach to understanding and telling history as a means to inclusive community engagement. I was interested in encouraging a participatory media culture throughout the documentary process and what that might mean for social change.

This Rural Civil Rights Project, in particular, is interested in drawing from a long history of community engagement and nontraditional screenings. The eight community screenings of *778 Bullets* held over the course of a year have brought together historically disparate communities within the city: public officials have joined the discussion as have those connected to the university and a growing population of people in the region concerned with issues of race. At this particular historical moment and with the exposure of systematic violence towards black men and increasing economic disparity, there is a growing unease about race and a lack of public opportunity for engagement about these issues. There is also a mounting public exigency about race that contributed to the cultural context of the community screenings of *778 Bullets*.

The February 14, 2012, screening for the Carbondale chapter of the American Association of University Women provided a lively discussion about collective memory and segregation on campus in the 1950s and 1960s. As a part of the Imagined Geographies' Voices of Southern Illinois interdisciplinary program in April 2013, the screening of the documentary involved people from the northeast-side neighborhood, the predominant African American community in Carbondale, activists, university students, and faculty. The audience members suggested that a film like *778 Bullets* contains helpful information essential to public memory and that future screenings should be made available to communities unaware of the shoot-out and the issues of racial justice that emerged from it. The suggested target audiences included city officials and law enforcement, in particular, to encourage community dialogue about historical patterns of violence between police and the predominantly black northeast-side community. The clear pattern is that Carbondale's historical pattern continues to inform contemporary racial politics. A continuing dialogue about these suggestions includes future documentary screenings programmed with a facilitator-led, restorative-justice dialogue. This framework attempts—in the words of political activist and scholar Angela Davis—to move the discourse beyond remembering and forgetting and into a space of transforming the existing social relationships.

Most of the public screenings and discussions surrounding *778 Bullets* took place around and after the verdict was handed down in the Trayvon Martin murder trail. On July 26 at the Church of the Good Shepherd, a week and a half after the verdict, in a basement with standing room only of sixty-plus people, everything I had experienced about the discourse of race in the Midwest, mostly polite silence, changed. The right combination of historical circumstances, rhetorical exigencies, and gathering of concerned citizens formed the beginning of a growing movement of people concerned about issues of racial justice in the region.

Directly after the verdict in the Martin murder trial, many in the local Carbondale community and across the country experienced a great deal of shock and had few words to express the impact of this event. This was echoed at a small rally demanding justice for Martin at the Carbondale Federal Building in late July 2013. The injustice served to Martin and the local context with the history of undocumented race relations and civil rights in Carbondale created a unique exigency for the screening of *778 Bullets*. A largely unknown but concrete example of excessive police violence based on fear and race emerged in an environment in which the emotions exposed in a highly publicized verdict began to root in a local story of Carbondale history. The systems of oppression connected across historical context and geographical place revealed themselves in discussions after the documentary on several occasions. In the process of discussing the film after the screenings, the actual act of violence on the screen stands in for a host of invisible and notable infractions concerning race in the local history. Collectively, the audience at the Church of the Good Shepherd began to piece together basic information about the shoot-out and to connect how these stories might be related to other acts of violence in Carbondale and across the nation. Most of the postscreening discussions led to a larger conversation about systematic violence toward African Americans more broadly. July 26 was one of those rare moments when people gather in physical proximity in the face of grave concern; a spontaneous call for collective organizing and for some form of public action was made. The people in the audience responded.

Much has happened since the community screening of the documentary in a church basement during late July 2013. My crew and I were invited to screen *778 Bullets* at Longbranch Coffeehouse as part of the Sustainable Living film series. Organizers of the film series were impressed with the audience turnout, which included two city council persons and other community leaders. One organizer noted, "I have been helping to host the Sustainable Film Series for three years now ... and found last night's gathering to be one of the more provocative and powerful times that we have had in the Back Room." This screening was a powerful engagement of audience members; people expressed a variety of viewpoints, and conflicting narratives were articulated. Family members of law enforcement were present and talked about the fear people had of each other and of the Black Panthers, in particular. One local community audience member tried to reinforce the common stereotypes of the Panthers. A discussion evolved about perceived and real threats, a thorny issue that plagues the Martin case as well as the fall 2013 cases of Jonathan Ferrell and Renisha McBride, who were shot and killed while trying to obtain help on a stranger's property after car accidents. The kind of discussion that emerged is not heard often among the different cultural factions of a rural small town. Finally, the City of Carbondale's Human Relations Commission hosted a screening during its monthly meeting as a means to discuss possibilities for a city-sponsored civil-engagement campaign around issues of race.

## Facilitating Social Change

The process of social change is complicated and difficult to qualify in terms of understanding patterns and describing processes and possibilities. The engagement of documentary and social change is bigger than the media screen; agitation begins before the film is fully conceptualized and continues long after the documentary screen is relevant. It involves bodies of people organizing, undocumented discussion, civic partnerships, and dozens of locally specific conditions. Central to this question is the activation of participatory media publics. The scholarly investigation of documentary and social change may require an experiential component, participatory visual and digital methods with source material for documenting processes outside the cinema screen. Without these methods, the documentary screen will continue as the primary site of agitation and leave so much of the process undocumented. Interdisciplinary engagement with critical ethnography, oral history, and communication in terms of the cultural production practice would greatly improve the broader understanding of documentary and social change.

In the case of *778 Bullets*, the documentary screen became a space of initiating conversation around historical detail, police violence, and history of discrimination locally. What has emerged from the grassroots organizing and public discussion after the documentary bought people together is a long list of unheard grievances and a desire to petition for a more equitable community. These concerns were organized under three main themes: (1) culturally sensitive education in schools, (2) race issues at the local campus, Southern Illinois University, and (3) concerns regarding race, the local police, and the court system. In a sense, the documentary screenings provided locations for people to gather around and an invitation to speak; a form of organizing took shape from the bodies available to take actions beyond the screening and the resources offered to that process.

Thomas Waugh's *Show Us Life: Toward a History and Aesthetics of the Committed Documentary* suggests committed documentary "attempt[s] to act, to intervene ... as films made by activists speaking to specific publics to bring about specific political goals."[16] Thus, I am arguing for the framework for guiding our understanding of documentary and social change, considering these dimensions:

(1) Social-change documentary informs political discourse bigger than the documentary itself.
(2) Social-change documentary intervenes in the process of transformation by facilitating action beyond the mere viewing of the documentary.
(3) A documentary is effective when it is connected in some way to an action focused in the present.
(4) Documentary media function to open up a space for participatory media culture and collective political action.
(5) Finally, as Nancy Fraser suggests, social justice is both a process of cultural recognition and economic redistribution.[17]

These dimensions of documentary engagement privilege the process of social change that requires a multi-modal method of study.

In the case of *778 Bullets*, the participatory historical documentary functions as a platform for public discussion and political intervention and does not stand in for it. The production process, in unexpected ways, opened up opportunities for creating structures, facilitating action beyond the documentary screening. This film has given rise to the Racial Justice Coalition, an activist community, organizing with other community groups, such as the Concerned Citizens of Carbondale and Nonviolent Carbondale. It is too soon to tell how this newly formed organizing around race will impact the resource inequities in Carbondale or increase the community acknowledgment and acceptance of historical voices that are largely ignored. I take comfort in the words of Margaret Nesbit, who first gave us access to the Black Panther story. While driving her to an interview with a regional news team reporting on the forty-third anniversary of the shoot-out, she mentioned, "I have not seen anything like this before." After a short pause, I asked, "In what way?" Without thinking she simply replied, "People are moving, things are getting done."

The relationship between contemporary documentary and social change is potentially promising as new spaces of civic engagement begin to flourish from and with the genre. Documenting the black experience is a critical part of this project. Additionally, the range of social change and the engagement opportunities for documentary span much more of the process than is typically addressed by scholars: from the inception of the idea in preproduction through and beyond distribution of the film. Yet, most documentary scholarship conceptualizes the thing we can get a hold of—the screen—as the motor of engagement. If we take the question of documentary and social change seriously, we need to rethink the primarily textual and traditional historical methods used to document the experience, especially since activist history is only partially archived, if at all. This is an urgent task in a world of new-media convergence and participatory production; issues of engagement and social change become a more primary concern. Interdisciplinary work in fields like cultural studies, communication, and critical anthropology could lend valuable insights in how to understand documentary as a cultural practice with patterns of influence.

I made *778 Bullets* with the intention of engaging privilege and historical memory because I was inspired by the possibilities for using the genre as a means to public deliberation and social change. *778 Bullets* has screened in over twenty festivals in major media markets, such as Los Angeles and New York City, played at notable festivals, such as the San Francisco and San Diego Black Film Festivals, screened at prestigious venues, such as Anthology Film Archive in New York City, and has been awarded two top documentary awards. California Newsreel, which is the home of the largest African American civil rights moving image archive in the country, has also picked up the short for distribution. From this production emerged a commitment to a larger project engaging the connections among theory, history, and practice as means to community engagement. This practice can be an essential contribution to documenting and archiving the black experience of rural civil rights, an oral history that threatens to pass along with the lives of those who experienced it. I would like to continue to expand the narrative agency of those whose stories are being told and think creatively about participatory elements of the project as the Rural Civil Rights Project develops.

What has been emerging from the community screening of *778 Bullets* has been the best teacher for my scholarly insights about documentary and social change. From my own practical experience, engaging social change with the documentary camera means entering a discussion that one does not control; one must sometimes be patient and work with the flow of the political climate. In these instances, I am translating and reading the rhetorical exigency more than I am willing a documentary into existence. There is a timing to social-change documentary that is undeniable, as I suppose there is for all films, but the stakes for documentary trying to engage the process of social change are often much higher compared to a concern for critical or box-office success.

Whenever I engage my media production work, informed theoretically and historically, the process provides an insight into how my academic biases and positions can be influenced by the experience of my arts practice. Yes, theory and history can shape how we approach art, but the documentation of production practice should shape how we understand documentary theory. There is no more essential moment to ground documentary theory in production practice as when issues of social change are of central concern.

## Notes

1. Rabinowitz, "Wreckage Upon Wreckage," 119–37.
2. Ellis, *Documentary Idea*, 78–79.
3. Ruby, "Speaking For," 50–52.
4. Duncan, "*778 Bullets* Raises Broad Discussion."
5. Gubrium and Harper, *Participatory Visual*.
6. Gatchet and Cloud, "David, Goliath, and the Black Panthers," 7–12.
7. Bush, "Civil Rights Movement," 42–67; Hall, "Long Civil Rights Movement," 1233–63; Umoja, "Repression Breeds Resistance," 3–19.
8. Hoerl, "Mario Van Peebles's," 219.
9. Van Deburg, *New Day in Babylon*.
10. Hoerl, "Panthers," 211.
11. Onion, "Map That Lincoln Used."
12. Gubrium and Harper, *Digital Methods*, 31.
13. Ginsburg, "Parallax Effect," 65.
14. Barnouw, *Documentary*.
15. Nisbet and Aufderheide, "Documentary Film," 450.
16. Waugh, *Show Us Life*, xiii.
17. Fraser, *Justice Interruptus*, 14.

## Works Cited

Barnouw, Eric. *Documentary: A History of the Non-Fiction Film.* New York: Oxford University Press, 1993.
Bush, Rod. "The Civil Rights Movement and the Continuing Struggle for the Redemption of America." *Social Justice* 30 (2003): 42–67.

Duncan, Dustin. "*778 Bullets* Raises Broad Discussion." *The Southern*, August 23, 2013. Accessed October 23, 2013. http://m.thesouthern.com/news/local/bullets-raises-broad-discussion/article_4e48ceb4–0baa–11e3–8c68–0019bb2963f4.html?mobile_touch= true.

Ellis, Jack C. *The Documentary Idea: A Critical History of English-Language Documentary Film and Video*. Englewood Cliffs, NJ: Prentice Hall, 1989.

Fraser, Nancy. *Justice Interruptus*. New York: Routledge, 1997.

Gatchet, Amanda Davis, and Dana L. Cloud. "David, Goliath, and the Black Panthers: The Paradox of the Oppressed Militant in the Rhetoric of Self-Defense." *Journal of Communication Inquiry* 37 (2012): 7–12.

Ginsburg, Faye. "The Parallax Effect: The Impact of Aboriginal Media on Ethnographic Film." *Visual Anthropology Review* 11 (1995): 64–76.

Gubrium, Aline, and Krista Harper. *Participatory Visual and Digital Methods*. Walnut Creek, CA: Left Coast Press, 2013.

Hall, Jacquelyn Dowd. "The Long Civil Rights Movement and Political Uses of the Past." *Journal of American History* 91 (2005): 1233–63.

Hoerl, Kristen. "Mario Van Peebles's Panther and Popular Memories of the Black Panther Party." *Critical Studies in Media Communication* 24 (2007): 206–27.

Nisbet, Matthew C., and Patricia Aufderheide. "Documentary Film: Towards a Research Agenda on Forms, Functions and Impacts." *Mass Communication and Society* 12 (2009): 450–56.

Onion, Rebecca. "The Map That Lincoln Used to See the Reach of Slavery." *Slate Group*, September 4, 2013. http://www.slate.com/blogs/the_vault/2013/09/04/abraham_lincoln_the_president_used_this_map_to_see_where_slavery_was_strongest.html.

Rabinowitz, Paula. "Wreckage Upon Wreckage: History, Documentary and the Ruins of Memory." *History and Theory* 32 (1993): 119–37.

Ruby, Jay. "Speaking for, Speaking about, Speaking with, or Speaking Alongside—An Anthropological and Documentary Dilemma." *Visual Anthropology Review* 7 (1991): 50–67.

Umoja, Akinyele Omowale. "Repression Breeds Resistance: The Black Liberation Army and the Radical Legacy of the Black Panther Party." In *Liberation, Imagination, and the Black Panther Party: A New Look at the Panthers and Their Legacy*, edited by Kathleen Cleaver and George Katsiaficas, 3–19. New York: Routledge, 2001.

Van Deburg, William L. *New Day in Babylon: The Black Power Movement and American Culture, 1965–1975*. Chicago: University of Chicago Press, 1992.

Waugh, Thomas. *Show Us Life: Toward a History and Aesthetics of the Committed Documentary*. Metuchen, NJ: Scarecrow, 1984.

# PART IV

# AND BEYOND: THE CONTEMPORARY BLACK STRUGGLE

# Sundown Nation

## *Living in the Aftermath of an American Holocaust*

### DAVID ROSSIAKY

Only a short distance from where I wrote this essay in Carbondale, Illinois, is the small town of Anna, Illinois, where no African Americans own residences. It is central to note that this is not by chance or strange coincidence; African Americans do not own residences in Anna *by design*. The reason for the absence of an African American population in this small, quaint Illinois town is shocking. In November 1909, Anna Pelley, a twenty-four-year-old white woman, was found dead in an alley in Cairo, thirty-five miles south of her hometown of Anna. Pelley had been strangled to death, and her clothes had been ripped from her body. Based solely on the tracking of bloodhounds, an African American man named Will James was arrested for the crime. Shortly after his arrest, lynch mobs from Pelley's hometown gathered at the jail where James was being held, with the intent of ensuring that "justice" was served. In an attempt to protect their prisoner, police secretly escorted the suspect across southern Illinois, seeking the safety of a larger law-enforcement department. They were discovered en route and transported back to Cairo, where a mob numbering in the thousands awaited. The sound of enthusiastic cheers and delighted singing filled the air as the horde hanged James, unloaded a hail of gunfire into his dying body, and dragged him through the streets. Before burning his mutilated corpse, the lynch mob cut out his heart. James's severed head was later displayed on a pole in a park in Cairo. Still thirsting for blood, the crowd returned to Anna and neighboring Jonesboro to drive out all of the African Americans residing in those towns.[1]

It is sad that this grotesque and inhumane spectacle of lynching and the subsequent removal of blacks from entire townships are not isolated events. The forceful eradication of African Americans from their homes and communities took place independently in every region of the United States between 1864 and 1920.[2] Film director Marco Williams calls this *banishment*, and Elliot Jaspin, author of *Buried in the Bitter Waters*, describes it as *racial cleansing*.[3] Additionally, sociology professor emeritus James W. Loewen discusses these events in his book by the same name as the rise of *sundown towns*. Regardless of the term used to describe this phenomenon, in each instance the pattern was the same: there was "an alleged crime against a white woman, the lynching of a black man, and the expulsion of the black community."[4] This essay examines the role of sundown towns in the transition from formal to modern racism in the United States. Beginning with the aforementioned banishment pattern, this essay explores the ways in which banishments typically unfolded, including discussions of both the physical and mental tolls exacted on those immediately affected in cases of racial exile. Of particular focus are Williams's documentary film, *Banished: How Whites Drove Blacks Out of Town* (2006), and its significance as a historical text and uniqueness of perspective and scope in documenting the black experience in the United States. This is followed by a chronology of how these events sent ripples cascading through time by means of property theft, government programs, media coverage, social norms, and the very language we use to discuss racism in the United States, which remain prevalent and relevant to this day.

Prior to discussing the aforementioned points, it is first important to explain the differences between formal and modern racism. While the formal system of slavery in the United States came to an official end in the nineteenth century, the formal and legalized system of racism did not. Throughout the twentieth century, institutional racism transformed continuously, weaving an unbroken thread through history that connects the practice of slavery to the realities of twenty-first-century America. This was possible because racism became a prominent social institution, or a learned system of behaviors and accepted norms. In this way, racism reacts to and interacts with societal trends, transforming as necessary to facilitate its continued existence. As this essay demonstrates, formal racism, which was once overt—acceptable to manifest physically and publicly—morphed slowly into modern racism, which is more often covert—it must be manifested privately and subtly. At the time of the rise of sundown towns and the years immediately following, evidence regarding their establishment and existence was hidden. Over time, the existence of sundown towns and the memories of their creation were not merely ignored but nearly forgotten entirely. As this essay illustrates, *Banished* brings to light that this process actively continues to this day, making it all the more important to discuss sundown towns openly and honestly.

Before discussing banishment, it is imperative to first examine the inciting allegations and lynching. Suspected crimes against white women, most commonly allegations of rape, were historically used to incite frenzied white mobs for a number of reasons. By gaining an understanding of the underlying motivations behind lynching and banishment, other than the broad concepts of unadulterated hate and ignorance, a deeper comprehension of banishments can be achieved.

The alleged crimes against white women, as precursors for the expulsion of black communities, are important because they speak to two of white men's greatest fears after the abolition of slavery in the United States. First, it is well understood that white men, particularly slave owners, were completely free under the law to rape black women. When slavery was abolished, white men were angered at losing this legal power over black women. Additionally, widely held stereotypes about black men portrayed them as sexually repressed brutes, which fueled the fears held by white men who imagined that all white women would be unsafe once black men were free to act upon their repressed desires.[5] As such, an alleged crime against a white woman was all that was necessary to instigate a lynching and subsequent banishment. Whites were wholly convinced by the allegations alone and rarely, if ever, conducted formal investigations to confirm or deny whether the African American male suspect had actually committed the crime. Such was the case during the 1908 riot in Springfield, Illinois, as well as Forsyth County, Georgia's banishment of the black community in 1912.[6]

Lynching, in cases of banishment, acted as *the* catalyst for the black community's forceful eradication. In the three-stage banishment model, lynching functioned as a means to instigate a mob and to introduce violence into the process. In the minds of whites, this violence was legitimized, as they believed it was retaliation for violence perpetuated by blacks against whites. In this way, whites circumvented the legal system that was in place to handle just such a scenario. If a crime was committed, the alleged perpetrator should be judged and, if found guilty, sentenced by this system. By straying from this formal structure in cases where African Americans were the alleged perpetrators, whites were making a clear distinction between themselves and nonwhites through the process of *othering*.[7]

Othering was crucially important to banishments, as it was the process by which whites made the distinction between *us* and *them*. Considering the prevalence of Christianity in the United States during this time period, othering was a necessary step for whites to take if they wished to banish African

American communities. Christianity firmly holds that all people are created in the image of God, and as such, it is extremely important to treat fellow humans with respect and kindness. Positioning blacks as savage brutes allowed whites to circumvent moral imperatives, because, after all, they were dealing with animals, not human beings. This is but one remnant of legalized slavery in the United States that is clearly articulated in the U.S. Constitution's three-fifths compromise. In this way, whites systematically and formally used legal and religious systems to other nonwhite people as less than humane, further legitimizing spectacle lynching, banishment, and mob law in the minds of whites across the country.

The prevalence of lynching in the United States became so normalized that lynchings in Georgia unfolded in the same manner as lynchings in Missouri. In *Making Whiteness: The Culture of Segregation in the South, 1890–1940*, Grace Elizabeth Hale describes the formula of a spectacle lynching:

> The well-choreographed spectacle opened with a chase or a jail attack, followed rapidly by the public identification of the captured African American by the alleged white victim or the victim's relatives, announcement of the upcoming event to draw the crowd, and selection and preparation of the site. The main event then began with a period of mutilation—often including emasculation—and torture to extract confessions and entertain the crowd, and built to a climax of slow burning, hanging, and/or shooting to complete the killing. The finale consisted of frenzied souvenir gathering and display of the body and the collected parts.[8]

Here we see not only the first two steps of the banishment process once again integrated into a formal system but also that the dehumanization of the victim(s) of the lynching, symbolically through emasculation and the gathering of souvenirs, including the commodification of parts of the body itself, was institutionally required as well. Thus, lynching was an integral link in the chain of events leading to banishment for a number of reasons: It created the frenetic mobs necessary to accomplish a banishing, reinforced othering through evasion of the legal system, and, finally, introduced violence as an effective agent of swift action, circumventing moral imperatives.

In 1906, a series of allegations of black men raping white women swept across Forsyth County, Georgia. Relying on weak evidence, the police arrested several suspects, which resulted in the formation of lynch mobs that only dissolved their plans to storm the jail after the intervention of state troops. Eventually, a young white girl was raped and murdered by an African American man named Ernest Knox, who admitted that he had committed the crimes. Although Knox had confessed and was in police custody, four more African Americans were inexplicably arrested and charged with partaking in the crime:

Ed Collins, Oscar Daniel, Trussie Daniel, and Rob Edwards. Again, a mob formed, and police whisked away Knox to another holding cell. Unfortunately, the four other suspects were left to the mob. Edwards was mutilated, shot, and killed, and his lifeless body was hung on a telephone pole for all to see.[9]

In this real-life example, the functions of lynching in the banishment model are clearly demonstrated. Following allegations of crimes against white women, the procedures of the legal system were circumvented when arrests were made prematurely. After one alleged perpetrator, Knox, confessed and was subsequently arrested for committing the crime, more arrests were made unnecessarily, working to further other African Americans from their white neighbors. Later, the lynching followed the spectacle model, including mutilation and the public display of the body. The lynching, carried out by a mob, demonstrates an escalation of violence that would continue through the banishing. Finally, Edwards was dehumanized, both during the lynching and afterwards when his body was hoisted into the air as one might lift up a recently caught fish to pose for a photograph. Chilling as it is, this comparison is apt, as it also describes the pride whites felt after the lynching, as well as the gruesome pleasure they derived from the spectacle and their desire to repeat or continue the event.

Continuing the above account of Forsyth County's 1906 banishment, Knox and Daniel were both convicted on the same day, and it is pertinent to note that "between them the two juries deliberated a total of sixty-two minutes before announcing their verdicts." The fact that the deliberations were so short demonstrates that the white jury believed black lives were cheap, a manifestation of the dehumanization of blacks perpetuated by the dominant ideology. On the night of Knox's and Daniel's convictions, the banishment began. White citizens of Forsyth County went door to door, demanding that African American residents immediately leave the town or die. Churches were burned, and homes served as targets for those with guns. Terror was the weapon of choice, as demonstrated at one African American home where no one answered the front door: "[The white mob] tied the family's cow to a stake in the yard, piled wood and brush around it, and burned the animal alive." Taking only what they could carry, the African American population fled Forsyth County, leaving jobs, property, and any remaining hopes of equality behind.[10]

In Forsyth, it was rumored that African Americans had threatened to dynamite the town in retaliation to a prospective lynching—a typical example of fearmongering preceding a banishment; however, after a lynching finally occurred, it was actually a white mob that used dynamite to destroy a black home, demonstrating the differences between how violence would be tolerated when perpetuated by whites versus nonwhites.[11] In 1921, white mobs in Tulsa,

Oklahoma, seized airplanes and dropped dynamite onto the African American community, making it the first "place in the contiguous United States to undergo aerial bombardment."[12] In 1913, three blacks—Ophelia Blake, Frank Smith, and Alex Graham—"decided it was safe to move back to Cumming [Georgia]. At 3 o'clock in the morning on February 19, 1913, a series of explosions shook the town. Someone had planted dynamite under their homes." While there were no fatalities, it became embarrassingly clear that Cumming was anything but safe.[13]

The extreme destruction employed in cases of banishment was so violent and so public it seems inconceivable that evidence of these events could be hidden to any substantial degree, but when the black population was completely decimated in one town after another, only members of the white mobs remained to chronicle what had happened, and they can certainly be said to have had an agenda in the little writing they did on the subject. In fact, the majority of what we know about this American holocaust comes from the oral tradition, passed down through African American families from one generation to the next. Often these stories are corroborated through all-but-forgotten newspaper articles paired with census data.

Importantly, documentarian Williams uses *Banished* as a net to catch these scattered fragments of history and assembles them like puzzle pieces to provide a larger and more cohesive portrait of this chapter in American history than can any existing individual source. With documentary film as his vehicle, Williams captures the devastation of banishments in an immediately accessible form that emotionally describes not only his findings but also the difficult search required to uncover these well-hidden facts.

In *Banished*, Williams examines three communities in which banishments took place: Forsyth County, Georgia; Pierce City, Missouri; and Harrison, Arkansas. In each case, Williams first describes the events leading up to the banishment of the black community, relying on archived newspaper articles and census data. These timelines are then corroborated and elaborated upon by journalists, researchers, and descendants of those who survived the banishments. Finally, Williams follows modern-day efforts made toward various forms of reconciliation as well as the obstacles, complications, and indifference impeding their realization.

Visiting Forsyth, Williams follows the struggles of the descendants of Strickland family members, who were forced to abandon their homes in the 1912 racial expulsion, wherein more African Americans were forcibly displaced than in any other known banishment.[14] The Strickland family returns to the Forsyth County property once owned by their ancestors to discover beautifully maintained luxury homes worth substantial sums of money, all built on land taken under duress through violence. In fact, the loss of property is one of the most visible and enduring consequences of African American banishment.

Jaspin makes an appearance in Williams's *Banished* and discusses his research: "With the black-owned land in Forsyth County, what you see is a sale from somebody to a black landowner, and then you don't see the next deed; there's no sale from Joe Smith, the black landowner, to John Doe, who is white. As you go back down the chain of title, what you find is that at some point you run into a hearing for adverse possession."[15]

Law professor Alfred Brophy further elaborates:

> Adverse possession is the way that people have of taking title to property without buying it, and it's of great relevance in these banishment cases because as soon as the African American owners are off the property, some white folks or other folks come on and start using it as though it's theirs and then, after a period of time, it is theirs. And so what you have is this combination of violence with the legal system: violence to run folks off and then the legal system to change title.[16]

The lasting economic consequences of what is ultimately property theft are substantial. While returning ownership of stolen land to African American descendants of banishment seems an impractical solution, certainly compensation for the present value of the land is one possibility. After the passing of one hundred years, the value of the homes and land that were seized from African Americans has doubled and redoubled several times over. It is important to remember that this is land that could have been passed down within a family for generations were it not stolen from its black owners.

Even this is difficult, however, to compare with the lasting emotional consequences of banishment. In many cases, survivors of banishments left behind not just their homes and property but their dead. When the Strickland family was banished from Forsyth County, they were forced to leave behind the family burial plot located on their property. A particularly painful moment in *Banished* depicts the descendants of the Strickland family returning to Forsyth County in the twenty-first century to visit the gravesites of their ancestors, only to find them on white-owned land, unkempt, littered with debris, and in plain sight of a Confederate-flag license plate, which is in stark contrast to the beautifully preserved residential expanses covering the rest of their former property.[17]

In addition to the Strickland family, Williams also documents descendants of banished African Americans living in Pierce City. There, the filmmaker interviews James Brown, whose family managed to survive the 1901 banishment. Brown describes how his family was nearly slaughtered as they fled from their neighbors: "My dad always told me that the family was run out of Pierce City.... They escaped when the bullets were coming through the house. They went to the cellar and then from there they crawled through the grass—hid by the well. Bullets were hitting the well, but then they ran off into the woods." Brown's family ran to Springfield, Missouri, where with other survivors, they once again found themselves starting from scratch. Former Pierce City Mayor Carol S. Hirsch corroborates Brown's report: "[T]he mob formed at the jail. They came down the street. They formed a line, they said that they stood shoulder to shoulder and just fired across [the railroad tracks] into what we believe was the black community.... It must have been horrible."[18]

Murray Bishoff, managing editor of the *Monett Times*, explains that there is no direct evidence in Pierce City that a banishment ever occurred, save for an archived newspaper article from 1901 and the lack of a black community today. The article's headline again confirms the sundown-town formula: "HEINOUS CRIME AT PIERCE CITY, a Young Lady Assaulted and Brutally Murdered. HER THROAT CUT FROM EAR TO EAR. Mob Law the Result. One Negro, Will Godley, Lynched and Two Others, Pete Hampton and Frank Godley, Riddled with Bullets and Their Bodies Burned in the House Where They Fell."[19] Importantly, the implication of "Heinous Crime at Pierce City" is in reference only to the assault and murder of a presumed white woman, which, certainly, is heinous regardless of race, but the headline conveys that the following mob *law*, consisting of lynching, murder, arson, terrorism, and banishment, is not intended to be described by the word *heinous*. Instead, those acts are reported as a natural and justifiable course of events. The fact that there remains no African American community in Pierce City today nor any easily accessible record that the 1901 attacks occurred at all demonstrates that banishments have a lasting effect that continues to be problematic in the twenty-first century.

Williams also follows the story of Charles Brown, who struggles to exhume and relocate the remains of his great-grandfather James Cobb. Cobb died before the Pierce City banishment, and in the chaos of the moment, his family was unable to stop and consider relocating his remains as they fled for their lives to Springfield. When Cobb's wife and immediate family members later passed, they were buried in Springfield, where his descendants, including Brown, remain today. Brown, based on an understandable feeling of being unwelcome in Pierce City and a desire to have his great-grandfather buried with the rest of his family, undertook an exhaustive investigation to locate James Cobb's unmarked burial plot. He is met with strong reluctance and flat-out refusal from Pierce City administrators at every step, turning what could have been a reconciliation into a drawn-out and painful process that did less to bring closure than to echo the dominant ideology of Pierce City in 1901.

While Pierce City and other sundown towns do not have monuments, placards, or memorials acknowledging the historical events that took place there, sundown towns commonly did employ signs at city limits to make the residents' endorsement of violence and terrorism against minorities perfectly clear. These signs varied in form, but the message was always the same. Specifically, signs across thirty-one states displayed such text as "Whites only within city limits after dark," "Don't let the sun go down on you in [insert name of town]," and "If you can read, you'd better run. If you can't read, you'd better run anyway."[20] Other towns used sirens to terrorize African Americans, sounding them to inform nonwhites that they were no longer welcome after a certain hour of the day. For example, in Villa Grove, Illinois, the siren sounded daily at 6:00 p.m. to alert African Americans to leave the city limits. This practice continued until 1998.[21]

The driving out of African American citizens was not limited to the South or to isolated areas. "Illinois, for example, had 671 towns and cities with more than 1,000 people in 1970, of which 475, or 71 percent, were all-white in census after census—almost all of these 475 were sundown towns." In the local region around Carbondale, confirmed sundown towns include Ava, Anna, Belknap, Benton, Campbell Hill, Carterville, Christopher, Dongola, Goreville, Herrin, Johnston City, Jonesboro, Karnak, Pinckneyville, Sesser, Steeleville, Tamaroa, West Frankfort, Wolf Lake, and Zeigler, and several others are suspected but not unequivocally confirmed.[22] That this pattern can be seen all over the United States, in Northern and Southern states alike, indicates that the mindset of the terrorists behind the banishments was, in fact, in line with this country's pervasive ideology.

Newspapers and other publications from sundown communities reflect the sentiments of many of the white inhabitants and reinforce the institution of sundown towns. Two such excerpts demonstrate the mindsets of at least the authors, if not a majority of the citizens of these towns as well. The first was written by the editor of the *Cairo Bulletin*. The premise of the article is that the citizens of Cairo, Illinois, were dissatisfied by the fact that from 1910 to 1920, the census showed a population gain of only 655 residents: "Disappointment was expressed by some that the figure was not larger but those who knew how the population was made up were gratified at the showing. It is estimated that more than 2,000 Negroes have left Cairo since the last census, making the increase in the white population nearly 2,700 people."[23]

Of a failed attempt to banish African Americans from Hall County, Georgia, Jaspin relates, "In an editorial, the *Gainesville News* deplored the attacks." While the intention may have been to speak out against the attacks, it seems to me that the effect was, nonetheless, racist. For example, the article states, "The law-abiding white man and the law-abiding Negro have no trouble. The

Negro with any sense does not have to be told his place—he already knows it and will keep it. The sentiment of the people is clear on the question and law and order must, and will, prevail." Jaspin goes on to note that the attacks continued unhindered.[24]

It is important to note that an examination of the history of banishments in the United States shows that what is said is just as enlightening as what is not said. The current ideology insists that with his 1863 Emancipation Proclamation, President Abraham Lincoln freed the slaves and succeeded in putting the country on the path to equal opportunity for all. Any minor imperfections in this monumental accomplishment were later reconciled during the Civil Rights Movement in the 1960s, as evidenced by the election of Barack Obama as President of the United States in 2008. Although this fairy tale is certainly more pleasant than reality, much is left unsaid, making it dangerous in its implications and far less enriching than the truth. That this ideological view of the past is able to exist at all is a symptom of historical omissions rather than a cause, making the rapid dissemination of information in the highly engaging and emotional form of documentary films, such as *Banished*, all the more vital to shining a spotlight on the misleading texts that have existed for so long.

Take, for example, *100 Years of Progress: The Centennial History of Anna*, a book published in 1954 by the Anna Centennial Committee. Bear in mind that Anna, Illinois, provides the backdrop for the banishment described in the opening of this essay. Remarkably, *100 Years of Progress*, an authoritative five-hundred-page volume on the history of Anna, which covers everything from the process for choosing horses for funeral processions to the day that Sunlit Bakery installed its first bread-slicing machine, conveniently fails to mention the 1909 banishment of the black community.[25]

For a book that claims to be the most complete and definitive historical record of Anna, these omissions are not just insulting, they play an active role in propelling the legacy of sundown towns into the future. In compiling and editing this watered-down historical text, the Anna Centennial Committee made a conscious decision to exclude references, implicit or explicit, to the most important event in the town's history. This is not mere ignorance or even disregard but the continued participation in and endorsement of the institution of racial discrimination in the United States. With that in mind, this audacious and offensive excerpt appears in the book's dedication, written by Howard Lam, chairman of the Anna Centennial Committee:

> May we as citizens of this community, both past and present, pause for just a moment in our thinking and try to recall some of the people who have been in some small way responsible for the privileges we now enjoy. As we think back

over the years, many memories will undoubtedly come to our minds—some happy, others sad. But, regardless of our concern at the present time, they all have a purpose in this theme of life.[26]

When Lam discusses "the privileges we now enjoy," the "we" he is referring to are, of course, the all-white citizens of Anna, and the "privileges" include the sustained dominance of the all-encompassing *white privilege* that remains a powerful societal force today. Viewed through this lens, the "people who have been in some small way responsible" can only be the lynch mob in Cairo in 1909 along with the white citizens who participated through their tacit compliance. This chilling sentiment is further evoked in the book's foreword, written by Mary H. Kent, one of the book's editors:

ONE HUNDRED YEARS OF PROGRESS, the history of Anna and her people, is now presented with the hope that it may bring its readers to a higher appreciation of the character and worth of the men and women who conquered the west and planted here the institutions which we enjoy today.

As the story of 100 years of growth and progress of the City of Anna unfolds, may the achievements of its citizens inspire the youth of this generation to write an even more glorious history in the future!

We wish to express our appreciation to the citizens of Anna who so willingly aided in accumulating the materials for this survey. Without their assistance this story could not have been written. Their fine spirit of cooperation is ample proof that the characteristics manifested by the early settlers of this community are still dominant in this community today.[27]

Only a precious few historical documents concerning the rise of sundown towns were written during the time period of their establishment, and the overwhelming majority of them were produced by whites. Many of these first-hand accounts have simply been lost to time, while others have been actively hidden or destroyed. For these reasons, texts written in recent years are especially significant, as they reintroduce banishments into public discourse and build a foundation for further research and discussion. Williams's *Banished* is of particular importance, as it literally allows the viewer to see and hear the stories of the families directly affected by banishments and is most certainly the most extensive text on the topic that comes from an African American perspective.

Unsurprising, the surge of banishments in the early twentieth century coincides with the rebirth of the Ku Klux Klan. Williams investigates this in a town where the KKK continues to maintain an active presence: Harrison, Arkansas, an unusual town in that its black citizens were actually banished twice, in both 1905 and 1909.[28] In an interview with Bob Scott, a white retiree who moved to Harrison, Williams asks what it is about Harrison that led him to retire there: "For two reasons; the low cost of living ... and probably more importantly than anything else is lack of blacks."[29] The two men share a prolonged and uncomfortable pause before Scott embarrassingly attempts to justify his answer.

Williams next visits the Harrison Chamber of Commerce, meeting with Layne Wheeler, who, in reference to the town's banishments, comes to the defense of Harrison and its residents, employing the common but flawed argument that "even in those days, it was a small percent of the population that was involved in that. And so while we want to acknowledge that, acknowledge the hurt of that, we know that we have moved past that, and that's not the community that we are today." In reality, while perhaps only a small group of Harrison citizens directly participated in the banishment of the black community, they never could have succeeded or continued to walk free without the consent of the majority of the town's white citizens, especially with two banishments occurring within the time span of only a few years. As to the second point, that Harrison continues to afford the Ku Klux Klan a comfortable home to this day, speaks against any notion that the people of Harrison have "moved past" the ideology of the early 1900s.

Williams asks, "The Klan is an easy target for blame, but are they really the cause of [Harrison's] negative image, or a symptom of it?" The Confederate flag waving outside the Harrison Chamber of Commerce is certainly not deterring the KKK. A point of heated contention, the Confederate flag is often defended as representing "heritage, not hate." It is important to remember, however, that both the traditional South and the United States as a whole share in a heritage *of* hate, built literally on the backs of the enslaved. The Confederate flag remains significant because the Confederate states seceded specifically to continue the institution of slavery. Those who continue to romanticize the Confederacy frequently argue that the seceding states were primarily concerned with state's rights. While there is truth to this claim, it is also misleading, because the cause of secession was the state's right *to endorse slavery*, contention over the Fugitive Slave Law of 1850 notwithstanding. This is clearly evidenced in the following excerpts from the Mississippi and Texas declarations of secession, which are two of four such documents; the other two existing declarations, from Georgia and South Carolina, use similar language and also make the ties between secession and slavery abundantly clear.

The second paragraph of *A Declaration of the Immediate Causes Which Induce and Justify the Secession of the State of Mississippi from the Federal Union* makes the link:

> Our position is thoroughly identified with the institution of slavery—the greatest material interest of the world. Its labor supplies the product which constitutes by

far the largest and most important portions of commerce of the earth. These products are peculiar to the climate verging on the tropical regions, and by an imperious law of nature, none but the black race can bear exposure to the tropical sun. These products have become necessities of the world, and a blow at slavery is a blow at commerce and civilization. That blow has been long aimed at the institution, and was at the point of reaching its consummation. There was no choice left us but submission to the mandates of abolition, or a dissolution of the Union, whose principles had been subverted to work out our ruin.[30]

*A Declaration of the Causes Which Impel the State of Texas to Secede from the Federal Union* echoes Mississippi's:

In all the non-slave-holding States, in violation of that good faith and comity which should exist between entirely distinct nations, the people have formed themselves into a great sectional party, now strong enough in numbers to control the affairs of each of those States, based upon an unnatural feeling of hostility to these Southern States and their beneficent and patriarchal system of African slavery, proclaiming the debasing doctrine of equality of all men, irrespective of race or color—a doctrine at war with nature, in opposition to the experience of mankind, and in violation of the plainest revelations of Divine Law. They demand the abolition of negro slavery throughout the confederacy, the recognition of political equality between the white and negro races, and avow their determination to press on their crusade against us, so long as a negro slave remains in these States.[31]

With this evidence in mind, it becomes vitally telling when contemporary discourse suggests a historical separation between race and American political policies. In 2010, for example, with a glaring lack of regard for historical significance, Virginia Governor Bob McDonnell declared April to be Confederate History Month, audaciously omitting any relationship between the Confederacy and slavery.[32] When viewed critically, this omission is a modern adaptation of that made by the aforementioned Anna Centennial Committee, again an endorsement in support of racial inequality in the United States now and in the future through the malicious decision to document only a portion of our shared history in such a consciously misleading fashion. Political writer Ann Pietrangelo notes, "We have made incredible strides, both socially and legally, but much work remains for civil rights advocates. But let's not kid ourselves. The bigots never really went away, they just got quieter when polite society forced the issue."[33] In this way, even pushes against institutional racism can fuel a resurgence of that same institution, making it all the more important to be attentive and honest when working toward and discussing racial equality in America.

As Jaspin and Williams explain, in 1987 Dean Carter, a citizen of Forsyth County, organized a brotherhood march to be held on Dr. Martin Luther King, Jr.'s holiday with the distinct goal of demonstrating that the racist mentality held by citizens of the region was a thing of the past and that all people were indeed welcome within the community. On the day of the event, Carter and the marchers were quickly reminded that racism was alive and well when an assemblage of white separatist groups, including the KKK, the Arian Nation, and the White Brotherhood, interrupted their demonstration. Members of the white-supremacist organizations overran the marchers' police escorts, forcing the marchers onto a bus in order to reach the end of their route.[34] As the footage from *Banished* demonstrates, the hateful white separatists carried the Confederate flag while disrupting the peaceful march, indicating that they perfectly understood its symbolic meaning. Images of this nature should serve to remind the Harrison Chamber of Commerce, as well as other states and the United States as a whole, that the Confederate flag is the embodiment of white supremacy.

Williams also explores the twisted connection between the KKK and Christianity, particularly in relation to the burning of crosses as an act of terror.[35] Briefly referenced in Texas's declaration of secession, this also relates directly to the African American critique of the myth of America as the Christian Nation: "If whites had a difficult time discerning the contradictions in the myth of the Christian Nation, blacks did not. If America was really a Christian nation, blacks pointed out, how could the institution of slavery possibly survive?"[36]

By the time the Great Depression occurred, African Americans who had been driven out of their homes had congregated into ghettos in the largest urban centers of the United States. These Americans clearly had been suffering from their own Great Depression for some time already. At that time, the New Deal policies enacted to pull the country out of its depression further strengthened the ties between race and class. In *When Affirmative Action Was White: An Untold History of Racial Inequality in Twentieth-Century America*, Ira Katznelson implores us, "Imagine two countries, one the richest in the world, the other amongst its most destitute. Then suppose that a global program of foreign aid transferred well over $100 billion, but to the rich nation, not the poor."[37] This is exactly what happened within the United States in the 1930s and 1940s, as Katznelson argues at length, as a result of Social Security, the labor laws of the New Deal and Fair Deal, and the GI Bill, all of which worked towards equality on paper but in reality further oppressed African Americans.

On a fundamental level, these government programs were designed to build up the American economy by strengthening and empowering the middle class. However, because African American communities were by and large forced from their homes and relegated to urban slums, the constitution of the upper and middle economic classes became overwhelmingly white, inextricably tying race to class. African Americans in the 1940s found themselves essentially right back where they were in 1865, having now been both literally and figuratively banished to the lowest level of American society. Through this link between race and class, the government policies enacted to strengthen the middle class, and thereby the economy at large, did so at the expense of the lower class, consisting primarily of minorities.

For as important and far-reaching as these issues are for modern society, very little is being done to bring them to light. One of the most intriguing issues concerning sundown towns, and, consequently, the problem that does the most to ensure their survival, is that so few people are consciously aware of them at all. In terms of educating the public, Andrew Hacker summarizes the contemporary segregation of schools, and Jonathan Kozol has dedicated an entire book to the subject.[38] However, the most striking comments I found concerning education in relation to race were from individual teachers, and I find that their experiences speak louder than observations of the national public schooling system, as they are more tangible and offer a glimpse into the human element of the equation. Linda Ledbetter is a history teacher at Forsyth County Central High School, and in an interview, she made the following comments about educating her students about Forsyth's history:

> [She] says that if students ask her about the racial cleansing, she pretends ignorance.... When she takes fifteen or twenty minutes in her one-semester course to teach students about the county's history, she never mentions the racial cleansing. "I generally don't go into the rape and all," Ledbetter says, "because I don't want to foster any bad racial issue and anytime anything in our history has been brought up it's to cause trouble. Like the race marches and all ... just created turmoil and trouble.... The more you discuss race here with Atlanta like it is, so totally black and so totally against whites, you just create problems."[39]

Notice that Ledbetter believes in order to squelch racism, it is best to ignore it, as evidenced by her feigned ignorance of the Forsyth County banishment when her students inquire about it directly. This is highly problematic, because by ignoring institutional racism, she is sending the message that there are no consequences for perpetuating racial inequalities. This mentality, combined with the fact that Ledbetter is both a teacher and a Forsyth County commissioner, and thereby a person of authority, is a crucial factor in the maintenance of the sundown-town legacy. Sad but not surprising, Ledbetter continues to be rewarded despite or perhaps as a result of her skewed views. Forsyth County responded in 2000 to her contribution to continuing racial inequality by naming her Forsyth County Central High School's Teacher of the Year.[40]

In a separate series of interviews, Loewen researched incidents of teachers openly and frequently using racial slurs in the classroom. He observes,

Such a wisecrack, coming casually from the person in charge, can make quite an impact on a classroom.... Sundown town rhetoric descends to its lowest point when speakers try to be funny.... Telling such a joke in a sundown town classroom lends it a special relevance.... The teller assumes, almost always correctly, that no one will object, and sharing such jokes bonds teller and audience into a racial in-group.[41]

Loewen concludes with a personal story about how he had unintention-ally told "a side-splitting joke in a sundown town." Speaking to an unnamed volunteer in Sheridan, Arkansas, about his research, he mentioned that Anna, Illinois, is said to stand for "Ain't No Niggers Allowed." The volunteer "laughed uproariously. People from multiracial towns, including white people, don't think it's funny."[42]

In discussing sundown towns, another absurdity is worth noting: There is a reversal mentality held by white residents within sundown towns. "In 1994, anthropologist Jane Adams found that a peculiar anxiety gripped residents of Anna ... about nearby Carbondale." As it turns out, there are people of Anna who are afraid to leave their own city limits after sunset for fear of African Americans in *other* communities. In another Southern Illinois community, "[a] former resident of Herrin ... relates that Herrin natives still warn each other, 'Don't go to Colp,' a nearby black-majority township, even during the daytime. Residents of independent sundown towns expressed particular anx-iety about visiting Atlanta, Detroit, or Washington, D.C., three cities they know have black majorities."[43] This demonstrates that the problem of banish-ment also entails the conditions of isolation and reclusion, which only act cyclically to further perpetuate the problem.

When reparations for African Americans are discussed, it is generally assumed that they must be made for slavery and in the form of money. This is both a dangerous and limited assumption. The danger in offering money as reparations for slavery lies in calculating and agreeing upon a monetary value commensurate to this American holocaust. How might this great destruction of human life be calculated? It should be immediately evident that the logic in attempting to set a fair monetary value for centuries of human suffering and death falls apart in equal measure whether it is done in the present and called slavery or done retroactively and called reparations. In the end, no amount of money can ever heal the wounds of enslavement, torture, and mur-der by one group of human beings against another. However, the problem does not inherently lie in making reparations with money or in making repa-rations specifically for slavery but in the combination of the two.

One possible method for calculating a dollar amount for reparations is to use property values. In cases of banishment, possessions, homes, and land were all left behind by communities fleeing for their lives, and this property was looted and seized shortly thereafter. The value of land and homes can readily be determined today. The problem is inherently in the disbursement of the reparations. Should they be paid only to direct descendants of victims of banishments? Should they be paid to all African Americans currently residing in the community, regardless of their families' relation to banishments? What happens to the money if there are no longer descendants of families subjugated to banishment?

Another potential solution is the creation of scholarships for African American students within the community. This is a more permanent solution that has a direct and positive impact on black communities and the entire populace of the town alike. If the scholarships apply to institutions within the town itself, they can also work towards reintegrating sundown towns, a major hurdle in the process of truly eliminating the sundown-town ideology. It is of course necessary to make the connection between the scholarship and banishment abundantly clear for this method to be effective. Many opponents of reparations ask where the money will come from. In cases of banishment, entire towns acted as a whole, its citizens exercising their agency either through direct participation or through tacit consent, and as such, reparations today must be publicly funded by these same towns. It is irrelevant whether individuals living today had any involvement in banishment; a sundown town is made as a collective decision, and reparations must be made in the same manner.

If monetary solutions are not enacted, monuments have the potential to go a long way toward reparations. At the very least, issuing a formal and sincere apology would be a tremendous step towards a process of reconciliation and reintegration of the community. Sundown towns are so incredibly damaging and problematic precisely because formal acknowledgements of their very existence are rare. This lack of recognition is especially hurtful, as it denies the legitimacy and significance of not only the history of banishment but also of the place of African Americans in contemporary society. The severe deficiency of acknowledgments of the history of so-called racial cleansing in the United States exemplifies the cultural shift to covert racism while providing a platform for its continuation into the future. It is for this reason that reparations are totally and completely necessary; inaction in the case of issuing reparations is essentially an action to not offer reparations. This would be only the latest decision to not act, following in the footsteps of the tacit consenters of banishment, the authors of *100 Years of Progress*, Forsyth County Central High School's 2000 Teacher of the Year, and Virginia governor McDonnell.

While Williams uses *Banished* to bring sundown towns to light and explore a variety of approaches toward reconciliation, he admits that there are no easy answers. However, in documenting this portion of American history, he has already taken the crucial first step in the reconciliatory process of opening a dialogue, moving this American holocaust from the margins of history into the spotlight. The road to reconciliation will be difficult, but it can no longer be ignored.

It is obvious that these contemporary conditions run deep in the hearts and minds of the American people and can be traced all the way back to slavery. The attempts made at equality up to this point are clearly having only minimalistic results, and gradualism has proved too slow and anything but steady. Small-town USA will not fix itself. Segregated urban centers will not fix themselves. The change must come unequivocally, universally, and with immediacy. It is the duty of every person with a sense of morality and responsibility to quell racism at the points of origin in their own communities, and we need local, state, and federal assistance toward this effort with leadership by example. I concede that discussing race like adults can unleash unpleasant feelings, but these are simple sacrifices in comparison to the emotional, physical, and economic trauma that we as a nation currently expend needlessly and constantly on ignoring and preserving the sundown-town legacy. I leave you with the thoughts of Marco Williams to contemplate:

> In the last 25 years, many victims of injustice have demanded reparations. Some demands have been met; others denied. In 1988, President Ronald Reagan signed a bill granting reparations to Japanese Americans interned during World War II. Since 2001, the German Foundation has distributed $5 billion to compensate victims of the Holocaust. For the past 15 years Michigan Congressman John Conyers has introduced a bill to provide reparations for slavery. The bill has never been passed. In 2003, a lawsuit for reparations was filed by African American survivors of the 1921 Tulsa riots. The U.S. Supreme Court dismissed the case. Of the thousands of African Americans violently expelled from their homes and land between 1860 and 1930, only four descendants from the Rosewood, Florida massacre have been compensated for their loss.[44]

## Notes

1. Loewen, *Sundown Towns*, 21–23, 172–75.
2. Chivonnie, *Reelblack TV*.
3. Williams, *Banished*; Jaspin, *Buried in the Bitter Waters*.
4. Williams, *Banished*.
5. Bogle, *Toms, Coons, Mulattoes, Mammies, & Bucks*.
6. Loewen, *Sundown Towns*, 175–76.
7. Said, *Orientalism*.
8. Hale, *Making Whiteness*, 203–4.
9. Jaspin, *Buried in the Bitter Waters*, 125–34.

10. Ibid., 129, 130, 125–34.
11. Ibid., 129.
12. Loewen, *Sundown Towns*, 310–11.
13. Jaspin, *Buried in the Bitter Waters*, 140.
14. Williams, *Banished*.
15. Ibid.
16. Ibid.
17. Ibid.
18. Ibid.
19. Ibid.
20. Loewen, *Sundown Towns*, 202–4.
21. Ibid., 310–11.
22. Ibid., 4–62.
23. Ibid., 48.
24. Jaspin, *Buried in the Bitter Waters*, 130–31.
25. Lam, Parks, and Rich, *100 Years of Progress*, 363–64, 358.
26. Ibid., i.
27. Ibid., ii–iii.
28. Williams, *Banished*.
29. Ibid.
30. Mississippi, "Confederate States," para. 2.
31. Texas, "Confederate States," para. 10.
32. "Apology Not Accepted."
33. Pietrangelo, "What Do Meathead and Archie."
34. Jaspin, *Buried in the Bitter Waters*, 140–51; Williams, *Banished*.
35. Ibid.
36. Hughes, *Myths America Lives By*, 79.
37. Katznelson, *When Affirmative Action Was White*, 142.
38. Hacker, *Two Nations*, 173–87; Kozol, *Shame of the Nation*.
39. Jaspin, *Buried in the Bitter Waters*, 150–51.
40. Ibid., 151.
41. Loewen, *Sundown Towns*, 311–12.
42. Ibid.
43. Ibid., 324.
44. Williams, *Banished*.

## *Works Cited*

"Apology Not Accepted, Lawmaker Says of McDonnell." *CNN Political Ticker*, April 8, 2010. Accessed April 9, 2010. http://politicalticker.blogs.cnn.com/2010/04/08/apology-not-accepted-lawmaker-says-of-mcdonnell-2/?fbid=E9BTKFKe7Km&hpt=T1.

Bogle, Donald. *Toms, Coons, Mulattoes, Mammies, & Bucks: An Interpretive History of Blacks in American Films*, 4th ed. New York: Continuum International, 2001.

Brundage, W. Fitzhugh, ed. *Under Sentence of Death: Lynching in the South*. Chapel Hill: University of North Carolina Press, 1997.

Chivonnie. *Reelblack TV: Marco Williams Discusses BANISHED*. December 3, 2007. Accessed January 5, 2010. http://www.youtube.com/watch?v=B8l89EsggFU&feature=related.

Darder, Antonia, and Rodolfo D. Torres. *After Race: Racism After Multiculturalism*. New York: New York University Press, 2004.

Feagin, Joe R. *Racist America: Roots, Current Realities, & Future Reparations*. New York: Routledge, 2000.

Georgia. "Confederate States of America—Georgia Secession." January 29, 1861. Avalon Project. *Lillian Goldman Law Library, Yale University*, 2008. Accessed April 13, 2010. http://avalon.law.yale.edu/19th_century/csa_geosec.asp.

Hacker, Andrew. *Two Nations: Black & White, Separate, Hostile, Unequal.* New York: Scribner, 2003.

Hale, Grace Elizabeth. *Making Whiteness: The Culture of Segregation in the South, 1890–1940.* New York: Vintage, 1998.

Hughes, Richard T. *Myths America Lives By.* Urbana: University of Illinois Press, 2003.

Jaspin, Elliot. *Buried in the Bitter Waters: The Hidden History of Racial Cleansing in America.* New York: Basic, 2007.

Katznelson, Ira. *When Affirmative Action Was White: An Untold History of Racial Inequality in Twentieth-Century America.* New York: Norton, 2005.

Kennedy, Randall. *Nigger: The Strange Career of a Troublesome Word.* New York: Vintage, 2002.

Kozol, Jonathan. *The Shame of The Nation: The Restoration of Apartheid Schooling in America.* New York: Three Rivers Press, 2005.

Lam, Howard, George E. Parks, and Robert L. Rich. *100 Years of Progress: The Cenntenial History of Anna, Illinois.* Cape Girardeau, MO: Missourian, 1954.

Loewen, James W. *Sundown Towns: A Hidden Dimension of American Racism.* New York: Touchstone, 2005.

Mississippi. "Confederate States of America—Mississippi Secession: A Declaration of the Immediate Causes Which Induce and Justify the Secession of the State of Mississippi from the Federal Union." January 1861. Avalon Project. *Lillian Goldman Law Library, Yale University*, 2008. Accessed April 13, 2010. http://avalon.law.yale.edu/19th_century/csa_missec.asp.

Pietrangelo, Ann. "What Do Meathead and Archie Have to Do with Health Care Reform?" *Care2*, March 22, 2010. Accessed March 22, 2010. http://www.care2.com/causes/politics/blog/what-do-meathead-and-archie-have-to-do-with-health-care-reform/.

Said, Edward W. *Orientalism.* New York: Vintage, 1978.

South Carolina. "Confederate States of America—Declaration of the Immediate Causes Which Induce and Justify the Secession of South Carolina from the Federal Union." December 24, 1860. Avalon Project. *Lillian Goldman Law Library, Yale University*, 2008. Accessed April 13, 2010. http://avalon.law.yale.edu/19th_century/csa_scarsec.asp.

Texas. "Confederate States of America— Declaration of the Causes Which Impel the State of Texas to Secede from the Federal Union." February 2, 1861. Avalon Project. *Lillian Goldman Law Library, Yale University*, 2008. Accessed April 13, 2010. http://avalon.law.yale.edu/19th_century/csa_texsec.asp.

Williams, Marco, dir. *Banished: How Whites Drove Blacks Out of Town in America.* Two Tone Productions and the Center for Investigative Reporting, 2007. DVD. 87 min.

# Portrait of Jason

## A Reappraisal

### GERALD R. BUTTERS JR.

The loosening of cultural mores in the 1950s and rampant sexual experimentation in the 1960s helped bring an end to motion-picture censorship in
the United States. These factors, coupled with the development of cinéma
vérité in the 1960s, led to a number of early documentary works that considered the gay male experience. Perhaps, one of the most provocative and controversial of these pre–Stonewall films is Shirley Clarke's *A Portrait of Jason*
(1967). Clarke's film is one of the first representations of an "out" African
American man. One may argue that the unusual film is technically not a documentary; it has proven to be almost impossible to place it into a distinct
generic category. Yet, the film is considered to have many documentary-like
tendencies and, thus, is considered as such for this essay. Film scholar Tony
Rains claims that if *Portrait of Jason* is anything, it is a "record of a performance," yet a "performance ably assisted by a filmmaker who most assuredly
knew what and who she was filming."[1] Questions of cinematic control, power,
and actualization need to be raised regarding this film, particularly as it has
reentered the public consciousness with its 2013 re-release.

Clarke began her creative life as a choreographer in the 1950s and eventually began making dance and movement-related films. She began a relationship with African American actor Carl Lee (son of the esteemed African
American actor Canada Lee) in the late 1950s. This relationship led to artistic
collaboration between the two that gave Clarke entrée into a world that otherwise may have been off limits to a white filmmaker—that of urban African
American culture. Carl Lee helped her create *The Connection* (1960), which

shows a group of jazz musicians waiting for a shipment of heroin; *A Cool World* (1963), which illustrates the lives of black teenagers in Harlem; and then, *Portrait of Jason*. All of these films are centered on black culture but were not widely distributed, as they were part of the sixteen millimeter, avant-garde world in which at the time of their releases relegated them to being screened primarily in art-house theaters.

Importantly, *The Connection*, *A Cool World*, and *Portrait of Jason* are considered Clarke's responses to the cinéma vérité style that had become so influential with the development of the handheld camera in the late 1950s and early 1960s and with the work of documentary filmmakers like D. A. Pennebaker, Jean Rouch, and Richard Leacock. Cinéma vérité emerged as a style of filmmaking that was conceived of as being more realistic than traditional Hollywood documentaries; made with simple movable equipment, it was believed that cinéma vérité avoids artistic effect and artificiality, and, therefore, these films are more "authentic."

The subject of Clarke's ninety-nine-minute film *Portrait of Jason* is Jason Holliday, né Aaron Payne, an aging, openly gay African American hustler who operated on the periphery of a number of worlds in post–World War II society, including urban African America, elite white culture, and the gay subculture. An off-camera voice tells Jason/Aaron in the latter third of the film, "I've never come to see you LIVE anywhere." Rootless, Jason is part of, yet not wholly a member of, any culture, as America's incessant homophobia, racism, and classism prevented that from happening.

Stories conflict regarding how Clarke and Holliday met. In one press release, he is described as a "friend of a friend of hers."[2] The *New York Times* claims that an actor in her first feature, *The Connection*, introduced her to Jason.[3] In an interview in the 1980s, Clarke states that Jason was a friend of her husband's father and that "Jason used to come around and clean my house when I didn't want to."[4]

It is also difficult to discover the truth about Holliday's actual life since much of it was either manufactured or embellished for narrative purposes and is not readily verifiable. Holliday claims he was born in Trenton, New Jersey, and that at five years old, he began his career "as errand boy for prostitutes, pimps, bootleggers, school teachers, doctors and lawyers, etc.—and anyone else I could get a buck out of. Lonely old men and hot hotel maids." Holliday dropped out of colleges in both New Jersey and Washington, D.C., and decided that "New York was where I belonged." He claims that in less than three weeks he became a "B'way Gypsy" as a chorus boy in various productions of *Carmen Jones*, *Finian's Rainbow*, and *Green Pastures*. This wasn't steady work, though, and Holliday "turned many tricks" between shows in order to survive.[5]

*Portrait of Jason* was filmed over a twelve-hour period, from 9:00 p.m. to 9:00 a.m. on December 3–4, 1966, in Clarke's New York apartment. Jason is filmed the entire time with the exception of short intervals during which the camera was being reloaded. He "performs" for the camera for almost the entire period and is provided a limitless quantity of alcohol and marijuana for the entire shoot. Throughout the film, Jason moves from politely drinking a cocktail to swigging from a bottle. As British queer theorist Gavin Butt argues, "It is precisely the degree to which *Portrait of Jason* fails to offer up acceptable 'positive images' of minoritarian identity that makes Clarke's film intriguing."[6] Clarke repeatedly contradicted herself over the years regarding the amount of "control" she had over Jason, the filmmaking process, and the construction of the film's narrative. Clarke told one journalist that "the main responsibility [for the filmmaking process is the director because he or she] symbolizes and always has symbolized the one in charge."[7] Yet, Clarke argued that in *Portrait of Jason*, "I gave up more control than I ever had in my whole 12 years of film making."[8] She had originally intended on doing a *Pop Art and Vernacular Cultures* two-hour feature on a singular personality in which "his humor, his tears, his terrors" would be revealed, with shooting to take place "all night and into the morning." This is largely the process Clarke followed. She had a skeleton film crew and several other onlookers on the set. Clarke's preconception of the process turned out wildly different from what she anticipated. She explained, "[T]he whole atmosphere in the room, all the energies were directed to and through Jason [the star].... Everything progressed with the reality of being lived and experienced in front of your eyes. It was extraordinary. I found I didn't have to control every breath of the actor and every frame the camera shot."[9]

Cinéma vérité strains to show a version of truth. In Clarke's production there is no truth; there is only performance as production. This "cinema of truth" is a style of documentary filmmaking that combines improvisation with the use of the camera to unveil truth or to highlight subjects hidden behind a veil of reality. Screenwriter Mick Eaton argues that the very presence of the camera in the cinéma vérité mode will create an atmosphere in which "people will act, will lie, will be uncomfortable."[10] *Portrait of Jason* is often discussed within the context of cinéma vérité. Clarke argued that this style of filmmaking "called to our attention that people are the most interesting subject. Yet, we have rarely allowed anyone to really speak for himself for more than a few minutes at a time. Just what might happen if someone was given his head and allowed to let go for many consecutive hours. I was curious and WOW did I find out."[11]

It is not uncommon for spectators to confuse cinéma vérité with the "actual" truth. Film critic Arthur Knight comments, "[W]hat the camera—

reputedly the most realistic of all artistic tools—gives back is not reality, but a version of reality.... [I]n a documentary, which uses life itself as its raw material, one is shown only an aspect, a segment of the total scene—a selection that corresponds to the personal vision, or the special bias, of the filmmaker himself."[12] The bandying about of this "cinéma vérité" status is often lost upon the public, who confuse it with direct cinema, which attempts to have a "fly on the wall" approach to filmmaking. David Miller, columnist for the *Los Angeles Occidental*, describes Clarke's filming of *Jason* as "the objective recorder par excellence."[13] This reached an absurd point when journalist Daniel Talbot of the New York Theater wrote Clarke in July 1967: "Where did you dig this guy up? He out-verites anything I've ever seen in cinema vérité."[14]

Cinéma vérité often involves stylized setups and an interaction between the filmmaker and the subject, even to the point of provocation. Although Jason is the only person on screen, he is not the only individual within the narrative of the film. Clarke and Lee bait Jason with questions during the shooting, and at least two other individuals off-camera are watching/participating in the proceedings. Much of what has been written about *Portrait of Jason* refers to it as a singular performance, but Clarke's and Lee's interventions in the proceedings are paramount to the production of the film and have been ignored by most film theorists and historians. The acting, lying, and discomfort take place both in front of and behind the camera.

Importantly, the camera is not objective during the shooting of *Jason*. The lens itself is unfocused for much of the initial dialogue, which adds substantially to two motifs that run through the documentary—the notion of multiple identities and the search for the true Jason/Aaron. Because Clarke was forced to change film every ten minutes, which causes the camera to slowly go out of focus, an action that inadvertently functions as a transition of sorts, Knight claims that the impact of this is "to emphasize the ritualistic, oddly impersonal nature of this true confession."[15]

Aaron/Jason claims that he renamed himself in San Francisco in order to "give himself another chance." Thus, just as performers have stage names and create new identities, Jason has attempted to do the same. As viewers are introduced to him, he says:

> My name is Jason Holliday.
> My name is Jason Holliday.
> My name is Aaron Payne.

Next, Clarke begins the "interview": "What do you do for a living, Jason?" He explains, while drinking an alcoholic beverage, "I'm a stone whore and I'm not ashamed of it. Everyone in New York has a gimmick. I'm a hustler, and I have more than one hustle." Jason's "hustle" obviously involves selling himself sexually, but the audience has only a limited idea of where he finds his clients who pay him for sex, and he does not describe these transactions. The hustles that Jason recounts more frequently refer to being someone's "maid, butler, flunky," "anything [to keep] from punching the clock from 9–5." For example, he served as an assistant or houseboy to a number of wealthier, older, white couples or individuals and to African Americans in the performing arts, including singer Carmen McCrae. Jason explains that while occupying such jobs, he attempted to do as little work as possible and that he often conceived of ways to steal from his clients. In one instance, he obtained a moving truck and removed an entire house full of antiques from a former employer.

Jason describes himself as a sexually active individual, and he, clearly, enjoys "balling," but it is difficult to consider him as a sexual being—his self-deprecation and painful honesty desexualize him.

Jason obviously endured a great deal of racism in his encounters with white employers. He explains, "I think as a houseboy I really suffered. They think you're a dumb little colored boy. They're going to use you as a joke." Jason recounts being called "spook" and "nigger" and how his employers used him as a form of entertainment, among other indignities. Clarke never interrogates the lack of economic opportunities that exist for Jason—his hustle is his career, and it is implied that his choices are his own and are not determined by larger economic, cultural, or racial factors.

Jason's goal is to be a nightclub or cabaret performer. Attempting to achieve this dream for more than ten years, he has borrowed money from a number of different people in order to stage his own production. He sees himself as a natural performer, and one can argue that the film is indeed a sort of screen test. Jason has clearly thought out his routine—he envisions it as a three-part act in which he embodies "a swinging hip cat who's been around," "a bitchy" personae, and a clown, "because all clowns are happy and sad." In true drag style, Jason performs as a number of Hollywood stars (and their on-screen roles), including Mae West, Barbra Streisand (singing "The Music That Makes Me Dance" from *Funny Girl*), Prissy and Scarlett O'Hara from *Gone with the Wind*, and various characters from *Carmen Jones*. He embodies both black and white and male and female characters; the trope of a flexible identity is paramount to Jason's personality. One may argue that it is critical to his survival or, perhaps, indicative of his lack of success. However, as the film progresses, it becomes abundantly clear that his cabaret act will never be successful. Jason is well past his prime, and his alcoholism, lack of self-control, and incessant clowning will destroy any possibilities of a hit act. Yet, he clearly loves being on stage and is thrilled that he is the subject of this film.

*Portrait of Jason* is fascinating because it illustrates the limited position of gay black men in a highly racist, homophobic, pre–Stonewall American culture. Clarke made this film at a time when America's long-standing patriarchal notions of race, gender, and sexuality were being challenged within society. As a black man unable to "contain" his homosexuality, Jason bears a double stigma that limits his economic opportunities even more. These pressures lead to a self-destructive personality in which he abuses alcohol and drugs to ease his pain. Jason laughs almost incessantly through the entire twelve hours of filming with the exception of the last hour. However, his laughter is mawkish, grating, and unrelenting, leading one to question the validity of what he is telling those present during the filming and audiences that would subsequently view the movie. However, the laughter also serves as Jason's coping mechanism, because the absence of the appearance of having a good time would illustrate the emptiness in his life and his hopeless future.

Jason doesn't appear to have anyone in his life that he can trust or depend on. He has burned bridges with former clients and employees by either refusing to be servile or by stealing from them. This includes individuals that went out of their way for him, including McCrae and Jason's mother, "who protected him till the day she died." Jason's father, Big Tough, "a gambler, bootlegger ... with muscles bulging for days," was embarrassed by him and frequently beat him with a razor strop for being effeminate. Jason describes that while administering the cruel punishment, his father would yell, "Don't move, don't holler, I'm gonna tear your natural ass." As Jason recounts the brutality of his father's rage, he, once again, laughs through the entire story.

Although viewers might assume that Jason was beloved by the filmmakers, as the film progresses, it becomes abundantly clear that he cannot trust Clarke, Lee, or the others who are present during the film's shoot. Perhaps blinded by either his love of the spotlight or the endless supply of drugs and alcohol, Jason does not seem to question Clarke's motives. Importantly, a review of the press that surrounded *Portrait* makes it clear that he needed to be concerned with the filmmakers. For example, Clarke comments to avant-garde filmmaker Jonas Mekas, "I suspected that for all his cleverness, his lack of the know-how of filmmaking would prevent him from being able to control his own image of himself." Furthermore, in 1967, the year the film was released, Clarke explained to Mekas,

> I discovered the antagonisms I'd been suppressing about Jason. I was indeed emotionally involved. Since the readers of this "conversation" haven't yet seen the film, I should say here that while Jason spoke to the camera, other people were in the room during the shooting, beside myself, who reacted to what Jason said and did, got involved with him. We had a tiny crew, plus two old friends of Jason who

knew all his bits and had suffered from his endless machinations as well as enjoyed his fun and games.[16]

Significantly, Shirley's daughter, Wendy Clarke, relates that Jason had a very obvious crush on Carl Lee. Thus, it is not a stretch to assume that this served as at least a partial rationale for the contempt that her mother held for Jason. In addition to resenting Jason as a result of his feelings for Carl, Shirley's claim that she had heard all of Jason's routine at least fifty times before the shoot and that she felt the simple need to expose him as an effeminate, queenish, two-bit hustler deeply complicated the relationship between the director and subject.[17] This is clearly evidenced in a 1983 interview with Brecht Andersch during which Shirley confesses, "I started out that evening with hatred, and there was part of me that was out to do him in, get back at him, kill him."[18]

Though it has gone previously unexplored, Shirley Clarke's perspective adds valuable insight into why *Portrait* becomes a "snuff film" of sorts in the last reel as she and Lee turn vicious toward Jason. In particular, the couple steers the subject away from the discussions about his relationships with former clients, his father, and his encounters with the law, which are the main focus of previous two-thirds of the film. Rather than continue along that trajectory, Clarke begins a vicious and personal indictment of Jason after he voluntarily describes his mother as a "nice colored lady ... who knew her place" but always protected him from his violent father and society at-large. Despite his loving description of his mother, Clarke changes the entire tone of the film when she bluntly asks him, "Did you hate your mother?" Because two commonly held stereotypes about gay men are that their mothers are responsible for making them queer and that gay men hate all women, in that moment Clarke becomes the perfect example of and purveyor of the dominant culture's rampant homophobia.

Clarke's and Lee's interrogations of Jason do not end with the question about his mother. By this point in the film, Jason is heavily intoxicated, having consumed an excessive amount of alcohol and smoked several joints, which affect his self-control. That those items were supplied by the filmmakers, who were well aware of the fact that he had suffered from mental health issues, further calls their intentions into question. In his extremely fragile state, Jason remains the perfect subject when he tells Richard, one of the off-screen participants whom Jason considers a friend,

> I love you, Richard. I do. You'll see.
> Don't trust me, Richard. 'Cause I'm out to get you.
> I'll hang you. Fuck you up so you'll be mine.

As Clarke loads the last role of film, Lee begins attacking Jason again:

> You remember those dirty rotten letters you wrote about me?
> Lying in the Bowery as a bum. What did you tell those for?
> Why'd you do that to me? Rotten queer.

It is unclear whether Lee is under the influence of drugs and alcohol at this point in the film since he is off-camera (Lee later died as a result of a heroin addiction). Regardless of his state of mind, he continues to berate Jason, "Just 'cause I wouldn't loan you a few lousy dollars. You evil shit." Like Clarke before him, he, too, is the embodiment of America's homophobia.

Much has been written about Jason's "exposure" in the last reel of the film as his laughing jester-like performance turns more somber and serious. However, critics and scholars have failed to effectively articulate the fact that his mood transforms as a result of the filmmakers' hateful accusations, which eventually cause him to cry. As he sobs, he tells Lee, "Without you I wouldn't know anything about anything. If you don't know, I love you." Completely unfazed by Jason's comments, Lee calls him a "vicious cunt." Jason responds by characterizing himself as a "real male bitch." Clarke then joins in on the action:

> CLARKE: Are you lonely? You should be lonely.
> HOLLIDAY: I should suffer.
> CLARKE: You're not suffering.

Lee tells Jason he's full of shit, and the walls of his performance are torn down. Jason begs Lee to "teach" him. In the single most emotion-filled moment in the film, Jason moans and groans from deep within—"YOU ... CAN ... TEACH ... ME." Lee responds: "Honest, motherfucker. Stop that acting. Goddamn liar. Just full of shit, man. You're full of shit." At this point, Jason becomes defensive: "Shut up!" Lee quickly responds, "Bitch. Fuck you." The last words heard on camera are from Clarke, who, in three different inflections, says, "The end ... the end ... the end," which is a powerful conclusion to a unique film experience.

Clarke, clearly, recognized that she had captured an emotionally charged and gripping moment on film that reveals just as much about her, Lee, and their observers as it does about Jason. In the 1967 interview with Mekas, she explained,

> How the people behind the camera reacted that night is a very important part of what the film is about. Little did I expect how much of ourselves we would reveal as the night progressed. Originally, I had planned that you would see and hear only Jason but when I saw the rushes I knew the real story of what happened that

night in my living room had to include all of us, and so our question-reaction probes, our irritations and angers, as well as our laughter remained part of the film.[19]

Indeed, *Portrait of Jason* provides a very telling glimpse into Lee's and Clarke's poor treatment of Jason that, at least in part, seems to stem from their homophobia. When the filmmaker yells "the end" to signal the conclusion of the film, she is also completing the end of a mental gay bashing. Thus, as professor Phillip Brian Harper contends, it is not Jason's flouting of convention that is most striking in the film but the "interrogator's ever more hostile examination of him [Jason]."[20]

Despite being an extremely problematic film that takes advantage of its subject, some critics heralded *Portrait of Jason*, which opened to mixed reviews. For example, Andersch, inaccurately, claims, "*Portrait of Jason* was Clarke's major contribution to the cinéma vérité canon."[21] Reviewing it for *Film Quarterly*, "E. C." builds up *Portrait of Jason*'s cinéma vérité style: "*Jason* proves that cinema may be among other things, compelling even if used as simple recording device for a single person."[22] As Clarke demonstrates, as the camera goes in and out of focus during the shoot, it is far from a "simple recording device," and, certainly, more than one individual is in this film. In contrast, Knight claims that "no significant shred of the man's [Jason's] past and personality have been uncovered or uncommented upon," and a reviewer for *Newsweek* argues, "What does not work at all is Miss Clarke's decision to bait and taunt her subject in the last few minutes of the film until he cowers and weeps."[23]

Clarke asserts that there is such a thing as documentary reality. This is certainly true in *Portrait of Jason*, as those behind the camera use insults and taunting to manipulate the "reality" in front of the camera. Film critic Melissa Anderson argues, "There is still an enormous power imbalance between Clarke, who wields the camera, and Jason, who performs for her (and the viewer)."[24]

Although some reviewers criticize Clarke's treatment of Jason, she remained unapologetic about her actions long after the film was released. Clarke, clearly, had intentions to destroy Jason Holliday when she invited him to her apartment that winter night in December 1966. She was frank with professor Lauren Rabinovitz about starting the filmmaking process filled with "hatred" and said that she wanted to "get back at him, kill him." Ironically, Clarke also recounted that as the evening progressed, she became more sympathetic to Jason and "developed more and more of a total ability to understand where he was coming from, leaping cultural gaps and his homosexuality."[25] If that was the case, then why did she attack him at the end of the film? If she developed this capacity to understand, then why did she and Carl Lee launch their "barrage of insults and epithets" at Jason?[26] Later in her life, discussing the film in an interview with Rabinovitz, Clarke provided more insight into *Portrait*'s production and her intentions: "At times he [Jason] was very funny, and there were times when he was very cruel and very dangerous." Because of Jason's erratic behavior, Clarke asked Carl Lee to be present for the filming since "they had a relationship ... over the years and ... Carl could confront Jason." As a "white lady director," she did not believe that she had the power to do so. When Rabinovitz asked Clarke whether she intended for the film to end with the confrontation, she responded, "Oh yea, I had every intention of having a climax of some kind take place. I knew that I would have to get Jason to face the truth at some point but I wasn't positive how. In other words, I was going to let Jason do whatever he wanted to do as long as I could, and then I was going to challenge him to come clean—tell the truth."[27]

Clarke's comment begs the question, "Tell the truth about what?"—the difficulty of being gay and African American in a homophobic society where economic and social opportunities were almost nonexistent? Unfortunately, her comments lead to more questions than answers for the behavior in which she and Lee engaged in that evening.

*Portrait of Jason* frankly deals with the subject's blackness and homosexuality. Documentary films that focus on a singular, gay black man run the risk of deemphasizing either race or homosexuality and, thus, open themselves up to criticism. Kevin Thomas in the *Los Angeles Times* declares that Jason Holliday is "no ordinary man. He is (1) Negro, (2) homosexual."[28] To others, Jason was nothing more than a "black male whore."[29]

The level of violent homophobia at the time of *Jason*'s release is shocking—even in publications that took a more liberal or radical stance toward social issues. In her *Village Voice* review of *Portrait of Jason*, critic Betty Kronsky explains how Clarke invited Holliday to spend an entire night in her apartment to "do his thing" in front of the camera. Kronsky then describes Jason as

> a paragon of failure, a man who has defiled over and over again on his dream of theatrical potency; a homosexual who had found ersatz sexual power in skilled repetitive games of using and being used; a negro ex-housemaid who knew the ins and outs of making men knaves to their manservants; a sensitive beautiful psychologizer who played on the nerves of psychiatrists and lived in terror that he would destroy their power to rescue him. She offered to this expert at failure the chance to redeem his image once and for all by doing his thing powerfully and effectively for one night of pure potentiality. Well, character is fate, and he fails again.[30]

From Kronsky's perspective, Jason is a monstrosity, one who is manipulative and is able to sexually control his victims, take advantage of employers, drive psychiatrists to madness, and transgress gender norms, yet ultimately end up a failure. Her description of Jason reaffirms popular perceptions of the day, which characterized homosexuals as dangerous. This perspective is also purported in 1967 when *CBS Reports* aired an hour-long documentary *The Homosexuals*, in which sensationalistic, gay men are portrayed as promiscuous, unstable, and threatening. *Portrait of Jason* seems to further confirm CBS's scathing report. Perhaps, *Cavalier*, a popular men's magazine, is more succinct in describing Jason as a "Negro fag."[31]

Since identity is predicated by a number of social and cultural factors, the various observable and nonobservable traits of an individual make up the complex human being. Jason, Thomas claims, "emerges as a desperate outsider, struggling to make something of his life yet knowing that he won't."[32] Unfortunately, Clarke was well aware of this and was willing to exploit Jason's life, dreams, and ambitions all for the sake of motion-picture notoriety. As she tells columnist Deac Russell in *Boston after Dark*, "For a time after the film premiered at the 1967 New York Film Festival, Jason had a 'dream' every time the telephone rang, it was MGM calling him with an offer."[33]

Shirley Clarke has rightfully been praised as a landmark female director. Film scholar Thomas F. Cohen claims that she has a "revered place in the history of cinema."[34] Rabinovitz, among Clarke's most ardent defenders, argues that Clarke is "always aware of her position as the sole woman filmmaker involved" and that her three feature films "present pictures of alienation and deep-seated unrest among those excluded from the American dream of success and power."[35] Furthermore, in *Points of Resistance*, Rabinovitz seemingly lets Clarke off the hook for exploiting Jason: "an African-American homosexual man's only power here comes from undercutting his victimization by the camera. Once again, Clarke addresses questions of power and resistance in relation to both sexual and social identities."[36] This argument ignores Clarke's personal relationship with Jason and separates the director from the cinematic apparatus. Jason "[plays] the victim" and "[manipulates] his position"; Clarke's and Lee's interrogations of Jason are treated in a neutral manner.[37]

Considering the way that the filmmakers manipulated their subject and for the film's rampant homophobia, I call for a reexamination of *Portrait of Jason*. The 2013 release of the film and the projected repackaging on DVD is introducing a new generation to this "cornerstone of LGBT filmmaking."[38] How did American culture go from *Today Show* critic Judith Crist's observation that Jason is "a desperate and pathetic human" to *Chicago Reader* columnist J. R. Jones's description of him as "full of life, proudly gay, and brutally, disarmingly frank about his sex life"?[39] Is Shirley Clarke a pioneer of women's filmmaking in the United States and a leader in the independent cinema movement of the 1950s and 1960s, as it is often claimed? Or is she a purveyor of homophobia and an opportunistic, manipulative filmmaker? Perhaps, the truth lies somewhere in between. In her interview with Rabinovitz, Clarke says, "So far as I know no one has ever suggested that Jason was exploited. As far as I know, there has never been anything written about it that doesn't see *Jason* as an exploration of what makes a particular human tick."[40] To that, I respond with a resounding, "Well, now there has."

## Notes

1. DVD notes.
2. Press release, Saidye Bronfman Centre of the University of Montreal Young Women's Hebrew Association and National Health Service, folder 3, box 1, Clarke Papers.
3. *New York Times*, July 9, 1967, folder 1, box 6, Clarke Papers.
4. Lauren Rabinovitz, interview with Shirley Clarke, final draft, folder 2, box 15, Clarke Papers.
5. Program, 5th New York Film Festival, September 1967, Lincoln Center for the Performing Arts, folder 6, box 5, Clarke Papers.
6. Butt, "Stop That Acting!" 41.
7. Shirley Storm dialogue, folder 1, box 1, Clarke Papers.
8. Ibid.
9. Ibid.
10. Eaton, "Production of Cinematic Reality," 51.
11. "Interview with Jonas Mekas," *Village Voice*, August 24, 1967, folder 1, box 1, Clarke Papers.
12. Knight, "Cinema Verite and Film Truth," 44.
13. David Miller, "*A Portrait of Jason* Film Reviewed at Cinematheque," *Los Angeles Occidental*, May 7, 1968, folder 1, box 6, Clarke Papers.
14. Daniel Talbot to Shirley Clarke, July 2, 1967, folder 6: "U.S. Motion Pictures Produced—Portrait of Jason," box 5, Clarke Papers.
15. Knight, "Cinema Verite and Film Truth," 44.
16. "Interview with Jonas Mekas."
17. Ibid.
18. Andersch, "Film as a Battleground."
19. "Interview with Jonas Mekas."
20. Harper, "Walk-on Parts and Speaking Subjects," 142.
21. Andersch, "Film as a Battleground."
22. Callenbach, review, 77.
23. Knight, "Cinema Verite and Film Truth," 44; Review of *Portrait of Jason*.
24. Anderson, "Vagaries of Verities," 59.
25. Rabinovitz, interview with Clarke.
26. Anderson, "Vagaries of Verities," 59; Betty Kronsky, "Jason Outjason's All Reviewers—This One Too," *Village Voice*, October 12, 1967, folder 1, box 1, Clarke Papers.
27. Rabinovitz, interview with Clarke.
28. Kevin Thomas, "*Portrait of Jason* at Cinematheque," *Los Angeles Times*, May 6, 1968, folder 1, box 1, Clarke Papers.
29. *Harper's Bazaar*, 19, folder 1, box 1, Clarke Papers.
30. Kronsky, "Jason Outjason's All Reviewers."
31. *Cavalier*, January 1968, folder 1, box 6, Shirley Clarke Papers.

32. Thomas, *Portrait*.
33. Russell, "Independent Filmmakers," 27.
34. Cohen, "After the New American Cinema," 57.
35. Rabinovitz, "Radical Cinema," 82–83.
36. Rabinovitz, *Points of Resistance*, 137.
37. Ibid.
38. Jones, "Bitch Is Back," 41.
39. Crist, *Today Show*, November 7, 1967, folder 6, box 5, Clarke Collection; Jones, "Bitch Is Back," 41.
40. Rabinovitz, interview with Clarke.

## *Works Cited*

Andersch, Brecht. "Film as a Battleground: Shirley Clarke's *Portrait of Jason*." *SFMOMA*, July 7, 2009. http://blog.sfmoma.org/2009/07/film-as-a-battleground-shirley-clarkes-portrait-of-jason/.

Anderson, Melissa. "The Vagaries of Verities: On Shirley Clarke's *Portrait of Jason*." *Film Comment* 35, no. 6 (November–December 1999): 56.

Butt, Gavin. "Stop That Acting! Performance and Authenticity in Shirley Clarke's *Portrait of Jason*." In *Pop Art and Vernacular Cultures*, edited by Kobena Mercer, 36–55. Cambridge: MIT Press, 2007.

Callenbach, Ernst. Review of *Portrait of Jason*. *Film Quarterly* 22, no. 1 (1968): 77.

Clarke, Shirley. Papers. Wisconsin Center for Film and Theatre Research, State Historical Society, Madison.

Cohen, Thomas F. "After the New American Cinema: Shirley Clarke's Video Work as Performance and Document." *Journal of Film and Video* 64, no. 1–2 (2012): 57–64.

DVD notes. *Portrait of Jason*. Directed by Shirley Clarke. Burlington: Second Run. DVD. 105 minutes.

Eaton, Mick. "The Production of Cinematic Reality." In *Anthropology—Reality—Cinema: The Films of Jean Rouch*, edited by Eaton, 48–55. London: British Film Institute, 1979.

Harper, Phillip Brian. "Walk-on Parts and Speaking Subjects: Screen Representations of Black Gay Men." In *Black Male: Representations of Masculinity in Contemporary American Art*, edited by Thelma Golden. 141–48. New York: Whitney Museum of Art, 1994.

Jones, J. R. "The Bitch Is Back." *Chicago Reader*, May 24, 2013, 41.

Knight, Arthur. "Cinema Verite and Film Truth." *Saturday Review*, September 9, 1967, 44.

Rabinovitz, Lauren. *Points of Resistance: Women, Power, & Politics in the New York Avant-Garde Cinema, 1943–71*. Urbana: University of Illinois Press, 1991.

_____. "Radical Cinema: The Films and Film Practices of Maya Deren, Shirley Clarke, and Joyce Wieland." PhD diss., University of Texas at Austin, 1982.

Review of *Portrait of Jason*. *Newsweek*, November 6, 1967.

Russell, Deac. "Independent Filmmakers Try Harder, Work Less." *Boston After Dark*, September 27, 1968, 27.

# Dancing as Voice

## *Krumping and Clowning in* Rize *as Black Vernacular Rhetoric*

### Joshua Daniel Phillips

Despite popular claims to the contrary, significant cultural issues, such as racism and classism, continue to plague contemporary American society. Although today's forms of oppression are more covert in their marginalization of people, the prevailing systems of white patriarchal power continue to push certain voices out of the public sphere and to the periphery. This constant attack on underprivileged citizens engaged in social resistance ensures that traditional voices perpetuate and, thus, maintain the dominant ideological status quo that guides the majority of our public conversations. This essay examines a form of social resistance that attempts to speak back to dominant ideologies. More specifically, this piece focuses on David LaChapelle's documentary film *Rize* (2005), using it to position the African American dance movements krumping and clowning[1] as forms of vernacular resistance that challenge dominant discourses, and asks the public sphere to continue developing as an inclusive space where all voices may be heard equally. To achieve that goal, this essay transitions through three sections. First, it discusses *Rize* within the theoretical framework of vernacular rhetoric. Second, this essay looks at the African American experience on film and places *Rize* within historical and contemporary cultural contexts. Finally, this essay highlights how *Rize* can work to expand cultural understanding of African American youth and their lives in the inner city.

Because *Rize* highlights a form of resistive empowerment, using the film can aid scholars in expanding their scholarship at the intersections of race, class, and vernacular rhetoric. Furthermore, the voices featured in *Rize* broaden understanding of the African American experience in contemporary America. As people become more inclusive of multiple voices within the public sphere, they are encouraged to wrestle with the current perceptions of democracy, social justice, and equal access. By providing the dancers featured in the film a platform to speak out, *Rize* ultimately gives its audience a new appreciation for what it means to grow up in South Central Los Angeles. While this documentary showcases the realities of poverty, broken families, drugs, and violence, it also highlights an encouraging perspective of creativity, ingenuity, hope, and resistive empowerment. For these perspectives, I position *Rize* as an important documentary that narrates a counterhegemonic space and elicits voice through dance.

## Rize *and Vernacular Rhetoric*

On the surface, it may be difficult to understand the political and social implications of documenting seemingly inconsequential forms of dance that evolved from a lower-class neighborhood plagued by racial oppression. However, vernacular rhetoric theorizes the importance of artistic movements in marginalized communities and, therefore, can assist in highlighting how dancing can bring voice to a community. In short, vernacular rhetoric is a text produced by a marginalized voice that can be used in an effort to draw attention to oppressive hierarchies.[2] In a more traditional sense, *text* commonly refers to written documents and public orations. However, a more generous understanding of *text* as a medium for vernacular rhetoric includes dancing, music, art, crafts, and storytelling as well as various other forms of expression.[3]

Having been rendered invisible by the larger culture, marginalized groups must often discover creative ways to tell their stories and transfer their cultural values to the next generation. This transference to future generations can happen through "informal discourse."[4] Using mediums such as dance, music, and storytelling as informal discourses allows a group to comply with dominant culture while resisting it. For example, a group is complicit with dominant culture by participating in an acceptable art form. Yet, the group also can be resistant by using that art form to critique dominant ideologies. Therefore, through vernacular rhetoric, a marginalized group can subtly counter the messages communicated by dominant ideologies while affirming the communicative mediums of the dominant culture.[5] Because all groups are trapped within a dominant system, a marginalized group cannot escape the systemic cultural powers that regulate the realities of the group's everyday life. Instead, historically disempowered groups must find ways to speak to the larger culture in a way that will showcase the value and worth of the group's cultural practices and beliefs.

Importantly, vernacular rhetoric is ultimately implemented as a means of controlling one's history.[6] Discussing the historical legacy of black music, in particular, widely known scholar Cornel West reminds us that "Afro-American popular music constitutes a crucial dimension of the background practices—the ways of life and struggle—of Afro-American culture."[7] In recounting the history of black America, a brief chronology would include slavery, emancipation, reconstruction, Jim Crow, the Harlem Renaissance, civil rights, voting rights, *Brown v. Board of Education*, ghetto isolation, the war on drugs, and President Barack Obama. Each of these examples contributes to the cultural fabric of black America, and from these examples, one can better appreciate how artistry has helped transfer the stories of a marginalized group by passing down and sharing cultural trials and triumphs from generation to generation. Without artistic expression, some aspects of black America's history might otherwise be lost. For example, important histories of slavery are captured in Negro spirituals, while important accounts of ghetto life are captured in rap and hip-hop. By recognizing and comprehending the cultural texts of black America, mainstream American culture is provided a better understanding of black America's cultural legacies and contemporary realities. Whether the medium is dance, music, or storytelling, what remains central to vernacular rhetoric is that it provides scholars with a vantage point that places invisible groups and inaudible voices at the center of discussion.[8]

## African Americans in the Movies

Placing marginalized groups at the center of discussion becomes increasingly important when looking at a popular form of expression, such as cinema. Since its emergence as a viable form of entertainment and expression, Hollywood cinema has failed to accurately capture the essence of the African American experience. This stems from a multitude of reasons but fits primarily into two categories. First, African American experiences have historically been largely ignored by the film industry and the general public. Second, when African American experiences have been depicted in film, black bodies have been grossly misrepresented and stereotyped.[9] Although movies such as *Nothing but a Man* (1964), *Antoine Fisher* (2002), and *Akeelah and the Bee* (2006) more accurately depict the multifaceted lived realities of African American communities, after the movies' releases, they were widely ignored by the vast majority of the viewing public and as a result are few and far between. Furthermore, such movies often receive far less exposure because larger studios refuse to back them, public relations refuses to sell them, or white audiences refuse to view them. Hence, the American film industry remains unable and/or unwilling to consistently produce films that more fully address the African American experience.[10]

While Hollywood continues to fall short in its portrayals of African American identity, in the past ten years a plethora of independently produced documentary features has shed light on lesser-known aspects of black life. LaChapelle's *Rize* is a prime example of the manner in which nonnarrative cinema is used to provide a voice to an otherwise marginalized segment of the African American population. Ironically, the film would most likely not have been made were it not for the interest of LaChapelle, a white filmmaker who had firmly established himself in the media industry as a photographer for magazines, such as *Vanity Fair*, *Vogue*, and *Rolling Stone*. Additionally, he has garnered respect for his directorial work on music videos. In 2005, LaChapelle, learned about krumping and clowning while shooting the "Dirrty" music video for Latina/white pop star Christina Aguilera.[11]

That two nonblack celebrities had to meet to bring a movie about lower-class, black, teenage dancers to the silver screen should not be understated. Understandable, nonblack celebrities touting a movie about an African American dance movement can be read as both voyeuristic and appropriation. While LaChapelle's and Aguilera's involvement in *Rize* might be read as problematic because of the racial differences between the producers and the subjects, it is important to remember that without financial backing and LaChapelle's reputation, "[h]ardly anyone outside of South Central Los Angeles would have known about this significant and important art form."[12] This sentiment might easily be read as LaChapelle taking on the role of the "great white savior" by giving voice to the experiences of black folks. However, in creating *Rize*, LaChapelle acts as a listener and removes himself from the narrative by employing a vérité style. More specifically, the film includes neither the voiceover narration, which is a staple of many documentaries, nor editorializing by the filmmaker. Thus, the dancers take center stage, and it is *their* voices that recount the evolution of krumping and clowning as well as their experiences living in South Central Los Angeles.

By capturing these experiences on film, the documentary helps the characters share their stories in the national spotlight. *Rize* details these experiences through the evolution of krump and clown dancing as a form of resistive empowerment for young, African American, inner-city teenagers. Having been relegated to the margins of America's unspoken caste systems, teenagers in

South Central L.A. created this art form as a way to express themselves as well as provide a safe afterschool activity. *Rize* focuses on several of the movement's central figures: Tommy the Clown, Larry Berry, Dragon, Lil'C, Tight Eyez, and Miss Prissy. Each of these thoughtful and intelligent dancers has a compelling story that helps create the larger narrative about krumping and clowning, and given that the dance forms emerged from an impoverished, oft-overlooked, predominantly black urban space and made it to the silver screen is an especially major feat.

As Harry Benshoff explains, part of the trouble with selling black-themed films to a wider and whiter viewing audience is predicated upon the notion that white audiences do not connect with the content, or, at the very least, white audiences *do not think they will* connect with the content.[13] Critical reviews discussing *Rize* clearly reflect this attitude. For example, online reviewer Ryan Rutherford writes: "When I first saw [the dance style], I laughed at it. To me it looked like nothing more than controlled flailing. Just swinging your arms around with balled fists, rolling your body like a stripper, jumping around, fake fighting and not much more. After seeing this documentary ... I realize that it is so much more than that. To the kids that are in that world, it is everything to them."[14] Another review, written by staindslaved, on the same website reads: "As an incredibly 'white' dancer myself I've always found this style of dancing ... um ... whack? But it was incredibly interesting and even remarkable to hear from the other side.... If these kids want to express themselves through intense free-style dance moves than [*sic*] all the power to them!"[15] Roger Ebert, who gave *Rize* three out of four stars, expresses similar sentiment, "*Rize* on the whole brings good news, of a radical social innovation that simultaneously sidesteps street gangs and bypasses hip-hop.... The most remarkable thing about *Rize* is that it's real."[16]

While it is encouraging to hear such positive reviews for a film focusing on lower-class African Americans from the inner city, many online reviewers note that they had stumbled upon *Rize* by accident, demonstrating that they had not heard of the film and probably would not have watched it otherwise. These sentiments juxtapose the wide availability and success of other African American films. For instance, films that have successfully crossed cultural and racial barriers tend to depict the African American, middle-class, suburban lifestyle.[17] These films include *Waiting to Exhale* (1995), *Soul Food* (1997), and *Why Did I Get Married?* (2007). Notably, many of these films come on the heels of what entertainment reporter Tony Armour calls the "Cosby effect,"[18] in reference to *The Cosby Show*'s (1984–92) ability to gain mainstream success while depicting the lives of upper-middle-class African Americans. *Cosby* and the aforementioned films are situated in the belief that white audiences feel like they will be able to connect with the characters on the screen because they are from a similar socioeconomic background. While this upper-middle-class reality is definitely a part of the black experience, this assiduously focused depiction of African Americans can also be problematic, as it perpetuates a worldview that marginalizes black experiences that do not fit into this very narrowly constructed mold. To clarify, there is definitely space for the aforementioned films and TV series; however, narratives that feature dignified African Americans living below the poverty line also warrant more mainstream attention. The black experience is rich and diverse, and these multiple realities need to be showcased.

## Dancing Oneself into Existence

*Rize* is perfectly positioned as a documentary that can reach a larger mainstream audience in an effort to narrate an important story from the ornately complex African American experience. In capturing the experiences and narratives of young black teenagers in South Central L.A., *Rize* also illustrates how dance can be effectively used as vernacular rhetoric. Largely ignored by the dominant culture, the young people in this film tell their stories of pain, struggle, hope, and triumph through a dance movement that was created locally and later gained national respect. For instance, one of the dancers featured in the film, Lil'C, went on to work as a choreographer for such artists as Missy Elliott, Jennifer Lopez, and Gwen Stefani and became a guest judge on Fox's *So You Think You Can Dance*.[19] In this regard, vernacular rhetoric is more than just a theoretical framework for categorizing various cultural experiences. More completely, vernacular rhetoric is a lifeline for speaking oneself into existence and communicating with the dominant ideologies on a more equal playing field. This eighty-four-minute film can be sectioned into three themes that highlight the experiences of those who are using dance as a way to narrate their lives.

## Communal Struggle

As *Rize* begins, the screen fades in from black and white letters explain, "THE FOOTAGE IN THIS FILM HAS NOT BEEN SPED UP IN ANY WAY." This disclaimer sets the stage for the fast-paced, convulsive, hyperfrenetic movements that comprise two radical dance styles—krumping and clowning. After the opening disclaimer, slow and steady gospel music begins to play as images from the 1965 Watts riots appear on the screen. The black-and-white news footage shows residents pummeling one another, police officers in riot gear advancing upon suspected looters, and burning buildings and shattered windows that demonstrate the fallout from the uprising. Suddenly, the news footage shifts to color as the filmmakers juxtapose the images from the Watts rebellion with the aftermath of the Rodney King verdict.[20] Nearly thirty years had passed between the Watts riots and the Rodney King riots, but the footage, which demonstrates the marginalized populations' response to systemic oppression, is eerily similar. Finally, a calm voiceover interrupts the violent mayhem: "This is our neighborhood. This is where we grew up. We were all kids back then when this happened, but we managed to grow from these ashes.... And this is where we still live." *Rize* then shifts to the present; intercutting images from the Watts and Rodney King riots is footage of dancers in a fenced-in parking lot, krumping and clowning. Thus, the dissatisfaction with social, economic, and political disenfranchisement that led to the riots has been harnessed into dance, which functions as a commentary on historical and contemporary inequality.

The cultural history that manifests within these contemporary dancers is a long and painful history that attaches black bodies to the ongoing struggle of inner-city life.[21] Although young, the dancers are mindful of the unjust legacy that permeates their community. Their aggressive dance moves not only articulate their frustrations with their current situations but also ostensibly mimic the police brutality Rodney King endured a decade prior. In *Rize*'s opening moments, a large crowd is gathered around three modern-day storytellers. One dancer bends over on the pavement while the two others dance around him, slapping, shoving, and pushing his helpless body. Eventually, the seemingly vulnerable dancer begins to rise from the pavement, the other two dancers step to the side, and this once-broken, black body takes center stage. Symbolically, he has risen from the ashes and danced his way back into existence.

Throughout the film, the audience is witness to several dimensions of this raw art form as dancers throw each other into fences, push each other into crowds, flip tables, and hang from light poles. In giving voice to what appears chaotic, Dragon most completely captures the motives behind these gatherings: "A lot of people think it's just, you know, 'Oh, they're just a bunch of rowdy, you know, just ghetto, just heathens and thugs.' No. No. What we are [is] oppressed." Although the dancing looks violent, no fighting takes place at these gatherings. Rather, these dancers have mutual love and respect for one another as they engage in a communicative style that constructively speaks back to the violence and oppression that each of them knows on the most personal levels.

Beyond the external systems of oppression that have plagued this South Central community for decades, there is also the everyday reality of a community fighting the internal demons of violence, drugs, and gangs. As *Rize* delves deeper and deeper into these dancers' lives, it also becomes apparent that many of them are from broken homes, as some of their parents are in jail, suffer from substance abuse, or absent altogether. As a result, many of the dancers are forced to fend for themselves with little to no adult supervision. One dancer's mother describes this environment as "the pit of snakes," and Lil'C's mom explains, "Kids these days have a whole set of anxieties." In the midst of such dire circumstances and limited resources, it can become difficult for young people to remain optimistic when navigating their communities. Therefore, in order to cope with these types of situations, black youth from impoverished communities must develop survival techniques.[22] For some, surviving the ghetto means joining a gang for protection, family, and resources. The dancers in *Rize* have the same desire to survive; however, instead of turning to gangs for protection, family, and resources, they turn to clown and krump crews.

The lure of gang life is exceedingly familiar for the dancing community's patriarch, Tommy the Clown, a former drug dealer who thanks God for going to jail because it helped him turn his life around. In no uncertain terms, Tommy boasts that he "aspired" to be a drug dealer when he was a young kid growing up in the inner city because dealers were the wealthiest guys in the neighborhood. He has since become a positive role model, ghetto celebrity, and father figure to nearly all of the young dancers. One young female dancer in particular speaks to his influence: "If I wasn't dancin' for Tommy, I'd probably be doing some bad things right now." The dancers' mothers also appreciate Tommy's role as a surrogate father and use him to help motivate their children to perform well in school. The extraordinary tasks of communal father, provider, and protector resonate intimately with Tommy as he describes saving kids' lives: "I catch you in a gang, you are in trouble.... I don't want you to wear them colors. And they listen to me and they do it. So I guess you could say that saved his life because if they would've worn that color, they would've went over to that neighborhood, they would've got shot, they would've been dead."

Near the end of *Rize*, the audience is witness to the unforgiving brutality of gang violence. On September 10, 2003, an innocent fifteen-year-old girl, Quinesha, was shot and killed while she and her friend walked to the corner store for a late-night snack. Reflecting on this violence, a classmate of Quinesha laments, "Just walking down the street you can get shot for no reason." The harsh reality of a murdered youth is not lost on the older people in South Central either. Austin Harris, the owner of Payless Caskets, comments, "Lots of people think the old folks the one all doin' all the dying, but you young folks beatin' us out of here boy. You know that. You're killin' yourselves. Don't make no sense."

Evaluating the context of this neighborhood as a whole, it is difficult to come to any conclusion other than South Central is a grueling place to grow up. From the outside looking in, it is easy for some to declare how hard work and personal responsibility would lift them out of similar situations. Yet, for these young dancers, South Central is all they know, and the 'hood brings comfort. Miss Prissy relates, "Some people don't feel safe outside of this place.... I've seen a lot of people come from Hollywood and come and visit my home and be like 'How do you live here? You live in South Central. Oh, it's so—it's so dangerous!' [I'm] like, 'It's not dangerous. It's life.'" Miss Prissy highlights her personal relationship with her neighborhoods and, ultimately, her dance crews. The familial bonds she feels with her neighborhood and her dance crew are central to self-identification and create a powerful sense of belonging.

## Communal Creativity

According to some estimates, as many as fifty clown groups exist in the Los Angeles area, and each one has a unique costume, makeup, theme, and name. They include Homeboy the Clown Entertainment, Cartoonz Clowns, Just Clownin', and Get 'Em Up Soldiers. There is also an Asian crew: Rice Track Clowns. Underscoring the significance of these crews showcases grassroots creativity on film. This contrasts the larger media landscape where many narrative films focus on the negative attributes of African American communities.[23] For instance, *Boyz N the Hood* (1991), *Precious* (2009), and *For Colored Girls* (2010) depict African American communities as inherently violent, uncaring, and unforgiving. While there is a space for these films, they are the predominant representations of blacks and black life, consistently depicting African American communities as places to escape from as opposed to communities also filled with creativity, hope, and love. Significantly, when films do highlight more positive attributes of African American communities, it is usually achieved with the help of a great white savior. For instance, *Dangerous Minds* (1995) and *Freedom Writers* (2007) both illustrate how struggling teenagers of color can overcome adversity or create positive changes in their lifestyles and communities. However, positive creativity is only sparked after white teachers intervene and transform the unruly behaviors of black and brown bodies. In both instances, white audiences are taught that inner-city teenagers cannot manage their own affairs and that mainstream America should fear the "growing populations of ostensibly uneducated and uncontrollable Youth of Color."[24]

In contrast to films that underscore inner-city teenagers' reliance on the outside help of white intermediaries, what audiences stand witness to in *Rize* is an inner-city community's ability to foster positivity and artistry from within in spite of limited resources. In a portion of his interview, Lil'C notes that teenagers in more affluent neighborhoods are given the opportunity to partake in dance forms, such as ballet, performing arts, tap, and jazz. In doing so, Lil'C simultaneously marks the absence of performing arts in South Central. Dragon expands upon this narrative, making it clear that for him, krumping and clowning are his resistive way of combating this marginalized status: "We don't have after-school programs.... There's always a football team because in the inner-city we're all thought to be sports players. Everyone does not play basketball and everybody does not play football.... Is there something else for us to do? So what we did is—is *a group of us got together and we invented this*" (emphasis added).

Dragon continues defining krumping and clowning as a "ghetto ballet" that is "just as valid" as any other form of dance that may come out of a more traditional and formal setting. However, he does mark one key difference in that this "ghetto ballet" is a movement that is "already implanted in us from birth." This is unlike the more classical forms of dance, which must be taught. In the film, we see this perceived predisposition to this type of dance as footage of contemporary krump dancing is interwoven with old footage of African ceremonies. The juxtaposed images of the aggressive krump and clown movements with those of African wrestling create an interesting parallel that is only strengthened by the fact that participants in both forms engage in face painting. Hence, *Rize* creates the sensation of kinship across the African diasporas, and the teenagers in South Central and the African tribal communities seem to be connected through time and distance.

In addition to creating sense of shared kinship with their African roots, music and dance are also outlets for the dancers to vent their frustrations, share their emotions, and pass on their culture. When discussing the emotional benefits of dance, Tight Eyez explains that these dance groups operate as both a means of escape and a medium to express his otherwise suppressed voice: "It's real hard for kids like me cuz, okay, you have school, you go to school, but you have gangbangers. You can't even wear certain colors around here so you tend to have an outlet and sometimes, most of the time your outlet is music ... and a lot of times dancin' comes out." In this regard, krumping and clowning are used as nonverbal forms of communication for expressing emotions that the dancers may not otherwise be able to express.

In sharing these emotions through dance, the dancers are simultaneously communicating stories about their culture. While most of these narratives are circulated and shared on the streets, the dancers at least once a year are provided the opportunity to communicate to a larger audience at BattleZone, a dance competition pitting the best krumping and clowning crews against one another. *Rize* chronicles BattleZone V at the Great Western Forum, the former home of the Los Angeles Lakers and Kings that has a capacity of about seventeen thousand. BattleZone was created in the spirit of a heavyweight boxing match, complete with entourages, robes, and a championship belt. Instead of formal judges determining the winners of each dance-off, the competition rests solely on the audience's applause. Integral to each team's success is the incorporation of various ages, genders, and body types. For instance, the Little Mama matches position two elementary school girls against each other, and the Big Boy matches position two heavyset men against one another. About the diversity of the dancers, Miss Prissy remarks, "Some of us may look gritty. Some of us may not have the prettiest smiles.... But we are krumpin.'" The crowd's energy and the inclusiveness of the competition create the quintessential communal event where everyone is encouraged to take part in the telling of the larger narrative.

Ultimately, BattleZone V ends with clear winners and losers. The winners dance around with their trophies and climb on the tops of the dressing-room lockers. Conversely, the losers are clearly upset at the outcome, even going so far as to suggest that they were cheated. Notably, the competitiveness of BattleZone does have the potential to remind community members and audiences about the same problematic rivalries that exist among the street gangs. Obviously, dance crews are not gangs, as the latter generally create division through violence and intimidation. However, as previously mentioned, the familial institutions of dance crews and street gangs fill similar psychological needs for protection, family, and resources. Additionally, in heated moments of competition, both have the potential to divide and harm the community, albeit in very different ways. Therefore, in the interest of community cohesion, events like BattleZone should strive to usurp the cyclical nature of division through competition and, instead, position their success on the merits of bringing the community together. Otherwise, South Central may unintentionally re-create a similar competitive atmosphere that leads to so many of the original problems among teenagers.

Regardless of whether the dancers won or lost, what is made clear during this portion of the film is that BattleZone depicts moments of creativity, victory, and defeat that uniquely belong to the dancers. First, these dancers created vibrant dance movement in the streets of South Central that captures the imagination of an entire community. Second, these dancers successfully transitioned this dance movement from the streets and proceeded to produce a massive event at an iconic sports arena. The event was so well marketed and widely popular that it generated enough social and economic capital to last multiple seasons. Most important, BattleZone was driven exclusively by the dancers. This internal creative power happened without the guidance of well-intentioned government policies or external white mentors. The self-guided success of this event should not be overlooked, and the dancers should be exceptionally proud of their ability to create, promote, and market an event that showcased their love of dancing and brought together a struggling community.

## Communal Hope

While celebrating his BattleZone V victory with his fellow dancers in the locker room, Tommy the Clown is abruptly interrupted when he receives a phone call informing him that his house had been broken into while he was performing in the competition. With tears flowing down his face and his voice cracking, Tommy presses his body against a concrete wall and states, "You try and work hard for these people, but people always doing stuff.... It's hard, man." In an attempt to comfort Tommy, Larry reassures him that burglaries do not matter because the dancers will ultimately move on to bigger and better things. These comforting words in a moment of heartache remind viewers that surviving difficult moments can sometimes take never-ending amounts of hope and faith. This hopeful theme is central in the final minutes of *Rize* when it highlights the community's dedication and faith in God's guidance and wisdom. Drawing a parallel between krumping and clowning and faith, Dragon's mother engages in the following exchange:

> DRAGON'S MOTHER: I can krump too. I get krump for Christ, but I get krump.
> INTERVIEWER: Is there a difference?
> DRAGON'S MOTHER: I don't think there is a difference. I think when [these performers] dance, they dance from the spirit. And when I'm—when I'm at church, I dance from my spirit.

*Rize* then shifts to a small church of about thirty people. Two of the krumpers, Miss Prissy and Dragon, are dancing in front of the congregation while the other parishioners sing gospel hymns and the pastor shouts scripture from behind the podium. Miss Prissy describes her reasons for attending church: "Dragon brought me back to Christ. One day we were getting krump in my garage, and he told me, 'You know, you'd be a lot better if you start going back to church.' I forgot what started me on my way, and it was God." In these moments, Miss Prissy's graceful movements unite the contradictory worlds of paroxysmal, spastic, and sexualized street performance with the elegant, modest, and holiness of church. Not only do these two worlds exist side by side but also the gritty streets and pristine church are interdependent. They are woven together out of the same African American experiences and cannot be separated. Quite profoundly, they need one another in order to survive.

Beyond uniting a complex community, these young dancers also have a profound passion for creating change in their community. Larry says he wants to use his talents as a dancer to make "smiles where there [were] no smiles. Laughter where there was no laughter." For these and other reasons, it remains vital to speak about these dancers as role models in the black community. Notably, each one of these performers is making an impact in his/her community through a movement that is "an inclusive, nonviolent form of social resistance."[25] Holistically, krumping and clowning are influential and persuasive methods of change. Not only are these dancers communicating stories and fashioning constructive art but they are also providing the younger generation with positive role models. Given most of the dancers' relatively young ages, this sense of responsibility is impressive.

In reflecting on role models, the default is to tokenize those African American leaders who have made it out of the 'hood and into the halls of the Ivy League and other historically white spaces. While we should celebrate the successes of such leaders as President Obama, Oprah Winfrey, and LeBron James, their stories should not be positioned as the quintessential stories of black success. Doing so only operates to undermine the achievements of African Americans still living in the 'hood who struggle daily with the realities of widespread indifference. Furthermore, tokenizing those African Americans who have "made it" strengthens the bootstrap mentality and mollifies to ideologies of personal responsibility and colorblind equality. Inequality exists, race still matters, and certain black communities remain marginalized regardless of who is sitting in the White House.

By focusing on those who remain in these marginalized communities, either by choice or by chance, *Rize* offers a more inclusive perspective of what a successful African American role model can look like. As Swoop says, "give me my respect for just doing something positive and not going negative." Here, Swoop uses his voice to offer pedagogical commentary about how racism and power operate. First, at the micro level, Swoop is telling spectators that he is not given the credit he deserves as a black male who is resisting dominant stereotypes about black masculinity. Second, at the macro level, Swoop is asserting himself as a progressive member of the black community who can transform his neighborhood without the assistance of white systemic intervention or pandering white endearment. This critical interpretation elevates

Swoop's value as a leader in his community and destabilizes the political imposition of how whiteness currently defines "good" role models.

In the end, places like South Central Los Angeles are often demonized for their lack of values and lack of role models. These spaces are ignored because tumultuous lifestyles are not something that most people aspire to. However, it is important to remember that these problems do not solely manifest within oppressed communities.[26] There remain both internal and external factors that subjugate these neighborhoods, and, in this regard, we might all soon discover how each of us is implicated in their demise. Because we are all intrinsically linked to one another's community, we should all be concerned about the condition of one another's community. Yet, we should also be humbled enough to know that we are not the experts on other people's neighborhoods and that no amount of outside help can uplift struggling communities unless the people within those communities are empowered.

From the outside, South Central may seem like a community that lacks leadership, but if there is any hope of transforming this disenfranchised environment, then scholars must concede that only those living within South Central have the wherewithal to create that transformation. Those living in South Central are the ones who most intimately understand the circumstances of their neighborhood, and these dancers are the ones who have the ability to change their community from the bottom up, as opposed to those who try to change things from the top down. What's more is that these young people already have the desire to rise above their situations. They don't need to be told what to do. They simply need people to hear them. This type of attitude uniquely situates these young men and women as the hope of their community. With that in mind, it is important to support the efforts of these dancers as well as look upon them for knowledge and guidance. These dancers are speaking to the outside world through dance, and now it is our obligation to listen to their voices.

*Rize* is a commanding documentary that highlights the narratives of young dancers whose voices had not been given a platform to be heard by mainstream audiences. As vernacular rhetoric, the dancing throughout *Rize* not only underscores a significant cultural art form but also, and more important, emphasizes how this art form is transforming a community. In situating krumping and clowning as vernacular rhetoric, audiences might more clearly appreciate how these dance movements capture the creativity of South Central as well as empower the citizens of the community to speak loudly within the surroundings of gangs, violence, drugs, and subjugation.

Additionally, cultural standards about materialism, consumption, wealth, and success can manipulate young inner-city teenagers looking to make a name for themselves in a world that remains callous toward their circumstances. Yet, krumping and clowning resist appropriation while telling a different story about the hopes, dreams, and desires of a struggling neighborhood. Tight Eyez asserts his commitment to the power of this art form: "We're not gonna be clones of the commercialized hip-hop world, because that's been seen for so many years. Somebody's waiting on something different: another generation of kids with morals and values that they won't need what's being commercialized.... I feel that we're custom-made and we're of more value than any piece of jewelry or any car or any big house that anybody could buy."

These words communicate a deeper understanding about the importance of these dance movements and how empowering these art forms are to these young dancers. Krumping and clowning were not created for mass consumption. Instead, they are about earning self-respect, finding one's voice, and rescuing a desperate community. Dragon likens his experience with krumping to reaching "out for that board" as one is drowning. In this regard, the process of communicating dance through film becomes important in that documentary cinema can help communicate these types of stories, experiences, and emotions that are oftentimes overlooked in broader culture.

Ultimately, *Rize* reflects the heart of this African American community's ability to strengthen itself through shared experiences. Some of the time, these shared experiences are uplifting, and other times, those experiences are downright depressing. In those instances, these dancers have found a way to compel hope within themselves as well as those around them while facing the violence and despair of an oft-disregarded neighborhood. The lesson from these dancers is that one might lose everything external, but one should never lose hope or one's sense of self-worth. There may not always be a happy ending in the traditional sense, but one's role in life is to keep moving forward, to keep being positive in the face of adversity. As Tommy the Clown eloquently summarizes in the aftermath of being robbed and evicted, "When they get to hatin', start shakin'."

## Notes

1. As defined by Rap Basement, krumping and clowning are freestyle dance forms that use high-energy, fast-paced, aggressive, and exaggerated movements to "release anger, aggression and frustration positively, and in a non-violent way." For more information, see www.rapbasement.com.
2. Ono and Sloop, "Critique," 29.
3. Howard, "Vernacular Mode," 242.
4. Hauser, *Vernacular Voices*, 11.
5. Ono and Sloop, "Critique," 22.
6. Bacon, "Declaration of Independence," 140.

7. West, *Cornel West Reader*, 474.

8. Phillips, "Engaging Men and Boys," 263.

9. Stewart, *Migrating to the Movies*, 27.

10. Sieving, *Soul Searching*, 202.

11. Gleiberman, "*Rize* review."

12. Roberts, "Rising Above Adversity."

13. Benshoff and Griffin, *America on Film*, 94–100.

14. "*Rize* Reviews."

15. Ibid.

16. Roger Ebert, "*Rize*," *Chicago Sun-Times*, accessed November 11, 2012, http://rogerebert.suntimes.com/apps/pbcs.dll/article?AID=/20050623/REVIEWS/50614004/1023.

17. Benshoff and Griffin, *America on Film*, 94–95.

18. Terry Armour, "African-American Films Ride 'Cosby effect,'" *Chicago Tribune*, November 18, 2007, accessed November 11, 2012, http://articles.chicagotribune.com/2007–11-18/news/0711160690_1_african-american-semi-autobiographical-film-idris-elba.

19. RealityBug.

20. During the earlier morning hours of March 3, 1991, Rodney King, a twenty-five-year-old African American male, led Los Angeles police on a high-speed chase. Police eventually stopped King's car, and a confrontation ensued. During the confrontation, five police subdued King with Tasers and batons. From an apartment complex across the street, George Holliday videotaped the incident. The video ignited a media firestorm over police brutality and indicated that King was unarmed, defenseless, and hit with a baton over thirty times. King suffered multiple broken bones, brain damage, and kidney damage. Four of the officers were charged with excessive force but were acquitted on April 29, 1992. For more information, see Gooding-Williams, *Reading Rodney King*, and Owens and Browning, *Lying Eyes*.

21. Smaill, *Documentary*, 54.

22. Majors and Billson, *Cool Pose*, 7.

23. Friedman, *Hollywood's African American Films*, 202.

24. Yosso and Garcia, "From Ms. J. to Ms. G.," 98.

25. Gonzalez, "Rize."

26. Choules, "Shifting Sands," 478.

## Works Cited

Bacon, Jacqueline. "Declaration of Independence: African American Abolitionists and the Struggle for Racial and Rhetorical Self-Determination." In *Critical Rhetorics of Race*, edited by Michael G. Lacy and Kent A. Ono, 139–58. New York: New York University Press, 2011.

Benshoff, Harry M., and Sean Griffin. *America on Film: Representing Race, Class, Gender, and Sexuality at the Movies*, 2d ed. Oxford: Wiley-Blackwell, 2009.

Choules, Kathryn. "The Shifting Sands of Social Justice Discourse: From Situation the Problem with 'Them,' to Situating It with 'Us.'" *Review of Education, Pedagogy, and Cultural Studies* 29, no. 5 (2007): 461–81.

Friedman, Ryan Jay. *Hollywood's African American Films: The Transition to Sound*. New Brunswick: Rutgers University Press, 2011.

Gleiberman, Owen. "*Rize* review." *Entertainment Weekly*, June 15, 2005. Accessed July 4, 2012. http://www.ew.com/ew/article/0,,1072752,00.html.

Gonzalez, Ed. "*Rize*." *Slant Magazine*, June 10, 2005. Accessed July 4, 2012. http://www.slantmagazine.com/film/review/rize/1557.

Gooding-Williams, Robert. *Reading Rodney King/Reading Urban Uprising.* New York: Routledge, 1993.

Hauser, Gerard A. *Vernacular Voices: The Rhetoric of Publics and Public Spheres.* Columbia: University of South Carolina Press, 1999.

Howard, Robert Glenn. "The Vernacular Mode: Locating the Non-institutional in the Practice of Citizenship." In *Public Modalities: Rhetoric, Culture, Media, and the Shape of Public Life,* edited by Daniel C. Brower and Robert Asen, 240–66. Tuscaloosa: University of Alabama, 2010.

Majors, Richard, and Janet Mancini Billson. *Cool Pose: The Dilemmas of Black Manhood in America.* New York: Lexington Books, 1992.

Ono, Kent A., and John M. Sloop. "The Critique of Vernacular Discourse." *Communication Monographs* 62, no. 1 (1995): 19–46.

Owens, Tom, and Rod Browning. *Lying Eyes: The Truth Behind the Corruption and Brutality of the LAPD and the Beating of Rodney King.* New York: Thunder's Mouth, 1994.

Phillips, Joshua Daniel. "Engaging Men and Boys in Conversations about Gender Violence: *Voice Male* Magazine Using Vernacular Rhetoric as Social Resistance." *Journal of Men's Studies* 20, no. 3 (2012): 259–73.

RealityBug. "So You Think You Can Dance Cast: Lil C." *RealityBug,* 2013. Accessed July 4, 2012. http://www.realitybug.com/soyouthinkyoucandance/cast/196-Lil-C.

"*Rize* reviews." *Rotten Tomatoes.* Accessed July 4, 2012. http://www.rottentomatoes.com/m/rize/.

Roberts, Geoffrey D. "Rising above Adversity." *Reel Talk Movie Reviews,* n.d. Accessed July 4, 2012. http://www.reeltalkreviews.com/browse/viewitem.asp?type=review&id=1347.

Sieving, Christopher. *Soul Searching: Black-Themed Cinema from the March on Washington to the Rise of Blaxploitation.* Middletown, CT: Wesleyan University Press, 2011.

Smaill, Belinda. *The Documentary: Politics, Emotion, Culture.* New York: Palgrave Macmillan, 2010.

Stewart, Jacqueline Najuma. *Migrating to the Movies: Cinema and Black Urban Modernity.* Berkeley: University of California Press, 2005.

West, Cornel. *The Cornel West Reader.* New York: Basic Civitas, 1999.

Yosso, Tara J., and David Gumaro Garcia. "From Ms. J. to Ms. G.: Analyzing Racial Microaggressions in Hollywood's Urban School Genre." In *Hollywood's Exploited: Public Pedagogy, Corporate Movies, and Cultural Crisis,* edited by Benjamin Frymer, Tony Kashani, Anthony J. Nocell II, and Richard Van Heertum, 85–104. New York: Palgrave Macmillan, 2010.

# Gender, the Streets and Violence

## *Ameena Matthews and Violence Interruptions in* The Interrupters

### Ashley Farmer

In February 2012, Ameena Matthews appeared on *The Colbert Report*. For a show that uses high-profile actors and authors to satirize the American political system, Matthews's appearance is somewhat of an anomaly. Sitting across from host Stephen Colbert, Matthews explained her guest spot by describing her unique work: "I am a Violence Interrupter in saving lives.... We stop the transmission from violence, one person to another. Where I work is where I used to live. In Chicago, Englewood ... people think that it's violent but it's not, it's just stricken by just poverty and lack of education and lack of jobs.... My goal is to save a life and to be proactive and reactive." When asked by the TV host why young people pay attention to her, Matthews responded, "I'm considered a credible messenger.... I've been there, and I've done that. I have been out there in the streets of Chicago."[1]

Matthews is one of the central characters in Steve James's and Alex Kotlowitz's documentary *The Interrupters* (2012). The film follows her and two other Violence Interrupters, Cobe Williams and Eddie Bocanegra, who work for CeaseFire, an organization designed to quell the rising number of violent crimes in urban spaces like the South Side of Chicago. James's and Kotlowitz's documentary developed out of their shared interest in Chicago, where they both reside, and Kotlowitz's interest in exploring CeaseFire's unique approach to grappling with violence.[2] Using a skeleton camera crew, the filmmakers follow the three protagonists as they attempt to break the cycle of violence by intervening in community conflicts. The documentary simultaneously celebrates the Interrupters' extraordinary courage and documents the causes and effects of their violent pasts.

This essay explores how *The Interrupters* challenges standard visual depictions of the inner city. In particular, it examines Ameena Matthews and the ways in which her role as a Violence Interrupter in the Englewood community creates new definitions of race, space, gender, and resistance. Through an investigation of Matthews's personal history, family life, and community activism, *The Interrupters* shows the shifting gendered landscape of the contemporary black community and offers diverse visual representations of black womanhood within the inner city.

## Black City Cinema: Contemporary Portrayals of the Inner City

The inner city has come to represent more than a collection of buildings, businesses, and residents that comprise a given locale. Rather, in the political and social context, which is largely shaped by national discourse, the inner city has become a marker of being black, male, poor, and dispossessed. The set of attributes assigned to urban areas ascribes race, gender, and economic labels that undermine the diversity of experiences of those who reside in inner-city spaces. African American women have often become the symbols of this public discourse. Visually, African American women in urban spaces have occupied a handful of stereotypical roles, including the welfare queen, the single mother, or the jezebel. These images further compound the perception of the inner city as a space of black dysfunction and destruction and place African American women at the epicenter.[3] As a result, the inner city has become a real and imagined space defined by its ability to confine and discipline black bodies and black minds.

In the 1990s, African American filmmakers embraced the inner city and its complicated race and gender constructs in order to counter dehumanizing narratives about the black community.[4] This cycle of films, known as "hood films," is defined by "visual and aural iconography" of the inner city and are "often engaged in a dialogue with its immediate socioeconomic, political, and industrial contexts."[5] John Singleton's *Boyz N the Hood* (1991) serves as a notable example of a hood film. It uses cultural symbols, contemporary politics, and the aesthetics of the inner city to counter narratives of black dysfunction and visually tie them to the larger systemic challenges that African Americans face. For example, *Boyz N the Hood* makes overt references to the inner city's economic and social realities. Statistics on black male mortality, the visual markers of poverty, and the specter of white surveillance in the Los Angeles Police Department are in the first scenes of the film. The film's protagonist, Tre (Cuba Gooding Jr.) comes of age as he navigates the negative forces that plague his community, including drugs, child neglect, and violence. Together, the sounds and visual symbols construct the inner city as a dystopian space to be conquered by young black men. This cinematic technique, coupled with the genre's inclusion of gansta rap stars (Ice Cube is in *Boyz N the Hood)* and music, connected with black youth culture made the films incredibly lucrative at the box office. As a result of their successes, films like *Boyz N the Hood*, *Straight out of Brooklyn* (1991), *Juice* (1992), and *Menace II Society* (1993) in the 1990s dominated the public's perception of black inner-city life.[6]

Traditionally, African American women occupied a marginal place in hood films with the black male experience taking center stage. As Paula Massood explains in *Black City Cinema*, on-screen depictions of African American women often characterized them as the "bane of the black man's existence" due to their role as single mothers or welfare recipients. This contributed to existing narratives that claim that African American women are the source of the black community's problems, perpetuating stereotypical images of African American femininity.[7] In other instances, they served the purpose of authenticating the "ghetto" context in which the storyline develops. For example, in *Boyz N the Hood*, women appear only in relation to the main male protagonists, Doughboy (Ice Cube), Ricky (Morris Chestnut), and Tre. As Gwendolyn Pough notes, Shalika (Regina King), Doughboy's girlfriend, represents the stereotypical "ghetto girl," wearing braids, drinking, and engaging in "unfeminine" behavior. Others, including Ricky's girlfriend Shanice (Alysia Rogers), perpetuate the image of the young, black single mother. Throughout the film, she is always featured with Ricky's child, serving as a reminder that the football star will always be tied to the inner city because of her choice to keep the baby, rather than their engagement in unprotected sex. In their critiques of the film, scholars Pough and Michele Wallace reveal how the focus on black men erases African American women's voices, aspirations, and experiences with violence.[8] Thus, African American women are situated both figuratively and literally outside of the inner-city frame, suggesting that the confluence of structural and social problems in the inner city does not affect their lives.

These marginal or negative characterizations of black women are widespread and have broader implications for women in the inner city. As sociologist Patricia Hill Collins explains, this "constellation of representations" in popular culture helps to justify current "social relations of hyper-ghettoization, unfinished racial desegregation, and efforts to shrink the social welfare state."⁹ The effects of these social relations are far-reaching and contribute to the systemic oppression that perpetuates the inner-city problems that are featured in James's and Kotlowitz's film. Furthermore, these images, and the matrix of inequality that they perpetuate, reveal the complex ways in which African American women have experienced oppression in the post–civil rights era.

*The Interrupters* shares some of the same visual and analytical tropes that characterize hood films. Yet, if films like *Boyz N the Hood* and *Menace II Society* are about black immobility, violence, and the demise of young black men, *The Interrupters* uses the documentary form to explore the roots of this violence and the individualized effects of racialized containment. The documentary expands the problem of violence beyond the street corners of Englewood and reveals it to be a citywide, multigenerational problem that affects all of the residents who come in contact with violence and its aftermath. This inversed perspective connects the coded elements of the inner city to larger structural institutions that perpetuate inequality, including the police force, lawmakers, and political institutions.

Hood films and documentaries focusing on the inner city consistently deliver conflicted and complicated depictions of these institutions and those who inhabit those spaces. While they highlight the sociopolitical context that perpetuates inequality, these images, at times, reinforce some of the most longstanding and negative African American stereotypes. As a result, some critics suggest that such films mythologize "the violent elements of urban life while jettisoning complexities of gender, ethnicity, sexuality, age, and economy."¹⁰ *The Interrupters* attempts to address some of the complexities of the inner city while linking these ideas to larger systemic issues that affect urban spaces. The filmmakers created their documentary as an attempt to "restart a conversation about [violence]" and as a step towards revealing the experiential diversity of the inner city "by showing some of the harsh realities [of Englewood] as well as the genuine hope that the interrupters elicit."¹¹

James and Kotlowitz faced challenges in creating a more nuanced picture of the inner city. In particular, producing a critically engaged examination of the black community was difficult given that the filmmakers are not minorities or members of the Englewood community. For the filmmakers, this is an ongoing concern. In his previous documentary, *Hoop Dreams* (1994), James drew both praise and criticism for his depiction of two young African American basketball players, Arthur Agee and William Gates, who were residents of Chicago's Cabrini Green housing projects. As James and his partners document Gates and Agee, two interrelated narrative strains develop: the economic and social realities of the inner city are complex, and "the desire to escape the ghetto is a natural aspiration."[12] The former narrative underscores the idea that the media has produced a one-sided picture of urban life, downplaying the nuances of inner-city residents. The latter reinforces some of the dominant discourses of black dysfunction by perpetuating the assumption that escape from urban spaces is the best way to achieve social normalcy. Thus, while an important step in documenting the black experience in inner cities, films like *Hoop Dreams* fall short of some of their critical intentions and reproduce some of the harmful narratives about inner-city life.[13]

In *The Interrupters*, James and Kotlowitz are more cognizant of the visual representation and narratives about the inner city. Their choice in protagonists reflects this point. The main characters of *The Interrupters* are two men—an African American and a Latino—and an African American woman. While the Violence Interrupters are overwhelmingly black and male, the filmmakers' choice to diversify the central characters indicates an interest in resisting the typecasting of Englewood and its inhabitants. The filmmakers' decision to depict alternative models of inner-city life marks a departure from hood films. Mirroring narrative films like F. Gary Gray's *Set It Off* (1996), which features four African American women battling everyday issues of poverty, racism, and sexism, *The Interrupters* highlights the experiences of African American women and documents their efforts to survive inner-city life.[14] Not only does this framework challenge essentialist characterizations of African American women but it also foregrounds African American women's gender-specific experiences with oppression, domination, and violence.

James and Kotlowitz further resist stereotyping Englewood by interweaving a discussion about the structural factors that lead to violence with the personal stories of the neighborhood's residents. For example, the filmmakers follow Cobe Williams into the home of Englewood resident and mother Latoya Oliver, whose two sons are in rival neighborhood gangs. After a tense scene where Oliver discusses the role that violence has played in her home, the film cuts to an interview with CeaseFire employer Dr. Gary Slutkin, who provides his theory on understanding and preventing violence: "Violence is like the great infectious diseases of all history.... What perpetuates violence can be as today as the microorganisms of the past were. I had been overseas for about ten years at World Health working on infectious diseases. Coming back to the U.S. the violence is unavoidable. But I saw it as behavior, not as bad people." The "invisible" forces that Slutkin refers to make a violent act not simply about retaliation but a product of ongoing inequalities that lead an individual to believe that in that moment a violent act is the only viable resolution. Tio Hardiman, the creator of the Violence Interruption Program, echoes Dr. Slutkin's remarks, "Violence is a learned behavior," or an act brought on by an individual's need to assert self-validation in the midst of perpetually dehumanizing circumstances.

The interviews with Slutkin and Hardiman reinforce one of *The Interrupters*' main themes, that violence is a disease "caught" by residents of the inner city rather than an act endemic to African Americans in urban spaces. To emphasize this point, viewers are consistently shown a textured crosscutting between Englewood residents' personal experiences with violence and an analysis of the social and economic conditions that lead Englewood residents to commit violent acts. In the case of Ameena Matthews, Englewood residents explain the poverty, overcrowding, abuse, and lack of resources that led her to turn to drugs and violence. The filmmakers juxtapose these images with present-day scenes, where Matthews describes how her violent past continually infringes upon her current attempts to live a family and faith-centered lifestyle. This contrast not only highlights the ubiquitous nature of systemic racism and economic oppression but it also personalizes the effects of this oppression to a greater extent than fictional films.

Finally, James and Kotlowitz reveal the complexities of the city in their depiction of Englewood by featuring the effects of violence on the physical terrain of the neighborhood. Interspersed between explanations of violence are striking images of dilapidated buildings, graffiti featuring gang signs, and memorials constructed to honor victims of neighborhood violence. These moments, which James admits are meant to cause "rumination by the viewer," reflect the ways in which Englewood residents, rather than the filmmakers, experience and respond to violence, poverty, and loss.[15]

Together, the editing, systemic explanations, and penetrating interviews signal key differences in James and Kotlowitz's cinematic approach to documenting Chicago. There is a conscious attempt to disassociate the violent behaviors and actions that take place in Englewood from the idea that these acts are intrinsically tied to race. In addition, by focusing on men *and* women who defy inner-city stereotypes, the documentary counters the popular perception of the inner city as an exclusively male space. Moreover, James and Kotlowitz challenge the narrative of a universal desire to leave the ghetto by focusing on those who work from within the inner city to change it. As a result, *The Interrupters* reframes traditional narratives about violence and counters depictions of powerlessness within the inner-city community.

*The Interrupters*, like 1990s hood films, explores the interrelationship among poverty, violence, and criminality in the lives of urban African Americans. James and Kotlowitz expand on this idea by using the documentary genre to explore the lives of the Violence Interrupters and the structural and economic factors that led these community workers toward a life of violence.

Indeed, the film's power lies in the tension between the dire realities of life in the inner city and the positive relationships forged by CeaseFire's Violence Interrupters. In particular, Matthews, a former gang member turned Violence Interrupter, embodies this tension.

## A New Kind of Enforcer: Ameena Matthews

Viewers are initially introduced to Ameena Matthews in a scene where she is seated in a Violence Interrupters staff meeting hosted on the University of Illinois at Chicago campus. Matthews's bright-red hijab is striking as she sits in the back of the meeting room. Sitting silent, she is an imposing figure, not only as a result of her seriousness but also because she is one of only two women in the room and in the Violence Interrupters program.[16] Poised, confident, and self-assured, Matthews's presence among a group of former violent, male offenders exemplifies important differences in *The Interrupters'* representation of inner-city life on screen. The hood films of the 1990s often portray African American women who only occupied traditionally female roles and spaces, as the appendages of men. In *The Interrupters*, viewers meet Matthews in a male-dominated public space where she is recognized as an individual in her own right, unattached to a male protagonist.

As viewers discover as *The Interrupters* progresses, Matthews is notable not only because she is one of the few women in a male-dominated profession but also because of her unique ability to confront, engage, and disrupt violence within the Englewood community. For example, when a fight breaks out on the street corner in front of CeaseFire offices, she intervenes immediately. She walks directly into the conflict and literally pulls a young man away from the scene and into her car. As she drives him away from the altercation, Matthews calms the young man down and speaks to him about the futility of violent retaliation. According to CeaseFire leader Hardiman, Matthews is an effective Violence Interrupter because she is able to "get in where a lot of guys can't get in." In this particular situation, Matthews's ability to effectively communicate with the young man helps her channel his energy into resolving the conflict by discussing the unintended consequences of his potential retaliation. Indeed, it is her training and personally informed response to violence in the black community that make Matthews so effective. Throughout the film, the many scenes of her talking to gang members, counseling families, speaking at funerals, and of course, disrupting violent acts show the extent of Matthews's activism and the high stakes of her commitment to ending violence in Englewood.

It is important to explain that Matthews's commitment to Englewood stems from her ties to Chicago's South Side communities. As the daughter of Jeff Fort, one of the most infamous gang leaders in Chicago history, Matthews witnessed the effects of violence from an early age. In 1966, Fort, along with Eugene "Bull" Harrison, founded the Black Stone Rangers, a notorious Chicago gang. The Stones were extremely powerful in the black community of Woodlawn, a South Side community adjacent to Englewood, acquiring local real estate, businesses, and commercial properties in order to control the area.[17] The gang's success was in part due to federal aid given to them by Lyndon B. Johnson's War on Poverty programming, a piece of 1964 legislation that funneled money into the inner city to reduce poverty and drug use. Specifically, the Stones and their rival gang, the Devil's Disciples, used federal funding to unite warring gangs and create job and housing opportunities for black residents. However, government oversight, gang wars, and drug trafficking erased the gains the Stones made.[18] In addition, state and federal law enforcement relentlessly pursued Fort and eventually tried and convicted him for plotting terrorist attacks against the United States.[19]

As a child, Matthews witnessed the cycle of violence, incarceration, and abuse perpetuated by gangs like the Stones and the Devil's Disciples. Yet, as Hardiman points out, "Ameena never lived off [Fort's name], she made her own name on the streets." In *The Interrupters*, Matthews details how she was one of the few women in an Englewood gang who was "taking care of the business," or selling drugs, hustling, and committing crimes. As she recounts the story of her past, youthful pictures of her appear on screen that reflect and authenticate her storied gang life. Matthews explains that she continued with this lifestyle until she was involved in an altercation in which she was wounded. That moment represents a turning point in her life because it made her reevaluate her circumstances. Matthews further comments that her father called her after this confrontation, vowing to seek revenge. Rather than looking for retribution, she decided that adding to the cycle of gang violence was not the answer. Instead, she told her father not to retaliate against her enemies, and she left her gang, finding solace in her faith and family. Matthews's revelation is an important moment in *The Interrupters*, as it is the first instance where personal triumph overcomes instances of extreme personal and community violence.

James and Kotlowitz use Matthews's personal history to explain the institutional structures, or lack thereof, that lead to the spread of violence. Sitting at the feet of her grandmother "Madea," Matthews describes that her father and mother were teenagers when she was born and that both were caught up in the street lifestyle. Her mother sent her to live with her grandmother after Matthews experienced mental, physical, and sexual abuse in her mother's home. For Matthews, her grandmother was her sole protector: "Once I got hip to the game, my goal was to get Madea up out of [her roach-infested apartment]. But I got caught up. I got caught up in that one more thousand, one more run, one more big hit." Thus, the desire to protect her loves ones and remove them from poverty drove Matthews to violence.

Matthews's life as a gang member sharply contrasts with the image of her as a Violence Interrupter. The juxtaposition is especially stark in the scenes that feature her and her family. These scenes include images of Matthews hosting her daughter's eighth birthday party at a roller-skating rink where she adopts the traditional roles of wife and mother. In these instances, Matthews appears happy and fully enriched by her family and religious community, a contradiction from her previous life of crime. James and Kotlowitz also use Matthews's roles as a wife and mother to explore her transformation. In a voiceover, Matthews says that it was her father that introduced her to Islam, but her continued practice of the faith comes from her desire to "do better" with her life. Her participation in Islam allowed her to meet her husband and start a family: "My family keeps me very, very grounded. At the end of the day I have to come home and cook dinner.... My family is my real job, out there in the community is a piece of cake for me." In her personal life, Matthews embodies the "respectable" form of black womanhood as a wife and mother.

By featuring Matthews's home life, rather than just her activist work, James and Kotlowitz reveal the complexity of her life and her relationship with the community of Englewood. Viewers learn that Matthews embodies two forms of black womanhood both intimately linked to the inner city. The first is the black female gang member; the second is the wife, mother, and local community activist. The former identity offers new visual representations of women, as films—documentary or otherwise—rarely feature women in positions of power within street culture.[20] The latter suggests that black women in the inner city can occupy powerful roles in both public and private spaces. In both instances, Matthews defies standard conceptions of black womanhood in the inner city by not fitting neatly into the stereotypical roles usually associated with African American women on screen in narrative films, like *Waiting to Exhale* (1995) or *Losing Isaiah* (1995).[21] Irrespective of the form of womanhood Matthews embodies, her identification as an African American woman is in a critical tension with the inner city and the matrix of inequality inherent in the urban spaces. As a result, violence, drugs, and the gendered code of the streets continually inform her decisions. Indeed, the documentation of Ameena Matthews in the past and present highlights the gendered frameworks that exist within the inner-city space and the complex relationship between African American women and urban spaces.

Matthews's role as a wife, mother, and reformed gang member further complicates on-screen depictions of African American women in the inner city. Scenes of Matthews acting as a wife and mother produce several new images of black womanhood within the inner city. Scenes featuring Matthews and her family suggest that even as her economic status and stability increased, she did not abandon the community in which she grew up. Instead, the film reflects her steadfast commitment to changing the Englewood community from within its boundaries. Thus, her work as a Violence Interrupter and her individual relationships with members of the Englewood community defy the idea that physical separation from the inner city is a necessary component of upward mobility and economic security.[22] In addition, the juxtaposition of Matthews as a respectable family woman and Matthews as a member of Englewood's street culture constructs a narrative of social change that derives its power from within the spatial confines of the inner city. Not only does this storyline produce a female-centered narrative of the inner city but it also resists attaching the destruction of the black community to African American women. This alternate narrative becomes a source of power for Matthews, affording her a certain degree of mobility and security in her neighborhood.[23] This mobility also produces an alternative model of African American prosperity, one in which African Americans reach across class boundaries in order to develop models of social change.

If Matthews's status defies progressive middle-class values in her choice to remain connected to Englewood, she reinforces other values and cultural markers as she embraces the role of wife and mother. As Collins describes in her study of post–civil rights era gender politics, the growth of the black middle class also "sparked changes in the treatment of gender and sexuality." In these instances, "representations of poor and working-class authenticity and middle-class respectability increasingly came in gender-specific form."[24] Collins contends that an important part of achieving middle-class status is the rejection of the stereotypical images of black womanhood "in favor of a politics of respectability."[25] As a form of resistance, African American women adopted "respectable" or traditional roles and behaviors in order to combat negative characterizations of their public and private lives. Matthews embraces these behaviors throughout the film through her conservative dress and her emphasis on her roles as a wife, mother, and caregiver. Adopting this stance allows Matthews to defy the standard images of the inner city. However, it also distances Matthews from the street culture that she once embraced and reinforces hegemonic gender constructs within the black community.

The tension between nontraditional and traditional gender roles in the black community remains unresolved, as the film only explores Matthews's perspective on this issue. Yet, the film showcases African American women's ability to navigate their violent surroundings in the inner city and adopt "appropriate" feminine behavior. Matthews is able to deploy both of these images of womanhood. And, as a result, she is able to "challenge and manipulate the constraining social and cultural expectations embedded in the gender code" of the streets.[26] The contrasting images of the Violence Interrupter show that there are multiple, and at times competing, iterations of black womanhood in the inner city. The film asks viewers to question notions of contemporary black essentialism particularly as it pertains to black women in urban spaces and to reconsider traditional narratives of African American women's role in inner-city decay.

## Ameena in Action: Women-Centered Community Building

The reconfiguration of gender roles is especially prevalent in scenes that feature Matthews's activism. For example, *The Interrupters* features an extended scene in which she works with the friends of a recently murdered child. The scene begins with Matthews and her fellow mosque members holding a vigil for Corey, a young man who was shot and killed while sitting in front of his home. Matthews breaks away from the prayer group to confront Corey's friends. The following scene features her in the middle of a group of adolescent men, preaching about Corey's senseless death and the need to end violent retaliation. As the camera pans across the faces of the young men in the circle, Matthews yells, "All of it is stupid! All of it is stupid! ... It is unacceptable for me to be holding this child's ... this young man's obituary. Schools, churches, your mama's house, cars.... Those are safe zones." As she talks, she walks up to different young men, looks them in the eye, and demands that they look back. She then pulls the youngest boy from the circle gathered around her and asks, "Who does this baby belong to? Who does this little shorty belong to? He's just hanging around y'all?" The young men respond in the affirmative. Matthews continues, "He just hanging around y'all, right? So he see everything that you all do, right? So if this brother right here catch a case and do a hundred years, who fault is it? It's his fault?" Matthews's question hangs in the air until the young men accept accountability for the boy and his future. She ends her lecture by telling the crowd, "Treat him righteous. Y'all got it? I'm looking to you." The scene concludes with the group of young men thanking her and promising to abide by her words.

Matthews's positioning in this scene serves as one example of the ways in which the focus on African American women can alter the cartographies of black bodies within the inner city. In this particular scene, she occupies the center of the circle, with young and older African American men encircling her. All eyes and bodies are focused on her. If, as Bill Nichols suggests, the on-screen body is a battle site of contested values and representation, then Matthews's appearance on screen becomes a meaningful marker of social difference.[27] Her physical positioning defies ideas of the acceptable spaces for respectable women because she is positioned as an authority figure on the "block."[28] Furthermore, Matthews is the literal and figurative epicenter of the conversation on the street, a position she uses to encourage the young men to resist violent behavior. Through this scene and others featuring Matthews, viewers witness a transformation whereby African American women—rather than violence, sports, or even African American men—are at the literal and figurative epicenter of communal transformation in the inner city.

James and Kotlowitz include multiple scenes of Matthews speaking in public spaces, whereas her male counterparts are often featured working in one-on-one relationships. As a result, the viewer repeatedly sees Matthews as a public figure transforming social and political spaces as former gang member and member of the community. Taken together, *The Interrupters* presents a visual and figurative narrative whereby Matthews and by extension African American women are at the center of contemporary resistance models. The filmmakers use Matthews as the conduit through which to "restart the conversation" about violence and construct alternative visions of the inner city. Indeed, in documenting Matthews, James and Kotlowitz reveal previously ignored gendered models for inspiring change in the black community.

The filmmakers intersperse these inspirational moments throughout the film, countering narratives of inner-city decline. For example, a significant subplot of the film is Matthews's relationship with a young woman from the neighborhood named Caprysha Anderson. Upon meeting Anderson, viewers learn that she is a hardened teenage girl who has already endured her share of abuse and neglect. Like many of her male counterparts, Anderson views drugs and violence as the only way to ensure personal survival and control. Matthews recognizes a younger version of herself in Anderson and attempts to mentor the young woman. James and Kotlowitz follow this relationship as Matthews and Anderson both navigate personal and communal experiences with violence. This narrative draws specific links between the experiences of African American women and the cycle of violence in the inner city.

Matthews and Anderson's relationship is defined by a collection of moments where both women attempt to navigate their abusive pasts in order to forge a prosperous future. James and Kotlowitz characterize this relationship through a series of tightly edited scenes that collectively show the bonds that African American women forge through shared experiences with violence. One of the first extended scenes between Matthews and Anderson occurs after Anderson is released from jail. As Matthews drives her home, Anderson tells her that she wants to obtain her high school diploma, go to college, and become a pediatrician so that she can take care of children and her siblings. The next glimpse into their relationship comes when Matthews takes Anderson out for the day. The film shows the two women riding a carousel at the local mall. Matthews's voiceover describes her personal connection with Anderson and how her story affects her as a mother more than as a community activist. Immediately following their carousel ride, the film cuts to the two women in a nail salon where Matthews treats Anderson to a manicure. As the camera focuses on the teenager, Matthews asks her how it feels to be treated nicely. She uses this moment to remind Anderson that she can be someone else, someone whose everyday life and every experience are not dictated by antagonism, violence, and abuse. Anderson's violent behavior becomes the subject of conversation, giving her time to reflect on the juxtaposition of herself as a violent offender and a young girl being pampered. As Anderson reflects, Matthews tells her, "You deserve to be happy. You deserve to be having girly stuff done." These words bring Anderson to tears to which Matthews responds, "It's ok to cry.... I cry.... Big girls cry." The scene ends with a close-up on Anderson's newly manicured nails as she thinks about Matthews's words.

*The Interrupter* also features moments of conflict between the two women where they are at odds over Anderson's life choices. For example, the filmmakers capture Matthews and her mentee together at a hair salon where Anderson is getting a new hairstyle for the first day of school. While in the stylist's chair, she reiterates her goal of graduating from high school, which makes Matthews beam with pride while offering words of encouragement. However, her happiness gives way to anger in the following scene when Matthews states that Anderson misled her and that school had actually begun three weeks prior to their visit to the hair salon. Angry, Matthews confronts Anderson on camera, "You didn't fight hard enough for you to get up in that school and do what you need to do." When Anderson responds that getting her life together takes time, Matthews balks at this and tells the teenager that she is manipulative. Pushing her face next to the young woman, she asks, "Do you want to be loved? Absolutely. Do you deserve to be loved? Absolutely. First thing, you got to love you." After an extensive lecture, Anderson walks away leaving Matthews to reflect on Anderson's life and her own past. Speaking to the camera, Matthews relates that she sees so much of herself in Anderson. Fighting back tears, she speaks about the regrets she has from her past and her fear that Anderson will end up in the same place if she continues down this self-destructive path.

In their attempt to show the beauty and vulnerability in the relationship between the two women, the filmmakers reveal important cues as to how black womanhood and black resistance function in the inner city. James and Kotlowitz create a clear distinction between the spaces in which Matthews connects with young men and the spaces where she connects with young women. The scenes in the nail salon and hair salon illustrate this point. Historically, semi-public spaces like the beauty salon have been places in which African American women could assert leadership and forge relationships with other women.[29] In the film, it is in these moments that Matthews is able to break through Anderson's tough exterior and in which the young girl opens up about her past and future. Thus, if Matthews and her body positioning defy standard concepts and characterizations of gender with the young men of Englewood, her relationship with Anderson reinforces these notions. As a result, the traditional connections of race and gender are challenged but not entirely remapped through Matthews's on-screen activism. However, the relationship between Matthews and Anderson reveals a lesser-known model of resistance and rehabilitation whereby black female misconduct and violence are countered with traditionally feminine, or as Matthews says, "girly," elements or acts. These touching moments between the two women reveal the ways in which black women work together to overcome the obstacles of inner-city life. The scenes also reveal the fact that African American women carve out gender-specific spaces to form community within the inner city. In turn, the documentary reveals an alternative cartography of counterpublic or safe spaces for African American girls and women.

Matthews's relationship with Caprysha Anderson is at once about defying the constraints of the inner city and about the recognition of black women's gender-specific experiences with violence. Many current-day programs center on ending gang violence and poverty among African American men as they are deemed to be at the highest risk for violent activity.[30] However, the film displays that African American women are equally affected by the cycle of poverty and violence that exists in many urban spaces. Matthews effectively explains this when she reflects on her relationship with Anderson: "It's true that it's only so much that I can do. And that's just one Caprysha. But it's hundreds of thousands of Capryshas out there." In this statement, as much as in her relationship with the young girl, Matthews is calling attention to the need to recognize the ways in which black women suffer within the inner-city infrastructure. In particular, their similar stories show the abuse and neglect often borne by African American women. The enormity of this recognition is not lost on Matthews or the filmmakers. Matthews also nods to the irony of her relationship with Anderson: "You know I remember being nineteen and being a scared girl like that.... If I could go back and make that pain go away for me today ... and that's so painful for me for her. Because she is going to be my age someday and it's going to be a whole bunch of regrets." Indeed, Matthews recognizes that the very person that she identifies with most is the same one that she is struggling, and to some extent failing, to save. The film's epilogue leaves the fate of Caprysha Anderson—and by extension young black women in the inner city—undetermined. In the final scenes of the film, the two women have reunited and are still continuing to build their relationship. Yet, they must rebuild and reconnect from inside prison walls, as Anderson is again incarcerated.

Matthews's relationships reveal that conflict resolution and violence interruption in contemporary African American communities are mediated by gender. At times, Matthews's challenges to the gender hierarchy are the key to her effectiveness. At other times, she reinforces traditional notions of men's and women's roles. However, these scenes also serve as healing moments or instances in which African American women are able to work together to address personal abuse and positive futures. There is still space for debate as to the critical message of *The Interrupters* in regards to gender, the inner city, and resistance. However, the relationship among Matthews, Anderson, and young men in Englewood reflects new "ethnographic imaginations" whereby African American women enter into official narratives about the inner city, community, violence, and power.[31]

James and Kotlowitz produce a real-life account of contemporary inner-city life and a deft historical analysis that spans beyond the life of the featured characters. As a result, *The Interrupters* goes further than facile projections of the inner city and suggests that the violence present in neighborhoods like Englewood is not simply due to its inhabitants. Rather, it is the legacy of civil rights failures, drug laws, deindustrialization, and unequal policy measures. While many viewers may comprehend that public discourses about inner-city residents are contrived, *The Interrupters* personalizes the effects of this discourse and pinpoints the effects of its naturalization.

By featuring Ameena Matthews and Caprysha Anderson, *The Interrupters* also highlights the gender-specific challenges African American women face. Not only does the film challenge narratives that marginalize African American women in urban spaces but it also reveals that African American women are also victims of the oppressive systems in the inner city. The film explores African American women's experiences in a rich and nuanced complexity that forces the audience to rethink traditional notions of women in urban spaces and their ability to resist and redefine the inner city for themselves. Matthews and Anderson reveal the gender-specific effects of discrimination and poverty but also the ways in which women, uniquely, continue to push for a new sense of possibility for themselves and each other. Most important, *The Interrupters* shows that critical attention to gender is necessary to gain a complete understanding of ideas of violence, poverty, and resistance in the inner city. The film carefully details the evolution of African American women in the inner city in a way that narrative films and popular culture have neglected and, thus, failed to portray. The result of the film is a dynamic framework for understanding the contemporary black condition in new, unique, textured, and thought-provoking ways.

## Notes

1. Matthews, "Ameena Matthews."
2. Alex Kotlowitz, "If Gang Shootings and Revenge Killing Were an Infectious Disease How Would You Stop It?" *New York Times*, May 4, 2008, A52; West and West, "Interrupting Violence," 21.
3. The idea that black women are the root of the black community's dysfunction is often attributed to the Moynihan report published in 1965. The Moynihan report claims "the deterioration of the Negro family" was the fundamental problem of the black community. Targeting black women specifically, the report also created the now infamous matriarchy thesis that blames black women for the deteriorating state of black communities. Moynihan, *Negro Family*, 29. More recent scholarship has explored the proliferation and modification of the discourse in the 1990s and 2000s, primarily through the tropes of the "welfare queen" and the "jezebel" in popular culture, film, and literature. For more information, see Campbell, *From Good Ma to Welfare Queen*. Perhaps the most thorough investigation of the stereotypical images of African American women comes from sociologist Patricia Hill Collins, "Mammies, Matriarchs, and Other Controlling Images," in Collins, *Black Feminist Consciousness*.
4. For an overview of these films, see Reid, "New Wave Black Cinema."
5. Massood, *Black City Cinema*, 1.
6. Ibid., 146–47.
7. Massood, "Street Girls with No Future," 232.
8. Wallace, "*Boyz N the Hood* and *Jungle Fever*," 215–17; Pough, *Check It*, 129–33.
9. Collins, *Black Sexual Politics*, 137.
10. McCarthy et al., "Danger in the Safety Zone," 282.
11. West and West, "Interrupting Violence," 21.
12. Kennedy, *Race and Urban Space*, 102.
13. Arthur and Cutler, "On the Rebound," 22–25.
14. For more on the film *Set It Off* and its portrayal of African American women, see Harris, "Interrogating."
15. West and West, "Interrupting Violence," 25.
16. Ibid., 23.
17. Moore and Williams, *Almighty Black P Stone Nation*, 2.
18. Mallory, *Understanding Organized Crime*, 214.

19. Moore and Williams, *Almighty Black P Stone Nation*, 2–5.
20. Notable exceptions to this point include the film *Just Another Girl on the IRT* (1992).
21. For more on these images, see Banks, "Women in Film," 80–82.
22. Years of research on upwardly mobile African American families suggest that a hallmark of the black middle class is their goal of living in decent and safe neighborhoods. For more information on the history of middle-class housing and development, see "Seeking a Good Home or Neighborhood," in Faegin, *Living with Racism*. This has been an ongoing debate among sociologists since the 1970s with major leaders in the field, such as William Julius Wilson, arguing that the black middle-class "exodus" from poor neighborhoods is responsible for black poverty and class stratification. For an overview of this literature and recent developments in this debate, see Adleman, "Neighborhood Opportunities, Race, and Class."
23. In her study of women in urban spaces, Nikki Jones shows that the reputation of being both a violent person and a kind person helps women negotiate violent situations in "It's Not Where You Live."
24. Collins, *Black Sexual Politics*, 122–23.
25. Ibid., 139.
26. Jones, *Between Good and Ghetto*, 11.
27. Nichols, *Representing Reality*, 232.
28. In her analysis of the constructs of the politics of respectability, Evelyn Higginbotham explains that "the street signified male turf" while "women who strolled the streets ... blurred the boundaries of gender." *Righteous Discontent*, 193.
29. For more on the role of beauty salons and African American women, see Gill, *Beauty Shop Politics*.
30. Studies show that American inner-city gangs are overwhelmingly male. Vigil, "Urban Violence and Street Gangs." Recently, scholars have paid increased attention to the role of women in gangs and to female gangs. However, preventative measures remain largely male-focused. See, for example, Miller and Decker, "Young Women and Gang Violence."
31. Nichols, *Representing Reality*, 228.

## Works Cited

Adleman, Robert M. "Neighborhood Opportunities, Race, and Class: The Black Middle Class and Residential Segregation." *City and Community* 3 (March 2004): 43–63.
Arthur, Paul, and Janet Cutler. "On the Rebound: Hoop Dreams and Its Discontents." *Cineaste* 21 (Summer 1995): 22–25.
Banks, Ingrid. "Women in Film." In *African Americans in Popular Culture, Volume 1*, edited by Todd Boyd, 67–88. Westport, CT: Prager, 2008.
Campbell, Vivyan Adair. *From Good Ma to Welfare Queen: A Genealogy of the Poor Woman in American Literature, Photography, and Culture*. New York: Garland, 2000.
Collins, Patricia Hill. *Black Feminist Consciousness: Knowledge, Consciousness, and the Politics of Empowerment*. Boston: Unwin Hyman, 1990.
_____. *Black Sexual Politics: African Americans, Gender, and the New Racism*. New York: Routledge, 2005.
Faegin, Joe R. *Living with Racism: The Black Middle-Class Experience*. Boston: Beacon Press, 1994.
Gill, Tiffany. *Beauty Shop Politics: African American Women's Activism in the Beauty Industry*. Urbana: University of Illinois Press, 2010.
Harris, Tina M. "Interrogating the Representation of African American Female Identity in the films *Waiting to Exhale* and *Set It Off*." In *African American Communication and*

*Identities: Essential Readings*, edited by Ronald L. Jackson II, 189–96. Thousand Oaks, CA: Sage, 2003.

Higginbotham, Evelyn Brooks. *Righteous Discontent: The Women's Movement in the Black Baptist Church, 1880–1920*. Cambridge: Harvard University Press, 1993.

Jones, Nikki. *Between Good and Ghetto: African American Girls and Inner City Violence*. New Brunswick: Rutgers University Press, 2010.

_____. "'It's Not Where You Live, It's How You Live': How Young Women Negotiate Conflict and Violence in the Inner City." *Annals of the American Academy of Political and Social Science* 595 (September 2004): 49–62.

Kennedy, Liam. *Race and Urban Space in Contemporary American Culture*. Chicago: Fitzroy and Dearborn, 2000.

Mallory, Stephen L. *Understanding Organized Crime*. Sudbury, MA: Jones and Bartlett, 2011.

Massood, Paula H. *Black City Cinema: African American Urban Experiences in Film*. Philadelphia: Temple University Press, 2003.

_____. "Street Girls with No Future: Black Women Coming of Age in the Inner City." In *Contemporary Black American Cinema: Race, Gender, and Sexuality at the Movies*, edited by Mia Mask, 232–51. New York: Routledge, 2012.

Matthews, Ameena. "Ameena Matthews." Interview by Stephen Colbert. *Colbert Report*. February 1, 2012. 6:57. http://www.colbertnation.com/the-colbert-report-videos/407605/february-01-2012/ameena-matthews.

McCarthy, Cameron, Alicia P. Rodriguez, Ed Buendia, Shuaib Meacham, Stephen David, Heriberto Godina, K. E. Supriya, and Carrie Wilson-Brown. "Danger in the Safety Zone: Notes on Race, Resentment, and the Discourse of Crime, Violence, and Suburban Security." *Cultural Studies* 11, no. 2 (1997): 274–95.

Miller, Jody, and Scott H. Decker. "Young Women and Gang Violence: Gender, Street Offending, and Violent Victimization in Gangs." *Justice Quarterly* 18 (2001): 115–40.

Moore, Natalie Y., and Lance Williams. *The Almighty Black P Stone Nation: The Rise, Fall, and Resurgence of an American Gang*. Chicago: Hill Books, 2011.

Moynihan, Daniel Patrick. *The Negro Family: A Case for National Action*. Office of Policy Planning and Research, U.S. Department of Labor. Washington, D.C.: GPO, March 1965.

Nichols, Bill. *Representing Reality: Issues and Concepts in Documentary*. Bloomington: Indiana University Press, 1991.

Pough, Gwendolyn. *Check It While I Wreck It: Black Womanhood, Hip Hop Culture, and the Public Sphere*. Boston: Northeastern University Press, 2004.

Reid, Mark A. "New Wave Black Cinema in the 1990s." In *Film Genre 2000: New Critical Essays*, edited by Wheeler Winston Dickson, 13–28. Albany: State University of New York Press, 2000.

Vigil, James Diego. "Urban Violence and Street Gangs." *Annual Review of Anthropology* 32 (2003): 225–42.

Wallace, Michele. "*Boyz N the Hood* and *Jungle Fever*." In *Black Popular Culture: A Project by Michele Wallace*, edited by Gina Dent, 123–31. Seattle: Bay Press, 1991.

West, Dennis, and Joan M. West. "Interrupting Violence: An Interview with Steve James and Cobe Williams." *Cineaste* 36 (Fall 2011): 21.

# About the Contributors

Angela J. **Aguayo** is an assistant professor in the Department of Cinema and Photography at Southern Illinois University. An award-winning writer, director, and producer of five documentary shorts, she has most recently published in *Visual Communication Quarterly* and *Studies in Documentary Film*.

Travis D. **Boyce** is an assistant professor of Africana studies and social sciences at the University of Northern Colorado. He has published in the *Journal of Pan African Studies* and *Journal of African American Males in Education* and was a contributor to *Before Obama: A Reappraisal of Black Reconstruction Era Politicians* (Matthew Lynch, ed., Praeger, 2012).

Gerald R. **Butters** Jr. is a professor of history at Aurora University. He is the author of *Black Manhood on the Silent Screen* (University Press of Kansas, 2002), and *Banned in Kansas: Motion Picture Censorship, 1915–1966* (University of Missouri Press, 2007). His articles have been published in *Cercles, Choice, Flow, Film/Literature Quarterly*, and *Journal for Multimedia History*.

Winsome **Chunnu-Brayda** is the associate director of multicultural programs at Ohio University. Her publications include articles in *Journal of Pan African Studies, Journal of Negro Education*, and the *Journal of Eastern Caribbean Studies*. She was a contributor to *Before Obama: A Reappraisal of Black Reconstruction Era Politicians* (Matthew Lynch, ed., Praeger, 2012).

Ashley **Farmer** is a postdoctoral fellow at the Clayman Institute for Gender Research at Stanford University. She is the author of several articles about African American women's civil rights and Black Power activism, featured in the *Black Scholar* and the *Black Diaspora Review*. She is working on a study of African American women's intellectual production during the Black Power Movement.

Michael **Graves** is an assistant professor of communication at the University of Central Missouri. His work includes the essays "'Go Back to the Part about You Reading': Transmedia Storytelling, Adaptation, and *Justified*" and "Keeping It Real: What Planning Can Learn from Reality TV," the latter of which was published in the *Journal of the American Planning Association*.

Kevin E. **Grimm** received a PhD in the history of American foreign relations from Ohio University. His research focuses on African American transnational racial identifications with Ghana and black American influence on President Dwight D. Eisenhower's foreign policy with Africa during the 1950s. His work has been published in the *Journal of Contemporary History* and *OFO: Journal of Transatlantic Studies*.

Novotny **Lawrence** is an associate professor in the Radio, Television, and Digital Media Department and an affiliate faculty member in the Africana Studies Department at Southern Illinois University. He is the author of *Blaxploitation Films of the 1970s: Blackness and Genre* (Routledge, 2007) and essays on such topics as *C.S.A: The Confederate States of America*, the comedy of Dave Chappelle, and *The Twilight Zone*. He is writing an article about *Akeelah and the Bee* (2006) and a book on *The Jeffersons*.

Joshua Daniel **Phillips** is a PhD candidate and lecturer in the Department of Communication Studies at Southern Illinois University and speaks nationally about ending men's violence against women. His book *1,800 Miles: Striving to End Sexual Violence, One Step at a Time* (Morgan James, 2010) recounts his stories from a 2008 advocacy walk from Miami to Boston.

Mike **Phillips** is a doctoral candidate in comparative literature at the Graduate Center, City University of New York (CUNY), and teaches film and media studies at Brooklyn College (CUNY) and Purchase College (State University of New York).

Eric **Pierson** is an associate professor and former chair of the Communication Studies Department at the University of San Diego. His work on black images and audiences has appeared in *Encyclopedia of African American Business History* (Greenwood, 1999), *Encyclopedia of the Great Black Migration* (Greenwood, 2006), *Journal of Mass Media Ethics*, and *Screening Noir*.

Charlene **Regester** is an associate professor in the Department of African, African American, and Diaspora Studies at the University of North Carolina at Chapel Hill and serves on the editorial boards of the *Journal of Film and Video* and *Choice Reviews*. She is the author of *African American Actresses: The Struggle for Visibility, 1900–1960* (Indiana University Press, 2010) and *Black Entertainers in African American Newspapers* (2 vols., McFarland, 2002 and 2010).

David **Rossiaky** is an independent scholar. His thesis project, "Sundown Nation," focuses on sundown communities or townships that became all-white after their white residents forcefully eradicated their black populations.

Melanie **Shaw** received a BA in creative writing and pan–African studies from California State University, Northridge. She is an editor for *Kapu Sens*, a journal of California State University, Northridge, and tutors with such organizations as 826LA, helping high school students with their writing.

Joseph L. **Smith** is a PhD candidate in philosophy and a graduate teaching assistant in the Department of Philisophy at Southern Illinois University. He is working on his dissertation, "The Niggarization of Black Bodies."

Sara **Tekle** received BAs from California State University, Northridge, where she studied psychology and pan–Africanism. Her articles include "Hillary Clinton: Wife, Mother, AND Politician," *CAPTURED Student Research Journal* (2012); "Why Are

There So Many Black Men in Prison?" *Black World News Magazine* (2012); and "Where Do We Go From Here? Black Males in the United States Criminal Justice System," *Kapu-Sens Journal* (2012).

Theresa Renée **White** is an associate professor in the Pan African Studies Department at California State University, Northridge. She is a producer and director of educational documentary films and her research has appeared in *British Journal of Medicine and Medical Research, Interactions, Studies of Communication and Culture, Journal of Black Studies, Journal of International Women's Studies,* and *Journal of Visual Literacy.*

# Index

*Numbers in* **bold italics** *indicate pages with photographs.*

access to education 58; voting rights 58
Acosta, R. Alexander 48
agitators, outside 58, 59
Aguilera, Christine 224
Ali, Muhammad 5, 76
All-England Club 97
Allen, Jo Ann 31
America, postracial 11, 20, 21, 25
*American Blackout* (2006) 2
American Civil Liberties Union (ACLU) 50
American Tennis Association (ATA) 94; Althea Gibson 96; New York State Junior Championship 96; Ora Washington 95
Anderson County School Board 33
Anker, Daniel 3, 10, 16, 25
Anna, Illinois 188; Anna Pelley 188; banishment 189; Jonesboro 188; racial cleansing 189; reverse mentality 203; sundown town 189; Will James lynching 188; *see also 100 Years of Progress*; sundown town
antebellum era 58
anti-integration 35
Ashcroft, John 48
Ashe, Arthur 105, 107
Association Tennis Club, Washington, D.C. 94
Australian Open 101
authenticity, black: in film 134, 139, 141, 145, 149

B-girl 162
Babatundé, Obba 117, 119
Baird, Maiken 5, 99, 101, 102, 103, 106, 109, 111; "An Open Letter to the Tennis Community" 110; USTA lawsuit 110; *see also Venus and Serena*
'Bama 138, 141; Great Migration 138
Bambara, Toni Cade 146
*Banished: How Whites Drove Blacks Out of Town* (2006) 6, 189, 197, 198; adverse possession 194; Strickland family 193–94; *see also* banishment; Forsyth County, Georgia, banishment; Harrison, Arkansas, banishment; Pierce City, Missouri, banishment; sundown town
banishment 6, 189; adverse possession 194; Anna, Illinois 189; descendants of 194; failed in Hall County, Georgia, 196–97; isolation 203; lynching as catalyst for 190; oral history 193; othering 190; pattern 189, 190; property theft 194; rebirth of Ku Klux Klan 198; reclusion 203; reparations 204; violent destruction 193; *see also* Forsyth County, Georgia, banishment; Harrison, Arkansas, banishment; Pierce City, Missouri, ban-

ishment; reparations; sundown town
Bar-Kays 132
Barnouw, Eric 2
Bates, Ruby 13, 14
Battle of the Sexes match 92, 93, 105
Beauchamp, Keith 43, 44, 45, 46, 47, 48, 53; *see also* Till, Emmett Louis; *The Untold Story of Emmett Louis Till*
Beck, Glenn 12, 21, 22, 23, 24, 26n2, 27n36
Belafonte, Harry 122, 123, 125
Bell, Al 135, 137, 138, 140, 145; independent label 140; Stax Records 135, 137, 138
*Berea College v. Kentucky* 29
Berry, Halle 128
*The Big Blow* (2000) 88n2
bigotry 38
bin Laden, Osama 65, **66**
black bodies 20
black experience 16, 21, 26n2, 134; missing narratives 155
black history and memory 3, 8, 11, 12, 16, 19–20, 22, 23, 24; collective memory 18, 20, 26n26, 179; moral imagination 18, 20, 26n26; Scottsboro Boys 11, 17, 22; silencing 3, 11
Black History Month 53
black identity: fear of 4; inner-city life 7
black liberation theology 24
Black Panther Party for Self-

Defense 6, 24; advocacy 58; Carbondale, Illinois 172, 173, 175; Carbondale 6, 177; fist 5; J. Edgar Hoover 174; movement 6, 23, 135; threatening 174

Black Peril 82, 83

Black Power 60, 61, 63, 68, 135, 154, 158; and capitalism 135; movement 60, 65, 134, 161, 174; polarizing 174; *Up Tight* (film) 137

black superhero: Isaac Hayes 133; Jack Johnson 75, 84; *Wattstax* marketing 133, 134

blaxploitation (Hollywood's black exploitation film movement) 6, 133, 136, 139, 145, 149; *Passing Through* 146–47; representations of black ghetto 142; *Super Fly* (1972) 143; *Sweet Sweetback's Baadasssss Song* 140, 141, 150n24; *Willie Dynamite* (1974) 143; *see also* soundtrack

Blue, Carroll Parrott: *Conversations with Roy DeCarava* (1983) 156

"Blue Black Jack" (2004) 75, 77, 84

Bob Jones University 51

Booker T. & the M.G.'s 134, 137, 144

boxers, black 78; against Tommy Burns 78; racist theories about 78, 82, 83, 84; unofficial Negro heavyweight championship 78

*Briggs et al. v. Elliot* (1954) 59

Brittain, principal D.J. 34, 35

Brown, Foxy 163

Brown, James 161

brown-paper-bag test 159

*Brown vs. the Topeka Board of Education* 4, 29, 31, 34, 37, 40, 41n1, 51, 55n39, 59, 223

Bryant, Carolyn 45, 49

Bryant, Roy 45, 48, 49

"Burn, baby, burn" 144

Burns, Ken 5, 74, 78, 81, 82, 85, 86, 87, 89n39, 89n47

Burns, Tommy 78

Bush, George W. 51, 55n39

business, black 60; entrepreneur 74

Butler, Duran 43

Cain, Bobby 31

California Newsreel 57, 157

capitalism: black 134, 135; Martin Luther King, critical of 134; Richard Nixon and black capitalist program 135, 136

Carbondale, Illinois 6, 172, 173, 177, 188; culture 174; distrust 176; Human Relations Commission 181; near slave-belt region 174; northeast side 180; *see also* Black Panther Party; *778 Bullets*; Southern Illinois University

Carlos, John 5

Carmen Jones/*Carmen Jones see* Dandridge, Dorothy

Carmichael, Stokely 60

Carter, Dan 11

Caswell, Anna Theresser 31

CeaseFire 238, 242, 244

Charleston, Mississippi 37, 39, 40, 42n19

Christ 232

Christianity 24, 201; African American 17; Christian Nation 201; eleven o'clock on Sunday morning 42n15; othering 190–91; white 86

cinema, nonnarrative truth 117

cinéma vérité 208; "authentic" 209

civil rights 50, 54, 69, 177, 223; activists 58, 60, 61, 75, 105; Dorothy Dandridge and 128; nonviolent methods 174; post–civil rights era 23, 53, 241; pre–civil rights era 58; radical turn 61; Rural Civil Rights Project 178; Till murder 49, 53, 54; *see also* Civil Rights Act of 1984; Civil Rights Movement

Civil Rights Act of 1984 23

Civil Rights Movement 6, 23, 43, 46, 52, 158, 173, 177, 197; antithetical to 126; during Orangeburg Massacre 57; mistrust of whites 135; and Watts Rebellion 142–43; *see also* civil rights

Civil War 58

Claflin University 57, 61

Clarendon County, South Carolina 59

Clarke, Shirley 7, 208, 215,

216; antagonism/hatred toward Jason 213, 214, 216; baiting Jason 212; *The Connection* (1960) 208; *A Cool World* (1963) 209; daughter, Wendy Clarke 214; exploitation of Jason 218; landmark female director 218; mental gay bashing 216; pioneer 218; *see also* Holliday, Jason/Aaron Payne; Lee, Carl; *A Portrait of Jason*

Clarke, Wendy 214

class 76, 84, 87, 156, 209, 221

Clijsters, Kim 106, 107, 108, 110

Clinton 12 31; D.J. Brittain 34; integration 32, 34, 39; segregation 32, 33, 36, 39; *see also* Green McAdoo Grammar School

Clinton, Bill 100

Clinton High School 36; first to graduate blacks 36

*The Clinton 12* (2006) 4, 30, 31, 32, 34, 35, 38, 40; *see also* Clinton 12

Coburn, Tom 51

Cold War 46, 52, 53

colonialism 23, 155; anticolonialism 25

*Color Adjustment* (1992) 2

color line: Althea Gibson 95, 99; boxing 76, 78, 79, 80, 82, 83, 84; John L. Sullivan and 78; Ora Washington 95

color, skin 157–62; Benjamin Payton 160; Chris Rock 161; dark 158, 160; Eurocentric 158, 159, 161; fair 159; *Good Hair* 161; James Brown 161; Johnny Ford 160; light 158, 159; "liver lips" 160; resentment toward lighter skin 159, 160; "skillet blonde" 160; "tar baby" 160; too black/dark 159, 160

colorism 158, 159, 161; brown-paper-bag test 159; effects 160, 161; resistance to, fading 161; *see also* color, skin

Columbia Pictures 132, 137, 145

communist conspiracy 59

Communist Party USA 11, 26n6

Compton, California 100, 101

Cone, James 27*n*36

Congress of Racial Equality (CORE) 135

Congressional Black Caucus 48

"Cosby effect" 225

Cosmopolitan Club 96

countermemory 16, 17, 19, 172, 176

couple, interracial 39, 51, 75, 83, 87; Dorothy Dandridge movies 125–26; *New York Times* criticism of 125, 126

Court, Margaret 93; Mother's Day Massacre 93

Cram, Bestor 57, 67; *see also Scarred Justice: The Orangeburg Massacre 1968*

criminalization 25

*The Crisis* 75

Crouch, Stanley 75

Dandridge, Dorothy 5, 116–131; Academy Award nomination 116, 117, 123; Albert Maysles 117; Brock Peters 121; Carmen de Lavallade 120; Carmen Jones/*Carmen Jones* 117, 120, 122, 123, 125; Clarence Muse 119; *Confidential* law suit 122; couch 117, 118, 128; Curt Jurgens 125; Cyril Dandridge 127; daughter 120, 127; death and funeral 127; drugs and alcohol 124; dubbing of singing 122, 123; Fayard Nicholas 121; Halle Berry 128; Harold Nicholas 127, 129*n*3; Harry Belafonte 122, 123, 125; *Hep* law suit 122; hypersexualization 117, 118, 119, 121, 125; interracial romance in movies 125–26; *Introducing Dorothy Dandridge* (1999) 129*n*3; *Island in the Sun* (1957) 125; Jack Denison 124, 127; Jasmine Guy 119, 121; Joe Adams 120, 121; John Justin 125; *The King and I* 124; Laurence Fishburne 121; Lena Horne 118, 120; major milestone 124; *Malaga* (1960) 126; marginalization 128; nightclub singer 117, 118, 120; Obba

Babatundé 117, 119, 129*n*3; Otto Preminger 122, 123, 124, 127; Peter Lawford 127; Rolonda Watts 121, 127; Ruby Dandridge 119; *Tamango* (1958) 124, 125; *Tarzan's Peril* (1951) 120; trailblazer 118, 119; Vivian Dandridge 119, 127; woman as spectacle in film 119; *see also Dorothy Dandridge: An American Beauty*; *Jet* magazine; *Porgy and Bess*; the press

Dandridge, Ruby 119

Dandridge, Vivian 119

Dash, Julie 156

Dassin, Jules 137

Davis, Miles: *A Tribute to Jack Johnson* (1971) 88*n*2

De Laine, Reverend J. A. 59

democracy 16; American 19, 20, 21, 22, 23, 24, 25

Denison, Jack 124, 127

desegregation 30, 32, 59, 62

discrimination 30, 36, 39, 41, 41*n*1, 143, 197

disenfranchisement 68

DJ Magnificent Montague 144

documentary cinema production 8

documentary cinema studies 8

Dodd, Christopher J. 50

dominance racial 80; white 80, 85

*Dorothy Dandridge: An American Beauty* (2003) 5, 116, 117, 124, 127, 128

*Dred Scott v. Sanford* (1857) 41*n*1

D'Souza, Dinesh 12, 21, 22, 23, 24, 25, 26*n*2, 27*n*36, 65, 67; *The Roots of Obama's Rage* 65; *2016: Obama's America* (2012) 24, 65

Du Bois, W.E.B. 3, 12; conception of the scholar 18, 19; historians 26*n*2; postracial America 21; site of knowledge 11, 16, 17, 18, 20, 26*n*21; textbooks as sites of knowledge 19; "unforgivable blackness" 75

Duryea, Etta 83, 89*n*43

DuVernay, Ava 6, 154, 156, 166; *Compton C Minor* (2009) 163; *I Will Follow*

(2011) 163; *Middle of Nowhere* (2012) 163; *This Is the Life* (2008) 163; *see also My Mic Sounds Nice*

EA Sports 88*n*2; *Fight Night Champion* (2010) 88*n*2

Early, Gerald 75

Earth, Wind & Fire soundtrack 140

*Ebony* magazine 127; Dorothy Dandridge 127, 129*n*1; *Shaft* merchandise complaint 141; Stax records 139

education 31, 58

Eisenhower, Dwight D. 47

Elliott, Missy 163

Emmett Till Justice Campaign 48

Emmett Till Unsolved Civil Rights Crime Act *see* Till Bill

Englewood, Illinois *see The Interrupters*

Epps, Gail Ann 31

equal protection 30

equality 61, 68, 69, 105; black as radical and dangerous 4; black female tennis players 93; fear of 57, 58; films and 54; gender 92; and Johnson-Jeffries fight 80, 81; pursuit of 57

Eve 163–64

Evers, Medgar 51

Evert, Chris 98

*Eyes on the Prize* (1987) 2

Facing History and Ourselves 52

Faubus, Orval 4

fear: of blacks/black identity 4, 61; easing of 69; framing 61, 68; white 61

Federal Bureau of Investigation (FBI) 49, 54, 63, 172, 174

*Fight Night Champion* (2010) 88*n*2

film audience, black 133, 140 and blaxploitation 133

filmmaker: black men 155; black women absent 155, 156

Fishburne, Laurence 121

flourishing of black individuals 16, 20, 22, 25

Forsyth County, Georgia

202; adverse possession 194; banishment 192; brotherhood march 200; Ernest Knox 191; lynch mob 191; Oscar Daniel 192; Rob Edwards, 192; Strickland family 193–94; trial 192; Trussie Daniel 192; *see also Banished*

Frazier, Edward 59

freedom rides 54

Freeman, Morgan 37, 39

French Open 97

friendships, interracial 39–40

Fugitive Slave Law of 1870 199

Garrison, Zina 5, 98–99, 102, 111

gay male 7, 208; *Cavalier* slur 218; as dangerous 217–18; difficulty of being 217; limited opportunities 213; *see also* homophobia

gender 8, 156, 213

ghetto, black: isolation 223; representations of 142; and white audience 148

Gibson Althea 5, 95–97, 99, 104, 111, 112*n*29; All-England Club 97; Wimbledon title 97

Goodman, Barak 3, 10, 16, 25

Gordy, Berry 139

gradualism 61

Grand Slam tournaments: Althea Gibson 98; Venus Williams 101, 104

*The Great White Hope* (1968) 75, 77, 84, 85, 86

great white savior 224, 229

Green McAdoo Grammar School 32, 34, 36

Gulf+Western 135, 137, 140

Guy, Jasmine 119, 121

Hamilton, Forrest 146

Harris, Luke Charles 157

Harrison, Arkansas, banishment 193; Bob Scott 198–99; Chamber of Commerce 199; Confederate flag 199; Ku Klux Klan 199; Layne Wheeler 199; *see also Banished*; banishment

Hayden, Ronald Gordon 31

Hayes, Isaac 132, 137, 147; Black Moses 133; *Hot Buttered Soul* (1969) 132; new

black superstar 133; *Shaft* (1971) (album) 132, 141, 147

heavyweight champion of the world: African American 74, 77, 78, 79; first black won 79; Jack Johnson 79, 81, 86; mantle of 88*n*18; symbol 79; white only 77; *see also* Johnson, Jack

hegemony, white 74, 78, 79, 84, 86; counterhegemonic space 222

Hemings, Sally 51, 55*n*39

Henderson, Edwin Bancroft 78

Hill, Lauryn 163, 164

*Hip Hop: Beyond Beats and Rhymes* (2006) 2

hip-hop and rap 159, 166; B-girl 162; and girls' childhood games 165–66; graffiti artist 162; MC 162; Nelly 165; patriarchal and misogynistic genre 162, 164, 166; sexism 164, 166

Holliday, Jason/Aaron Payne 209, 217; background 209; and Carmen McCrae 212, 213; drugs and alcohol 210, 211, 213, 214, 313; father, Big Tough 213, 214; goals 212; identity 218; laughter as coping mechanism 213; mother 213, 214; racism 212; sex 212; trust 213; work 211–12; *see also* homophobia; *A Portrait of Jason*

homophobia 209, 214, 215, 217, 218

Hoover, J. Edgar 174

Horne, Lena 118, 120

*Hot Buttered Soul* (1969) 132

Houghton-Mifflin Publishing 52, 55*n*39

House Committee on the Judiciary 50

Howard University 94

icons, black: Dorothy Dandridge 116; Venus and Serena Williams 109

independence 87

Independent Television Service (ITVS) 157

inequality 31, 69, 167, 200, 241; and violence 68

Innis, Roy 135

integration 30, 40; anti-

integration 35; school 31, 32, 34, 35, 37, 40

International Labor Defense 11

International Law and Order League 86

*The Interrupters* (2012) 7, 238, 239; black women's experience 242; Caprysha Anderson 249–53; complexities of city 243; Englewood, Illinois 238, 241, 242, 244; hope 241; inner city 239; positioning of Matthews 249; as public figure, Matthews 249; reconfiguration of gender roles 248; structural factors of violence 251; systemic repression 241; violence as disease 243; *see also* James, Steve; Kotlowitz, Alex; Matthews, Ameena

*Introducing Dorothy Dandridge* (1999) 129*n*3; *see also* Dandridge, Dorothy

*Island in the Sun* 125; *see also* Dandridge, Dorothy

"Jack Johnson" (1994) 75, 77, 79, 84, 89*n*50

Jackson, Jesse 49, 132, 136; attack on Hollywood 136–37; natural image 161; Operation Breadbasket 136; Operation PUSH (People United to Save Humanity) 136

Jackson, Samuel L. 75

James, Steve 7, 238, 241, 242, 243, 245, 246, 250, 252; *Hoop Dreams* (1994) 241; *see also The Interrupters*

Jane Balfour Films 157

Jay-Z 163

Jefferson, Thomas 51, 55*n*39

Jeffries, Jim 78, 80, 81, 83

*Jet* magazine: *Confidential* law suit trial 122; coverage of Dorothy Dandridge 116, 124, 129*n*1; divide between black and mainstream press 127; Dorothy Dandridge and Harry Belafonte 123; interracial couple in *Tamango* 125–26; Otto Preminger 122, 124, 127; promoting Dandridge in *Tamango* 125; Stax records

139; Till photographs 44, 48; *see also* the press
Jim Crow 12, 13, 14, 15, 22, 32, 35, 46, 51, 59, 62, 75, 223; Jack Johnson 82, 84
Johnson, Fred 96
Johnson, Jack 74–90; Belle Schreiber 84; "Black Peril" 82, 83; black superhero 75, 84; Booker T. Washington 82; boxer Jack Jefferson as 75, 88n6; Burns-Johnson fight 79–80; and class boundaries 81; dislike of 75; Etta Duryea 83, 89n43; Everleigh Club brothel 83; first African American heavyweight champion of the world 77, 87; heavyweight champion of the world 79, 81, 86; Johnson-Jeffries fight 80–81, 89n32; Johnson-Willard fight 85–87; Lucille Cameron 89n50; Mann Act incarceration 83, 85, 87, 89n50; New Negro 85, 89n39; "perpetual threat" 74, 75, 77; racial pride 79, 80, 81, 82; and social mores 81; transmedia persona 76; and white women 74, 76, 81, 82, 84, 85, 87, 89n50; *see also Unforgivable Blackness*
Johnson, Lyndon B. 23, 142, 245
Jones, James Earl 84
Jones, Minnie Ann Dickie 31
Jordan, David 49
Jordan, Michael 77
Jurgens, Curt 125
justice, racial 15, 18, 20, 22, 25, 26n6, 179; and films 54; injustice 16, 205; issues 3; Scottsboro Boys 11, 25; seeking 59
Justin, John 125

Kasper, John 35, 38
Kelly, Robin 11
Kennedy, Robert F. 63
Kent State University 57
Kilby Prison 15
*The Killings of Stanley Ketchel* (2005) 88n2
King, Billie Jean 102; Battle of the Sexes match 92, 93; Wimbledon Ladies Champion 92

King, Coretta Scott 49
King, Martin Luther, Jr. 3, 21, 23, 49, 60, 63, 107, 135, 137, 173, 174; Letter from the Birmingham Jail 42n15; March Against Fear 60
King, Rodney 158, 227
King-Riggs match 92
Kotlowitz, Alex 7, 238, 241, 242, 243, 245, 246, 250, 252; *see also The Interrupters*
krumping and clowning 7, 224, 226, 227, 231, 234, 235; BattleZone 231–32; clown groups 229; description 230; as resistive empowerment 224, 230, 235; *see also Rize*
Ku Klux Klan 3, 38, 199, 201; "rebirth" 198; "uptown" 60
L.A. Rebellion/L.A. School of Black Filmmakers 146, 147, 151n45; Toni Cade Bambara 146
L.A. School of Black Filmmakers *see* L.A. Rebellion
LaChapelle, David 7, 221; "great white savior" 224
Lady of Rage 163
Lange, Ted 148
Latham, William R. 31
Lead Belly (1912): "The Titanic" 88n2, 89n51
Leahy, Patrick 50
Lee, Carl 208, 213, 214, 215, 216, 217; attacking/baiting Jason 211, 215, 216; interventions 211; *see also A Portrait of Jason*
Leibowitz, Samuel L. 11
Lemmons, Kasi 156
Lewis, John 50
*Liberators: Fighting on Two Fronts in World War II* (1992) 2
Lil' Kim 163
Little Milton 143
Los Angeles Coliseum 132, 143, 144
Los Angeles Police Department 144, 150n24, 158
*Loving v. Virginia* (1967) 41n1
Lucy, Autherine 54n14
lynching 1, 12, 13, 52, 82, 83, 87, 188, 189; as catalyst 190; legal 15; mobs 12, 14, 188; 1901–10 89n47; othering

191; same geographically 191; souvenir gathering 191; spectacle lynching 191; *see also* sundown town

Macci, Rick 102–103
Major, Michelle 5, 93, 99, 101, 102, 103, 106, 109, 111; "An Open Letter to the Tennis Community" 110; USTA lawsuit 110; *see also Venus and Serena*
*Malaga* (1960) 126; Dorothy Dandridge kissed 126
Malcolm X 107
Mamoulian, Rouben 126
Mann Act 84, 85, 88n6, 89n50; James Robert Mann 84
Marble, Alice 96, 97
March Against Fear (1966) 60
March on Washington 3
marketing: conspicuous consumption 143; to urban consumers 138, 141
marriage, interracial 39, 41n1; *see also* Johnson, Jack
Marsalis, Wynton 75
Marshall, Thurgood 33
Martin, Trayvon 43, 172, 180
Matthews, Ameena 7, 238, 253; ability 244; abuse 245; activism 248, 251; *Colbert Report* interview 238; disrupting violence 244; father Jeff Fort 245; former gang member 244, 246, 247; Islam 247; as mother 246; relationship with Caprysha Anderson 249–53; turning point 245; as Violence Interrupter 239
Maysles, Albert 117
MC 162; female 163; lack of female 167; sexually exploitative images 165
MC Lyte 163, 165
McAdoo, Green 32
McCrae, Carmen 212, 213
McCullough, Barbara: *Fragments* (1980) 156
McDaniel, Keith Henry 31, 32, 34, 35
McDonnell, Bob 200; April, Confederate History Month 200
McDuffie, Emanuel 95
McEnroe, John 100

McKissick, Floyd 135
McLane, Betsy A. 2
McNair, Robert 57, 60, 62, 63
McSwain, Alvah 31
*McSwain et al. v. County Board of Education of Anderson County, Tennessee* 32, 33, 34
Memphis Sound 138, 139, 141; against Motown Records 139; *see also* Stax records
Mfume, Kweisi 48
*Midnight Ramble* (1994) 2
Milam, J.W. 45, 48, 49
Miles, Bill 2
Miller, Benjamin Meeks 14
Minaj, Nicki 163, 164, 166
miscegenation 35, 39, 83, 125, 126; *see also* race mixing
Mississippi declaration of secession, excerpt 199–200
Monroe, Marilyn 5, 116, 119
Montgomery, Olen 10, 15
Montgomery Bus Boycott 3, 46, 54n14
Montgomery County High School 42n19
Monumental Tennis Club, Baltimore 94
Mos Def (Dante Terrell Smith) 75, 84, 88
Mother's Day Massacre 93
Motown Records Berry Gordy 139; *Lady Sings the Blues* 139
*The Murder of Emmett Till* (2003) 4, 44, 47, 51, 53, 54
Murray, Donald Gaines 29
Muse, Clarence 119
music, black: historical legacy 223; increasing popularity of 139; spirituals 223
Muslim 64, 65
mutual flourishing and racial justice 3, 11, 12, 21, 25
*My Mic Sounds Nice* (2010) 6, 155, 162–67

Nastase, Ilie 92
National Association for the Advancement of Colored People (NAACP) 33, 48, 50, 51, 59; pressure on Hollywood 140
National Education Association (NEA) 154
National Guard: Alabama 14; Ohio 63; South Car-

olina 62
nationalism, black 134, 135, 138, 158; philosophies 174
Navratilova, Martina 98, 99
Neblett, Touré 67
*The Negro Soldier* (1944) 2
Nelly 165; "Country Grammar (Hot Shit)" 165
Nelson, Marilyn 52; *A Wreath for Emmett Till* 52
Nelson, Stanley 44, 45, 46, 47, 51, 54; *see also The Murder of Emmett Till*
Nesbit, Margaret 176, 177, 183
New Negro/New Negro Movement 85, 89n39
New York State Junior Championship 96
Newcombe, John 92
Nicholas, Fayard 121
Nicholas, Harold 127, 129n3
1968 Mexico City Olympics 5
1965 Watts Rebellion 6, 132, 133, 135, 142, 143, 226, 227
Nkrumah, Kwame 46
Norris, Clarence 10, 15, 20, 25

Obama, Barack 4, 12, 21, 22, 25, 30, 68, 197, 223, 233; as black militant 64, 65, *66*, 67; *Dreams from My Father* 24; *New Yorker* cartoon 64, *66*; struggle/resistance 24
Obama, Michelle 65, *66*
*Obama's America* (2012) 25; *see also* Dinesh, D'Souza
*On the Shoulders of Giants* (2011) 2
*100 Years of Progress: The Centennial History of Anna* (1954) 197; Anna Centennial Committee 197, 200; excerpt 197–98, 198; lynch mob 198; white privilege 198; *see also* Anna, Illinois
Operation PUSH (People United to Save Humanity) 136
oppression 3, 222, 227
Orangeburg, South Carolina 57, 69
Orangeburg Massacre 60, 61, 68; cause 68; riot 62–63; shooting 63; *see also Scarred Justice: The Orangeburg Massacre 1968*

*The Original Johnson* (2009–11) 5, 75, 77, 79, 84, 87, 88
Osborne, John 75
othering 67, 190, 191

Paint Rock, Alabama 13
Parks, Rosa 3, 107, 173, 174
*Passing Through* (1977) 146–47; Larry Clark 146–47, 150n40; Roderick Young 147; Ted Lange 147
Patterson, Haywood 10, 13, 15
Payne, Aaron/Jason Holliday *see* Holliday, Jason/Aaron Payne
Payton, Benjamin 160
Peters, Brock 121
Peters, Margaret 95
Peters, Roumania 95
Pickett, Wilson 144
Pierce City, Missouri, banishment 193, 194, 195; Charles Brown 195; James Brown 194–95; *see also Banished*
*Plessy v. Ferguson* (1896) 41n1, 51, 55n39, 59
police: Los Angeles Police Department 144, 150n24, 158; South Carolina Highway troopers 57
politics, racial 94, 95, 99
*Porgy and Bess* (1959) 126–27; abuse during 127; Brock Peters 126; and Civil Rights Movement 126; Dandridge's personal problems during 127; Otto Preminger 127; Rouben Mamoulian, firing of 126–27; Sammy Davis, Jr. 126; Samuel Goldwyn 126; Screen Directors Guild strike 126; Sidney Poitier 126
*A Portrait of Jason* (1967) 7, 208–19; actualization 208; call for reexamination of 218; cinematic control 208; cornerstone of LGBT filmmaking 218; director-subject relationship 214; filmmakers' intention 214, 217; "interview" 211; Jason's "exposure" 313; limited opportunities 213; mental gay bashing 216; New York Film Festival 218; no truth 210–11; poor treatment

216; power 208; production 210; "reality" of 216; reviews of 216; slur 215; "snuff film" 214; *see also* Holliday, Jason/Aaron Payne

Powell, Ozie 10, 15

Preminger, Otto 122, 123, 124, 127

the press, African American: and Dorothy Dandridge 116, 121, 128; *Ebony* 129*n*1; *Our World* 129*n*1; *see also Jet* magazine

the press, mainstream: *Confidential* libel suit 121, 122; *Cosmopolitan* magazine 129*n*1; and Dorothy Dandridge 116, 121, 128; *Life* magazine 128*n*1; *Los Angeles Times* 116, 122, 123, 125, 126, 127; *New York Times* 116, 123, 125, 126, 127; *Time* magazine 128*n*1

Price, Victoria 13, 14

pride, racial 79, 80, 81, 82, 87

Progressive Era 86

*Prom Night in Mississippi* (2008) 4, 30, 37, 39, 40

protests: interracial, equality 11; Orangeburg 61

Pryor, Richard 146, 148, 149, 150*n*21; as Chorus figure 148

Public Enemy 159, 163

Purity Crusade 86

Queen Elizabeth II 97

Queen Latifah 163, 164

*A Question of Color* (1993) 6, 155, 157–62; California Newsreel 157; colorism 158; Independent Television Service (ITVS) 157; Jane Balfour Films 157; Luke Charles Harris 157; self-esteem/self-perception 162; self-worth 160, 162; *see also* colorism; skin color

race 8, 24, 53, 84, 156, 182; and American democracy 10, 25; crisis 68; Jack Johnson 76, 79, 84, 87; Midwest 180; patriarchal notions of 213; race and sports 110

race mixing 35, 39; *see also* miscegenation

racial cleansing 189

racism 3, 6, 23, 38, 39, 52, 65, 158, 189, 205, 209, 221; Arthur Ashe and 107; cleansing 41, 204; covert 204; difference between formal and modern 189–90; Dorothy Dandridge and 118; Facing History and Ourselves 52; generational phenomenon 38; institutional 200; textbooks 154; USLTA policies 96; white 59, 94; Williams sisters 106, 107, 108

Rah Digga 163

Rangel, Charles 48

rape 13, 14, 59, 190, 192, 202

rappers: black female rappers 6, 162, 163; hypersexualized 163; male dominance 6, 162

Ray, Brenda 75

Reconstruction 19, 20, 58, 154

reparations 51, 203–4; apology as 204; Holocaust victims 205; for Japanese Americans 205; monuments as 204; for scholarships as 204

reprisal, economic 60

research fatigue 176

resistance 3, 5, 7, 22, 24, 60, 87, 161; black, as dangerous 60; hip-hop 159; Jack Johnson as signifier of 85; Venus and Serena Williams 105; white 94

Richardson, Judy 57, 67; *see also Scarred Justice: The Orangeburg Massacre 1968*

Richburg, E.E. 59

Riggs, Bobby 92, 93; Battle of the Sexes match 92, 93; King-Riggs match 92; Mother's Day Massacre 93

Riggs, Marlon 2

riot 61, 62; Detroit 63; whites after Johnson-Jeffries fight 81

*Rize* (2005) 7, 221–35; BattleZone 231–32; central characters 225; Christ 232; Christine Aguilera 224; clown groups 229; "Cosby effect" 225; counterhegemonic space 222; creating change 233; culture 230; dance 222; Dragon 225,

227, 230, 232, 235; drugs 222; faith 232; familial bonds 229; vs. hip-hop 235; hope 232, 234; imagination of community 231; informal discourse 222; inner city 221, 224, 227, 230, 234; Larry Berry 225; Lil'C 225, 226, 230; lure of gang life 228; marginalized group 222, 223, 230; mass consumption 235; Miss Prissy 225, 231, 232; nonviolent social resistance 233; oppression 222, 227; positivity 230; reviews 225; role model 233, 234; South Central Los Angeles 7, 222, 224, 225, 226, 227, 229, 231, 234; Tight Eyez 225, 230, 235; Tommy the Clown 225, 228, 232, 235; vernacular rhetoric 221, 222–23, 226, 234; violence 222, 227, 228; voice 224; *see also* krumping and clowning

Roberson, Willie 10, 15

Roberts, Randy 75

Robinson, Ruth Adkins 116; *see also Dorothy Dandridge: An American Beauty*

Rock, Chris 100; *Good Hair* 161

Romney, Mitt 67

*The Roots of Obama's Rage* 65

Rosewood, Florida, massacre 205

Run DMC 163

Rural Civil Rights Project 178, 179

Rush, Bobby 48

Salt-N-Pepa 163, 164

Saltzman, Paul 37, 39; *see also Prom Night in Mississippi*

Sandler, Kathe 6, 154, 156; awards 157; *Beah: A Black Woman Speaks* (2003) 157; *The Friends* (1995) 157; *Remembering Thelma* (1981) 157; *see also A Question of Color*

Sanford, Florida 43

*Scarred Justice: The Orangeburg Massacre 1968* (2009) 4, 57, 60, 61, 63, 67

Schlitz Brewing Company 137, 149*n*14

Schreiber, Belle 84
Schumer, Charles E. 48
Schwerner, Michael 51
Scott, Ridley 88n2
Scott Free Productions 88n2
Scottsboro: An American
 Tragedy (2001) 3, 11, 15,
 20, 21, 22, 25
Scottsboro Boys 10–28, 59;
 accusers, Victoria Price and
 Ruby Bates 11, 13, 14; black
 history and memory 2, 22,
 23, 24; Communist Party
 USA 11; confrontation 13;
 International Labor De-
 fense 11; interracial protests
 for equality 11; Jim Crow
 12, 15; postracial America
 25; rape 13; Samuel L. Leibowitz 11; social-economic-
 political structures 11; trial
 14, 15, 20; see also Scottsboro: An American Tragedy
Seals, J.W. 59
segregation 68; Black History
 Month presentation 53;
 Briggs et al. v. Elliot 59;
 eleven o'clock on Sunday
 morning 42n15; law of the
 land 58; Letter from the
 Birmingham Jail 42n15;
 school 4, 29, 30, 31, 32, 36;
 school prom 37, 38, 39;
 sororities 41; tennis 94, 96;
 unconstitutional 59; Watts
 143; see also desegregation;
 Jim Crow
Sellers, Cleveland L., Jr. 58,
 61, 62, 63
separate but equal doctrine 13,
 14, 29, 32, 33, 41n1, 55n39
778 Bullets 6, 171–84; Black
 Panthers 173, 177, 183;
 Church of the Good Shep-
 herd 172, 180; community
 interest 172; community
 screenings 172; Concerned
 Citizens of Carbondale
 182; countermemory 172,
 176; Elbert Simons 176;
 grassroots history 176;
 grievances 182; Margaret
 Nesbit 176, 177, 183; no
 deaths 172; Nonviolent
 Carbondale 182; objections
 to 178; people's history 177;
 police 172, 173, 174, 176,
 178, 180, 182; Racial Justice
 Coalition 182; Rural Civil

Rights Project 178, 179,
 183; rural struggle 172, 173,
 183; screening 179, 181,
 183; shoot-out 176, 177; social change 178, 181, 182,
 183, 184; social-change documentary 173, 179, 182,
 184; Trayvon Martin 172,
 180; truth 178; see also Carbondale, Illinois; southern
 Illinois
Shaft (1971) (album) 132,
 133, 147; Communiplex ad
 campaign 141; sales 141; see
 also Hayes, Isaac
Shaft (1971) (film) 150n24;
 merchandise 141
Shaft, John 133; fantasy 141
Shanté, Roxanne 163, 165
sharecropper/sharecropping
 51, 59, 60
Shaw, Larry 139; Operation
 Breadbasket 138; seg-
 mented marketing 138; Stax
 records 138, 149n12
Shriver, Pam 98, 99
Simons, Elbert 176
site of knowledge 11, 26n21,
 26n26
Sixteenth Street Baptist
 Church 3
slave/slavery 1, 22, 30, 41n1,
 83, 125, 133, 154, 155, 157,
 158, 160, 189, 190, 223; enslaved 199; Mississippi declaration of secession 199–
 200; reparations 203; Texas
 declaration of secession
 200; three-fifth compro-
 mise 191
slur 160, 215, 218; nigger, use
 of word 14, 48, 78, 106,
 148, 203, 212
Smith, Dante Terrell see Mos
 Def
Smith, Tommie 5
Soles, Maurice 31
soundtrack, motion-picture
 blaxploitation and 136,
 149; Earth, Wind & Fire
 140; market 137, 140; Stax
 sound 140; see also Uptight
South Carolina State College
 (SCSC) 57, 61, 63; Benner
 C. Turner 60; demonstra-
 tion 57–58; trial 58
South Central Los Angeles,
 California 7, 222, 224, 225,
 226, 227, 229, 231

South Side of Chicago 7, 238,
 245
Southern Christian Leadership Conference (SCLC)
 135
southern culture 13
southern Illinois 172, 173,
 174, 188
Southern Illinois University
 176, 177; Jeffrey Haas, The
 Assassination of Fred Hampton: How the FBI and the
 Chicago Police Murdered a
 Black Panther 177; radical
 activism event 177; Robbie
 Lieberman 177
Southern Poverty Law Center
 50, 51
sports 100
Staple Singers 132, 150n16
star image 77
Stax records 6, 132, 135, 137,
 140, 149';Bama image 138;
 Booker T. & the M.G.'s
 134, 137, 144; Carla
 Thomas 132, 134; Chicago
 and Stax sound 141, 147;
 Estelle Axton 134, 140;
 Gulf+Western 135, 137,
 140; identity to black,
 urban milieu 141; Jim Stewart 134, 135, 137; Memphis
 Sound 138, 139; movies,
 black-themed 141; Otis
 Redding 133, 135; soul
 music 134, 138; Southern
 "roots" 139; "Stax sound"
 140, 141; urban consumers
 138, 141; Warner Brothers
 135; see also Bell, Al; Shaw,
 Larry; Thomas, Rufus;
 Wattstax
Stilson, Jeff: Good Hair 161
Stokes, Carl 61
Strider, Clarence 59
Strom, Pete 62, 63
Stroman, John 61
struggle against inequality 33,
 167; black 20, 22, 23, 24;
 for civil rights 63, 172;
 Dorothy Dandridge 118,
 119; for equal
 treatment/equality 30, 60,
 85, 105; Venus and Serena
 Williams 111; women's
 rights 93
Struggles for Representation:
 African American Docu-
 mentary Film and Video 2

Stuart, Mel 6, 132, 137, 144, 145, 147, 148
Student Nonviolent Coordinating Committee (SNCC) 58, 60, 62
students: Claflin University 57–58, 60, 61, 68; John Stroman 61; riot 62–63; South Carolina State College (SCSC) 57–58, 60, 61, 62, 68; *see also* Orangeburg Massacre
Sugar, Bert 75
Sullivan, John L. 78
sundown town 6, 7, 189, 198; Anna, Illinois 188; Cairo, Illinois 196; Illinois 196; modern racism 189; pattern 189, 190; reconciliation 205; reintegrating 204; reverse mentality 203; rhetoric 203; signs 196; unawareness of 202; Villa Grove, Illinois 196; *see also* banishment
Supreme Court of the United States 29, 30, 31, 51, 59, 205
Sweatt, Herman Marion 29
*Sweatt v. Painter* 29
*Sweet Sweetback's Baadasssss Song* 140, 141, 150*n*24; Communiplex ad campaign for 141
Sykes, Alvin 48, 51

Tallahatchie River 45, 49
*Tamango* (1958) 124; interracial couple in 125–26; promoting Dandridge in 125
*Tarzan's Peril* (1951) 120
Taylor, Elizabeth 5
Taylor, Johnnie 143
Taylor, Robert L. 33
tennis: Battle of the Sexes match 105; "great white woman" 93; historical overview 94–99; second class 96; women's professional 92; *see also* Williams sisters
terrorism 23, 24
Texas declaration of secession, excerpt 200, 201
Texas State Constitution 29
textbooks, school: and blacks 154; racism 154
Thacker, Robert 31
Third World 46, 47

Thomas, Carla 132
Thomas, Rufus 132, 134, 143, 149*n*14; world's oldest teenager 143
*Thrilla in Manila* (2008) 2
Till, Emmett Louis 3, 4, 43, 59; Carolyn Bryant 45, 49; father's ring 45; justice for 51; J.W. Milam 45, 48, 49; kidnapping and murder 44–47, 50; Mamie Till 45, 47, 48; negative reaction 47; other participants 48; PBS website 51; reopening case 47, 48, 49, 53; Roy Bryant 45, 48, 49; Sheriff Clarence Strider 59; Till Bill 49–51, 54; trial and verdict 46; *A Wreath for Emmett Till* 52
Till, Mamie/Mamie Till Mobley 45, 47, 48
Till Bill/Emmett Till Unsolved Civil Rights Crime Act 50, 53, 54
Tillman, Ben 58
"The Titanic" (1912) 88*n*2
Tom Russell Band 5, 75, 79, 84, 88, 89*n*50
torture 12
A Tribe Called Quest 163
*A Tribute to Jack Johnson* (1971) 88*n*2
Trouman, James 95
Truth 18, 26*n*21, 133
Tulsa, Oklahoma 192–93; banishment 193
Turner, Benner C. 60, 62
Turner, Paul 35
Turner, Regina 31
Tuskegee Institute 94

*Unforgivable Blackness: The Rise and Fall of Jack Johnson* (2005) (book) 74
*Unforgivable Blackness: The Rise and Fall of Jack Johnson* (2005) (film) 5, 74, 75, 77, 78, 82, 87
Unger, Robert 25
United Arab Emirates's Dubai Duty Free Championships 112*n*42
U.S. Department of Justice 46, 48, 50, 53, 84
U.S. Information Agency 47
U.S. Lawn Tennis Association (USLTA) 94; racist policies 96, 97

U.S. National Lawn Tennis Association (USNLTA) 94; blacks barred from 94; *see also* U.S. Tennis Association
U.S. Open 95, 110; Serena Williams 100
U.S. Tennis Association (USTA) 94; lawsuit against *Venus and Serena* 110
University of Alabama, Tuscaloosa 41; first black student 54*n*14
*University of Maryland v. Murray* 29
Unsolved Civil Rights Crime Investigative Office 50
Unsolved Civil Rights Era Crimes Unit 50
*The Untold Story of Emmett Louis Till* (2005) 4, 43, 47, 48, 51, 53
*Up Tight* (1968) 137–38; blaxploitation 138; Booker T. & the M.G.'s (soundtrack) 137; Jules Dassin 137; *Up Tight* (film) 137–38

Van Peebles, Melvin: soundtrack, Earth, Wind & Fire 140; *Sweet Sweetback's Baadasssss Song* 140, 141
*Venus and Serena* (2012) 5, 99–111; before national prominence 99; Indian Wells Final and boycott 106–7, 108; producer Alex Gibney 110; Toronto Film Festival 109; USTA lawsuit 110
vernacular rhetoric 221, 222–223, 226, 234
Villa Grove, Illinois, siren 196
violence 14, 61, 180, 222; antiblack 52; apprehension about 68; boxing's glorification of 86; economic reprisal instead of 60; movie 125; racial 46; roots of 241; state 20
Violence Interrupter 7, 238, 243, 133, 248; black male 242; CeaseFire 238, 242, 244; Cobe Williams 238, 242; cycle of violence 238; Eddie Bocanegra 238; South Side of Chicago 238,

245; Tio Hardiman 242,
244; *see also* Matthews,
Ameena
Von Eeden, Trevor 75, 83, 84,
87, 90*n*63
Voting Rights Act of 1985 142

Waka Flocka Flame 163
Walker, Buddy 96
Wallace, George 15
Ward, Geoffrey C. 74
Warner Brothers 135
Warren, Earl 29
Washington, Booker T. 82
Washington, George 1
Washington, Ora 5, 95, 99, 111
Watts, Rolonda 121
Watts Summer Festival 132,
137; commercialization
133; Los Angeles Police De-
partment 144, 150*n*24;
Tommy Jacquette 144
*Wattstax* 6, 132–52; actors in
145; Al Bell 137, 145; the
Bar-Kays 132; and blax-
ploitation 134, 137; Carla
Thomas 132, 144; Colum-
bia Pictures 132, 137, 145;
criticism 147; David
Wolper 137, 145; financing
137; Forrest Hamilton 146;
Johnnie Taylor 143; Larry
Clark 146, 147; Little Mil-
ton 143; Los Angeles Coliseum 132, 143, 144, 145;
motto 144; race films 145;
rated R 134; Richard Pryor
146, 148, 149; Roderick
Young 147; Schlitz Brewing
Company 137; Staple
Singers 132; Summit Club
143; Ted Lange 148; vio-
lence 142; Wilson Pickett
144; *see also* black capitalism; black nationalism;
"Burn, baby, burn"; Hayes,
Isaac; Stuart, Mel; Thomas,
Rufus
Weathermen 24

Weems, Charlie 10, 15
West, Kanye 163
*Westminster School District v.
Mendez* 29
White Citizens Council 60
white flight 143
White Hope/Great White
Hope 80, 81, 83, 88*n*6
white supremacy 76, 160,
200; defiance of 76; doc-
trine 79; ideology 97; lega-
cies of 11, 16, 20, 25; logic
16, 17, 19, 21, 77
white woman/female 13, 14;
and Jack Johnson 74, 76, 81,
82, 87; part in banishment
195; purity of 14; Scottsboro Boys and 59
Willard, Jess 85, 86, 87,
90*n*60
Williams, Alfred 31
Williams, Eugene 10, 15
Williams, Marco 189, 193,
2016; fragments of history
193; *see also Banished: How
Whites Drove Blacks Out of
Town*
Williams, Oracene 102, 103,
110
Williams, Richard 101, 102,
103, 106, 110
Williams, Serena *see*
Williams sisters
Williams, Venus *see* Williams
sisters
Williams sisters (Venus and
Serena) backlash 105; be-
fore national prominence
100–102; Compton, Cali-
fornia 100, 101; Indian
Wells (California) Final,
boycott 106, 107; injury/ill-
ness 101, 103, 108; Irina
Spirlea 105; Isha Price 104,
105, 106; Kim Clijsters 106,
107, 108, 110; Olympics
109; Oracene Williams
102; Reebok 102, 104;
Richard Williams 101, 102;

Rick Macci 102–103; spe-
cial bond 193; training 102;
2031 campaign 93, 99, 101;
United Arab Emirates's
Dubai Duty Free Champi-
onships allegations 112*n*42;
U.S. Open Final 104, 105,
108; *Venus and Serena* 109;
Wimbledon 108, 109;
Women's Tennis Associa-
tion (WTA) 94, 104;
Yetunde Price 108
Wimbledon 92, 95; Althea
Gibson, first black player to
win 97; Billie Jean King 92;
Serena Williams 100; Venus
Williams 104; Zina Garri-
son 98
Wolper, David 137, 145
woman, black: gender-
specific experiences with violence 251, 252, 253; in
inner city 239; marginal
place in hood films 240;
oppression 241; in rap 164;
and resistance 251; *see also
The Interrupters*
woman, great white 93
Women's Liberation Move-
ment/women's movement
92, 156
women's professional tennis,
black 93; equality 93;
triple oppression 93
Women's Tennis Association
(WTA) 93, 94, 98, 112*n*29
*A Wreath for Emmett Till* 52
Wright, Andrew "Andy" 10,
15
Wright, Jeremiah A. 27*n*36
Wright, Moses (Mose) 44
Wright, Roy 10, 15

Young, Roderick 147

Zanuck, Darryl F. 126
Zimmerman, George 62